T0137804

Integration of Natural Language and Vision Processing

Computational Models and Systems

Edited by

Paul Mc Kevitt

Dept. of Computer Science, University of Sheffield, U.K.

Reprinted from Artificial Intelligence Review
Volume 8, Nos. 2–3 and 5–6, 1994–1995

Springer Science+Business Media, B.V.

Library of Congress Cataloging-in-Publication Data

```
Integration of natural language and vision processing : computational
  models and systems / edited by Paul McKevitt.
      p.    cm.
   "Reprinted from Artificial intelligence review 8:2/3 and 5/6
  1994."
   Includes bibliographical references.
   ISBN 978-94-010-4121-8     ISBN 978-94-011-0273-5 (eBook)
   DOI 10.1007/978-94-011-0273-5
   1. Natural language processing (Computer science)  2. Computer
  vision.   I. Mckevitt, Paul.
  QA76.9.N38I55  1995
  006.3'5--dc20                                          95-12
```

ISBN 978-94-010-4121-8

Printed on acid-free paper

Table of Contents

About the Authors

Shinji Abe obtained both his B.E. and M.E. in Nuclear Engineering from the Hokkaido University in Japan in 1984 and 1986, respectively. In 1986, he joined the Human Interface Laboratories of Nippon Telegraph and Telephone Corporation, where he was involved on research and development of video applications. Currently he is a senior researcher at the Artificial Intelligence Department of ATR Communication Systems Research Laboratories which he joined in 1993. His primary research interests are in Qualitative Reasoning about Physical Systems including Mathematical Model Generation and the System Identification Problem.

René Ahn obtained a Master's degree in theoretical physics from the Eindhoven University of Technology. He worked for six years as a software scientist at Philips Research Laboratories and is currently employed at the Institute for Language Technology and Artificial Intelligence (ITK). His main interests are in automatic reasoning and cognitive modelling.

Robbert-Jan Beun is working as a researcher at the Institute of Perception Research (IPO) in Eindhoven. He received his Master's degree in electrical engineering from the Eindhoven University of Technology (1983) andhis Ph.D. in linguistic pragmatics at the University of Tilburg (1989). His main interests are in dialogue modelling, discourse analysis and formal pragmatics.

Kellogg S. Booth is Professor of Computer Science and Director of the Media and Graphics Interdisciplinary Centre at the University of British Columbia. Prior to that, he was Professor of Computer Science and Director of the Institute for Computer Research at the University of Waterloo, where he was on the faculty from 1977 to 1990; he was also a member of the research staff in the Computation Department of the Lawrence Livermore National Laboratory, where he worked in the computer graphics group from 1968 to 1976. His research interests include high performance graphics workstations, scientific visualization, computer animation, user interface design and analysis of algorithms. He received his B.S. in mathematics from Caltech in 1968 and his M.A. and Ph.D. in computer science from UC Berkeley in 1970 and 1975. He is a member of the Canadian Human-Computer Communications Society, the IEEE Computer Society, and the ACM. He served as chair of ACM SIGGRAPH, the Association for Computing Machinery's Special Insterest Group on Computer Graphics, from 1985 to 1989 and then as past chair from 1989 to 1993. Dr Booth is a consultant to government and industry in the US and Canada on computer graphics and related areas of computer science. He has written over fifty technical papers and journal articles and serves as a referee for a number of journals, conferences and granting agencies.

Tijn Borghuis received his Master's degree in philosophy from the University of Amsterdam in 1989. Since 1990 he has been working on his Ph.D. project on the interpretation of modalities in typed lambda calculus, at the Faculty of Mathematics and Computing Science of the Eindhoven University of Technology. His current interests (besides completing his thesis) are type theory and intesional logic.

Harry Bunt graduated in physics (Utrecht) in 1969 and obtained a doctorate in Linguistics in 1981 with a dissertation on formal semantics (Amsterdam). He conducted research in Artificial Intelligence at Philips Research Laboratories from 1970 to 1983. Since 1983 he is Professor of Computational Linguistics at Tilburg University. Since its foundation in 1988 he is Director of the Institute for Language Technology and Artificial Intelligence (ITK). He initiated and directs the DenK project.

Andrew Csinger is a Ph.D. candidate at the Department of Computer Science of the University of British Columbia. He received his Bachelor's degree in Electrical Engineering from McGill University in 1985, and his M.Sc. in Computer Science from UBC in 1990. Several years in industry, first as software designer and then as consultant, convinced him that a retreat to academia was necessary. His research interests include the application of artificial intelligence techniques to problems in the real world. Andrew believes that computer systems must begin to shoulder some of the responsibility for effective interaction, and that user-modelling in intelligent multimedia interfaces is a promising direction.

Deborah A. Dahl received her Ph.D. in linguistics from the University of Minnesota in 1984. After completing a post-doctoral fellowship in cognitive science at the University of Pennsylvania Dr. Dahl joined the Natural Language Processing Group at Unisys Corporation (then Burroughs) and has been actively involved in the design and implementation of natural language processing software since that time. Dr. Dahl began working on extending written language processing work to spoken language in 1989 and since then has led several spoken language application development efforts at Unisys. Dr. Dahl is actively involved in spoken language standards efforts, and is currently the chair of the government-sponsored planning committee defining formal spoken language evaluation metrics.

Brigitte Dorner was born in Erlangen, Germany. She studied technical mathematics at the Technical University, Graz, Austria and is currently finishing her Master's degree in Computing Science at Simon Fraser University, Canada. Her research interests include computer vision, digital image processing, and visualization.

Niall Griffith is 44 and completed his Ph.D. in Computer Science at the University of Exeter in 1993. The topic of his dissertation was the use of neural networks in modelling the tonal structure of music. He has a Master's degree in Computer Science awarded by the University of Essex in 1988, and a Bachelor's degree in Archaeology and Anthropology awarded by the University of Cambridge in 1972. He is currently working within a research group at the University of Exeter that is investigating the use of artificial neural networks in software engineering. His principal reserach interests are the modelling of cognitive structure in music perception, the development of modular neural nets, and the abstraction of sequential structure and categorical attention. More generally he is interested in the implications of the computational metaphor of mind, and the relationship between representation and process in computational models.

Eli Hagen completed her Master of Science degree in the School of Computing Science, Simon Fraser University, Canada in 1993 and her Bachelor of Science degree in the Department of Computing and Information Science, Queen's University, Canada in 1991. Her M.Sc. thesis work consisted of designing a computational model of American Sign Language, which is aimed at being used in a natural language interface to a deductive database. Currently she is working as a research assistant in the School of Computing Science, Simon Fraser University.

Gerd Herzog was born in 1963 in Bad Kreuznach, Germany. He is a full-time researcher in the Special Collaborative Program on Artificial Intelligence and Knowledge-based Systems (SFB 314) of the German Science Foundation (DFG), project N2: VITRA, at the Universität des Saarlandes, Saarbrücken, Germany. He joined the VITRA group as a research assistant in 1985, when the project was started. He began to carry out full-time research in VITRA after completing his Master's degree in Computer Science, which was obtained from the Universität des Saarlandes in 1988. He is co-supervisor of the VITRA project since 1991. His primary research interests are in high-level scene analysis for the integration of natural language and vision processing. He is also interested in Multimedia and the general area of Intelligent Interfaces.

Fumio Kishino is the head of the Artificial Intelligence Department of ATR Communication Systems Research Laboratories. He received the B.E. and M.E. degrees from Nagoya Institute of Technology, Nagoya, Japan, in 1969 and 1971, respectively. In 1971, he joined the Electrical Communication Laboratories, Nippon Telegraph and Telephone Corporation, where he was involved in work on research and development of image processing and visual communication systems. In mid-1989, he joined ATR Communication Systems Research Laboratories. His research interests include 3D visual communication and image processing.

Marcia C. Linebarger received her Ph.D. in linguistics from MIT in 1980. Her experience includes college teaching (at Swarthmore and Hampshire Colleges), a post-doctoral fellowship in cognitive science at the University of Pennsylvania, and NIH-supported research on language processing in aphasia, a language disorder resulting from brain damage. Dr. Linebarger joined the Natural Language Processing Group at Unisys (then System Development Corporation) in 1985: she has been involved primarily in the development of the syntactic and semantic modules of the spoken language processing system.

Mark Lipshutz has worked since receiving his M.S.E. degree in Computer and Information Science from the University of Pennsylvania in 1982 in the computer science field as a researcher, knowledge engineer, systems analyst, consultant and instructor. Prior to that he was a teacher of secondary mathematics, during which time he served for a year as a Fulbright Exchange Teacher in London, England. His investigations have ranged from applied AI (automated configuration, item management for logistics) to his current focus on knowledge representation and reasoning for document understanding. The latter, ongoing for three years, includes the functional and logical analysis of documents provided in hardcopy form and the automatic generation of hypertext from legacy documents. Mr. Lipshutz is also interested in image processing and multi-disciplinary approaches to real-world problems.

Wolfgang Maaß is 29 and comes from Zülpich, Germany. Since 1992, he has cooperated in the project VITRA (Visual Translator) of the research program "Künstliche Intelligenz und wissensbasierte Systeme, Sonderforschungsbereich 314" in Saarbrücken, Germany, which is supported by the German Research Community (DFG). Since 1993, he has also participated in the Cognitive Science Program at the University of Saarbrücken. From 1985 till 1990, he studied Computer Science at the University of Aachen, Germany, where he obtained his Bachelor's degree. From 1990 till 1992, he studied at the University of Saarbrücken where he gained his Master's degree in Computer Science. His primary research interests are in visuo-spatial knowledge processing and Multimodal Communication. He is also interested in related research areas such as Geography, Environmental Psychology, Cognitive Psychology, and the Philosophy of Mind.

Paul Mc Kevitt is 31 and comes from Dun Na nGáll (Donegal), Ireland on the Northwest of the EU. He is a British EPSRC (Engineering and Physical Sciences Research Council) Advanced Fellow in the Department of Computer Science at the University of Sheffield in England, EU. The Fellowship, commencing in 1994, releases him from his tenured Lecturership (Associate Professorship) for 5 years to conduct full-time research on the integration of natural language, speech and vision processing. He is currently pursuing a Master's degree in Education at the University of Sheffield. He completed his Ph.D. in Computer Science at the University of Exeter, England, EU in 1991. His Master's degree in Computer Science was obtained from New Mexico State University, New Mexico, USA in 1988 and his Bachelor's degree in Computer Science from University College Dublin, Ireland, EU in 1985. His primary research interests are in Natural Language Processing including the processing of pragmatics, beliefs and intentions in dialogue. He is also interested in Philosophy, Multimedia and the general area of Artificial Intelligence.

Tsutomu Miyasato received the B.E. degree in Electronic Engineering from the University of Electro-Communications, Tokyo, Japan in 1976, and the M.E. degree in Electronic Systems from Tokyo Institute of Technology, Tokyo, Japan, in 1978. He received the Ph.D. degree from Tokyo Institute of Technology in 1991. From 1978, he was with the Research and Development Laboratories of the Kokusai Denshin Denwa (KDD) Co., Ltd., Tokyo, Japan, and worked in the field of high efficiency coding of handwritten signals, image processing in videotex. Since 1993, he joined ATR Communication Systems Research Laboratories where he is currently engaged in research on a teleconference system based on virtual reality technology.

Hans-Hellmut Nagel received the Diplom degree in Physics from the Universität Heidelberg in 1960 and the Doctor's degree in Physics from the Universität Bonn in 1964. After 18 months as a Visiting Scientist at M.I.T., he worked on the automatic analysis of bubble chamber film at the Deutsche Elektronen-Synchrotron at Hamburg as well as at the Physikalische Institut der Universität Bonn from 1966 through 1971. In Fall 1971 he became Professor für Informatik (computer science) at the Universität Hamburg. Since 1983 he has been Director of the Fraunhofer-Institut für Informations- und Datenverarbeitung at Karlsruhe, in a joint appointment as Full Professor at the Fakultät für Informatik der Universität Karlsruhe. In addition to his primary interest in the evaluation of image sequences and associated questions in computer vision, AI and pattern recognition, his interests include the implementation and use of higher level programming languages for the realization of image analysis systems. Dr. Nagel is a member of editorial boards of various international journals in the field of computer vision, AI, and pattern recognition.

Roslyn Weidner Nilson received her M.S. in Computer Science from Villanova University in 1990 and her B.S. in Electrical Engineering from Lehigh University in 1982. Roslyn Nilson has thirteen years of experience ranging from systems engineer, software analyst and designer, software implementer, and systems test. She was a programmer for RCA (1980 and 1981), a systems software analyst for Singer–Kearfott (1982–1984), and has worked on various projects and tasks since joining Unisys (then Burroughs) in 1984. Since joining the research staff she has worked as system integrator and interface designer for the IDUS system.

Lewis M. Norton holds a Ph.D. in Mathematics from the Massachusetts Institute of Technology. He has been a member of the research staff at MITRE Corporation (1966–1969) and the Division of Computer Research and Technology of the National Institutes of Health (1969–1983). He joined Unisys (then System Development Corporation) in 1983, and has been a member of Unisys' Spoken Language Systems Group since 1989. Dr. Norton's research has been in the areas of computational linguistics, automated reasoning, knowledge representation, and expert systems.

Seán Ó Nualláin holds an M.Sc. in Psychology and a Ph.D. in Computer Science from Trinity College, Dublin. He is currently on sabbatical leave at the National Research Council of Canada from his lecturing post at Dublin City University, where he initiated and directed the B.Sc. in Applied Computational Linguistics. He is the author of a book on the foundations of Cognitive Science: *In Search of Mind* (in press).

Ryuichi Oka is a manager of Theory and Novel Functions Department at Tsukuba Research Center of the Real World Computing Partnership (RWC Japan). He is also a chief of the Information Interactive Integration System Project of RWC. His research interests include motion image understanding, spontaneous speech understanding, self-organisation information base, movable robot, integration of symbol and pattern, and super parallel computation. Oka received his Ph.D. degree in Engineering from the University of Tokyo.

Patrick Olivier is a lecturer in Computer Science at the Centre for Intelligent Systems at the University of Wales, Aberystwyth.

4

After obtaining a Bachelor's degree in Physics from King's College, Cambridge, and a Master's degree in Artificial Intelligence from the University of Wales, he worked for two years as a researcher at the Centre for Computational Linguistics, in the Department of Language and Linguistics, UMIST (UK), where he is also currently a doctoral candidate. His current research interests include the mediation of information from the verbal to the visual domain, qualitative spatial reasoning and representation, and functional reasoning and representation in engineering domains.

Cornelius W.A.M. van Overveld is working in computer graphics since spring 1985 as a staff teacher and researcher in the Dept. of Mathematics and Computing science of Eindhoven University of Technology (EUT). He has an M.Sc. in physics and a Ph.D. in nuclear physics, also at EUT. In graphics, his main interests are in fundamental aspects of raster algorithms (discretisation, rendering), 3-D modelling, computer animation, dynamical simulation, and direct manipulation techniques for user interfaces.

David Poole is an Associate Professor in the Department of Computer Science at the University of British Columbia, and a Scholar of the Canadian Institute for Advanced Research. He obtained his Ph.D. from the Australian National University in 1984. He was part of the Logic Progrmaming and AI Group at the University of Waterloo from 1984–1988, and has been at the University of British Columbia since 1988. His main research interests are automated logical and probabilistic reasoning for diagnosis, common sense reasoning and decision making. He pioneered assumption-based logical reasoning, developed the system 'Theorist' which has been used for both default and abductive reasoning, and has more recently worked on representations and algorithms combining logic and probability.

Jeffrey Siskind received a B.A. in Computer Science from the Technion and an S.M. and Ph.D. in Computer Science from MIT. He did a postdoctoral fellowship at the University of Pennsylvania Institute for Research in Cognitive Science and is currently a visiting assistant professor at the University of Toronto Department of Computer Science. He pursues reserach on visual event perception, computational models of child language acquisition, and advanced compilation techniques.

Arnold Smith is coordinator of the Intelligent Human-Computer Interface Program at the Institute for Information Technology, National Research Council of Canada, where he recently moved from SRI International's Cambridge Research Centre in England. He was educated at Harvard and Sussex Universities, and his current research interests are in natural language processing and visualization.

Rohini Srihari received her B. Math in Computer Science from the University of Waterloo, Canada. She received her Ph.D. in Computer Science from the State University of New York at Buffalo in 1992. She was Assistant Professor of Computer Science, Canisius College, Buffalo, during 1985–1989. At present she is a research scientist at the Center of Excellence for Document Analysis and Recognition (CEDAR) and a Research Assistant Professor of Computer Science at SUNY at Buffalo. Dr. Srihari's Ph.D. dissertation was on using collateral text in interpreting photographs. Her current reearch centers on using linguistic information in interpreting spatial (visual) data. She is Principal Investigator on two projects: "Language Models for Recognizing Handwritten Text", an NSF/ARPA funded project on Human Language Technology, and "Use of Collateral Text in Understanding Photos in Documents", a DoD/ARPA funded project.

Suzanne Liebowitz Taylor received her Ph.D. in Electrical and Computer Engineering from Carnegie Mellon University in 1989 before joining the research group at Unisys. Dr. Taylor is researching techniques to analyze document images using image understanding, optical character recognition, and text interpretation. This work has resulted in the development of the Intelligent Document Understanding System (IDUS) which manipulates document images for input to either a text retrieval application or for a hypertext system. Previous work at Unisys includes the development of a prototype forms recognition system using a combination of neural networks and model-based approaches.

Yuri A. Tijerino received a B.S. in Computer Information Systems from the Department of Mathematics, Natural Science and Technology of Brigham Young University-Hawaii Campus in 1987. He obtained a M.S. and a Ph.D. from Osaka University in 1990 and 1993, respectively, majoring in artificial intelligence with emphasis on knowledge acquisition for knowledge-based systems. At Osaka University he helped design and implement MULTIS, a well-known knowledge acquisition system based on two-level intermediate ontologies. Since May 1993, he has been a post-doctoral fellow at the Artificial Intelligence Department of ATR Communication Systems Research Laboratories. His current interests include applying virtual reality technology to artificial intelligence research, generating reusable common sense visual ontologies for use in visual reasoning systems, and understanding how people combine natural language with hand gestures and/or face expressions so that highly intuitive interfaces for interactive computer graphics can be designed.

Jun'ichi Tsujii is 45 and from Kyoto, Japan. He is the Professor of Computational Linguistics and heads the Centre for Computational Linguistics (CCL), in the Department of Language and Linguistics, UMIST (UK). He was an Associate Professor in the Department of Electrical Engineering at Kyoto University and moved to the UK in 1988. He completed his Ph.D. in Computer Science at Kyoto University in 1978. His Master's degree and Bachelor's degrees were obtained in 1973 and 1971 from Department of Electrical Engineering, Kyoto University. He was engaged in a Japanese National Project on Machine Translation (Mu Project) from 1982 to 1986. His research interests are in machine translation, natural language processing and knowledge acquisition from corpora. He has become interested in multimedia communication in which language plays a partial but significant role. He is also interested in issues related to Artificial Intelligence and Cognitive Science in general.

Peter Wazinski was born in 1963 and he is from Mönchengladbach, Germany. Currently, he is a full-time researcher in the Special Collaborative Program on Artificial Intelligence and Knowledge-based Systems (SFB 314) of the German Science Foundation (DFG), project N2: VITRA, at the Universität des Saarlandes, Saarbrücken, Germany. He received his Master's degree in Computer Science from the Universität Koblenz, Germany, in 1991. His Master's thesis has been carried out at the German Research Center for Artificial Intelligence (DFKI), Saarbrücken. During his stay at the DFKI he worked as a research assistant in the project WIP, which is concerned with knowledge-based information presentation. He joined the VITRA project as a full-time researcher in 1991. In 1994 he will leave Saarbrücken and move to Freiburg, Germany. His primary research interests are in the representation of spatial knowledge including spatial reasoning. He is also interested in multimedia systems and the general area of Artificial Intelligence.

Carl Weir has over twelve years of experience as a computational linguist. He joined Unisys in 1987, assuming a leading role in integrating linguistic analysis algorithms with general knowledge representation and reasoning techniques. Dr. Weir chaired the first AAAI workshop on statistically based NLP techniques and is actively involved in issues involving the formal evaluation of NLP systems. He has authored and co-authored papers which have been published in the proceedings of AAAI, ACL, NSF, and ARPA-sponsored conferences. Dr. Weir specializes in data extraction techniques, and has been a member of the planning committee for government sponsored text understanding (MUC) evaluations for the last six years.

Preface

Although there has been much progress in developing theories, models and systems in the areas of Natural Language Processing (NLP) and Vision Processing (VP) (see Partridge 1991, Rich and Knight 1991) there has been little progress on integrating these two subareas of Artificial Intelligence (AI). In the beginning the general aim of the field was to build integrated language and vision systems, few were done, and two subfields quickly arose. It is not clear why there has not already been much activity in integrating NLP and VP. Is it because of the long-time reductionist trend in science up until the recent emphasis on chaos theory, non-linear systems, and emergent behaviour? Or, is it because the people who have tended to work on NLP tend to be in other Departments, or of a different ilk, to those who have worked on VP? There has been a recent trend towards the integration of NLP and VP and other forms of perception such as speech (see Denis and Carfantan 1993, Dennett 1991, Mc Kevitt 1994a, 1994b, 1994c, Pentland 1993 and Wilks and Okada (in press)). Dennett (1991, pp. 57–58) says "Surely a major source of the widespread skepticism about "machine understanding" of natural language is that such systems almost never avail themselves of anything like a visual workspace in which to parse or analyze the input. If they did, the sense that they were actually understanding what they processed would be greatly heightened (whether or not it would still be, as some insist, an illusion). As it is, if a computer says, "I see what you mean" in response to input, there is a strong temptation to dismiss the assertion as an obvious fraud."

Heretofore social trends in science in general have been towards reductionism. Pure reductionism argues that the social nature of experimentation is irrelevant to scientific outcome (see Popper 1972) where the interactions between scientists should have no effect upon their results. In contrast, the effort on integration required here will certainly involve social interaction between researchers in each field which might not have occurred otherwise (see Kuhn 1962). What matters to scientific progress is not the conducting of experiments per se, but rather the determination of which experiments are worth conducting. In such contexts, 'worth' is clearly a sociological, as opposed to a scientific, matter. Our hope is for a reversal of the unfortunate reductionist influence, through the re-unification of currently disparate strands of enquiry. Already, science has started to move in this direction (see, for example, Gleick 1987, Langton 1989 and Rowe and Mc Kevitt 1991).

This book is a compilation of two Special Double Issues of Artificial Intelligence Review (AI Review) Journal which focus on the Integration of Natural Language and Vision Processing. There are other books to follow on intelligent multimedia and theory. The books include site descriptions, papers and book reviews. Here, we have one site description, fifteen papers and three book reviews. We begin with a site description by Ryuichi Oka on the Real World Computing Program (RWC) which is a Japanese $500 million project at Tsukuba, Tokyo running until 2001. The RWC has as its objective the development of flexible and advanced information technologies to process diversified information such as images, speech, and text. Again Japan has spotted a creative research goal in the real world and has invested in it long term. The RWC will carry on from the successes of the Fifth Generation Project although it is not a simple extension.

Next we have a set of fifteen papers reflecting current work on integration. The papers seem to fall into at least one of three categories: (1) semantics for integration, (2) spatial relations, and (3) applications. First we have (Seán Ó Nualláin and Arnold Smith) and Ryuichi Oka looking at integration in general and the possibility of a common semantics. Oka uses a parallel and distributed model which can label images with words in a hierarchical manner. Such bottom-up emergent computation is certainly in vogue today. Ó Nualláin and Smith are engineering a system called SI which incrementally reconstructs a visual scene from descriptions spoken by a human user. The work is based on the sound philosophical work of Vgotsky (1962) and Wittgenstein (1963) and on Ó Nualláin's theories themselves (see Ó Nualláin 1995).[1] Ó Nualláin and Smith use SI to investigate two of the most interesting problems in integration: (1) the relation between a semantics for each, and (2) the notion of symbol grounding. They point to the fact that a shift from neat to scruffy which Wittgenstein (1961, 1963) and Schank (1972, 1977) had gone through reaching Vgotsky (1962) may be crucial for a common semantics. Oka describes the Cellular Frame Model (CFM) which can learn to label images such as pictures of animals with information such as *eyes, nose, mouth, finger* and so on. Oka points out that although he has built a model and implementation which can label parts of images it will be more difficult to model emotions like *love, think* and *beautiful* assuming these can be represented in images. Ryuichi may not have to wait long as Naoko Tosa at Musashino Art University has already developed, *Neuro Baby*, a 3-D digital child which simulates emotional patterns based on those of humans (see Graves 1993). Neuro Baby responds to inflections in human voice input, and if ignored will pass the time by whistling, and when addressed directly will respond with a cheerful *Hi*. I think we'll see more work on emotions coming from Japan and elsewhere in the future.

Spatial relations and their respective semantics is one of the crucial focusses for language and vision integration. This is reflected by the number of papers at the recent AAAI-94 workshop on the topic (see Mc Kevitt 1994b) and the next four papers here, some more than others, focus on this issue. Patrick Olivier and Jun-Ichi Tsujii discuss how space is reflected with prepositions in language and they propose a model which integrates qualitative conceptual representations with quantitative potential fields. Spatial relationships between objects like chairs and tables and meanings of phrases like *in front of*, and *beside* are investigated.

The next three papers by Maaß, (Herzog and Wazinski), and Nagel focus on issues such as giving route descriptions and objects like cars moving in visual environments. Hence, they also touch on spatial relations. Maaß focusses on how agents can discuss what they see in visual environments and he describes a model and system called MOSES where two questions are investigated: (1) how is visually obtained information used in natural language generation? and (2) how are the modalities coordinated? He focusses on the interaction between spatial and presentation representations for natural language descriptions. MOSES is a subproject of VITRA (VIsual TRAnslator) concerning the design and construction of integrated knowledge-based systems capable of translating visual information into natural language descriptions. In VITRA domains such as traffic scenes and videos of soccer matches are investigated. VITRA is discussed by Herzog and Wazinski in the next paper. These papers from Saarbrücken in Germany reflect a number of projects ongoing there on language and vision integration and we will see more papers from there, especially on intelligent multimedia, in future.

Hans-Helmut Nagel at Karlsruhe discusses the extraction of vehicle trajectories from image sequences of traffic scenes and association of them with motion verbs. His aim is to use machine vision for controlling road vehicles. In order to do that a grammar of complex driving activities is formulated. Nagel cooperates with Saarbrücken as VITRA can be used in the automatic generation of descriptions of trajectories of vehicles in real world image sequences. An interesting question which he asks is that of whether the computer-internal model of driving manoeuvres is the same as surface level warnings, signs, and complete natural language sentences.

Following the papers on space, route descriptions and driving we have three papers discussing useful applications of language and vision integration. First, Tijerino et al. discuss a project at ATR in Japan where a virtual teleconferencing system is being developed which involves the integration of Virtual Reality, Computer Supported Cooperative Work, and the generation, manipulation and modification of 3-D shapes based on verbal descriptions and pointing/gestures. They coined the term WYSIWYS (What You Say Is What You See) for this framework. The work, similar in spirit to that of Ó Nualláin and Smith, provides a framework for interactive indexing of knowledge-level descriptions of human intentions to a symbol-like representation based on deformable superquadratics[2]. Brigitte Dorner and Eli Hagen discuss the development of an interface for American Sign Language (ASL) where the machine interprets sign language and maps it into its respective natural language meaning. A hand tracker extracts information from image sequences and Definite Clause Grammars[3] (DCGs) are used to record non-manual and spatial information over the course of an ASL-discourse. This is very exciting work and language and vision processing will have many applications for the handicapped in the years to come.

Taylor et al. discuss the development of a system called IDUS (Intelligent Document Understanding System) which integrates natural language processing with document understanding where a document is being interpreted from its image form. IDUS employs several technologies including image processing, optical character recognition, document structure and text understanding. These areas have produced the most benefit for integration of natural language and image processing. IDUS supports the applications of text retrieval and automatic generation of hypertext links. We shall see much more work coming out on the integration of NLP with image processing and how information retrieval can be enhanced in this framework.

The next paper by Rohini Srihari gives a general overview of current computational models for integrating linguistic and visual information. She uses the *correspondence problem* (how to associate visual events with words and vice versa) as a key issue while looking at implemented systems which span several areas such as knowledge representation, natural language understanding and computer vision. She notes that the complexity of integrating the intrinsically difficult sub-disciplines of NLP and VP has meant that researchers have kept away from integration. Yet, she also points out that information from such diverse sources can simplify the individual tasks as in collateral-text based vision and using vision to resolve ambiguous sentences. For discussions on the latter see Simon (1969). Rohini also points to the surge of activity in multimedia processing where there has been an increased focus in the area of integration and applications inlcude natural language assisted graphics and information retrieval from text/picture databases (see Maybury 1992).

Jeffrey Siskind investigates the grounding of language in perception and describes an implemented computer program that recognises the occurrence of spatial motion events in simulated video input. He suggests that *support, contact* and *attachment* are crucial to specifying many spatial motion event types and gives a logical notation that incorporates such notions as primitives. Naive physics is used to conduct simulations to recover the truth values of primitives from perceptual input. Again, Jeffrey's work is tackling fundamental problems in integration and sees spatial relations as a central focus. In fact, we saw above that spatial relations may be the key to integration!

Niall Griffith looks at computational models of music. Niall describes a connectionist Kohonen Feature Map model of tonal structure. The model categorises sequential patterns of notes into representations of key and degrees of musical scale where the patterns are derived from abstractions of musical sounds identified with pitch and interval. Niall points out that the organisation of tonal organisation for music is analogous to the acquisition of a language and that the connectionist representations correspond directly to images used by musicians to represent key relations.

Next, there are three papers on applications of integration. Rohini Srihari looks at the use of natural language processing over captions on photographs in order to augment image interpretation of those photographs. Srihari has developed a system called PICTION which uses captions to identify humans in accompanying photographs and is computationally less expensive than traditional methods of face recognition. A key component of the system is the use of spatial and characteristic constraints from the caption for labelling face candidates. This work can be used for applications such as information retrieval. Work on the integration of natural language and image processing is one of the central focusses of integration and this is exemplified by the number of papers at the recent AAAI-94 workshop (see Mc Kevitt 1994b).

The next paper by Rene Ahn et al. focusses on the use of mathematics and logic for integration. Ahn et al. investigate the use of Type Theory for the DenK-system (Dialogue Management and Knowledge Acquisition) which is a cooperative interface combining linguistic and visual interaction. The DenK system integrates results from knowledge representation, communication, semantics, pragmatics and object-oriented animation. An application domain is represented visually and the interface acts as a cooperative assistant with its state represented in a rich form of Type Theory. Andrew Csinger et al. look at the problem of video authoring and point out that a model of the user is needed to enable presentations to be tailored to individual users. They discuss an abductive recognition process for the selection of a best user model which can then be used to abduce the best presentation. They describe, *Valhalla*, a prototypical system implemented to demonstrate authoring using video. The video is from the University of British Columbia (UBC) Computer Science Department Hyperbrochure which is an introduction to the Department giving interviews with its faculty and staff.

There are three book reviews here and each book is relevant to the topic of integration. Ó Nualláin's book entitled *The Search for Mind* is directly relevant as it focusses on semantics and grounding issues for integration. Nigel Ward's book focusses on a connectionist model of language generation and emergent/connectionist models such as this will certainly be important for integration. Creativity is relevant and any system which can be creative with language, art, and/or music will pass the ultimate test. Hence, Rowe and Partridge's book on creativity is reviewed here. These books from Ablex and Intellect reflect new lines of innovative work in the field. As I scan the papers here once more I see a number of names being called for integration: Herskovits, Jackendoff, Marr, Pentland, Schank, Talmy, Waltz and Winograd. They crop up regularly in my search for visions of language.

The articles here have been in response to a call by Masoud and myself which went out in December '93. I note that the USA, Japan, the EU (Britain, Germany, Ireland, and The Netherlands) and Canada are well-reflected showing up the fact that integration is a truly international issue. All of the papers have been reviewed by at least one reviewer other than myself and have been subsequently revised. Reviewers Andrew Csinger, Debbie Dahl, Jerry Feldman, John Gammack, Gerd Herzog, Robbert-Jan Beun, Mark Maybury, Hans-Helmut Nagel, Ryuichi Oka, Oliviero Stock, Yuri Tijerino and Neil Todd are to be thanked for the time and effort they have put into this process and I shall not say which reviewers reviewed which papers! The development

ment of this first (and further) books on language and vision would not be possible without Bill George (Desk Editor, Editorial Department), Polly Margules (Kluwer Inhouse Editor, Humanities and Social Sciences), Melanie Willow (Journals Editorial Office), and Masoud Yazdani (The Editor of *AI Review*), and they are to be thanked for all their cooperation. Melanie and Bill have worked very hard with authors and reviewers to enable this to happen.

That sums up the set of papers for this first book and we can get a feel for visions of language by reading these. With the development of computational models for language and vision there will undoubtedly be problems and some like *synesthesia* (see Cytowic 1992) which we have seen with people. I can't help but feel that language and vision systems will have a lot to say with respect to any road we take in the direction of SuperInformationHighways. There's more to come on that and other issues and I am looking forward... :)

Oiche mhaith,

Paul Mc Kevitt*
Dun Na nGáll (Donegal)
Ireland, EU

and

EPSRC Advanced Fellow in Information Technology
[1994–2000]
Department of Computer Science
University of Sheffield
England, EU.
June 1995

Notes

* Paul Mc Kevitt is currently funded for five years on an Engineering and Physical Sciences Research Council (EPSRC) Advanced Fellowship under grant B/94/AF/1833 for the Integration of Natural Language, Speech and Vision Processing.
[1] This book is reviewed here by Nadine Lucas and Jean-Baptiste Berthelin from LIMSI-CNRS in France.
[2] Superquadratics is a mathematical function of volumetric ellipsoids easily modifiable with a small set of parameters.
[3] Definite Clause Grammars (DCGs) were first developed by Pereira and Warren (1980) as a tool to be used in Prolog for natural-language processing.

References

Cytowic, R.E. (1992). *The Man Who Tasted Shapes*. Abacus: London, England.
Denis, M. and M. Carfantan (eds.) (1993). *Images et langages: multimodalité et modelisation cognitive*. Actes du Colloque Interdisciplinaire du Comité National de la Recherche Scientifique, Salle des Conférences, Siège du CNRS, Paris, France, April.
Dennett, Daniel (1991). *Consciousness Explained*. Penguin: Harmondsworth.
Gleick, J. (1987). *Chaos – Making a New Science*. Viking/Penguin: Harmondsworth.
Graves, Gaye L. (1993). *This Digital Baby Responds to Coos and Goos*. Tech Watch, Computer Graphics World **16**, July.

Kuhn, T.S. (1962). *The Structure of Scientific Revolutions*. University of Chicago Press: Chicago.

Langton, C. (1989). Artificial Life. In *Artificial Life*, C.G. Langton (ed.), 1–47. Addison-Wesley: Wokingham.

Maybury, Mark (ed.) (1992). *Intelligent Multimedia Interfaces*. AAAI Press: Menlo Park, CA.

Mc Kevitt, P. (1994a). Visions for Language. In *Proceedings of the Workshop on Integration of Natural Language and Vision Processing, Twelfth American National Conference on Artificial Intelligence (AAAI-94)*, Seattle, Washington, USA, August, 47–57.

Mc Kevitt, P. (ed.) (1994b). *Proceedings of the Workshop on Integration of Natural Language and Vision Processing*. Twelfth American National Conference on Artificial Intelligence (AAAI-94), Seattle, Washington, USA, August.

Mc Kevitt, P. (ed.) (1994c). *Proceedings of the Workshop on Integration of Natural Language and Speech Processing*. Twelfth American National Conference on Artificial Intelligence (AAAI-94), Seattle, Washington, USA, August.

Ó Nualláin, Seán (1995). *The Search for Mind: A New Foundation for Cognitive Science*. Ablex: Norwood, NJ.

Partridge, Derek (1991). *A New Guide to Artificial Intelligence*. Ablex: Norwood, New Jersey.

Pentland, Alex (ed.) (1993). *Looking at People: Recognition and Interpretation of Human Action*. IJCAI-93 Workshop (W28) at the 13th International Conference on Artificial Intelligence (IJCAI-93), Chambéry, France, EU, August.

Pereira, Fernando and David Warren (1980). Definite Clause Grammars for Language Analysis – A Survey of the Formalism and a Comparison with Augmented Transition Networks. In *Artificial Intelligence* **13**: 231–278.

Popper, K.R. (1972). *Objective Knowledge*. Clarendon Press: Oxford.

Rich, Elaine and Kevin Knight (1991). *Artificial Intelligence*. McGraw-Hill: New York.

Rowe, Jon and Paul Mc Kevitt (1991). An Emergent Computation Approach to Natural Language Processing. In *Proceedings of the Fourth Irish Conference on Artificial Intelligence and Cognitive Science*, University College Cork, IRL-Cork, Ireland, European Union (EU), September.

Schank, Roger, C. (1972). Conceptual Dependency: A Theory of Natural Language Understanding. In *Cognitive Psychology* **3**(4): 552–631.

Schank, Roger C. and Robert P. Abelson (1977). *Scripts, Plans, Goals and Understanding: An Inquiry into Human Knowledge Structures*. Lawrence Erlbaum Associates: Hillsdale, NJ.

Simon, Herbert A. (1969). *The Sciences of the Artificial*. MIT Press: Cambridge, MA.

Vgotsky, V. (1962). *Thought and Language*. MIT Press: Cambridge, MA.

Wilks, Y., and N. Okada (eds.) (in press). *Computer Language and Vision Across the Pacific*. Ablex: Norwood, NJ.

Wittgenstein, Ludwig (1961). *Tractatus Logico-Philosophicus (translated by D.F. Pears and B.F. McGuinness*. Routledge and Kegan Paul: London. (Original work published 1921).

Wittgenstein, Ludwig (1963). *Philosophical Investigations (translated by G.E. Anscombe)*. Blackwell: Oxford.

Artificial Intelligence Review **8**: 105–111, 1994.

The Real World Computing Program

RYUICHI OKA

*Real World Computing Partnership, Theory and Novel Functions Department,
Tsukuba Mitsui Building 13F, 1-6-1, Takezono, Tsukuba-shi, Ibaraki, Japan 305,
E-mail Address: oka@rwcp.or.jp*

The Real World Computing Program (RWC) is a national research program
funded by Japan's Ministry of International Trade and Industry (MITI) with a
budget of $500 million for 10 years (1992–2001). The RWC has as its overall
technical objective the development of flexible and advanced information technologies, that are capable of processing a variety of diversified information
(such as images, speech, texts, and so forth). The RWC emphasizes technologies that match the flexibility of human information processing capabilities
such as pattern recognition, handling of incomplete information, learning and
self-organisation, all of which are manifested in the way people solve problems
in the real world.

The approach to the objectives of RWC research program may be structurally
explained as follows. The flexible information processing will be based on four
types of functions: understanding, learning, inference, and control. Since patterns
and symbols are basic and common information, found in the real world, the
above functions will be required to carry out the integration of symbols and
patterns. The integration will be realized by exploring both problems of representation and algorithms which occur in the real world. Representation concerns
the framework for modeling the real world and is also strongly related to parallel
systems including optical systems. Algorithms concern the dynamics for solving
problems formulated in terms of the representation. Neural models are seen
promising candidates to realize both representation and algorithm.

Five major research themes, described here, will give a more concrete image
of the technical objective.

THEORETICAL FOUNDATIONS

The theoretical foundations for flexible information processing will provide
new methods for solving ill-posed problems by the integration of symbols and
patterns in connection with learning and self-organization. In order to promote
integration of conventional methods, theories for pattern recognition, multivariate
data analysis, probabilistic and statistic inference, neural computing, and machine
learning will be deepened and unified.

13

NOVEL FUNCTIONS

The goal is to develop the technologies for flexible information processing that conventional technology lacks in terms of robustness, openness, and real-time capability. Specific research goals include:

(i)   establishing schemes for flexible recognition and understanding of multi-modal information, including moving images, speech, texts, and gestures, and developing interactive information systems with which humans can communicate through such information media, and

(ii) developing flexible systems that are able to autonomously sense and understand and also control their real world environment.

MASSIVELY PARALLEL COMPUTING

Massively parallel systems (called RWC-1 and RWC-2) which will be developed to support the 'real world computation'. Research goals include:

(i)   providing multiple computation paradigms such as shared memory, message passing, data parallel, multi-threading and neural networks,

(ii)   establishing flexible adaptation to the execution status of problems and computation resources, i.e. such parallel systems will have the mechanisms for being adapted to the system load condition, variety of properties of information, requirements of real-timeness, robustness both for hardware and software, etc.,

(iii) providing computation and memory capacity to permit an unpredictable amount of computation which will allow programmers to give primitive description of their problems, and

(iv)   providing extremely fast interconnection networks and synchronization mechanisms, both of which are essential for massively parallel processing and the implementation of neurons and elements of other novel models.

The software architecture of the massively parallel system consists of the kernel, implementation language, base language, operating system, and programming environment layers. The base language supports the notion of object-orientation, reflection, and time-dependent programming. Using reflection, the programming language semantics as well as the resource management strategy is modified by the programming language itself. The new language functionalities might be easily constructed by the base language. Since we have to consider "time" in the real world, the base language provides the facility to describe the real-time system.

NEURAL NETWORK SYSTEMS

Here the goal is to establish a new type of neural model or computation, which is different from conventional models such as back-propagation, Boltzmann machine, and so forth. Connectionist models will be pursued as candidates that will provide a new scheme for representation of the real world. The domain of 'neural' research should be extended to deal with noisy, uncertain and incomplete information encountered in the real world.

OPTICAL COMPUTING SYSTEMS

The RWC aims at establishing basic technology for
(i)   optical interconnection devices and networks,
(ii)   optical neural models, devices, and systems,
(iii)   optical logic devices, circuits, and digital systems, and
(iv)   advanced opto-electronic integrated circuits development environments.

SUMMARY

The objectives of the RWC meet the challenging problems in pattern recognition and artificial intelligence in both conceptual and computational aspects.

First, the approach towards the integration of symbols and patterns should lead to new models and algorithms suitable to realize functions with robustness and openness beyond that of conventional pattern recognition and artificial intelligence. Scalable algorithms with simplicity and transparency will also be expected to process a large amount of information such as images, speech, text and so forth.

Second, real-time realization of these models and algorithms will require a new architecture of massively parallel computation which posses a wide spectrum of real time Input/Output channels, that make close contact with the real world.

Typical applications of RWC will include the realization of information systems capable of supporting human activities, such as: (i) a new viewpoint for humans in their creative activities by means of automatic search and inference of information in large databases including images and speech, (ii) an interface between humans and their environment e.g. supporting disabled people by means of intelligent monitoring.

In conclusion, the RWC programme is not a simple successor of the Fifth Generation Computer Project, but will promote challenging research to solve intrinsic problems related to artificial intelligence and pattern recognition. The key concept of the RWC is thus the integration of symbols and patterns, which allows the computer to communicate in terms of pattern like images and speech, while using symbolic representation for the information processing.

ACKNOWLEDGEMENTS

The author would like to thank Dr. J. Shimada of the Real World Computing Partnership and Mr. Matthias Janzen. The author is grateful to the anonymous referees for their comments to improve the representation of this site description.

15

APPENDIX

The research themes of the Program currently pursued by the Partnership are the following:

TSUKUBA RESEARCH CENTER (TRC) AND DOMESTIC DISTRIBUTED LABORATORIES

- Ecological and Evolution Models for Massively Parallel/Distributed Systems (Theory Fujitsu Laboratory)
- Statistical Inference as a Theoretical Foundation of genetic Algorithms (Theory GMD Laboratory)
- A Vision Processor in Neural Architecture (Theory Mitsubishi Laboratory)
- Computational Learning Theory of Probabilisitc Knowledge Representations (Theory NEC Laboratory)
- Information Integrating Interactive Systems (TRC Information Integration Laboratory)
- Real World Autonomous Systems (TRC Active Intelligence Laboratory)
- Learning and Growth Functions for Autonomous Mobile Robot (Novel Functions Fujitsu Laboratory)
- Information Integration Technology for Applying Sign Language Recognition (Novel Functions Hitachi Laboratory 1)
- Deskwork Support based on Episodic Memory (Novel Functions Hitachi Laboratory 2)
- Self-Organizing Information Bases (Novel Functions Mitsubishi Laboratory)
- Generic Tasks for Symbol Information Processing and Pattern Information Processing (Novel Functions MRI Laboratory)
- Parallel Information Processing Mechanisms and Attention Mechanisms in the Brain (Novel Functions NTT Laboratory)
- Cooperative Problem Solving Based on Heterogeneous Knowledge (Novel Functions Oki Laboratory)
- Vision Based Autonomous Systems (Novel Functions Sanyo Laboratory)
- Multi-Modal Human Interface with secretary Agents (Novel Functions Sharp Laboratory)
- Programming Interactive Real-Time Autonomous Intelligent Agents (Novel Functions SICS Laboratory)
- Active Perception Cognition (Novel Functions SNN Laboratory)
- Flexible Storage and Retrieva of Multimedia Information (Novel Functions ISS Laboratory)
- Adaptive Evolution Computers (TRC Neural System Laboratory)
- A New Model of Neural Networks Called Neural Logic Networks (Neuro ISS Laboratory)
- Pattern Recognition Based on Structured Neural Networks (Neuro Toshiba Laboratory)
- Massively Parallel Computation Model, OS, Programming Language and Environment (TRC Massively Parallel Software Laboratory)

- Massively Parallel Execution Models and Architectures (TRC Massively Parallel Architecture Laboratory)
- Development, Implementation, and Evaluation of a Programming Model for Massively Parallel Systems (Massively Parallel Systems GMD Laboratory)
- Massively Parallel Object-Oriented Models (Massively Parallel Systems Mitsubishi Laboratory)
- Massively Parallel Programming Environment (Massively Parallel Systems MRI Laboratory)
- Adaptive Massively Parallel Systems (Massively Parallel Systems NEC Laboratory)
- Resource Management in the Massively-Parallel Computing (Massively Parallel Systems Sanyo Laboratory)
- A Massively Parallel Machine with Optical Interconnection (Massively Parallel Systems Toshiba Laboratory)
- Special Light Deflectors (Optoelectronics Fujikura Laboratory)
- Optical Interconnection by Wavelength Domain Addressing (Optoelectronics Fujitsu Laboratory)
- Wavelength Tunable Surface Emitting LD Array (Optoelectronics Furukawa Laboratory)
- Optical Interconnection and Signal Processing Exploiting through Optical Frequency Addressing (Optoelectronics Hitachi Laboratory)
- Stacked Optical Computing Systems (Optoelectronics Matsushita Laboratory)
- Optical Neurocomputing (Optoelectronics Mitsubishi Laboratory)
- Electro-Photonic Processor Networks (Optoelectronics NEC Laboratory)
- Optical Bus Interconnection Systems (Optoelectronics NSG Laboratory)
- 3-Dimensional Optoelectronic Interconnection (Optoelectronics Oki Laboratory)
- Research of 3D-Integrated Stacked Optical Devices for Optical Computing Systems and their Applications (Optoelectronics Sanyo Laboratory)
- Parallel Optical Interconnection by Optical Fibers (Optoelectronics Sumiden Laboratory)
- Multi-Functional Surface Optical Devices for Optical Interconnection (Optoelectronics Toshiba Laboratory)

OVERSEAS SUBCONTRACTORS

- Learning a Map with a Stereo-Vision Based System (Istituto per la Ricerca Scientifica e Tecnologica)
- Hybrid Evolutionary Programming: Development of Methodology and Applications in Softautomation for High Autonomous and Intelligent Robotic Systems (Goedel School Software Development Company)
- Integrated Information Processing for Pattern Recognition by Self-Organization, Proto-type Optimization and Fuzzy Modeling (University of Sydney)

DOMESTIC SUBCONTRACTORS

Theory/novel functions

- Bi-Directional Translation of Pattern and Symbol Information (Takashi Omori, Department of Electronics and Information Science, Tokyo University of Agriculture and Technology)
- Modeling of Visual Recognition Based on the Interaction between Pattern Information and Symbolic Information (Masumi Ishikawa, Department of Control Engineering and Science, Kyushu Institute of Technology)
- Discrimination of Spoken Languages and Dialects (Shuichi Itahashi, Institute of Information Sciences and Electronics, University of Tsukuba)
- Spontaneous Speech Understanding (Tetsunori Kobayashi, Department of Electrical Engineering, Waseda University)
- Example-Based Translation on Massively Parallel Computers (Satoshi Sato, School of Information Science, Hokuriku Advanced Institute of Science and Technology)
- Acquisition of Linguistic Knowledge for Natural Language Processing from Text Corpora (Takenobu Tokunaga, Department of Computer Science, Tokyo Institute of Technology)
- Natural Language Understanding Based on Massively Parallel Processing (Tsunenori Mine, College of General Education, Kyushu University)
- Unified Planning of Recognition and Action in Changing Environments (Yoshiaki Shirai, Department of Mechanical Engineering for Computer-Controlled Machinery, Osaka University)
- Description/Understanding of Images and Performance Evaluation of Image Processing Algorithms (Keiichi Abe, Department of Computer Science, Shizuoka University)
- Parallel Cooperative Image Understanding Systems (Takashi Matsuyama, Department of Information Technology, Okayama University)
- Adaptive Object Model for Changing Environment (Michihiko Minoh, Integrated Media Environment Experimental Laboratory, Kyoto University)
- Image Understanding of Presentation Media by Integration of Multiple Information Sources (Yuichi Ohta, Institute of Information Sciences and Electronics, University of Tsukuba)
- Computer Vision Algorithms Based on Cooperative Computation (Naokazu Yokoya, Information Technology Center, Nara Institute of Science and Technology)
- Active-Control Robot Head for Vision-Sound Information Integration (Hirochika Inoue, Department of Mechano-Informatics, University of Tokyo)
- Task Execution System with Multi-Sensor Fusion in Human Robot Cooperative Work (Tomomasa Sato, Research Center for Advanced Science and Technology, University of Tokyo)

Neural systems

- Dynamics of Neural Networks (Shuji Yoshizawa, Department of Mechano-Informatics, University of Tokyo)

- Feedback Learning on Neural Network (Yoichi Okabe, Research Center for Advanced Science and Technology, University of Tokyo)
- Modeling 3-D Visual Information by Neural Processing Systems (Yuzo Hirai, Institute of Information Sciences and Electronics, University of Tsukuba)
- Neural Mechanisms and Information Representation for Color Vision (Shiro Usui, Department of Information and Computer Sciences, Toyohashi University of technology)
- Constraints Satisfaction Systems Using Hopfield Neural Network Modules (Yutaka Akiyama, Institute for Chemical Research, Kyoto University)
- Temporal-Pattern Dependent Learning Rule and a Model of the Hippocampal Cortical Memory System (Minoru Tsukada, Department of Information and Communication, Tamagawa University)
- Computational Dynamics of Chaotic Neural Networks (Kazuyuki Aihara, Department of Mathematical Engineering and Information Physics, University of Tokyo)

Massively parallel systems

- Real Time Music Information Processing Based on Parallel Processing (Yoichi Muraoka, Department of Information and Computer Science, Waseda University)
- Flexible Computer Assisted Analysis Systems for Non-Liner Problems (Shinichi Oishi, Department of Information and Computer Science, Waseda University)
- Distributed Shared-Memory Systems for Massively Parallel Processing Systems (Kei Hiraki, Department of Information Science, University of Tokyo)
- Super Parallel Architecture Based on Functional Model (Toshio Shimada, Department of Information Electronics, Nagoya University)
- Object-Oriented Concurrent Description Frameworks for Massively Parallel Computing (Akinori Yonezawa, Department of Information Science, University of Tokyo)

Optical systems

- Semiconductor Laser Diodes for Optically Triggered Digital IC's (Takeshi Kamiya, Department of Electronic Engineering, University of Tokyo)
- Optical Properties of Quantum Well Structures in a Micro Cavity and those Application for Semiconductor Laser Switches (Masahiro Tsuchiya, Department of Electronic Engineering, University of Tokyo)
- Optical Parallel Digital Computers (Yoshiki Ichioka, Department of Applied Physics, Osaka University)
- Architecture and Packaging Technique of Optical Computer (Jun Tanida, Department of Applied Physics, Osaka University)
- Development of an Integrated Optical Neural Network Module (Toyohiko Yatagai, Institute of Applied Physics, University of Tsukuba)
- Learning Capabilities and Massively Parallel Processing (Masatoshi Ishikawa, Department of Mathematical Engineering and Information Physics, University of Tokyo)

19

Artificial Intelligence Review **8**: 113–122, 1994.
© 1994 *Kluwer Academic Publishers. Printed in the Netherlands.*

An Investigation into the Common Semantics of Language and Vision*

SEÁN Ó NUALLÁIN

Computer Applications, Dublin City University, Dublin 9, Ireland,
E-mail address: onuallains@dcu.ie

ARNOLD G. SMITH

Institute for Information Technology, National Research Council of Canada,
Ottawa, Ontario K1A 0R6, Canada, E-mail address: arnold@ai.iit.nrc.ca

Abstract. This paper describes a project currently being undertaken at the National Research Council. The project addresses itself to two much-discussed topics:
- the relation between the semantics of language and vision
- the notion of symbol-grounding.

We discuss some of the parallels and differences between the linguistic and visual channels of perception, and then describe a computer system we are designing that exploits both. This system accepts verbal scene descriptions and re-constructs a three-dimensional display of the virtual model of the world that it builds up in the process of interpreting the input.

Key words: natural language, graphics, vision, grounding, visualisation.

1. LANGUAGE, VISION AND OTHER SYMBOL SYSTEMS

In terms of function, the differences between language and vision are profound. The role of visual perception is to keep us informed about the world we inhabit. The role of language is almost exclusively to exchange experiences with and help us collaborate with other humans. Yet function alone is not the whole story: it is now commonplace to posit analogies between visual processes and those of natural language. These analogies may focus on the syntactic level of each (Jackendoff 1987) or insist that language does not have a separate and unique semantics but shares its semantics with vision. Alternatively, in the approach taken by one of the co-authors (Ó Nualláin in press), a range of common features may be predicated not only of language and vision, but may usefully be extended to symbol-systems like music. Whether vision can be considered as a symbol-system in the same sense as language is a moot point (Gombrich (1962) would claim that this is certainly the case for the "vocabulary" of pictorial representation); the following characterisation is valid in any case.

* The Canadian Government's right to retain a non-exclusive, royalty-free licence in and to any copyright is acknowledged.

21

Language and vision share the following:

- A hierarchical organization. In language, this reveals itself as a chain of command from the level of sentences through further analysis into NP, VP etc. down to the terminal elements. In vision, we can usefully purpose a counterpart in the distinction between the level of recognition of objects through scene analysis by generalised cylinders to lower-level processes.
- At each level, hypotheses are lined up in parallel from recognition of an object or distinct text interpretation at the top level through constituent recognition at the intermediate level. The interaction between levels is a function of the degree of restriction of context: in a very restricted context, a change of orientation of a letter can change a whole language script. Likewise, alteration of a single point can cause re-identification of the object in vision.
- A syntax-semantics division. The situation for language is clear: in the case of vision, it is also useful to distinguish between the types of syntactic process implicated in edge-detection and those involved in object-recognition.
- Ambiguity. Again, the situation in language is clear: in vision, such illusions as the old hag/young woman indicate the same possibility. This illusion is one where the same drawing looks like one's daughter or grandmother, depending on one's interpretation: it is possible voluntarily to switch from one interpretation to the other.

We might, in further speculation, wish to extend the parallels to posit a "native language" of vision to complement that of language (for example, the alleged inability of some jungle-dwellers visually to judge distance would add support to this notion); to assume that an analogous situated cognition analysis might be valid for both; to propose critical periods in the ontogenesis of each system which determine whether certain crucial building-blocks may or may not be acquired; or, as is the case here, we may wish to further investigate aspects of the putative common semantics of language and vision. A first question that arises is: of what can this semantics consist? The most likely explanation, and one spelled out at length in Ó Nualláin (in press), is knowledge, initially of one's physical experience of the world, and later of a more conceptual nature, which Piaget termed "operational knowledge". We need to distinguish this from the formal symbol-system, which can be captured in terms of a syntax of the symbols in the medium in question: one consequence, noted below, is that the complexity of the system, be it music, language or whatever, can be characterized. Johnson-Laird (1988, pp. 264–265) gives examples of the grammar of a jazz musician's improvisations; the case for language does not bear repetition here; Gombrich's (op. cit.) analysis of the development of pictorial representation could also be extended in this fashion. Piaget can describe syntax only as an example of the more encompassing notion of operational knowledge, in this case extremely sophisticated sensorimotor sequencing. The debate surrounding this approach is outside the scope of this article – see chapter 3 of Ó Nualláin (in press).

We do not need to follow Piaget in denigrating the autonomy of symbol-systems to accept the reality of operational knowledge. We can insist with Vygotsky (1962) that this type of knowledge interacts with the (evolutionarily independent) formal symbol-system in idiosyncratic context-dependent ways. In fact, this interaction may be the essence of grounding. That notion of their common grounding is the leitmotif of this examination of language and vision.

The perspective on semantics taken in this paper merits more explanation. Perhaps the best way to introduce it is via the path taken by the Schankian school in the 70's. The reader will recall the famous original set of primitives (Ptrans, Mtrans, etc.). All were actions: Ptrans involved the physical movement of entities, Mtrans the type of "mental transfer" epitomized by giving information. (Interestingly, Jackendoff (1987, p. 150) has attempted a similar project and has come up with primitives like Object, Place, Action, Event. The line of attack is obviously different from Schank's in that Action is treated as being in some sense of the same type as the other entities). However, in contrast to his earlier work (Schank 1972), the later Schank (Schank *et al.* 1977) refused to separate form from content so rigorously. "Scripts" were introduced to characterize the sort of stereotyped sequences of actions implicated in visiting and eating at a restaurant, enduring diplomatic visits, etc. It was no longer claimed that the original primitives could be applied in precisely the same manner to any language-task. In order to function within scripts, they were explicitly related to specific words within the text in the context of a prior model of the expected events. In short, the operational knowledge characterized by the primitives and the expected action-sequence was interrelated with the symbols of the language.

Given Wittgenstein's (1961, 1968) famous transformation from a "neat" to a "scruff", Schank's conversion, though superficially different in kind, was similarly motivated and should not be surprising. The early Wittgenstein also attempted to describe all of language in terms of primitives ("atomic propositions" which could be mapped onto "logical atoms" in the world). However, he came to reject this approach, and his later theory insists that language can properly be considered only with respect to its use in specific behavioral contexts. This perspective on language is termed the theory of "language-games". It is compatible with the work of Vygotsky. For Vygotsky, the evolutionary antecedents of "language" can be seen in such a conceptual activity as birdsong, and of "thought" in the type of behavior exhibited in animals' (including "birds") problem-solving behavior. It is only in humans that Vygotsky discerns their interaction (see Ó Nualláin, in press, for a much fuller account of these ideas, as well as a much fuller account of how grounding is implemented by this type of interaction in context-specific ways).

Let us re-examine this point. The viewpoint taken here is that symbol-systems like music, language and vision all have a distinct syntax, i.e. rules of well-formedness. In some cases, we can characterise the complexity of this syntax precisely, e.g. $a^n b^n$ for language, pentatonic for some folk-musics. We may contrast these symbol-systems with "thought" (as in the thought and language debate), which is distinct both in ontogenetic and evolutionary terms. For example, we can observe thought-free "language" in birdsong. It has been argued (ibid) that it is with humans that thought for the first time achieves linguistic expression, and language becomes conceptual. The interaction with "thought" is what grounds symbol-systems, and it is this grounding which are investigating here. Now, it could indeed be argued, as we do elsewhere (Ó Nualláin *et al.* 1994b) that this is only one possible mechanism of grounding (though the one most appropriate here), i.e. mapping onto a putative language of thought, common to both vision and language: the type of grounding described in connectionist sub-symbolic work (see Barnden *et al.* 1991) is equally valid for its own type of application.

2. PROJECT GOALS

We are building a computer system in which to experiment with the computational implications of simultaneously supporting language and vision. In particular we want to investigate what requirements are imposed on a system for understanding natural language when the conversational context is modeled and fully visualized on the screen as the dialogue between human and computer proceeds. In effect the visualization grounds the language – albeit in a rather unusual way.

The task for the computer consists of the incremental interpretation and reconstruction of verbal scene descriptions as they are spoken (or initially, typed) by a human user. The idea is to allow a person to give a very sparse description of an environment that he wishes to create a model of, and to have the computer system instantiate and display an almost photo-realistic, three-dimensional model that is consistent with everything the user has said so far, and whose additional details are in some sense typical for the domain. As the user's description proceeds, some of the details and parameters of objects in the scene that will have initially been given default or randomized values will change to the specific values mentioned by the user. New objects can be introduced into the scene by simply mentioning that they are there, and these new objects too will initially appear in canonical orientations, in "reasonable" places, and with sizes, colours and other attributes taking on values that are randomly distributed around appropriate norms. The defaults will often of course be inappropriate to the model that the human user has in mind, but as (s)he continues to specify salient details of his or her own view of the world, the computer's internal model (and the screen view) change correspondingly, and new subsidiary defaults come into play. Of course, most of the detail is registered subsidiarily (in Polanyi's 1958, sense) if at all: to do so focally would cause the type of information overload from which Luria's (1970) famous mnemonist suffered.

A user's description of a scene might proceed as follows. The visualization window on the screen is initially black, and the system waits for the user to begin.

- User: "You are standing on a suburban street corner"
  (immediately a scene appears, consisting of typical suburban houses with lawns, sidewalks along the edge of the street, trees etc.)
- User: "The house on the corner has a red door, and green trim around the windows"
  (scene adjusts to fit the new descriptive detail. Note the phrase "on the . . . corner" occurs again, with a different interpretation because the dominating node is a house rather than a person.)

- User: "Walk down the street to your left, which is Rowan Crescent."
  (a street sign appears, with the new name on it, and the scene changes to reflect movement of the observer. The database is incrementally instantiated to include additional detail required to fill in the scene. The compass-point orientation of streets is still undetermined.)
- User: "There is a large apartment building on the next corner."
  (a large 10-storey building appears situated on the near-side corner of the next cross street).
- User: "No, it is on the north-west corner."
- System: "Which direction are you facing?"
  (presumably the apartment is in the wrong place, and the user is attempting to correct it. However, the system has not so far determined a compass orientation for the scene, so it attempts to clarify by asking the user a supplementary question)
- User: "West."
  (the apartment building relocates to the opposite side of the cross street, being replaced in its original position by just another variant of a typical house. The system now has a calibration of its internal orientation grid in terms of the compass.)
- User: "It is an eight-storey building"
  (the apartment building shrinks by two storeys).
- User: "There are no sidewalks on Rowan Crescent, but there are small three-foot posts every 20 metres along the edge of the road"
  (sidewalks disappear, and posts to specification appear).
- User: "Each post has a ring on top of it".
  (. . .)
- User: "Turn around"
  (could be done with mouse control as well) (scene pans to the view in the opposite direction).

3. RESEARCH AGENDA

In order to maintain a plausible, detailed and consistent visual scene as the user speaks, a great deal of default reasoning must be performed – much more than is usually considered necessary for language understanding systems. This is because in the visual domain, few things can be left unsaid, and values of some kind must be assigned to all the unspecified parameters. You cannot display a wall that may or may not have a gate in it, nor a door whose colour is indeterminate. A linguistic description may leave these details unspecified, but an unrestricted view reveals all.

Intuitively, we seem to carry out a process of this kind when we listen to people describing situations. Johnson-Laird (1983) and others have argued that we do this even when we would be better off constructing a propositional representation of what we hear. In any case, requiring the computer to construct and display a scene corresponding to its current interpretation of a discourse forces us to be explicit about much of the "common sense" that pertains to a domain, and provides excellent feedback to a user about whether the computer is correctly interpreting his utterances. Again, we emphasise that only patent absurdities will transit from subsidiary to focal awareness. If the process of interpretation is sound enough to allow the system to construct a fully-instantiated model of the world being described, one can make a fairly strong claim on equivalence of semantics.

Actually, of course, even constructing a model in sufficient detail to allow a "photo-realistic" display does not fully ground the description or understanding process in the way that the actual world would. Dimensions will still be represented only to a certain accuracy, surface characteristics will vary perfectly smoothly up to sudden discontinuities, etc. But grounding is in any case a matter of degree. The world has infinite detail at every point (*pace* quantum mechanical considerations), and this detail goes well beyond the capabilities of language to express or human cognition to comprehend.

As indicated, typicality and the choice of defaults is a central issue for the project. The emphasis initially is more on the normal kinds of static relationship that pertain in everyday worlds than on dynamics (elementary kinematics and naive physics). In particular, the focus on the structures and relations in the world is in the spirit of Hayes' Naive Physics Manifesto (Hayes 1985): later, we hope to extend the work to a point at which common sense reasoning moves toward centre stage (Hobbs and Moore 1985). The interpretation of locative expressions describing spatial relationships of objects is an important aspect, though we will be dealing with only a subset of even the common locatives.

From yet another perspective this is an investigation of methods of specifying simply the translation relation between language-oriented meaning representations and vision-oriented models. Meaning representations are derived in the process of semantic analysis of linguistic input. Their structure is defined by the composition of templates stored in the lexicon, with variables which are bound during the reference resolution process to salient dialogue items. The domain models are defined by the requirements of scene modelling, implemented by the instantiation of object types and aggregates in an object-oriented framework.[1] (This kind of organization of knowledge is quite general, and applies just as well to database query and other natural language interface tasks as to the kind of graphically modelled domain we are using here).

As a basis for this translation process we are using the abductive equivalential translation method (AET) developed at SRI Camrbridge for database access (Rayner and Alshawi 1992, Alshawi *et al.* 1992), and described briefly below. As developed in that project, AET is insufficient by itself to handle the spatial relationships that are important in our task. The required extensions for spatial relationships will initially be procedural (actually object-oriented generic functions specialized on the classes of the two objects involved in the relations), but we hope to construct a declarative generalization to AET to subsume these extensions later in the project.

4. AET

The basis of AET is a set of bidirectional equivalences, which express valid correspondences between expressions in two languages (in our case the language of linguistic meaning representations and the langauge of visualizable models). An equivalence expression can be represented as

$$A \Leftrightarrow B$$

where A and B are expressions containing terms from the object languages and connectives representing negation and conjunction (the expressions are constrained to be in conjunctive normal form, eliminating the need for a disjunction operator). Terms in A will all be from one language and terms in B will all be taken from the other. Here is a slightly simplified example of a relation that is used in the interpretation of the sentence "You are standing on a street corner":

$$hearer(X1), stand(E1, X1), located(E1, X2) \Leftrightarrow viewer\_position(X2).$$

Informally, some of the conjuncts will be read as qualifications, or contextual conditions, on the validity of the basic equivalence being expressed. But it is unnecessary to make separate provision for equivalence conditions – it is enough to declare simply that if A is true is one language, then B is true in the other language. Operationally, if A is the case, or is provable, then B can be asserted or instantiated. And in general the relation is symmetrical – it can be used to translate from the language of B to the language of A just as readily. A restricted first-order prover is used to carry out the translations.

In AET, the equivalences are augmented by a set of assumable axioms, which can be added to the stock of known facts by the prover if required to complete a translation and if they do not contradict any "explicit" facts about the world being modeled. In the example given, the *viewer_position* predicate defines the projection reference point ("eye-point") for the scene to be 1.7 metres vertically above the position denoted by its argument, because the reference position for the viewer of the scene is taken to be the viewer's point of gravitational support, and the viewer's (single) eye is taken to be 1.7 metres above that. This would of course not be true if the viewer were lying down, so we want to be able to assume *in the absence of information to the contrary* that the viewer is erect. Again simplifying a little, the form of an assumable is:

$$assumable(\langle goal \rangle, \langle cost \rangle, \langle user\_message \rangle, \langle conditions \rangle)$$

and the relevant instance in this case is

$$assumable(stand(E, X), 0, hearer(X)).$$

If the prover needs the fact that X is standing, and fails to prove it directly, it will look it as the goal term of an assumable. However, before adopting the assumption, it will first try to prove its negation. For this purpose, since we don't have a general treatment of negation available, rules of the form

$$neg(Goal) \leftarrow Body$$

27

can be defined for precisely this purpose. In this case

$$neg(stand(E, X)) \leftarrow lying\_down(E, X).$$

Assumables are used to supply default values for details required by one language but which may have been left unspecified in the other. But they are used for other purposes as well, for example to supply a presupposition necessary to interpret a user's linguistic utterance. As shown above, each assumable has an associated cost. If the cost is zero, the prover can use that assumption whenever it helps the task (as long as it is not contradicted by facts already known). But in general it tries to minimize the cost of assumptions made, and if the cost of an assumption exceeds a threshold, the user is informed of the assumption in English, so that potentially far-fetched assumptions are not made invisibly!

As implied above, the domain-oriented model is constructed by instantiating object types which correspond, to a first approximation, to the concrete common nouns particular to the application domain. Each of the types is parameterized with size, orientation, location, colour, material, and various kinds of connectedness attribute, all of which can be referred to by adjectival and other attributive means. The default values for object attributes are supplied by a process of constraint resolution involving dependency relations between objects (support, containment, attachment), naive physical laws (non-interpenetration, gravity), and normality (standard orientations, high-entropy distributions).[2]

5. APPLICATION DOMAIN

Initial experimentation on this project has been carried out using a domain of urban street environments, as illustrated by the sample conversation above. There is interest in applying the software to several other domains, one of which is robot navigation planning (in collaboration with the robotics research group at the national Research Council). The robot's task in this instance is to retrieve an object from an area that has been contaminated by radioactive debris. The person controlling the robot must be able to describe the features of the area that the robot will pass through on its way to the object. The description must contain sufficient detail to allow the robot to correctly recognize where it is at any point, and to orient itself in any recognized context, but the required level of detail is nowhere near what would be needed by an architect or an interior designer. Only salient details, such as would be given to a human making the same trip, are required. Once the robot gets close enough to its target object, for which it will normally have a full CAD-level design model, it will switch to using that model for recognizing the object's orientation and planning the necessary manoeuvres to pick it up.

So the (approximately real-time) response to the user's description of the scene is a full 3-dimensional projection of the model that the computer has constructed in interpreting his or her English statements, with animation facilities for "walking through" the model, and for providing a robot's-eye view of the path to its destination. For this particular task, this degree of feedback is perhaps more than is strictly required. But it does enable the user to check that his or her description has been correctly interpreted, and that (s)he has not omitted salient details.

But the paradigm also lends itself to many other applications: let's consider one, admittedly speculative, line of thought. Throughout the fields of design and illustration, wherever the designer might find it useful to articulate in words some of the relationships in what (s)he is trying to create, a system of this kind that worked well could prove invaluable. We are used to a world where images of imagined things have been expensive and laborious to create. That may soon cease to be true.

6. IMPLEMENTATION AND CURRENT STATUS

Implementation of the system is not yet complete, but we have a version running on a Sun workstation that supports dialogs similar to those shown, and we are currently porting it to the Macintosh environment for some parallel development there. We are using the Alvey Natural Language Tools grammar and parser (Grover et al. 1993) for syntactic and semantic analysis of the English input; we are building the domain models and translation mechanisms in CLOS (the Common Lisp Object System); and the graphical visualization facility is currently implemented directly in Common Lisp with some use of CLOS as well.

It was mentioned above that we consider common semantics as a "language of thought" mechanism for grounding. The data we have so far from our project establishes a set of relationships between the logical form expressions produced by ANLT and the naive physics of the streets and blocks worlds. We believe that we shall have to experiment not just with different domains of application, but also with different semantic formalisms in order to derive principles of relation. The isolation of these principles is important enough to justify the effort.

NOTES

[1] There are numerous books these days on modelling for virtual worlds and an object-oriented modelling in general. For an architect's perspective on the former, see (Best 1994).
[2] By *high-entropy* distributions we mean distributions of objects that spread the objects out in the available space rather than for example crowding them all into one corner.

REFERENCES

Alshawi, H., Carter, D. M., Crouch, R., Pulman, S. G., Rayner, M. & Smith, A. G. (1992). CLARE: A Contextual Reasoning and Cooperative Response Framework for the Core Language Engine – Final Report. SRI International: Cambridge, England.
Barnden, J. A. & Pollock, J. B. (eds.) (1991). *High Level Connectionist Models*. Ablex: Norwood, N.J.
Best, K. (1994). *The Idiot's Guide to Virtual World Design*. Little Star Press: Seattle.
Gombrich, E. (1962). *Art and Illusion*. Phaidon: London.
Grover, C., Carroll, J. & Briscoe, E. (1993). The Alvey Natural Language Tools Grammar 4th Release. Technical Report, Cambridge University Computer Laboratory: Cambridge, England.

Herskovits, A. (1986). *Language and Spatial Cognition.* Cambridge University Press: Cambridge.

Hayes, P. (1985). The Second Naive Physics Manifesto. In Hobbs, J. and Moore, B. (eds.) *Formal Theories of the Commonsense World.* Ablex: Norwood, N.J.

Hobbs, J. & Moore, R. (eds.) (1985). *Formal Theories of the Commonsense World.* Ablex Publishing: Norwood, N.J.

Jackendoff, R. (1987). *Consciousness and the Computational Mind.* MIT Press: Cambridge, Mass.

Johnson-Laird, P. N. (1983). *Mental Models: Towards a Cognitive Science of Language, Inference and Consciousness.* Cambridge University Press: Cambridge, England.

Johnson-Laird, P. N. (1988). *The Computer and the Mind.* Fontana: London, England.

Luria, A. R. (1970). *Une Prodigieuse Mémoire; Étude Psychobiographique.* Neuchâtelt, Delachaux et Niestlé.

Ó Nualláin, S. (in press). *The Search for Mind: A New Foundation for Cognitive Science.* Norwood, N.J.: Ablex.

Ó Nualláin, S., Smith, A. & Farley, B. (in press). The Spoken Image System. AAAI workshop on the integration of Natural Language and Vision Processing, Seattle.

Polanyi, M. (1958). *Personal Knowledge.* Routledge and Kegan Paul: London, England.

Rayner, M. & Alshawi, H. (1992). Deriving Database Queries from Logical Forms by Abductive Definition Expansion. Third Applied ACL, Trento, Italy.

Rayner, M. (1993). *Abductive Equivalential Translation and Its Application to Natural Language Database Interfacing.* PhD Thesis, Stockholm University.

Schank, R. (1972). Conceptual Dependency. *Cognitive Psychology* **3**: 552–631.

Schank, R. & Abelson, R. (1977). *Scripts, Plans, Goals and Understanding.* Lawrence Erlbaum: Hillsdale, NJ.

Vygotsky, V. (1962). *Thought and Language.* MIT Press: Cambridge, Mass.

Wittgenstein, L. (1961). *Tractatus Logico-Philosophicus.* Translated by D. F. Pears & B. F. McGuinness Routledge and Kegan Paul: London. Original work published 1921.

Wittgenstein, L. (1968). *Philosophische Untersuchungen; Philosophical Investigations.* Translated by GEM Anscombe. Macmillan: New York. Original work published 1953.

Artificial Intelligence Review **8**: 123–145, 1994.
© 1994 *Kluwer Academic Publishers. Printed in the Netherlands.*

Hierarchical Labelling for Integrating Images and Words

RYUICHI OKA

Real World Computing Partnership, Theory and Novel Functions Department, Tsukuba Mitsui Building 13F, 1-6-1, Takezono, Tsukuba-shi, Ibaraki, Japan 305, E-mail address: oka@rwcp.or.jp

Abstract. This paper proposes a parallel and distributed computational model called Cellular Frame Model for hierarchical labelling of partial and global parts of images by words. The labelling is regarded as a process for integrating images and words. An objective model world is described by defining a set of labels ordered in a hierarchy by means of a Cellular Frame knowledge representation. The existence reliability of each label is determined for each location of an array in the Frame. It is determined by a state equation whose initial condition is given by an input primitive label-pattern. The state equation is of the form of local, parallel and iterative computation. The computational process described by the state equation is considered as a process of aggregation (based on input label patterns) of label knowledge introduced for the model description. In this paper, the model description of the Cellular Frame is discussed from two viewpoints: (1) label hierarchy and (2) graphical interpretation of the model. Convergence of the labelling process is ensured by the fact that the state equation always converges. In addition, several hypotheses have been ascertained by showing an example model and a simulation of the labelling process by a state equation.

Key words: vision understanding, natural language, relaxation, cellular automaton, knowledge aggregation.

1. INTRODUCTION

The weakness of mutual interaction between image processing (Marr 1982, Ballard 1982) and natural language processing (Joshi 1991) has been widely known in the field of artificial intelligence. The situation is caused by the following two reasons.

The first one is due to the difference of forms for representing images and natural language. An image pattern is merely a two-dimensional distribution of pixels with numerical values indicating grey level of colour information. Natural language is represented by a set of symbol sequences each of which usually indicates a sentence or utterance.

The second one is due to the semantic gaps between meanings represented by images and those by natural language. Meaning indicated by images yields both ambiguity and incompleteness from the viewpoint of natural language and vice versa. It becomes a hard problem to make correspondences between parts of an image and sentences because of the different characteristics of semantic granularity, hierarchy and modality existing in each of them. The granularity of images is reflected by the size of focused region, while the granularity of natural language is reflected by the conceptual item determined by a set of sentences.

The hierarchy of image can be categorized into three, that is, early vision (Marr 1982), middle vision (Poggio *et al.* 1987) and high level vision (Feldman 1985). In the case of motion images, each category contains time parameters. Natural language processing consists of morphological, word, phrase, parse tree, lexical constraint levels and so on. Modality of images emerges from both different attentions and viewpoints of observers or subjects. There is the same situation in the case of natural language except that the domain under consideration is based on a stream of sentences.

According to these reasons, hereupon, the mutual interaction has been so restricted that only methods for information retrieval using index labels attached to images are now available to link images with natural language.

In order to overcome the difficulties mentioned above, we will propose an approach in this paper which is a new type of labelling method based on relaxation. Relaxation is an incremental method for satisfying constraints to obtain a semi-optimal solution of a combinatorial problem. Hereupon, the aim of the method is to integrate images and words by means of a labelling process for each location on images using a set of labels. The set is enough to provide the components for producing natural language sentences.

Our motivation is in the following. Two approaches are possible towards the integration of images and natural language. One is to realise the situation that natural langauge emerges from images, and the other is that images arise from natural langauge. The former seems intrinsic from the view-point of integration of them. The intrinsic progress in the former approach is to make correspondences between images and words for clarifying relationships between images and sentences. Without flexible correspondences between images and words in the former approach, the integration of images and natural language remains still in the toy model world. If we would obtain a word set by applying the proposed algorithm to real images, it will be required to solve hard problems of selection and ordering of the words to produce natural language sentences. This is another difficult problem. This paper should be followed by solutions of the open problem for producing sentences based on the results of this type of labelling process.

2. RELAXATION LABELLING APPROACH

Since the relaxation method (Young 1954) which conventionally had been used in numerical analysis of partial differential equations was introduced into image processing by (Rosenfeld and Zucker 1976), it has been applied widely to the problems of line and edge enhancement, noise elimination, matching, etc. (Sakaue *et al.* 1980). A standard relaxation method for applying image processing has four components: (1) labels, (2) compatibility coefficients between two labels,

(3) variables representing existence reliabilities of labels and (4) an iterative rule to renew values of variables. For solving an edge enhancement problem by a relaxation method, both a pair of a label and a variable are assigned to an edge feature with a direction, and a compatibility coefficient is typically defined by the correlation value between two edges, and a suitable renewal rule is determined (Sakaue 1980). Then a converged state of a variable provides a semi-optimal value indicating an existence reliability of a label. The function of labelling by a relaxation method is quite different from that of 3-dimensional reconstruction of scene images (Marr 1982; Ballard 1982). Because a labelling processing provides a symbolic description which represents an interpretation result of scene images, while a 3-dimensional reconstruction process produces merely a numerical representation of objects from scene images.

However, there are few applications of the relaxation method to image understanding using knowledge on images represented by a set of words with tree/network structure such as one in a thesaurus dictionary. According to (Matsuyama 1984), the reason for this is that labels and compatibility coefficients, each of which is defined for each label pair, used in relaxation labelling lack ability for describing of complex scenes, and uniform processing in overall space is too simple to handle various complex situations. To compensate for these drawbacks to relaxation labelling, the papers (Tsotsos 1981; Davis and Rosenfeld 1978) proposed improved algorithms of relaxation labelling employing hierarchical structures. The approach by (Tsotsos 1981) tries to enhance the model description ability of expert system type by introducing a hierarchical structure of part-whole for temporal events. The approach by (Davis and Rosenfeld 1978) only utilizes relaxation for calculating reliability of hypotheses, and the central mechanism for controlling the recognition processes is realised separately. Matsuyama's criticism is that by either proposal the relation between the relaxation and the control based on recognition processes is not smooth (Matsuyama 1984).

In this paper, we propose an algorithm of hierarchical labelling called the Cellular Frame Model (CFM). The CFM is an iterative labelling method similar to relaxation labelling, but its algorithm is based on an analogue cellular automaton and does not employ so called the support vector nor the compatibility coefficients which are defined in conventional relaxation labelling methods. More precisely, the CFM is not categorized as a relaxation labelling algorithm defined by Rosenfeld et al. (Rosenfeld et al. 1976). Compared with the relaxation algorithm using the hierarchical structure described in (Tsotsos 1981; Davis and Rosenfeld 1978), the CFM has the following two excellent features: (1) it is capable of describing a model having both graphical and hierarchical structure because it utilizes a special scheme for description called a Cellular Frame. The graphical structure by Cellular Frames gives model worlds higher description ability so that it seems to be superior to that of the conventional relaxation model which uses only flat structure by labels and compatibility coefficients between label pairs; (2) while the CFM also has a labelling process similar to relaxation, heterarchical control for hierarchical structure of a label set is embedded intrinsically in the labelling process. This type of control is obtained by the characteristics of definition of relationships amongst labels. As it is described in the next section, the label definitions by Cellular Frames represent partial, mutual, and hierarchical relationships between labels. All of those relationships usually are required for labelling on real images, and they lead the control of relaxation process to be heterarchical. Thus the connection between the labelling and the control structure becomes quite tight.

We explain CFM description and its labelling process with image understanding capability together with simulation experiments.

3. THE CELLULAR FRAME MODEL

The Cellular Frame Model deals with a labelling problem under the conditions that an input distributed pattern of labels (called primitive image labels) obtained from raw image data is given, and a model of the image world is described by a label set including primitive image labels. The CFM is composed of the following:

(1) a model description by label definition using Cellular Frames;
(2) Cellular Frame state equation to determine the two-dimensional distribution of the existence reliability of each label.

3.1. *Cellular Frame*

A Cellular Frame (CF) (see Fig. 1) is a box frame composed of 3×3 intra-boxes, when the treated objects are two-dimensional image patterns and $3 \times 3 \times 3$ intra-boxes, when the objects are 3-dimensional patterns. Hereafter, we deal only with two-dimensional cases, although we can deal similarly with 3-dimensional cases. Intra-boxes in CF are numbered as indicated in Fig. 1. Each box contains a label. For simplicity, by CF we mean that it is a frame of 3×3 intra-boxes each of which contains a label. Let the label contained in box 9 (definee) be defined by labels contained in boxes 1 to 8 (definers). Each non-null definer label in each Cellular Frame is categorized into a positive label or a negative label. A positive label increases the evidence of the definee label in box 9, while a negative label decreases it.

4	3	2
5	9	1
6	7	8

Fig. 1. The numbers indicating the intra-boxes of a Cellular Frame.

In principle, each of the labels in boxes 1 to 8 represents a object part of what the label in box 9 represents. Moreover, the number of the box is significant, the label in box 1, for example, is significant in the sense that it exists at the right of box 9. Similar situations hold for other numbers. It is significant that boxes 1 to 8 (= n) exist in its direction with $(n - 1) \cdot \pi/2$ seen from box 9. No direct connective relation between adjacent labels is defined, even if two intra-boxes are neighbouring.

3.2. Model world by Cellular Frames

3.2.1. Examples of Cellular Frame

In the CFM a model of an image world is represented by a set of CFs. We show an example. Let us assume that an image in Fig. 2(a) [except character parts] is given. Suppose that the image represents a part of the body of a human being or a monkey. Then we can attach the name of each part as its label as is shown by characters in Fig. 2(a).

Intuitively, we can give a hierarchy shown in Fig. 2(b) to the labels. Five Cellular Frames in Fig. 3 are concerned with representing the label 'Body,' where a label is hereafter indicated with '–.' Figure 3(a) is the CF representing 'Leg

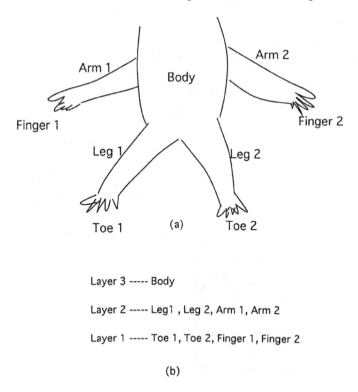

Layer 3 ----- Body

Layer 2 ----- Leg1 , Leg 2, Arm 1, Arm 2

Layer 1 ----- Toe 1, Toe 2, Finger 1, Finger 2

(b)

Fig. 2. (a) The labels for representing a pictorial object represented by the label 'Body' and (b) the heuristic hierarchy among the labels.

1' which indicates that if 'Body' exists at upper right and 'Toe 1' at lower left, then there exists 'Leg 1.' Let a blank box contain a null label meaning 'don't care.' As has been explained in 3.2., no connectivity is assumed between labels in a CF. Therefore, the CF does not indicate that 'Leg 1' and 'Body,' or 'Leg 1' and 'Toe 1' are connected directly. Figures 3(b), (c) and (d) define 'Leg 2,' 'Arm 1' and 'Arm 2,' respectively, meaning that in order for 'Body' to exist, it is necessary for 'Arm 1' to exist at its left, for 'Arm 2' to exist at its right, for

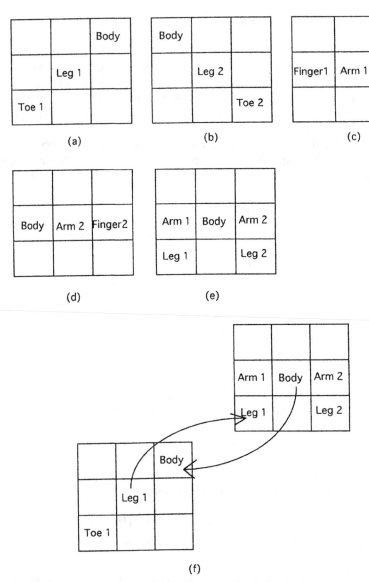

Fig. 3. The description of the label 'Body' by five Cellular Frames.

'Leg 1' to exist at its lower left and for 'Leg 2' to exist at its lower right. Each of 'Leg 1,' 'Leg 2,' 'Arm 1' and 'Arm 2' used in this definition is defined by other CFs. On the other hand, 'Toe 1' used in the definition of 'Leg 1' is not defined as a CF, but is corresponding to the raw image pattern data (for instance, a two-dimensional 0–1 pattern). Each label determined from a raw image pattern data such as this is called a primitive image label in this paper. No primitive image label is defined by a CF.

On the other hand, this paper does not discuss the algorithm to determine primitive labels from raw image patterns. We assume that given input patterns are two-dimensional patterns on which primitive labels are distributed.

We investigate the description ability of CF for the example model. Herein, we describe hierarchical characteristics of a model through the definitions of 'Leg 1' and 'Body' by the CF. Intuitively, since what 'Body' represents includes what 'Leg 1' represents, we assume that the level to which 'Body' belongs is higher than the one to which 'Leg 1' belongs. The intuitive level is reflected formally in the definition of labels by the CF. Specifically, we apply the principle of defining labels by the CF such that, based on the intuitive part-whole relationship among labels, we select the definee label to be of a higher level than the definer label. The definer label denotes the label which enters box 9 of CF, and the definee label denotes that which enters boxes 1 through 8. In addition to the aforementioned principle, however, CF is characterized such that the label hierarchically higher than the definee label in the part-whole relationship is allowed to enter the definer label. For instance, in the definition of 'Leg 1,' 'Body' is considered at higher level than 'Leg 1.' However, in the definition of 'Leg 1' it is required that 'Body' is included in a box at the upper right of 'Leg 1,' which may seem contradictory from part-whole relationship. On the other hand, the relation between 'Toe 1' and 'Leg 1' satisfies the part-whole relationship of definition.

Although most label definitions satisfy the fore mentioned principle, the following example may be observed because another definition is allowed. In the CF of 'Body' shown in Fig. 3(e) 'Leg 1' must exist at the lower left of 'Body'. Furthermore, in the definition of CF of 'Leg 1,' 'Body' must exist at the upper right. Therefore in the definitions of 'Body' and 'Leg 1' one defined the other at the intra-box (see Fig. 3(f)). The label 'Leg 1' occupies an intra-box numbered 5, that is, one of definer parts of the CF for defining 'Body,' and vice versa except that the label 'Body' occupies an intra-box numbered 2. This is the hierarchical representation of our model.

3.2.2. Graphical interpretation of model

We now describe graphical features of the example model defined by the CF. Let us consider the label defining process by the CF, when the model is produced. The defining process is interpreted such that a graph on two-dimensional lattice space is produced where the definer/definee relation of labels is represented by arcs (reciprocal directions are allowed and arc directions are determined corresponding to the numbers assigned to intra-boxes as shown in Fig. 1 between node labels. We explain this by the example given in Fig. 4.

Let us assume that the CF is produced in a sequence of (1) to (5) in Fig. 4(a). The sequence is regarded as a quite simple model world made by an image sequence for describing a story in a picture book. Each CF in Fig. 4(a) indicates a scene of the story, and labels such as A, B, C etc. represent objects in the scenes.

The incremental step to construct a graph is described in the following. It is assumed that the location of label A is given.

(i) The relation among the definee label A and the defining labels C, D and F from the CF in Fig. 4(a)(1) indicates that the labels C/D/F are located on the lines. The lines end at the label A. At this time, however, the positions of labels C/D/F are not yet determined. The label having an incoming arrow represents a definee label. The label A in Fig. 4(b) is the definee label.

(ii) Next, let us define label B by the CF in Fig. 4(a)(2). This definition indicates that D is located at the left of B, C at the upper left of B, and E at

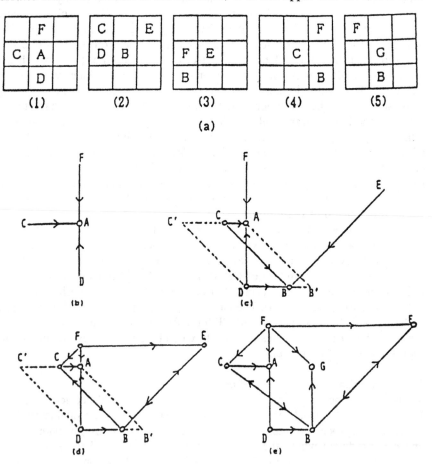

Fig. 4. (a) The sequential definition of Cellular Frames and (b, c, d, e) its interpretation from the viewpoints of construction of a graph.

the upper right of B. Addition of this definition to Fig. 4(b) leads to the configuration where, assuming the length of the graph segment AD being unity, C is located on graph segment C'A, B is on the graph segment DB', and B and C are located such that graph segments CB and AB' are parallel. While E is located on a line in the upper right direction to B, its position is indefinite.

(iii) Furthermore, we define labels E and C by the CFs in Figs. 4(a)(3)(4). As shown in Fig. 4(d), the positional relation among labels E, F and other labels is definite, but at this stage labels B and C still have uncertainty shown in Fig. 4(c).

(iv) We define label G by the CF of Fig. 4(a)(5). The relation between label B and F is determined through label G. As a result, positional relations among B, C, E and F is determined and all labels have definite locations (Fig. 4(e)).

As mentioned in the foregoing discussion, the model defining process using CFs is regarded as that of graphical construction of the model.[1] Although we have locally limited label directions exactly to eight, we can assert global characteristics such that the label to be put in box 9 can be defined so that the label in box 2 lies within a range between 22.5° to 67.5°.

Furthermore, when we define labels. To provide a model with flexibility, we can positively use positional uncertainty among labels. The state equation described later executes model labelling with uncertainty assumed.

We consider that model description ability of CFs is high because of the hierarchical structure of the model, and the graphical structure of the described model whose nodes are labels.

4. IMAGE UNDERSTANDING BY LOCATION LABELLING

The representation of a model by a set of CFs constitutes a graphical network whose nodes are labels as described in Section 3. We can expect that a part of the set of labels are primitive image labels appearing in an input image, but most of the labels are determined as knowledge constituting the model world of images. Let us consider an image sequence of a story in a pictorial book as a model world. Primitive labels are obtained by pattern matching between reference patterns (corresponding primitive labels) and each local area of images. However, we should take account of a large amount of words to extract and represent more semantical meanings of the sequence of images. There are hierarchy levels based on the definition of relations among labels. A definee label positions on higher hierarchy level than its definer labels. In the next section, a state equation is introduced. The function of the state equation is to calculate the distribution of reliability values of each label on a two-dimensional array. Each location of the array has a value indicating the existence reliability at that location for each of non-primitive labels. The reliability values of partial nodes of the network model are determined by primitive labels (given reliability unity) appearing in an input pattern. Locations with high reliability values of existence are determined using a bootstrap way. Each label has an array for representing status of understanding. Each element of array has a value indicating the reliability of existence of the label (word) at the location. Let us consider an example which has three labels 'Monkey,' 'Look' and 'Box'. Then, if we can find the three locations from 'Monkey'-array, 'Look'-array, 'Box'-array whose reliability values exceed a threshold value, then a sentence such as 'A monkey looks at a box' can be produced. Every work is located in a network which represents a model world made by CFs. A verb such as 'Look' is also determined by CFs.

When we calculate the reliability of labels belonging to higher levels of the hierarchy, given as knowledge in the model world, this process can be described as the knowledge being aggregated through overall label reliability computation. A model world by CFs is represented by a network which locate each of nodes on a two-dimensional array. For real world images, it is impossible to expect that locations of input labels match with the model world. Moreover the appearance of every labels necessary for constructing non-primitive labels can not be expected. In order to obtain an algorithm with the ability for robust aggregation of knowledge, the allowance of both uncertainty of label positions and defection of labels for input images is especially required. Since the state equation allows for uncertainty of label positions in the network and there exist the mutual and partial definitions among labels through CFs, this leads to robust and reasonable assignment of label reliability. We can also look upon the aggregation process of label knowledge as a kind of understanding process of an input primitive image label pattern.

5. CELLULAR FRAME STATE EQUATION

Execution of location labelling in the CFM is carried out by application of a state equation to an input pattern of primitive labels.

5.1. *Notation*

Let us consider labels of different kinds (except primitive labels) which are used to describe a model world. Let the total number of the non-primitive labels be N, and let the l-th non-primitive label be denoted $L(l)$, where $1 \leq l \leq N$. Generally, $L(l)$ does not correspond to a single definee of the CF in the model world, but plural ones. This is because the object represented by a given $L(l)$ can appear in various images. For instance, in Fig. 3 let 'Body' belong to a monkey. If the monkey moves around, then various images are generated. In these images, the relation between 'Body' and other parts can not be represented by a single CF, but must be done using several.

Let us assume that there exists (K_l) CFs which define label a given label $L(l)$. Since labels put in boxes 1 to 8 of the CFs can occur in different box locations (l), we distinguish the same label by denoting $L(l)$ corresponding to k-th CF within K_l as $L(l_k)$ as (l, k).

Now let us assume that there exists a Cellular Space (written as CS) which is a two-dimensional lattice plane, corresponding to a CF denoted by (l, k). We define the CS whose elementary cell at a lattice point has nine intra-cells composed of one accumulation intra-cell and eight propagation intra-cells as shown in Fig. 5.

If a label $L(l)$ occupies the same definee in (K_l) CFs, a set of (K_l) CSs is generated. If the model world is made of N labels of different kind, there exist $(\sum_{l=1}^{l=N} K_l)$ CSs. We call the total set of CSs *Computation Space* of Cellular Frame Model.

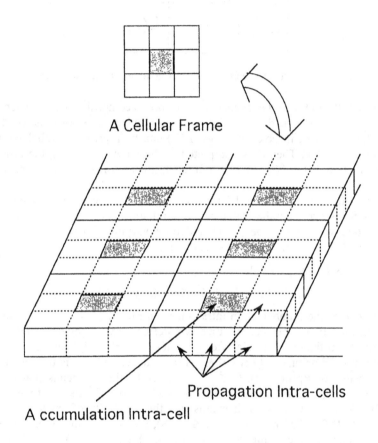

A Cellular Frame

Propagation Intra-cells

A ccumulation Intra-cell

Fig. 5. Building block of Cellular Space.

5.2. *Cellular Frame state equation*

To consider the state equation, we define symbols shown in Fig. 6 for the CF indicated by (l, k). A number i ($1 \le i \le 8$) of $L(l_k^i)$ assigned to each box (intra-cell) in Fig. 6 corresponds to a number of box (intra-cell) in Fig. 1.

The expression $L(l)$ indicates the l-th label which has K_l Cellular Frames with $L(l)$ as definee. Each CF for each label is denoted by (l, k). The label in box 9 of the CF (l, k) is denoted by $L(l_k)$ and the label in box i ($1 \le i \le 8$) is

41

$L(l_k^4)$	$L(l_k^3)$	$L(l_k^2)$
$L(l_k^5)$	$L(l_k)$	$L(l_k^1)$
$L(l_k^6)$	$L(l_k^7)$	$L(l_k^8)$

Fig. 6. The notation for representing labels in the set of Cellular Frames.

denoted by $L(l_k^i)$. In Fig. 6 the labels in 8 of the boxes composing a CF are denoted by $L(l_k^i)$ $(1 \leq i \leq 8)$ that define $L(l_k)$; l_k is the number of set of CSs to which label $L(l_k^i)$ contained in box i belongs; $L(l_k^i)$ can be a primitive label without definition by the CF. Then l_k^i is interpreted as the number denoting the array of the input pattern. If the $L(l_k^i)$ is not a null label, it is a positive label or a negative label.

We assume that an intra-cell from the aggregation cells in each building block of CS has a real-number value denoting reliability of a label at the location. Let the state value range be [0, 1] and time varying. Then the state value $P_i^{l,k}(x, y, t)$, $(t = 0, 1, 2, 3, \ldots)$ is described as follows:

(1) $0 \leq P_i^{l,k}(x, y, t) \leq 1$,

(2) $1 \leq l \leq N$, $1 \leq k \leq K_l$, $1 \leq i \leq 9$, $(x, y) \in I \times I$,

where i denotes the number of an intra-cell as in Fig. 1, (x, y) is the coordinate of a point on a two-dimensional lattice (we define x-axis rightward, and y-axis downward from the origin); t signifies time; $l(1 \leq l \leq N)$ is the number of theset to which this CF belongs; $k(1 \leq k \leq K_l)$ is the k-th set of CS; I is the integerset.

If the value of $P_i^{l,k}(x, y, t)$, $(1 \leq i \leq 8)$, is unity, then it means that for the CF denoted by (l, k), *the label in the i-th box of this CF exists* at time t with reliability 1. If the value is 0, it means that the reliability of existence of the label is null. If $0 < P_i^{l,k}(x, y, t) < 1$, $(1 \leq i \leq 8)$, then the reliability of existence is proportional to the value of P; $P_9^{l,k}(x, y, t)$ *indicates the reliability of existence of label* $L(l_k)$ *at* (x, y, t).

We assume that an input image pattern of primitive labels is available by processing a brightness image pattern. The primitive labels are for instance 'Toe 1,' 'Toe 2,' 'Finger 1,' 'Finger 2,' etc., as shown in Fig. 3 which are not defined by the CF. The state equation whose initial condition is defined by an input primitive label pattern is:
(1) defined in Cellular Space;
(2) of the form of local, parallel, iterative computation;
(3) that in which the process of iterative computation represents updating reliability of existence.

42

The equation performs an iterative computation where each cycle consists of an accumulation computation among CSs and a propagation computation in each CS. The accumulation computation is characterized by the relationship between label definitions by the CF. The propagation computation means two-dimensional propagation of state values to provide state values to different areas on a CS where accumulation computations are carried out.

The state equation is described from the viewpoints of initial condition and updating procedure for state of each intra-cell, state value of $L(l_k)$, and state value of the label $L(l)$ as output.

Initial condition for intra-cell state
We describe the input primitive label pattern as:

(3) $\{A(x, y) \mid (x, y) \in I \times I\}$

then the initial condition of the state value becomes:

(4) $P_i^{l, k}(x, y, 0) = \begin{cases} 1 & \text{if } L(l_k^i) = A(x + \xi_{i, 2}, y + \eta_{i, 2}) \neq \text{null} \\ 0 & \text{otherwise} \end{cases}$

for $1 \leq i \leq 8$, $1 \leq l \leq N$, $1 \leq k \leq K_l$, where null indicates a null label, and a pair of parameters, $(\xi_{i, 2}, \eta_{i, 2})$, determines a neighbouring point of (x, y). The 8 pairs are:

(5) $\begin{cases} (\xi_{1, 2}, \eta_{1, 2}) = (1, 0) & (\xi_{2, 2}, \eta_{2, 2}) = (1, -1) \\ (\xi_{3, 2}, \eta_{3, 2}) = (0, -1) & (\xi_{4, 2}, \eta_{4, 2}) = (-1, -1) \\ (\xi_{5, 2}, \eta_{5, 2}) = (-1, 0) & (\xi_{6, 2}, \eta_{6, 2}) = (-1, 1) \\ (\xi_{7, 2}, \eta_{7, 2}) = (0, 1) & (\xi_{8, 2}, \eta_{8, 2}) = (1, 1) \end{cases}$

The initial condition of ninth intra-cell is determined by:

(6) $P_9^{l, k}(x, y, 0) = 0,$

for $1 \leq l \leq N$, and $1 \leq k \leq K_l$.

Updating procedure for intra-cell state
The updating of intra-cell states for aggregation is executed independently through each CF. Eight labels $L(l_k^i)$, $1 \leq i \leq 8$, exist in the CF corresponding to the label $L(l_k)$. If we represent the result of updating the label $L(l_k)$ at point (x, y) and time t by $P_i^{l, k}(x, y, t)$, then it is determined as follows for $t \geq 0$, $1 \leq i \leq 8$, $1 \leq l \leq N$, $1 \leq k \leq K_l$ and $q = $ the label number assigned to the label $L(l_k^i)$, $(1 \leq q \leq N)$:

(7) $P_i^{l, k}(x, y, t+1) = \max \begin{cases} P_i^{l, k}(x, y, 0) \\ \max_m \dfrac{1}{\sum_{j=1}^{J=8}|c_j^{q, m}|} \sum_{j=1}^{J=8} c_j^{q, m} P_j^{q, m}(x, y, t) \\ \sum_{a=1}^{a=3} P_i^{l, k}(x + \xi_{i, a}, y + \eta_{i, a}, t). \end{cases}$

Index $a(= 1, 2, 3)$ of Equation (7) is used for calculating an average value using

43

three neighbouring states on the same array. The parameters, $(\xi_{i, a}, \eta_{i, a}) = (1[i + a - 2], 1[i + a])$, where

$$(8) \qquad 1[x] = \begin{cases} 1: & X = 0, 1, 2, 8, 9, 10 \\ 0: & X = -1, 3, 7, 11 \\ -1: & X = 4, 5, 6 \end{cases}$$

determines a neighbouring location of (x, y). The set of neighbouring locations used in Equation (7) are different depending on i as shown in Fig. 7.

Let us consider the case of $i = 2$ at (x, y) in Fig. 7. Then we have $(\xi_{2, 1}, \eta_{2, 1}) = (1, 0)$, $(\xi_{2, 2}, \eta_{2, 2}) = (1, -1)$, $(\xi_{2, 3}, \eta_{2, 3}) = (0, -1)$, so that the part of Equation (7), $\sum_{a=1}^{a=3} P_2^{i, k}(x + \xi_{2, a}, y + \eta_{2, a}, t)$, shows that three state values are locally propagated from the locations $\{(x + \xi_{2, a}, y + \eta_2) \mid a = 1, 2, 3\}$ to the location (x, y) on the same array. We call this calculation the *propagation computation* of our method.

The parameter $c_j^{q, m}$ of Equation (7) which is defined by:

$$(9) \qquad C_j^{q, m} = \begin{cases} 1 & L(l_m^j) : \text{positive label} \\ 0 & : \text{null label} \\ -1 & L(l_m^j) : \text{negative label}. \end{cases}$$

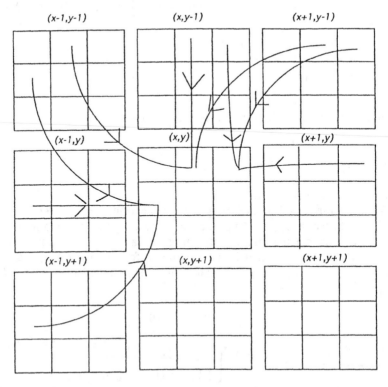

Fig. 7. The definition of neighbourhoods used in our propagation computation part of Cellular Frame state equation.

indicates a weight value used for accumulating 8 intra-cell values. The definition of q means the selection of CSs each label of which matches with $L(l_k^i)$. The parameter m of Equation (7) is used for selection the maximum value amongst them. The middle part of the right side of Equation (7) means: (1) the calculation to obtain a weighted average value for 8 values of intra-cells, and it is also normalized by the sum of absolute weight values; (2) the selection of the maximum one. We call this calculation the *accumulation computation* of our method.

We will now explain what the Equation (7) means. The state value of label $L(l_k^i)$ at the i-th box of each CF is updated by selection the maximum value amongst (1) the initial condition, (2) the maximum accumulation value by selection the maximum one amongst ones each of which is calculated by using its own definer intra-cells with the same definee label $L(l_k^i)$ and (3) the propagated value from neighbouring intra-cells on its own array.

Using this kind of propagation, we can extend the possible directions of propagation within the present framework of 8 directions. Let us pick up an i-th direction out of (7). Then for the i-th intra-cell in a Cellular Space cell, the range of directions of propagation of state values (possible for interactions based on directions) is within $i \times 45° + 45°$ and $i \times 45° - 45°$ as shown in Fig. 7. This leads to the continuous covering of direction range 90° when the number of iterations of propagation increases.

State value of label $L(l_k)$
The state value $P_9^{l, k}(x, y, t+1)$ at time $t + 1$ corresponding to label $L(l_k)$ is determined by averaging the intra-cell state values $P_i^{l, k}(x, y, t + 1)$, $(1 \leq i \leq 8)$. If the label in an intra-box is null, the intra-box is irrelevant to calculation of average value. This is described as follows for $t \geq 1$, $1 \leq l \leq N$, $1 \leq k \leq K_l$:

$$(10) \quad P_9^{l, k}(x, y, t+1) = \frac{1}{\sum_{i=1}^{8}|c_i^{l, k}|} \sum_{i=1}^{8} c_i^{l, k} P_i^{l, k}(x, y, t+1)$$

where the averaging indicates average of $P_i^{l, k}$ as to i such that $L(l_k^i) \neq$ null $(1 \leq i \leq 8)$. The parameter $c_i^{l, k}$ is the same weight defined by Equation (8).

Output state value of label $L(l)$
There exist (K_l) CFs determine label $L(l)$. We define the existence reliability of label $L(l)$ at point (x, y) and time $t + 1$ by the maximum amongst $P_9^{l, k}(x, y, t+1)$, $1 \leq k \leq K_l$. Let it be represented by:

$$(11) \quad Q^l(x, y, t+1) = \max_{1 \leq k \leq K_l} P_i^{l, k}(x, y, t+1)$$

5.3. Convergence of state equation

It is obvious that $P_i^{l, k}(x, y, t)$ increases monotonically at any point (x, y) because of Equation (7). Moreover, it takes a value in $[0, 1]$. Therefore, $P_i^{l, k}(x, y, t)$ converges as to t and at the same time $P_9^{l, k}(x, y, t)$ and $Q^l(x, y, t)$ also converge.

5.4. *Dynamic adaptation for changing images*

The function of the initial condition embedded in the Equation (7) is to provide for each time t the source which springs out a unit value from a location on the two-dimensional array. The location is where a primitive label is directly extracted from the image pattern. The source is used as a driving force for propagating and accumulating by means of increasing the values of states. The hierarchical levels of these labels are higher than those of the primitive labels. If the Equation (7) releases the initial condition term after a certain computation time T, then all of the state values will begin to decrease because of losing the source. Also, the mechanism works well for adapting the system to the change of input image. If the initial condition terms of Equation (7) is determined by a changing image and also it is synchronized with changing time, then the labelling computation can adapt to the change of image. Let us describe the formulation assuming that a changing input image is represented by $\{A(x, y, t) \mid (x, y) \in I \times I\}$. Then the initial condition term of Equation (7), $P_i^{l, k}(x, y, 0)$, should be replaced by $D_i^{l, k}(x, y, t)$ which is defined by:

$$(12) \quad D_i^{l, k}(x, y, t) = \begin{cases} 1 & \text{if } L(l_k^l) = A(x + \xi_{i, 2}, y + \eta_{i, 2}, t) \neq \text{null} \\ 0 & \text{otherwise} \end{cases}$$

In this case, the labelling process leads to a kind of interacting between images which are different from each other.

6. SIMULATION EXPERIMENT

A computational model of CFM has been developed and a simulation has been carried out for the following objectives:
(1) to show an example of model world representation where various input primitive label patterns are expected;
(2) to examine knowledge aggregation through the computation of label reliability from lower to higher levels based on the definitions of hierarchical labels (bottom-up mechanism);
(3) to investigate compensation for an input primitive label pattern as an incomplete input from higher to lower (top-down mechanism);
(4) to verify that global relationship between labels by means of propagation is free from the local restriction of 8 directions on model representation by 3×3 boxes;
(5) to check whether high reliability is assigned at a higher level at the point on two-dimensional lattice coordinates where reliability is intuitively high;
(6) to observe the speed of convergence of the state equation.

Let us consider a situation which combines an image world and a sentence expression such as 'A monkey looks at a box.' Let Figs. 8(a) and (b) be objective image patterns.

These images are samples from a sequence of image showing a story in a pictorial book for children titled 'Curious George' (Ray 1947). In the book

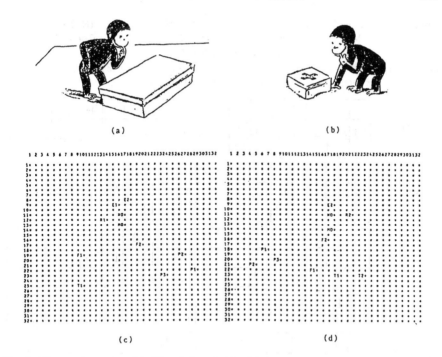

Fig. 8. The raw image data (a), (b) and the primitive label patterns (c), (d) corresponding to (a), (b), respectively.

there are also sentences associated with each image. Children can understand almost content of the story without reading the sentences. In order to produce these sentences by processing only the sequence of images, we should reveal the mechanism about how images and words are integrated with each other.

We assume that the primitive label patterns shown in Figs. 8(c) and (d) are extracted from the images. The primitive labels in Fig. 8(c), (d) are 'Eye 1' (E1), 'Eye 2' (E2), 'Ear 1' (R1), 'Ear 2' (R2), 'Nose' (NO), 'Mouth' (MO), 'Finger 1' (F1), 'Finger 2' (F2), 'Toe 1' (T1), 'Toe 2' (T2), 'Plane 1' (P1), 'Plane 2' (P2), 'Plane 3' (P3). The primitive labels belong usually to results of so-called early vision or image processing using pattern matching algorithms for raw image data. This extraction of primitive labels is carried out by another process which is not described in this paper. A method proposed by (Yamada et al. 1993) is useful for extracting primitive labels from images. We only discuss the aggregation problem under the condition that the primitive label patterns are assumed.

The model world description by CFs is depicted in Fig. 9, with 9 kinds of labels representing macroscopic objects and 13 kinds of primitive labels representing microscopic objects. Each row of Fig. 9 indicates a set of Cellular Frames which defines a label. Cellular Frames exceeding 5-the one in the labels 'Arm 1,' 'Arm 2' and 'Box' are dropped in this figure. An expression like '–Arm 1' indicates a negative label.

Rrimitive Labels : Eye 1 (E1), Eye 2 (E2), Ear 1 (R1), Ear 2 (R2), Nose (NO),
Mouth (MO), Finger 1 (F1), Finger 2 (F2), Toe 1 (T1), Toe 2 (T2),
Plane 1 (P1), Plane 2 (P2), Plane 3 (P3)

Non-primitive Labels: Arm 1 (A1), Arm 2 (A2), Leg 1(L1), Leg 2 (L2), Body (B),
Face (FA), Monkey (MN), Look (LO), Box (Bx)

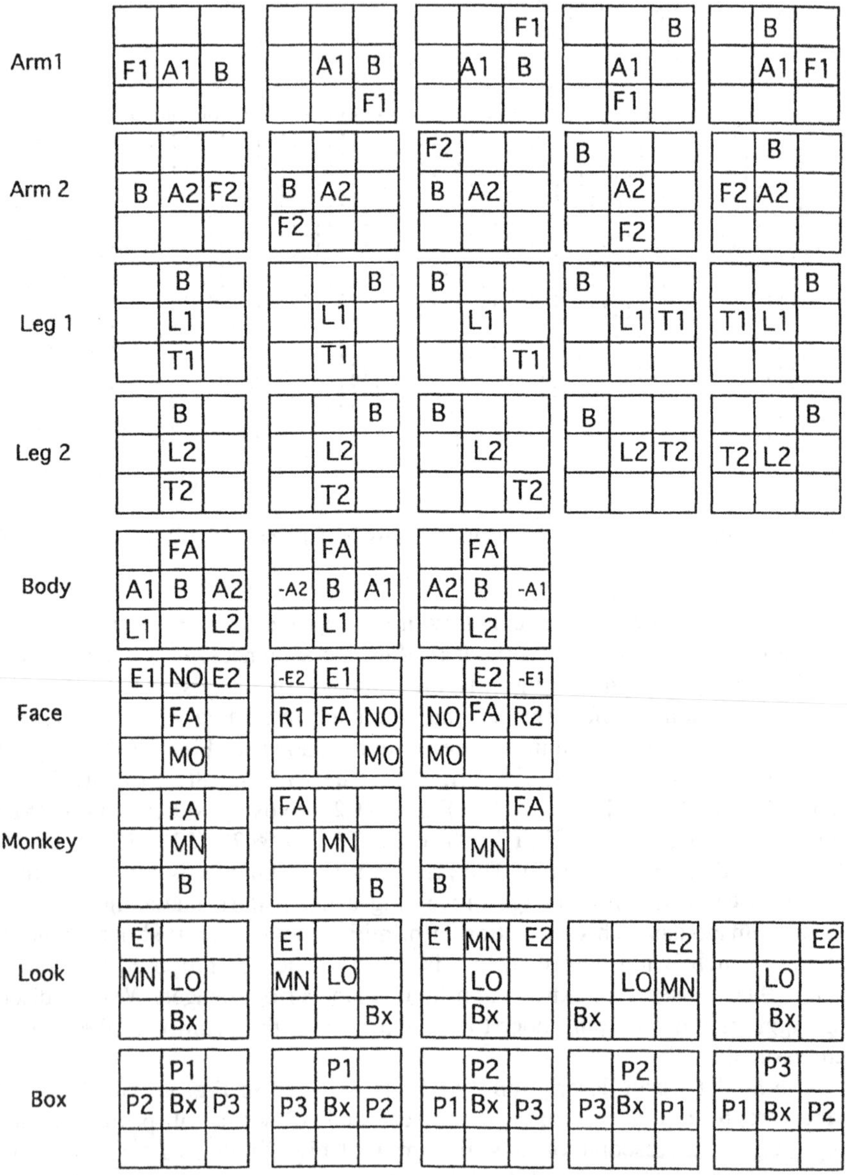

Fig. 9. An example of an image model world description by Cellular Frames.

48

In Fig. 9, each label indicating a macroscopic object uses plural CFs for its definition. It reflects the fact that an image world of the situation 'A monkey looks at a box' has a variety of image label patterns. For example, 'Body' has 3 CFs. The first one defines 'Body' when the monkey faces the observer directly. The second and third ones define 'Body' when the monkey faces the observer to the right and left, respectively. In the second CF for 'Body,' 'Arm 2' has a negative symbol. It means that when the monkey faces the observer to the right, 'Arm 2' must not exist at the left of 'Body.' In the third CF, 'Arm 1' and 'Body' indicate a converse situation. There are 5 CFs which define label 'Look,' each of which includes 'Monkey' and 'Box,' either or both of 'Eye 1' and 'Eye 2'. The difference between the CFs stems from the distinction of configurations amongst labels. It reflects the difference of scenes seen by the positions of the monkey. Similar situations apply to other labels.

There is a hierarchy among labels determined by definition relations of CFs. If we represent a set of labels belonging to a level j by R_j, then $R_1 = \{$'Face', 'Box'$\}$ makes one level, and $R_2 = \{$'Arm 1', 'Arm 2', 'Leg 1', 'Leg 2'$\}$ makes another level. Between R_1 and R_2 there is no upper-lower relation. Above R_1 and R_2, exists $R_3 = \{$'Body'$\}$. Above R_1 and R_3, $R_4 = \{$'Monkey'$\}$; above R_1 and R_4 is $R_5 = \{$'Look'$\}$ which is the highest level. This is the description for objective (1).[2]

In the model world model of Fig. 9, there are 9 different labels (not primitive labels). If they are numbered from the top $l = 1, 2, 3, \ldots, 9$, then the time-varying pattern of output state value $Q^l(x, y, t)$ $(1 \le l \le 9)$ on a two-dimensional plane $(x, y) \in I \times I$ shows the formation process of label reliability. The simulation results of the state equation where initial condition is set by Fig. 8(c) are depicted in Figs. 10(a), (b), which are distributions of $\{Q^l(x, y, t) \mid (x, y) \in 32 \times 32\}$, $(1 \le l \le 9)$ on a two-dimensional lattice plane at time $t = 5$ and 17, respectively. In Fig. 10 for each label, the horizontal axis is x, vertical axis is y, and the size of square is proportional to the value of $Q^l(x, y, t)$.

In Fig. 10, when the number of iterations is small, that is, at an early stage, reliabilities of 'Arm 1' and 'Leg 1' have smaller absolute values. Their final reliability, however, becomes relatively larger than that of 'Body.' This is because the definitions of 'Arm 1' and 'Leg 1' includes image labels, and they are lower labels (R_1) themselves, (2). When they start to be processed, label 'Body' at a higher level (R_3) is also processed, (2). Processing of 'Body' simultaneously accelerates the processing of 'Arm 1,' 'Arm 2,' and 'Leg 1,' (3). The reliability of 'Face' and 'Box' is formed only from image labels (2). When 'Face' and 'Body' are formed, 'Monkey' is accelerated (2). Processing 'Monkey' also contributes to the formation of 'Look' (2). 'Monkey' has no other labels with which it accelerates formation mutually. Processing of 'Look' gradually synchronizes with processing of 'Monkey.' It is because 'Look' includes 'Monkey' in its definition which is processed slowly and synchronized, while it includes other rapidly processed labels such as 'Box,' and primitive labels 'Eye 1' and 'Eye 2' (2).

On the other hand, the definition of 'Leg 1' has primitive label 'Toe 2,' which does not exist in the input primitive label pattern, so at the beginning its

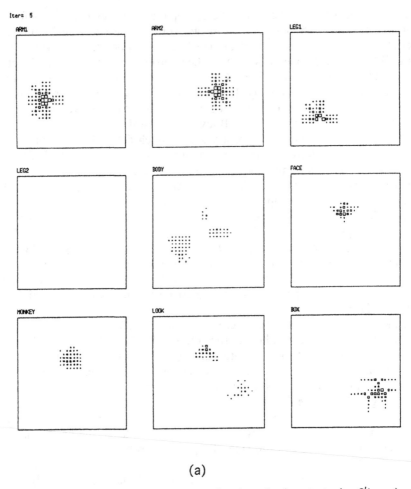

(a)

Fig. 10. The process of knowledge aggregation shown by the output value $Q^l(x, y, t)$.

reliability 0. While 'Body' increases the existence reliability through formation of 'Arm 1,' 'Arm 2,' 'Leg 1,' 'Face,' etc., the reliability value at this time, however, is half of that of 'Body.'

Next we look at directions of propagation. As we have seen typically in formation of reliability of 'Arm 1'/'Arm 2' can be in process, although they are not located directly to the right/left. Formation of other high level labels is similar. It indicates that global relationship between labels is free from the 8 directions of local constraints of CF **(4)**.

As we have seen typically in processing labels 'Face' and 'Box', etc., the high reliability value appears at the lattice coordinate points which are intuitively considered to have high reliability **(5)**. We can also see that at $t =$ 17 in the 32 × 32 lattice plane, the state value has fairly converged **(6)**.

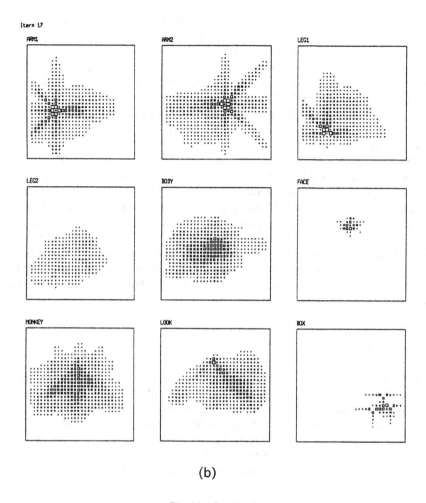

(b)

Fig. 10. (Continued).

7. CONCLUSION

We have proposed the Cellular Frame Model (CFM) of hierarchical labelling. In the CFM, we represent the objective model world by defining a set of labels with a scheme called Cellular Frame. The existence reliability of each label at each array location is determined by a state equation whose initial condition is given by an input primitive label pattern. The state equation is of the form of local, parallel and iterative computation. We can regard the computational process of the state equation as a process of hierarchical aggregation of label knowledge introduced for model description (based on an input primitive label pattern). In this paper we have investigated the CFs model description ability from two viewpoints: hierarchy of the set of labels and its graphical interpretation of the model world. Convergence of labelling is ensured by the fact that the state equation always converges. We have shown simple examples of modelling and results of simulation of the labelling process based on state equations for these examples to ascertain several hypotheses.

Further problems to be solved are: (1) to provide strong connection between CFs and raw image data; (2) to consider learning functions for automatic label acquisition by means of Cellular Frames and deletion based on input data of raw images; (3) to naturally introduce the function of attention; (4) to provide wide and tight relationships between activation patterns of Cellular Space and natural language.

Amongst these problems, the last one (4) is the most essential. The fundamental function of the CFM is to combine words (labels) with a two-dimensional distribution of primitive labels obtained from a real image. The words are used to describe in sentences what images mean. However the sentence description procedure is not shown in this paper. It is still an open problem to be solved. The words used in the simulation are restricted to the words which indicate parts of an image. A more difficult problem is to expand a set of words in order to represent human emotions or abstract concepts such as 'Love,' 'Think,' 'Beautiful,' 'Elegant' assuming that those are possible to represent by using images.

ACKNOWLEDGEMENTS

The author would like to thank Mr. E. Arita and Dr. J. Shimada of the Real World Computing Partnership, and Dr. K. Yamamoto, chief of the Image Understanding Section, Electrotechnical Laboratory for support of this work. The author would also like to thank Dr. M. Yamada and Dr. R. Baldwin for discussions in developing his ideas. The author is grateful to the anonymous referees and Prof. Paul Mc Kevitt of the University of Sheffield for their thoughtful comments which improved the presentation of the paper.

NOTES

[1] This graph is not necessarily a two-dimensional graph. Since the graph has a hierarchical structure, it seldom becomes a two-dimensional graph.
[2] From now on objective numbers are shown in brackets.

REFERENCES

Ballard, D. H. & Brown, C. M. (1982). *Computer Vision*. Prentice-Hall Inc.: New Jersey.
Davis, L. S. & Rosenfeld, A. (1978). Hierarchical Relaxation for Waveform Parsing. In Hanson, A. R. & Riesman, E. M. (eds.) *Computer Vision Systems*. Academic Press: New York.
Feldman, J. A. (1985). Connectionist Models and Parallelism in High Level Vision. *Computer Vision and Image Processing* 31: 178–200.
Joshi, A. K. (1991). Natural Language Processing. *Science* 253: 1242–1249.

Landy, M. S. & Hummel, R. A. (1986). A Brief Survey of Knowledge Aggregation Methods. In Proceedings of *The Eighth International Conference on Pattern Recognition*, 248–252.

Marr, D. (1982). *Vision*. W. H. Freeman and Company: New York.

Matsuyama, T. (1984). Knowledge Organization and Control Structure in Image Understanding. In Proceedings of *The Seventh International Conference on Pattern Recognition*, 1118–1127.

Nagao, N. (1984). Control Strategies in Pattern Analysis. *Pattern Recognition* 17(1): 45–56.

Oka, R. (1982). Extraction of Cell Features from Images. *Trans. Institute Electronics Communication Engineers, Japan* **J65-D**(6): 1219–1226.

Poggio, T. & the Staff (1987). MIT Progress in Understanding Images. In Proceedings of *Image Understanding Workshop*, 41–54.

Ray, H. A. (1947). 'Curious George', Houghton Mifflin Company: Boston.

Rosenfeld, A., Hummel, R. A. & Zucker, S. W. (1976). Scene Labeling by Relaxation Operations. *IEEE Trans. System, Man and Cybernetics* 16: 420–433.

Sakaue, K., Tamura, H. & Takagi, M. (1980). Overview of Image Processing Algorithms. *Bull of Electrotechnical Laboratory* 44(7–8): 43–55.

Toriwaki, J. & Yokoi, S. (1980). Algorithms of Image Processing. *Japanese Information Processing Society*, Japan 21(6): 613–619.

Tsotsos, J. K. (1981). Temporal Event Recognition – An Application of Left Ventricular Performance. In Proceedings of *The Seventh International Joint Conference on Artificial Intelligence*, 900–907.

Yamada, H., Yamamoto, K. & Hosokawa, K. (1993). Directional Mathematical Morphology and Reformalized Hough Transformation Analysis of Topographic Maps. *IEEE Trans., Pattern Analysis and Machine Intelligence* 15(4): 380–387.

Young, D. (1954). Iterative Methods for Solving Partial Differential Equation of Elliptic Type. *Transactions of the American Mathematical Society* 76: 92–111.

Zucker, S. W. (1976). Relaxation Labelling and the Reduction of Local Ambiguities. In Proceedings of *The Third International Conference on Pattern Recognition*, 852–861.

Artificial Intelligence Review **8**: 147–158, 1994.
© *1994 Kluwer Academic Publishers. Printed in the Netherlands.*

Quantitative Perceptual Representation of Prepositional Semantics

PATRICK OLIVIER

Centre for Intelligent Systems, University of Wales, Aberystwyth, Dyfed SY23 3DB, UK. E-mail address: plo@aber.ac.uk

JUN-ICHI TSUJII

Centre for Computational Linguistics, University of Manchester, Institute of Science and Technology, Manchester, M60 1QD, UK. E-mail address: tsujii@ccl.umist.ac.uk

Abstract. In this paper we concentrate on spatial prepositions, more specifically we are interested here in projective prepositions (eg. "in front of", "to the left of") which have in the past been treated as semantically uninteresting. We demonstrate that projective prepositions are in fact problematic and demand more attention than they have so far been afforded; after summarising the important components of their meaning, we review the deficiencies of past and current approaches to the decoding problem; that is, predicting what a locative expression used in a particular situation conveys. Finally we present our own approach. Motivated by the shortcomings of contemporary work, we integrate elements of Lang's conceptual representation of objects' perceptual and dimensional characteristics, and the potential field model of object proximity that originated in manipulator and mobile robot path-finding.

Key words: Subject Areas: semantics, spatial prepositions, visualisation.

1. INTRODUCTION

The recent rise of cognitive linguistics, and interest in how the structure of our perceptual system is reflected in our linguistic system, has led to a number of studies in the semantics of spatial descriptions. At the same time, technological advances in the fields of computer vision, multimedia and virtual reality have given rise to a need for practical natural language interfaces to such technology. Effectively mediating the interchange of information between the verbal and the visual domains involves constructing both a meaningful semantics for spatial descriptions and procedures for encoding and decoding descriptions. We argue that this necessarily requires the integration of perceptually structured and quantitative representations of the objects and speaker/viewer.[1]

In this paper we concentrate on spatial prepositions, more specifically we are interested here in projective prepositions (e.g. "in front of", "to the left of"). We demonstrate that projective prepositions are in fact problematic and demand more attention than they ave so far been afforded; after summarising the important components of their meaning, we review the deficiencies of past and current approaches to the decoding problem. Finally we present our own approach. Motivated by the shortcomings of contemporary work, we integrate elements of Lang's conceptual representation of objects' perceptual and dimensional characteristics, and the potential field model of object proximity that originated in manipulator and mobile robot path-finding (Khatib 1986).

2. THE SEMANTICS OF PROJECTIVE PREPOSITIONS – THE PROBLEMS

In this section we classify the components of the spatial meaning of projective prepositions that have motivated our treatment. Throughout, the decoding problem, that is, generating adequate meanings for a locative expression in a particular situation, is our benchmark for representational adequacy.

The spatial meaning of a projective prepositional predication (e.g. "the chair is in front of the desk") can include: a constraint on the proximity of the located (LO) (e.g. "the chair") and reference objects (RO) (e.g. "the desk"); a directional constraint on the LO relative to the RO; and a relative orientation between the speaker, LO and RO. Constraints are of an intrinsically fuzzy nature such that different relative positions and orientations of the speaker, RO and LO satisfy the predication to different degrees, and combinations of constraints on the RO and LO originating from different predications must be readily accommodated.

2.1. *Reference frames*

Intrinsic, deictic and extrinsic interpretations of projective prepositions differ according to the reference frame with respect to which the directional constraint is characterised (Retz-Schmidt 1988). Figure 1 is an example of a scene that might give rise to predications which invoke each of these reference frames.

Intrinsic. In the intrinsic case the reference frame is centred at the RO and adopts the intrinsic orientations of the RO. Thus LO deemed to be "in front of" the RO under an intrinsic reading if it is located in the direction defined by the vector that is the half-plane of the *front* of the RO. In Figure 1 stool number 1 is intrinsically "in front of the desk".

Deictic. The reference frame for a deictic interpretation is centred at the speaker and adopts the speaker's orientation; deictic readings can be invoked explicitly with qualifications such as "from where we are standing"; when the RO has no intrinsic or extrinsic sidedness relating to the preposition used; or when intrinsic or extrinsic interpretations are ruled out on other grounds (e.g. the impossibility of spatially arranging the objects as required by the interpretation). In Figure 1 stool number 2 is deictically "in front of the desk".

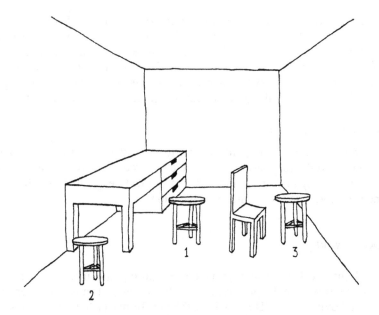

Fig. 1. Intrinsic, deictic and extrinsic uses of "in front of".

Extrinsic. Extrinsic readings can occur when the RO has no intrinsic sides relating to the locative preposition (e.g. for objects such as trees) but is in close proximity to another object that is strongly sided (e.g. such as a house); in which case the reference frame capturing the intrinsic orientations of the stronger sided object can be adopted by the RO. Referring to Figure 1 the chair is extrinsically "in front of stool number 3"; here the stool has inherited an extrinsic front from the right wall.

2.2. *Proximity constraints*

Projective prepositions necessarily place a constraint on the proximity of the located object and the reference object. Predications such as "the chair is in front of the desk" constrain the "desk" and "chair", to some degree, to be proximal to each other. Conversely projective prepositions such as "away from" predicate a distal relationship between the located and reference object. The degree of the proximity expressed in any projective prepositional predication varies according to a number of considerations including: the spatial context (the spatial extent and content of the scene described); and the absolute and relative sizes of the LO and RO (e.g. a car that is "left of" a lorry is typically less proximal than an apple and orange similarly described).

2.3. *Directional constraints*

In addition to the constraint on the proximity of the LO and RO, projective prepositions place a constraint on the position of the LO relative to a particular side of the RO. In the case of the intrinsic interpretation (see Section 2.1) of a predication such as "the stool is in front of the desk", the "stool" is located in some region of the space defined by the half-plane that is the intrinsic front of the "desk". Intuitively, the closer the "stool" is to the region of space defined by the projection of the desk's dimensions into this space, the more the spatial arrangement conforms to the prototypical interpretation of the predication.

2.4. *Interacting constraints*

Typically an object is located with respect to more than one RO by the means of multiple spatial predications. This places a requirement on the meaning representations of spatial predications that they must be capable of being easily combined, to give rise to a cumulative meaning.

3. RELATED WORK

Nearly all the work in recent years on computing the meanings of spatial prepositions stems from the prototype semantics of either Herskovits (Herskovits 1985) (Herskovits 1986) (Herskovits 1988) or Talmy (1983). In their system SOCCER, Schirra and Stopp (1993) adopt Herskovits' notion of a core meaning, and implement this as a typicality field (which is closely related to the potential field model, see Section 5.1). The ability to sum fields of different predications satisfies the compositionality requirement. Yet representational poverty exists with respect to the spatial and perceptual characteristics of the objects, as whilst directionality and proximity constraints are adequately captured for the intrinsic reference frame and set of objects, variation in the degree of constraint (for example, depending on the size of the reference object) and the potential for ambiguity arising from interpretations with respect to different reference frames are not accounted for.

Underlying Kalita's work (Kalita and Badler 1991) uses a conceptualisation of the space around a reference object as six orthogonal rectangular projected regions (based upon an enclosing cuboid idealisation of the object) due to Douglas and Novick (1987). Using this model and following Talmy's work, the semantics of projective prepositions are lexicalised as geometric-relation schemas. For example, the meaning of "behind (X, Y)" is encoded as the complex schema:

```
{g-union
geometric-relation:
    spatial-type:                    positional
    source-constraint-space:         back-half-axial-plane (X)
    destination-constraint-space:    back-half-axial-plane (Y)
geometric-relation:
    spatial-type:                    positional
    source-constraint-space:         centroid (X)
    destination-constraint-space:    back-zone (Y)}
```

Reference frame ambiguity is not addressed; directionality is too tightly restricted to locations with the region back-zone(X, Y), and proximity constraint is left to the "underlying constraint satisfaction techniques and the use of a weight slot in the template for constraint representation".

Within the framework of the LILOG project (Maienborn 1991) Ewald Lang implemented the two-level approach to the semantics of dimensional adjectives in which the perceptual and dimensional properties of objects are conceptually represented as object schemata (Bierwisch and Lang 1989). Further developed for projective spatial predications, Lang's object schemata are capable of distinguishing deictic and intrinsic readings, though without explicit reference to quantitative space (i.e. actual scenes and observers). In the following section we integrate Lang's object schemata with a quantitative representation of space, thus allowing us to determine the actual direction corresponding to a reading of a projective predication in a particular reference frame. Having selected the direction of the predication we use the potential field model to represent the directional and proximity constraints of the predication in a manner that is both dependent on the dimensions of the RO and LO concerned, and allows combinations of spatial predications.

4. PERCEPTUAL CHARACTERISTICS AND QUANTITATIVE MODELS OF SPACE

Even in systems where an explicit spatial reference is constructed (in a quantitative cartesian space) such as Kalita's implementation of Talmy's schema, and Schirra's use of typicality fields in the SOCCER system, projective prepositions are interpreted with respect to the intrinsic reference frame alone.

4.1. *Lang's object schemata*

In contrast to Schirra and Kalita, Lang's two-level treatment of the semantics of dimensional adjectives and prepositions includes the explicit representation of both the dimensional and perceptual characteristics of objects. Amongst the perceptual characteristics are the notions of intrinsic and deictic sidedness. For example, the conceptual representation of a desk is as follows:

a	max	b	vert	c	across
a1	i-left	b1	i-bottom	c1	i-front
a2	i-right	b2	i-top	c2	i-back

In this first schema a, b and c label three orthogonal axes centred at the object each of which can be instantiated by one or more dimensional assignment parameters (DAPs);[2] a1-a2, b1-b2 and c1-c2 are corresponding half-axes. Each half axis is labelled either nil or with an intrinsic side (e.g. i-front).

When the object is positioned in a scene the deictic sides of the object are assigned relative to the position of the speaker/viewer, that is, the deictic axis system. Deictic sides in the conceptual schema are prefixed by d-. For example if a desk is positioned "against the left wall" as in Figure 1 would result an instantiated conceptual schema for the "desk" of:

a	max	b	vert	c	across
a1	i-left	b1	i-bottom	c1	i-front
	d-front		d-bottom		d-right
a2	i-right	b2	i-top	c2	i-back
	d-back		d-top		d-left

In this second schema it can be seen that Lang's object schemata explicitly represent the sidedness of object in the spatial context in which it occurs. The preposition "behind" references the region of space projecting out from the object in direction c2 under the intrinsic interpretation, and a2 under the deictic interpretation.

4.2. Object sides and the depiction of the scene

The objects in the actual scene are positioned within a quantitative cartesian space centred at the speaker, we term this the depiction coordinate system (DCS). Further, the half-axes of the object schemata have a qualitative relationship with the DCS on the basis of the deictic side assignment. A half-axis tagged with d-right points in the $+x$ direction, d-top tagged axes in the $+y$ direction, and d-back tagged axes in the $+z$ direction. We can therefore directly relate the directions corresponding to both intrinsic and deictic interpretations to actual directions in our DCS.

4.3. Quantitative models of objects

Quantitative dimensional properties of an object are specified relative to a, b and c axes of the object schemata. The choice of spatial model for an object is a separate consideration, dependent on the graphical display package, the only condition being that the quantitative description maps onto the intrinsic side assignments of the half-axes of a, b and c. Consistency requires that rotations of the object schemata in satisfying a constraint on the orientation of the object must always be accompanied by a corresponding rotation of the quantitative spatial model of the object.

5. REPRESENTING SPATIAL CONSTRAINTS

Having outlined the mechanism by which intrinsic and deictic reference frames can be related to the DCS, the next task is to represent the directional and proximity constraints that comprise the meaning of a projective preposition within the particular reference frame identified.

5.1. *The potential field model*

The potential field model (PFM) was first used to model spatial occupancy in path-planning for robot manipulators (Khatib 1986). Objects in the workspace were characterised by potential fields that decreased in strength away from the object boundary. The field was viewed as a repulsive force and thus by summing the component fields for a cluttered workspace, the minimum potential contours are likely to lie along object-free paths.

Potential fields were first used in NLU systems in the SPRINT (SPatial Relation INTerpreter) system (Yamada *et al.* 1988, 1992), and a related concept of typicality fields in the SOCCER system (Schirra 1993). In SOCCER spatial predications are modeled in terms of sets of typicality fields where the value of the field strength at a point corresponds to the likelihood that the located object at this point is the referent of the predication. The cumulative field comprises a probability density function for the set of constraints which is solved (that is the most probable interpretation in terms of a LO position in the scene) by computing the location of the field's maximum. In SPRINT potential fields were used purely to capture the notion of the directionality of a spatial predication, whereas in SOCCER potential fields model both directionality and proximity. However, both systems are deficient in that they do not account for different reference frames (i.e. they only consider intrinsic interpretations); and fix the strength of potential fields for particular prepositions, thereby not allowing variation in the degree of spatial constraint according to the dimensions of the reference object.

In the previous section we solved the reference frame problem by integrating Lang's perceptual categorisation of objects and the quantitative DCS. Using Lang's qualitative representation of sidedness we identify the side of a reference object corresponding to readings under deictic or intrinsic reference frames; the next step is the construction of the preposition's characteristic potential field projecting out from the identified side of the object. To capture the dependency of the directionality and proximity of a predication on dimensional properties of the RO, we modify the three parameters of the potential field that quantify the degree of these constraints, computing their values based on quantitative knowledge of the reference and located objects.

5.2. *Gradual Approximation*

The fundamental component of the PFM is a potential function by which the cost of a spatial configuration is computed – the function can vary between 0 and $+\infty$, and the lower the value the more plausible the configuration. Spatial constraint is characterised by potential fields, and thus the potential field for a combination of constraints arising in a description is naturally handled by the linear combination of the component potential functions. The point of minimum potential in the field is the most plausible interpretation, and where there is more than one minimum an ambiguity exists.

The minimum for a potential field can be simply computed using an incremental gradual approximation based on the gradient of the field, though this method is well known to suffer in the case of fields with local minima.[3] Consider a potential function $P(x, y)$, assuming that the LO is placed at some arbitrary point (x', y') then the next approximation to the global minimum is given by $(x' + \Delta_x, y' + \Delta_y)$ where:

(1) $\qquad \Delta_x = -C \dfrac{\partial P}{\partial x}$,

(2) $\qquad \Delta_y = -C \dfrac{\partial P}{\partial y}$.

C is a positive constant.

5.3. *Potential functions*

5.3.1. *Potential functions to capture proximity*
The PFM can be used to represent the qualitative constraint, for example, resulting from the predication "the chair is near the desk". In this case there is no constraint on either the orientation of the located entity, nor on the direction of the region extending from the reference RO. We therefore adopt a simple elastic potential function, $P_{prox}(x, y)$, analogous to that of a mechanical spring:

(3) $\qquad P_{prox} = \dfrac{K_{prox}}{2} (\sqrt{((x - x_0)^2 + (y - y_0)^2)} - L_{prox})^2.$

Here K_{prox} is the spring constant (the strength of the spring), L_{prox} is the original length, (x_0, y_0) is the DCS coordinate of the fixed end of the spring (fixed at the position of the reference object), and (x, y) the position of the located entity in the field.

5.3.2. *Potential fields to capture directionality/proximity*
Spatial constraints arising from predications such as "the chair is in front of the desk", consist of both a proximity constraint and an additional constraint on the direction of the LO relative to the RO.

The latter notion is captured using a linear potential function as given in Equation (4).

(4) $\qquad P_{dir} = \dfrac{K_{dir}}{2} (x - x_0)^2.$

The proximity and directional constraint comprising the meaning of "in front of" is captured by the linear combination of P_{dir} and P_{prox}. The resulting field is shown in Figure 2 below.

Positions for objects constrained by multiple spatial predications are similarly computed from the linear combination of the potential fields characterising each predication. Figures 3 and 4 are screen shots of the *visualisations* generated by our prototype language visualizer, and illustrate the PFM satisfying the compositionality requirement. Figure 3 is the visualization of the predication "a chair is in front of the left desk". When the additional predication "the chair

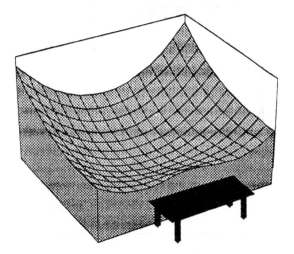

Fig. 2. Combined proximity and directional potential field.

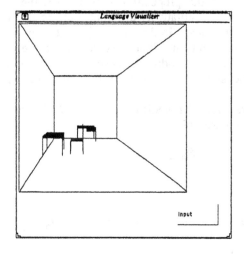

Fig. 3. Intrinsic interpretation of "a chair is in front of the left desk".

is near the back desk" is added the minimum energy configuration is calculated for the combined fields the resulting visualisation of which is shown in Figure 4.

5.3.3. *Object knowledge tuning of potential functions*
Consider the two predications:

"The chair is near the desk"
"The car is near the house"

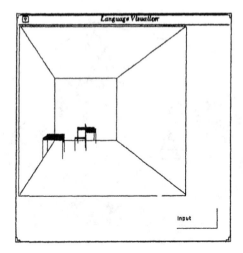

Fig. 4. Adding the predication "the chair is near the back desk".

Both expressions use the preposition ("near") yet their meanings whilst qualitatively similar are quantitatively different – the "car" and "house" are far more likely to be further apart. In the case of projective prepositions the quantitative variations in proximity and directional constraints are similarly dependent on RO and LO dimensions.[4] Modifying the potential function constants on the basis of object dimensions is a mechanism by which this dependency can be captured.

Taking the general case of a predication $Prep_{proj}(X, Y)$ where X is the located object and Y the reference object:

(5) $P_{\frac{X}{Y}} = P_{prox, \frac{X}{Y}} + P_{dir, \frac{X}{Y}}$

where,

(6) $P_{prox, \frac{X}{Y}} = \dfrac{K_{prox, \frac{X}{Y}}}{2} (\sqrt{(x - x_0)^2 + (y - y_0)^2} - L_{prox, \frac{X}{Y}})^2,$

(7) $P_{dir, \frac{X}{Y}} = \dfrac{K_{dir, \frac{X}{Y}}}{2} (x - x_0)^2.$

The shape and extent of the potential field $P_{X/Y}$ is governed by the three constants:

1. $K_{prox, X/Y}$
    Directly proportional to the proximity localisation of the minimum energy configuration.

2. $L_{prox, X/Y}$
    The distance of the minimum energy configuration from the reference object.

3. $K_{\text{dir}, X/Y}$

Directly proportional to the directional localisation of the minimum energy configuration.

In our language visualizer (Figures 3 and 4) values for $K_{\text{prox}, X/Y}$, $L_{\text{prox}, X/Y}$, and $K_{\text{dir}, X/Y}$ are linearly dependent on the dimensions of the RO and LO, which gives rise to intuitively more plausible depictions for the same preposition with different reference and located objects.

6. CONCLUDING REMARKS

By integrating Lang's representation of perceptual characteristics of objects with a quantitative model of the objects, deictic and intrinsic axis systems can be related to actual directions in the DCS. Once the directions corresponding to deictic and intrinsic interpretations of a projective preposition and the coordinates of the reference object have been identified, the potential field model of proximity and directionality constraints can be constructed, and the minimum energy configuration computed and displayed.

Issues that remain to be addressed include: determining how and when extrinsic interpretations should be invoked; how constraints arising from the spatial context can be accounted for by potential field tuning (e.g. the positions of nearby objects); and how factors relating to the perceptual context can be incorporated (e.g. interpretations that lead to the located object being hidden from view should in general be disallowed).

NOTES

[1] This research was kindly funded by the Matsushita Electric Industrial Company Limited.

[2] DAPs are not of direct interest here although they are fundamental to the process of dimensional designation and important where dimensional assignment might result in a reorientation of the conceptual object (e.g. "the pole is high").

[3] Due to the rarity of very complex combinations of constraints it is unlikely that local minima will be a problem.

[4] This is of course one of many factors, for example, functional dependency.

REFERENCES

Bierwisch, M. & Lang, E. (1980). *Dimensional Adjectives: Grammatical Structure and Conceptual Interpretation*. Springer-Verlag: Berlin-Heidelberg-New York.

Douglas, S. & Novick, D. (1987). Consistency and Variance in Spatial Reference. In Proceedings of *The Ninth Annual Cognitive Science Society Meeting*, 417–426.

Herskovits, A. (1985). Semantics and Pragmatics of Locative Expressions. *Cognitive Science* 9: 341–378.

Herskovits, A. (1986). *Language and Spatial Cognition – An Interdisciplinary Study of the Prepositions in English*. Cambridge University Press: Cambridge, UK.

Herskovits, A. (1988). Spatial Expression and the Plasticity of Meaning. In Rudzka-Ostyn, B. (ed.) *Topics in Cognitive Linguistics*, 403–427. Benjamins: Amsterdam-Philadelphia.

Kalita, J. & Badler, B. (1991). Interpreting Prepositions Physically. In Proceedings of *The Ninth National Conference on Artificial Intelligence*, 105–110. Anaheim, CA.

Khatib, O. (1986). Real-Time Obstacle Avoidance for Manipulators and Modile Robots. *The International Journal of Robotics Research* **5**(1): 90–98.

Lang, E. (1993). A Two-Level Approach to Projective Prepositions. In Zelinsky-Wibbelt, C. (ed) *Semantics of Prepositions*. Mouton de Gruyter: Berlin.

Maienborn, J. R. (ed.) (1991). *Processing Spatial Knowledge in LILOG*. IWBS Report 157, IBM Germany.

Retz-Schmidt, G. (1988). Various Views on Spatial Prepositions. *AI Magazine* **9**(2): 95–105.

Schirra, J. R. J. & Stopp, E. (1993). ANTLIMA – A Listener Model with Mental Images. In Proceedings of *The International Joint Conference on Artificial Intelligence, 1993*. Chambery, France.

Talmy, L. (1983). How Language Structures Space. In Pick, H. & Acredolo, L. (ed.) *Spatial Orientation: Theory, Research, and Application*, 225–282. Plenum Press: New York.

Yamada, A., Nishida, T. & Doshita, S. (1988). Figuring out Most Plausible Interpretation from Spatial Descriptions. In Proceedings of *The 12th International Conference on Computational Linguistics (COLING-88)*, 764–769.

Yamada, A., Yamamoto, T., Ikeda, H., Nishida, T. & Doshita, S. (1992). Reconstructing Spatial Image From Natural Language Texts. In Proceedings of *The 16th International Conference on Computational Linguistics (COLING-92)*, 1279–1283. Nantes, France.

Artificial Intelligence Review **8**: 159–174, 1994.
© 1994 *Kluwer Academic Publishers. Printed in the Netherlands.*

From Vision to Multimodal Communication: Incremental Route Descriptions*

WOLFGANG MAAß

Cognitive Science Program, Universität des Saarlandes, D-66041 Saarbrücken,
E-mail: maass@cs.uni-sb.de

Abstract. In the last few years, within cognitive science, there has been a growing interest in the connection between vision and natural language. The question of interest is: How can we discuss what we see. With this question in mind, we will look at the area of *incremental route descriptions*. Here, a speaker step-by-step presents the relevant route information in a 3D-environment. The speaker must adjust his/her descriptions to the currently visible objects. Two major questions arise in this context: 1. How is visually obtained information used in natural language generation? and 2. How are these modalities coordinated? We will present a computational framework for the interaction of vision and natural language descriptions which integrates several processes and representations. Specifically discussed is the interaction between the spatial representation and the presentation representation used for natural language descriptions. We have implemented a prototypical version of the proposed model, called MOSES.

Key words: spatial cognition, wayfinding, multimodal presentation, object representation.

1. INTRODUCTION

Recently in cognitive science there has been a growing interest in the connection between vision and natural language. The reductionist approach to separate each of these topics tends to ignore the fact that human beings integrate both abilities to act and communicate in their environment.

In the project VITRA (Visual Translator), we are investigating the connection between vision and multimodal communication in dynamic environments from a computational point of view (cf. Herzog and Wazinski, this volume). In a subproject, we are specialising on the generation of multimodal incremental route descriptions which combine natural language and spontaneous gestures[1] (cf. Maaß 1993). The main question for this kind of communication is how to lead a person to his/her destination by describing the route during the trip itself. Then persons were asked to give incremental route descriptions always used different modalities, e.g. speech and spontaneous gestures, to describe the route. Thus, two of the interesting subquestions are: (1) How is visually obtained information used in natural language production? and (2) How are these modalities coordinated? Our model, called MOSES, is led by the psychological results

of (cf. Allen and Kautz 1985). This report states that humans mentally partition the continuous and complex spatial environment into segments of information. These segments represent a partial view of the actual environment. We
propose two selection steps: the visual selection and the presentation selection.
These selections reduce the complexity of information and the complexity of
computation, making it possible to describe the route efficiently.

In Section 2, we suggest some of the major concerns which are central for
incremental route descriptions, followed by a discussion of related research.
For the process of incremental route descriptions, we have designed a computational model which is presented in Section 3. Two separate input processes
determine the behaviour of the entire process: the visual recognition (Section 3.1)
and the determination of path information obtained from maps (Section 3.2).
The interaction between the spatial representation and the linguistic representation, underlying the presentation processes is presented in Section 3.3. In Section
4.1 we demonstrate how to plan the presentation structures in order to effectively communicate the obtained information. The modespecific generators for
natural language and gestures are briefly mentioned in Section 4.2 and, in Section
5, we give a conclusion and a projection on some open questions.

2. MOTIVATION

Route descriptions are common communicative actions in everyday life which
can be divided into two classes: *complete* (or *pre-trip*) route descriptions and
incremental route descriptions. In order to give a description of the whole route
we use complete route descriptions. Here, a well-known problem for the route
finders is remembering many details at one time. En route to their destination,
they normally cannot ask the same person for more details. In *incremental route
descriptions*, e.g., descriptions given by a co-driver, the route finders receive
relevant route information as it is needed. This reduces the cognitive load. Central
to incremental route descriptions are temporal constraints on both the generation and following of route descriptions. The construction of a presentation
involves, a minimum of the following phases: determination of new information, determination of a presentation structure, transmission of the information,
and consideration of the length of time the hearer will presumably require to
understand and verify the information. Furthermore, the information must be
presented in accordance with the strengths of each presentation mode, while taking
into account the information to be presented and the current environment. In
this work, we address the first two phases. In the scenario considered here, the
speaker, SP, and hearer, H, travel by car in an urban environment. The task for
SP is to give adequate information to H. With the term *adequate* we mean that
SP must determine what is relevant to the hearer.

In this project we are not concerned with the use of long-term mental representations of spatial information, often called *cognitive maps*, but rather with
the phenomena which arise when the speaker uses both a map and visible information of the current environment to determine and describe a route in unknown

territory. For everyday route descriptions, various kinds of maps are used. The use of maps for description generation, be they street maps, region maps, world maps or anatomic maps, is quite standard. If one desires to go from point A to point B one first tries to orient oneself within the map and environment. In the next phase, one looks for an appropriate path from A to B while keeping track of the intended route. Both phases, *orientation* and *wayfinding*, are fundamentally guided by vision. Successful navigation requires a consideration of the underlying spatial structure of the environment. On a map of Australia, for instance, types of landmarks and types of paths differ between big cities and the Australian outback. In a city, houses and road signs play an important role whereas in the outback sacred sites and the four cardinal points are the main guidelines.[2] In this work, we deal mainly with urban environments.

When we consider the connection between vision and natural language, we must take into account that both sides have different requirements for the representation of spatial information. In the field of vision, there are some attempts to represent shape information about objects formally. For instance, Marr's 3D model represents an object's shape by compositions of cones (cf. Marr 1982) or Biederman's generalized cone representation (cf. Biederman 1990). On the linguistic side, representations use geometrical and conceptual information of objects and topological information of path segments as an underlying structure for generating descriptions of spatial arrangements. There are some approaches which try to connect vision and natural language production by defining an interface between the spatial representation and the linguistic representation (cf. Landau and Jackendoff 1993; Glasgow 1993).

Psychological experiments have been conducted concerning the human ability to process and represent information about the spatial environment (e.g., cf. Tolman 1948; Piaget *et al.* 1960; Siegel and White 1975; Yeap 1988). In the field of Environmental Psychology (cf. Stokols and Altman 1987), there is a well-known distinction between *route knowledge* and *landmark knowledge* (cf. Piaget *et al.* 1960; Siegel and White 1975). Route knowledge and its connections to other human abilities has been investigated through several approaches (cf. Blades 1991; Garling 1989; Hayes-Roth and Hayes-Roth 1979). In this context, complete route descriptions have been thoroughly examined for psychological (cf. Streeter *et al.* 1985; Thorndyke and Goldin 1983) and linguistic (cf. Klein 1982; Wunderlich and Reinelt 1982; Meier *et al.* 1988; Habel 1987) reasons, but little is known about incremental route descriptions. Klein and Wunderlich *et al.* have divided the communication of complete route descriptions into four phases: introduction, main part, verification and final phase. The sentence structures in complete route descriptions have been found to be extremely restricted and sometimes schematic. What is supported by route descriptions in our corpus where we found 31 different descriptions of spatial relations and 13 different verbs of movement. Furthermore, results showed that, in general, the syntactic structure of each sentence is very restricted.

Within the research field of cognitive maps, a distinction is made between *route knowledge*, which has more procedural aspects, and *survey* or *map knowledge*, which has more abstract aspects (cf. Thorndyke and Hayes-Roth 1982; Gluck

1991). In computational models route knowledge has been more intensively investigated than survey knowledge (cf. Kuipers 1978; McCalla and Schneider 1979; Leiser and Zilbershatz 1989; Gopal *et al.* 1989).

3. THE PROPOSED COMPUTATIONAL MODEL

From a phenomenlogical point of view, we determine two major phases during the generation of route descriptions. First, the speaker, SP, looks for an appropriate path from the starting point to the destination; this is called *wayfinding*. To do this, SP may use different media, but most common is the use of maps or mental representations. After the determination of the next path segment, SP describes the route. Usually this description is dominated by speech and spontaneous gestures but it can also include sketches. As SP moves through the dynamic environment and gives step-by-step descriptions, SP mentions landmarks, regions and spatial relations obtained by vision. This process is in contrast to the human ability to describe a route using only a cognitive map of a specific area. In this paper, we assume the speaker has had no experience with the given environment and must use a map to find his/her way.

On the process level, we assume interaction between the wayfinding and the presentation. It would otherwise be difficult to justify a description compiled from information obtained from a map or visible information of the current environment. While describing a non-trivial route, it is common to switch between wayfinding and presentation. Therefore, we assume a process which controls the interaction between both phases.

We have developed a model of the process of *multimodal, incremental route description*. Its basic architecture consists of a visual recognition process, a wayfinding process, a planning process, and two presentation processes (see Fig. 1). The wayfinding process models the human ability to look for a route while using a map and information received by vision. Interactions between vision, wayfinding and presentation processes are supervised and coordinated by the planning process. In general, all subprocesses depend on temporal aspects concerning the coordination of communication and the current environment, on presumed properties of the questioner, and environmental parameters such as weather, time, and light.

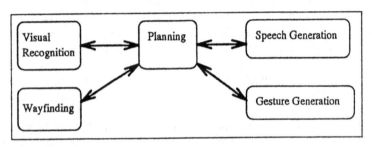

Fig. 1. Process model.

Different representation structures are associated with each process. Visual perception receives information from the current environment. We follow Neisser, who proposes that visual perception is led by schemata which enable us to select specific information even in complex and dynamic environments (cf. Neisser 1976). We use the term *visual percept* to denote an object-oriented representation structure. It is a dualistic representation consisting of an *object representation* and a *generalized representation* (see Fig. 3). The object representation integrates a *geometric* and a *conceptual* representation of an object. Landau and Jackendoff investigated that people use abstract spatial representations of objects (generalized representation) to determine spatial relations between objects. But on the other hand, Landau and Jackendoff discovered that in order to describe an object verbally we need a geometrical (cf. Landau and Jackendoff 1993) and a conceptual representation (cf. Jackendoff 1987).

The wayfinding process extracts path information from a map, for this, we also use a dualistic representation. On one hand, the speaker, SP, has survey information of the entire path. This information is necessary for a global orientation and to provide abstract information about distance to the destination. On the other hand, SP matches this general information to an exact topographical partition of the path which leads his/her movement and the description for the current time interval.

Information obtained by vision and maps is integrated by the planning process into a central spatial representation structure, called *segment* (see Fig. 2). Because of the incrementality of the entire process, this structure is extended step-by-step. Using this representation, the planning process extracts object information and interrelates relevant objects to construct a linguistic-oriented presentation structure. A segment provides information about objects, path segments, and spatial relations which are to be selected for the *presentation representation*. Because of the incrementality, the presentation representation can influence the spatial representation. In order to describe an object uniquely, the presentation planner may ask for more information than is presently available by the spatial representation. In this case the visual recognition must focus on this object to obtain more information. The same holds for path information. When the next path segments are needed, the wayfinding process searches for new path information.

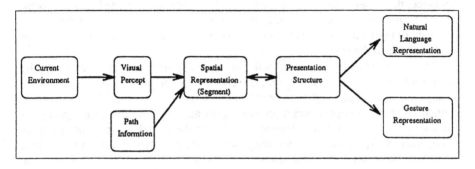

Fig. 2. Structure model.

Because our interviews have shown that the linguistic structure of route descriptions is limited, we use a schematic approach to present relevant information about the environment. These schemata disassociate presentation information into parts: Natural language generation and spontaneous gesture generation (see Section 4.1).

3.1. *What is the role of vision in our model?*

In our model, we do not deal with low-level aspects of visual perception, (cf. Marr 1982) rather we start on a higher level where specific areas in the current visual field are focused on. This is similar to the focussing technique used in linguistically oriented approaches (e.g., Grosz 1981). The current focus defines an *inner* visual field, in which we can identify, categorize and select distinct objects. The current visual focus also determines the main landmarks which are used in the presentation; Vision leads communication. If the visually accessed information is not sufficient, vision will be led by the demands of the presentation. Thus, we ask: How can high-level visual data be processed efficiently for use in multimodal communication? Our approach is based on psychological investigations by Ittelson (cf. 1960), Neisser (cf. 1976), and Schneider and Shiffrin (cf. 1977). Ittelson has performed a number of experiments involving visual space cues, whereas Neisser has developed a schema-based approach to visual perception. Schneider and Shiffrin found that a visual search can be divided into *automatic* and *controlled processes.*

Considering these results, the visual recognition process generates two different spatial representations of landmarks: *An object representation* and a *generalized representation.*

In our model, we use cuboids and rectangles to generate geometric representations. Associated with geometric properties, the model of a landmark is the conceptual model which includes size, colour, distance to the speaker's position, and functional properties (cf. Gapp 1994; Maaß *et al.* 1994). The generalized representation is a cuboid which surrounds the landmark associated with two kinds of axis: *generating axis* (e.g., top/down, see Fig. 3) and *orienting axes* (e.g., front/back, left/right, see Fig. 3). A generating axis is central to Marr's accounts of object shape and determines the object's principal axis (cf. Marr 1982). For instance, the generating axis of a human body is vertically oriented. In our model, the orienting axes are orthogonal to the generating axis and to one another (e.g., corresponding to the front/back and side/side axes; for more details cf. (Landau and Jackendoff 1993)).

Recent studies support the hypothesis a nonlinguistic disparity, between the representation of *what* and *where*, underlies how language represents objects and places (cf. Landau and Jackendoff 1993). Kosslyn asserts that the spatial component of mental imagery preserves *where* information about the meaningful parts of a scene and their relative locations, whereas the visual component preserves *what* information about how an image looks (cf. Kosslyn 1987). In this sense, the object representation of a landmark is used to determine *what* information, whereas the generalized representation serves for *where* information. Thus, geo-

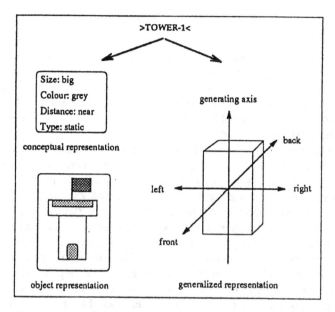

Fig. 3. The object representation and generalized representation of landmark Tower-1. The generating axis is the vertical axis, whereas the orienting axes are horizontal.

metrical or physical and conceptual information about landmarks refer to the object representation. Spatial relations between speaker, hearer, and landmarks are determined by using generalized representations.

In our model, we use restricted salience criteria: size, shape, and colour. The visual recognition process identifies landmarks without request (automatic visual recognition) or demand of the planning process (controlled visual recognition). The planning process uses domain-specific strategies to request specific landmarks. These strategies provide alternative objects if the visual recognition process cannot find the requested object. Thus, the visual recognition process can be described as follows:

1. While there is no request, identify objects with the strongest saliency (automatic visual recognition)
2. If there is a request for a specific object look for it in a default region (controlled visual recognition)
3. If this specific object cannot be found report it to the planning process and go to step 1.

An example for automatic visual recognition is the identification of a red telephone box in a German city. We see this telephone box although we might not be looking for it. An example of controlled visual recognition is, driving a car towards a crossing. In this case, the following strategy is normally used: First look for a traffic light somewhere in the upper right visual area. If the visual recognition process cannot find a traffic light, look for a traffic sign. If there is no traffic sign, supply the most salient object.

3.2. *How is map knowledge used for wayfinding?*

Visual recognition provides visual reconstruction access to the immediate environment. To find a non-trivial path, we commonly use maps to orient ourselves and to determine an optimal path considering several constraints. When humans use a map, they choose an abstract path. This is mainly determined by a direct connection line between the starting point and the destination and a spatially restricted search area around this path. This area, which we call the *rough path*, is determined before the speaker, SP, starts navigating and is elaborated upon, stepwise, while moving towards the destination. Incremental use of the map appears to be due to the limited capacity of working memory. We have developed a waysearch process that is based on this type of incremental searching.

In work done by Klein, the construction of the primary plan for complete route descriptions is divided into two techniques: advanced and stepwise planning. Klein proposed that these techniques can be used in combination. Advanced planning means that the route description process is mostly sequential, i.e. that first the wayfinding process determines the entire path. Then this path is described without going back to the wayfinding process. In contrast to this, stepwise route planning implies that there is an interaction between the wayfinding and the route presentation process (cf. Klein 1982). Gluck remarks that the relevant potential optimizing functions for the wayfinding process are not restricted to minimal distance or even minimal effort (cf. Gluck 1991). The wayfinding process in the TOUR model is a simple and slow approach to finding a way (cf. Kuipers 1977). In the TRAVELLER model proposed by Leiser and Zilbershatz an incomplete wayfinding process is used which cannot find partial paths in the cognitive map (cf.Leiser and Zilbershatz 1989).

We distinguish between the selection of a path that is known by experience (experience-based wayselection) and the search for a path using a map (cf. Elliott and Lesk 1982). In the TOUR model (see cf. Kuipers 1977) and in the TRAVELLER model (cf. Leiser and Zilbershatz 1989) experience-based approach is emphasized. Both models are based on a graph network which represents a 'mental' model of the spatial environment and concentrate on integrating new knowledge about the *external* world. Leiser and Zilbershatz divide route knowledge into a *basic network*, for the main routes, and a *secondary network*, for other routes. This division is based on experiments done by Pailhous (cf. 1969) and Chase (cf. 1982). A similar approach is presented by Gopal *et al.* In their NAVIGATOR model (cf. Gopal *et al.* 1989), they use a hierarchical structure for representing knowledge about the spatial environment.

The waysearching process is not as well understood as the experience-based wayselection process. In most of the relevant work, the route that must be presented is always previously known or generated by some straightforward algorithm like the A*-algorithm.[3] The waysearch process must also observe various kinds of constraints. If the person goes by car, the search process must consider streets accessible by cars and the type of street. For instance, for long-distance trips, car-drivers prefer to use highways as opposed to side-paths. Also relevant are external influences, such as the weather, rush-hour, accidents, or brightness. If it rains it is preferable to describe a covered path to a walker. There is some evidence that the cognitive ability of wayfinding combines the experience-based wayselection process and the waysearch process. For example, it is not usual that we remember paths in a large-scale space without searching for path segments. We combine wayselection and waysearch when we navigate along a route.

When we asked people to find a non-trivial path they tended to use a restricted area in which they attempted to determine path segments. This area was mainly determined by an imaginary line between the starting point and the destination and by an area around this line. People, unfamiliar with the given map, determined the path stepwise.

Based on these results, we have developed an incremental search algorithm which integrates most of the above mentioned constraints. This algorithm is a modified version of the RTA*-algorithm (cf. Korf 1990). One of the main features of this algorithm is that a search is directed by a spatial corridor, which serves as a model for a rough path. The search algorithm prefers paths inside the corridor. Paths outside of the corridor are considered, but weighted according to their distance from the corridor. The algorithm computes the following path segment from the current turning-point to the next turning-point. Thus it transforms the rough path into topographical path segments.

3.3. *Integration of map knowledge and visually acquired knowledge*

Information about landmarks and path segments acquired through visual recognition must be interrelated with topographical information obtained from a map. In each situation the speaker must combine four different kinds of information to describe a route while navigating along the path. First, the rough path is used to keep track of global orientation and it restricts the search area in a map. With the help of a rough path, a local topographical piece of the path is selected from a map. After that, the speaker must identify the path segment in the current environment. Representations of landmarks obtained by vision, is the third type of information. On the fourth level, those spatial relations are noted which have been established between speaker, hearer, and landmarks as perceived from SP's position (cf. Gapp 1994). All four kinds of information are integrated in a central structure, called a *segment* which serves as the internal spatial representation used for route descriptions.

Consider for instance a path segment where the speaker stands at position A and is oriented towards point B (see Fig. 4). The topographical path segment between point and B is a projection of the rough path on the map. In this case A and B are turning-points. Associated with this path segment are landmarks, tower-1 and house-4, determined by salience criteria.

A segment guides the speaker's orientation, navigation and route description for a specific time interval. The length of this interval depends on the underlying spatial structure and the kind of navigation. If a non-trivial route must be described, the speaker does not keep a description of the whole route readily mentally accessible, but only the part which is currently relevant. Segments are

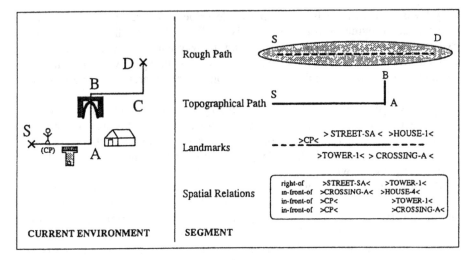

Fig. 4. Complete segmentation structure: How to derive a segmentation strucutre from an environment.

mainly determined by large changes in orientation. For instance, if SP turns left at a crossing, SP usually enters a new spatial environment which was not visible before the turn. Information necessary before SP turned left, is normally useless after the turn, but it is still accessible and SP can refer to it which demands a mental long-term representation. Each segment is added to a general spatial representation format, called the *segmentation structure*. The segmentation structure is the whole spatial representation from the starting point, to the current situation, as seen from the speaker's perspective.

A segment is the basis for the presentation planning process. We will present an example to clarify what is meant by a segment and by a segmentation structure. Assume the spatial configuration shown in Fig. 4. The goal of SP is to present a route from the *starting point*, S, to the destination, D. On the chosen route, there are three turning-point landmarks (A, B, and C). Between S and A is one landmark, a tower on the right side, and between A and B are two landmarks, namely a house on the right side and a bridge over the street. The streets are labelled by *street-1* to *street-4* starting at S.

The topographical path level of a segment represents path segments between the starting point S, the turning-points, A, B, C, and the destination D. Empirical data shows that turning-points are frequently used landmarks in route descriptions (cf. Klein 1982; Wunderlich and Reinelt 1982; Habel 1987; Meier *et al.* 1988; Hoeppner *et al.* 1990).

In the third step, all landmarks accessed by vision such as like house, trees, human beings, and animals are integrated. The difference between the second and the third level is that we switch from *large-scale space* to *small-scale space*. "Large scale space is space whose structure cannot be observed from a single viewpoint (Kuipers 1978)". In contrast to this, small-scale space includes all spatial objects which can be seen from a single viewpoint. A reason to use large-scale space information in route descriptions is that it is not necessary to perceive the next turning-point from the current position. Small-scale space information is needed when we mention a house on the right side. It is then necessary that the house be currently visible.

Every time SP leaves the current path segment, SP must determine the next one. For example, if SP turns left at A, SP leaves SA and enters AB which now becomes the current path segment. Now, to describe the transition from segment AB to BC, SP must first determine path segment BC.

The total segmentation structure is incrementally generated along the way from starting point to destination. This reflects the observation that SP at first does not know the entire topographical path in detail at the beginning. Another observation is that, for humans, it is easy to choose a new path if they have gone the wrong way. In our proposed model, a new rough path, the new segment and its successor must all be determined before proceeding. Starting from a given segment, the planning process determines a central presentation structure. Here, the spatial representation and the linguistic representation are integrated, similar to the approach of Landau and Jackendoff (cf. Landau and Jackendoff 1993). Those parts of the segmentation structure to be integrated in the communication are selected by the planner.

4. PLANNING PROCESS

The integration of spatial knowledge and path information, for use in natural language descriptions, requires flexible control processes. Therefore, we decided to use a plan-based approach. A central planning problem handles the temporal aspects of both the generation and following of route descriptions; this problem has received relatively little attention in previous planning research. Temporal relations, e.g., "Turn left *immediately/after 5 minutes*", are an important part of incremental route descriptions. Spatial relations involved in imperatives of movement ("Keep going along the field!") only hold for a set length. Thus, the planner needs to integrate both spatial and temporal information. Beside these content-dependent temporal relations, the planning process must also consider *external* temporal constraints given by relations between speaker, hearer, and the current environment. For instance, time the speaker and hearer need until they reach the crossing. Also, different strategies must be evaluated, to choose and apply the best strategy in a given situation.

4.1. *How do we plan the presentation?*

In *complete route description*, there are two competing strategies: planning in advance and stepwise planning (cf. Klein 1982, p. 7). Because of the incrementality, the process can be characterized as a stepwise planning process. At the starting point there is only a *rough path* to the destination point and the information for the first segment. The main task of the planning process is converting spatial information into presentation-oriented information, but it also determines the temporal structure of the presentation.

In our approach, the planning process deals with two major problems: Landmark selection and establishment of spatial relations. Salience of landmarks depends on various parameters, e.g. form, colour, and function of a landmark, light and weather conditions etc. (see Section 3.1). We define a *spatial relation* by specifying certain conditions for each landmark in a spatial configuration. Spatial relations are considered to be independent of any particular natural language and they form the basis for analysis of spatial prepositions within the framework of reference semantics (cf. Schirra 1990; Gapp 1994).

Landmarks, selected by vision, are not isolated from one another, but can be interrelated by spatial relations. Following Landau and Jackendoff, spatial relations mainly depend on boundedness, surface, or volumetric nature of a landmark and its axial structure (cf. Landau and Jackendoff 1993, p. 232). For instance, in Fig. 4 the landmarks bridge-1, house-4, and tower-1 can be described by object features or by their spatial relationship with one another.

The transformation of information, extracted from a segment, into a presentation structure is achieved using two techniques: schematic and non-schematic (cf. Maaß 1993). It is clear that the usage of schemata depends on familiarity of the current environment and the intended description. In addition to hearer and environment dependencies, external parameters, like time of day, are important. For example, a landmark may be relevant in the night because it is illuminated, but not during the day.

In general, no problems arise when switching between verbal and gestic presentation modes if SP desires to inform the hearer about, for example, a red house on the right side of a street. In MOSES, SP presents route descriptions by verbal expressions or pointing gestures. Therefore, we propose a central presentation representation. When the planning process selects items of a segment to be integrated into the presentation representation, it considers the cross-referentiality of information (cf. Wahlster *et al.* 1992). This means that an item can be parallely presented in different modes. To solve this problem the planning process keeps track of the valid use of information in different presentation modes.

The planning process distributes information for the presentation representation according to the individual strength of each presentation mode. For presentation processes we use several approaches (cf. Herzog *et al.* 1993; Maaß 1993). To explain of the main points, we give a simple example where the turn from path segment SA into AB is represented by two presentation structures (see Fig. 4.1):

The modespecific presentation structure (cf. Fig. 4.1) provides global information, such as the presentation mode and the way the questioner moves (M-TYPE). By using this and the action type (ACTION), a movement verb is determined. The presentation structure also contains information about the current path segment, ACTUAL(type(street-1)), and the following path segment, NEXT(type(street-2)). Another important item of the structure is the next turning-point, UNTIL(type(crossing-1)), which defines the connection to the next path segment. The time interval, t_i, describes the moment when the information is expected to be presented. All landmarks selected by the presentation planner are collected in the landmark list (LM). Spatial relations between these landmarks

VERBAL(	M-TYPE	by-feet
	TIME	(t_1)
	ACTUAL	(type(street-1))
	UNTIL	(type(crossing-1))
	ACTION	(move-straight))
VERBAL(	M-TYPE	(by-feet)
	TIME	(t_2)
	LM	(type (house-4, attr(colour, grey)))
	SPATIAL-REL	(in-front-of,turn-point-1,house-4)
	SPATIAL-REL	(left-of, street-2, street-1)
	ACTION	(turn-left))

Fig. 5. Two presentation structures for natural language generation.

and the speaker, which are to be described, are given by a list (SPATIAL-REL).

With this presentation structure, the speech process generates the following description:

> Go down the street, until you reach the next crossing.   (during t_1)
> In front of the grey coloured house, turn left.   (during t_2)

4.2. Modespecific presentation processes

In MOSES, we use several presentation modes: 2-dimensional graphical projection, perspective graphical animation, incremental natural language, and pointing gestures. The environment is represented by a 3-dimensional geometric model (see Fig. 6).

Survey knowledge, about the region in question, is represented by a 2-dimensional projection onto the horizontal plane. This presentation mode alone is not optimal because of the cognitive effort the user must invest matching the projected landmarks or crossroads with their actual visual appearance. Here views, simulating the speaker's perspective, can help. Both graphical presentation modes can be supplemented with several display techniques, such as highlighting, flashing, etc.

In MOSES, the incremental generation of surface structures is achieved with an incremental generator for German and English (cf. Finkler and Schauder 1992), based on Tree Adjoining Grammars (cf. Joshi 1983). For spontaneous gestures, we have developed a prototypical module for generating arrow-based pointing gestures.

5. CONCLUSION

Research on route descriptions, guided by vision, leads to the conclusion that we need to assume at least four subprocesses: a visual recognition process, a wayfinding process, a presentation process, and a planning process. Central to the representation of spatial information is the incrementally generated segmen-

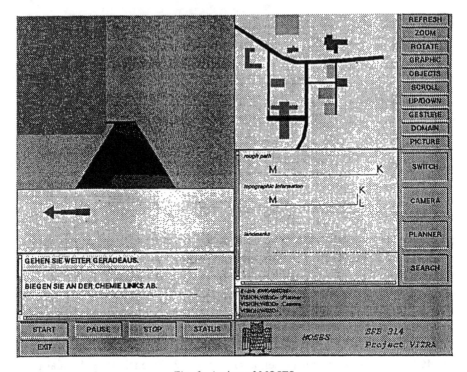

Fig. 6. A view of MOSES.

tation structure. The interaction between spatial information and presentation is directed by the planing process. The planning process enables convergence of information from the segmentation structure by selecting relevant information and by establishing spatial relations between landmarks and the speaker's position. Information about landmarks is obtained from a dualistic object representation.

We have presented a global framework, which still needs refinements and perhaps modifications. Our model will also need to be compared with the results of future psychological research. Specifically the interaction between the sub-processes and the representation structure needs to be examine more closely. Our current work is concerned with the seamless integration of temporal constraints. We also evaluate whether the spatial representation and the presentation representation are sufficient for route descriptions in dynamic scenes.

NOTES

* This work is funded by the cognitive science program *Graduiertenkolleg 'Kognitionswissenschaft'* of the German Research Community (DFG). I am grateful for Jörg Bau, Joachim Paul, Roger Knop, and Bernd Andes, and Amy Norton.
[1] Spontaneous gestures are a beginning research topic (cf. Sitaro 1993). Sitaro considers spontaneous gestures as a supporting mode for speech. Also, it seems that gestures can also carry information on their own. For instance, when we say "Go there!" and give a spontaneous gesture showing a trajectory rightwards.

[2] David Lewis has made some interesting investigations concerning the wayfinding ability of aboriginies in the Australian outback (cf. Lewis 1976).
[3] It is very unlikely that common heuristic search algorithms, like A*, are similar to human search ability in maps.

REFERENCES

Allen, J. F. & Kautz, H. A. (1985). A Model of Naive Temporal Reasoning. In Hobbs, J. R. & Moore, R. C. (eds.) *Formal Theories of the Commensense World*, 251–267. Ablex: Norwood, NJ.

Biederman, I. (1990). Higher-Level Vision. In Osherson, D. N., Kossyln, S. M. & Hollerbach, J. M. (eds.) *Visual Cognition and Action: An Invitation to Cognitive Science* (Volume 2), 41–72. MIT Press: Cambridge, MA.

Blades, M. (1991). Wayfinding Theory and Research: The Need for a New Approach. In Mark, D. M. & Frank, A. U. (eds.) *Cognitive and Linguistic Aspects of Geographic Space*, 137–165. Kluwer: Dordrecht.

Chase, W. G. (1982). Spatial Representations of Taxi Drivers. In Rogers D. R. & Sloboda J. A. (eds.) *Acquisition of Symbolic Skills*. Plenum: New York.

Elliott, R. J. & Lesk, M. E. (1982). Route Finding in Street Maps by Computers and People. In Proceedings of *AAAI-82*, 258–261. Pittsburgh, PA.

Finkler, W. & Schauder, A. (1992). Effects of Incremental Output on Incremental Natural Language Generation. In proceedings of *The Tenth ECAI*, 505–507. Vienna.

Gapp, K.-P. (1994). On the Basic Meanings of Spatial Relations: Computation and Evaluation in 3D Space. To appear in: Proceedings of *The Twelfth AAAI-94*. Seattle, WA.

Garling, T. (1989). The Role of Cognitive Maps in Spatial Decisions. *Journal of Environmental Psychology* 9: 269–278.Glasgow, J. (1993). The Imagery Debate Revisited: A Computational Perspective. *Computational Intelligence* 9(4): 309–333.

Gluck, M. (1991). Making Sense of Human Wayfinding: Review of Cognitive and Linguistic Knowledge for Personal Navigation with a New Research Direction. In Mark, D. M. & Frank, A. U. (eds.) *Cognitive and Linguistic Aspects of Geographic Space*, 117–135. Kluwer Academic Publishers: The Netherlands.

Gopal, S. & Smith, T. (1989). NAVIGATOR: A Psychologically Based Model of Environmental Learning Through Navigation. *Journal of Environmental Psychology* 9: 309–331.

Grosz, B. J. (1981). Focusing and description in Natural Language Dialogues. In Joshi, A., Webber, B. L. & Sag, I. A. (eds.) *Elements of Discourse Understanding*, 84–105. Cambridge, Cambridge University Press: London.

Habel, Ch. (1987). *Prozedurale Aspekte der Wegplanung und Wegbeschreibung*. LILOG-Report 17, IBM, Stuttgart.

Hayes-Roth, B. & Hayes-Roth, F. (1979). A Cognitive Model of Planning. *Cognitive Science* 3: 275–310.

Herzog, G., Maaß, W. & Wazinski, P. (1993). VITRA GUIDE: Utilisation du Language Naturel et de Représentation Graphiques pour la Description d'Iténitaires. In *Colloque Interdisciplinaire du Commitée National "Image et Langages: Multimodalité et Modélisation Cognitive"*. Paris.

Hoeppner, W., Carstensen, M. & Rhein, U. (1990). Wegauskünfte: Die Interdependenz von Such- und Beschreibungsprozessen. In Freksa, C. & Habel, C. (eds.) *Informatik Fachberichte* 245, 221–234. Springer.

Ittelson, W. H. (1960). *Visual Space Perception*. Springer: New York.

Jackendorf, R. (1987). On Beyond Zebra: The Relation of Linguistic and Visual Information. *Cognition* 26: 89–114.

Joshi, A. K. (1983). Factoring Recursion and Dependencies: An Aspect of Tree Adjoining Grammars (TAG) and a Comparison of Some Formal Properties of TAGS, GPSGS, PLGS, and LPGS. In Proceedings of *The Twenty-First ACL*, 7–15, Cambridge, MA.

Klein, W. (1982) Local Deixis in Route Directions. In Jarvella, R. J. & Klein, W. (eds.) *Speech, Place, and Action*, 161–182. Wiley: Chichester.

Korf, R. E. (1990). Real-Time Heuristic Search. *Artificial Intelligence* 42: 189–211.

Kosslyn, S. (1987). Seeing and Imaging in the Cerebral Hemispheres: A Computational Approach. *Psychological Review* **94**: 148–175.

Kuipers, B. (1977). *Representing Knowledge of Large-Scale Space*. PhD thesis, MIT AI Lab, Cambridge, MA. TR-418.

Kuipers, B. (1978). Modelling Spatial Knowledge. *Cognitive Science* **2**: 129–153.

Landau, B. & Jackendoff, R. (1993). "What" and "Where" in Spatial Language and Spatial Cognition. *Behavioral and Brain Sciences* **16**: 217–265.

Leiser, D. & Zilbershatz, A. (1989). THE TRAVELLER: A Computational Model of Spatial Network Learning. *Environmental and Behaviour* **21**(4): 435–463.

Lewis, D. (1976). Observations on Route Finding and Spatial Orientation among the Aboriginal Peoples of the Western Desert Region of Central Australia. *Oceania* **XLVI**(4).

Maaß, W., Baus, J. & Paul, J. (1994). *Visually Accessed Spatial Information Used in Incremental Route Descriptions: A Computational Model* (submitted).

Maaß, W. (1993). A Cognitive Model for the Process of Multimodal, Incremental Route Description. In Proceedings of *The European Conference on Spatial Information Theory*. Springer.

Marr, D. (1982). *Vision: A Computational Investigation into the Human Representation and Processing of Visual Information*. Freemann: San Francisco.

McCalla, G. & Schneider, P. (1979). The Execution of Plans in an Independent Dynamic Microworld. Proceedings of *The Sixth IJCAI*, 553–555.

Meier, J., Metzing, D., Polzin, T., Ruhrberg, P., Rutz, H. & Vollmer, M. (1988). *Generierung von Wegbeschreibungen*. KoLiBri Arbeitsbericht 9, Fakultät für Linguistik und Literaturwissenschaft, Universität Bielefeld.

Neisser, U. (1976). *Cognition and Reality*. Freeman: San Francisco.

Pailhous, J. (1969). Representation de l'espace urbain et cheminements. *Le Travail Humain*, 32–87.

Piaget, J., Inhelder, B. & Szemenska, A. (1960). *The Child's Conception of Geometry*. Basic Books: New York.

Schirra, J. R. J. (1990). Einige Überlegungen zu Bildvorstellungen in kognitiven Systemen. In Freksa, C. & Habel, C. (Hrsg.) *Repräsentation und Verarbeitung räumlichen Wissens*, 68–82. Springer: Berlin, Heidelberg.

Schneider, W. & Shiffrin, R. M. (1977). Controlled and Automatic Human Information Processing. 1. Detection, Search, and Attention. *Psychological Review* **84**: 1–66.

Siegel, A. W. & White, S. H. (1975). The Development of Spatial Representation of Large-Scale Environment. In Reese, W. (ed.) *Advances in Child Development and Behaviour*. Academic Press: New York.

Sitaro, K. (1993). *Language and Thought Interface: A Study of Spontaneous Gestures and Japanese Mimetics*. Ph.D. thesis, University of Chicago.

Stokols, D. & Altman, I. (eds.) (1987). *Handbook of Environmental Psychology*, volume 1 & 2. John Wiley & Sons.

Streeter, L. A., Vitello, D. & Wonsiewicz, S. A. (1985). How to Tell People Where to Go: Comparing Navigational Aids. *Intentional Journal of Man-Machine Studies* **22**: 549–562.

Thorndyke, P. W. & Goldin, S. E. (1983). Spatial Learning and Reasoning Skill. In Pick, H. L. & Acredolo, L. P. (eds.) *Spatial Orientation: Theory, Research, and Application*, 195–217. Plenum: New York, London.

Thorndyke, P. W. & Hayes-Roth, B. (1982). Differences in Spatial Knowledge Acquired from Maps and Navigation. *Cognitive Psychology* **14**: 560–582.

Tolman, E. C. (1948). Cognitive Maps in Rats and Men. *Psychological Review* **55**: 189–208.

Wahlster, W., Andre, E., Finkler, W., Graf, W., Profitlich, H.-J., Rist, T. & Schauder, A. (1992). WIP: Integrating Text and Graphics Design for Adaptive Information Presentation. In Dale, R., Hovy, E., Rösner, D. & Stock, O. (eds.) *Aspects of Automated Natural Language Generation: Proceedings of* The Sixth International Workshop on Natural Language Generation, 290–292. Springer: Berlin, Heidelberg.

Wunderlich, D. & Reinelt, R. (1982). How to Get There From Here. In Jarvella, R. J. & Klein, W. (eds.) *Speech, Place, nd Action*, 183–201. Wiley: Chichester.

Yeap, W. K. (1988). Towards a Computational Theory of Cognitive Maps. *Artificial Intelligence* **34**: 297–360.

Artificial Intelligence Review **8**: 175–187, 1994.
© *1994 Kluwer Academic Publishers. Printed in the Netherlands.*

VIsual TRAnslator: Linking Perceptions and Natural Language Descriptions

GERD HERZOG and PETER WAZINSKI

SFB 314, Project VITRA, Universität des Saarlandes, D-66041 Saarbrücken
Email: vitra@cs.uni-sb.de

Abstract. Despite the fact that image understanding and natural language processing constitute two major areas of AI, there have only been a few attempts toward the integration of computer vision and the generation of natural language expressions for the description of image sequences. In this contribution we will report on practical experience gained in the project VITRA (VIsual TRAnslator) concerning the design and construction of integrated knowledge-based systems capable of translating visual information into natural language descriptions. In VITRA different domains, like traffic scenes and short sequences from soccer matches, have been investigated.

Our approach towards *simultaneous* scene description emphasizes concurrent image sequence evaluation and natural language processing, carried out on an *incremental* basis, an important prerequisite for real-time performance. One major achievement of our cooperation with the vision group at the Fraunhofer Institute (IITB, Karlsruhe) is the automatic generation of natural language descriptions for recognized trajectories of objects in real world image sequences. In this survey, the different processes pertaining to high-level scene analysis and natural language generation will be discussed.

Key words: computer vision, high-level scene analysis, natural language access.

1. INTRODUCTION

Computer vision and natural language processing constitute two major areas of research within AI, but have generally been studied independently of each other. There have been only a few attempts towards the integration of image understanding and the generation of natural language descriptions for real world image sequences.

The relationship between natural language and visual perception forms the research background for the VITRA project (cf. Herzog *et al.* 1993), which is concerned with the development of knowledged-based systems for natural language access to visual information. According to Wahlster (1989, p. 479), two main goals are pursued in this research field:

1. "The complex information processing of humans underlying the interaction of natural language production and visual perception is to be described and explained exactly be means of the tools of computer science."

2. "The natural language description of images is to provide the user with an easier access to, and a better understanding of, the results of an image understanding system."

It is characteristic of AI research, that, apart from the cognitive science perspective (1), an application-oriented objective is also pursued (2). From this engineering perspective, the systems envisaged here could serve such practical purposes as handling the vast amount of visual data accumulating, for example, in medical technology (Tsotsos 1985; Niemann et al. 1985), remote sensing (Bajcsy et al. 1985), and traffic control (Wahlster et al. 1983; Neumann 1989; Walter et al. 1988; Koller et al. 1992b; Kollnig and Nagel 1993). The main task of computer vision is the construction of a symbolic scene representation from (a sequence of) images. In the case of image sequence analysis, the focus lies on the detection and interpretation of changes which are caused by motion. The intended output of a vision system is an explicit, meaningful description of visible objects. One goal of approaches towards the integration of computer vision and natural language processing is to extend the scope of scene analysis beyond the level of object recognition. Natural language access to vision systems requires processes which lead to conceptual units of a higher level of abstraction. These processes include the explicit description of spatial configurations by means of spatial relations, the interpretation of object movements, and even the automatic recognition of presumed goals and plans of the observed agents. Based upon such high-level scene analysis, natural language image descriptions have the advantage, that they allow variation of how condensed a description of visual data will be according to application-specific demands.

In VITRA, different domains of discourse and communicative situations are examined with respect to natural language access to visual information. Scenarios under investigation include:

- Answering questions about observations in traffic scenes (cf. Schirra et al. 1987).
- Generating running reports for short sections of soccer games (cf. André et al. 1988; Herzog et al. 1989).
- Describing routes based on a 3-dimensional model of the University Campus Saarbrücken (cf. Herzog et al. 1993a; Maaß et al. 1993).
- Communicating with an autonomous mobile robot (cf. Lüth et al. 1994).

In this survey, we will concentrate on our joint work with the vision group at the Fraunhofer Institute (IITB, Karlsruhe) regarding the automatic interpretation of dynamic imagery.

2. THE VISUAL TRANSLATOR

The task of the vision group at the IITB is to recognize and to track moving objects within real world image sequences. Information concerning mobile objects and their locations over time together with knowledge about the stationary background constitutes the so-called *geometrical scene description*. In Neumann (1989) this intermediate geometrical representation, enriched with additional world knowledge about the objects, has been proposed as an *idealized* interface between a vision component and a natural language system.

First results had been obtained in the investigation of traffic scenes and short sequences from soccer matches (cf. Fig. 1). Apart from the trajectory data supplied by the vision component ACTIONS (Sung and Zimmermann 1986; Sung 1988), synthetic data have been studied in VITRA as well (c.f. Herzog 1986). Since an automatic classification and identification of objects is not possible with ACTIONS, object candidates are interactively assigned to previously known players and the ball. The more recent XTRACK system (Koller 1992; Koller *et al.* 1992a) accomplishes the automatic model-based recognition, tracking, and classification of vehicles in traffic scenes.

Fig. 1. Three frames from the soccer domain.

Research described in Rohr (1994) concentrates on the model-based 3D-reconstruction of *non-rigid* bodies. A cylindric representation and a kinematic model of human walking, which is based on medical data, is utilized for the incremental recognition of pedestrians and their exact state of motion. This approach for the geometric modeling of an articulated body has been adopted in VITRA in order to represent the players in the soccer domain (cf. Herzog 1992b). In Fig. 2 different movement states of the walking cycle are shown.

The goal of our joint efforts at combining a vision system and a natural

Fig. 2. Geometric model of a human body.

language access system is the automatic *simultaneous* description of dynamic imagery. Thus, the various processing steps from raw images to natural language utterances must be carried out on an *incremental* basis. Figure 3 shows how these processes are organized into a cascade within the VITRA system.

An image sequence, i.e., a sequence of digitized video frames, forms the input for the processes on the sensory level. Based on the visual raw data, the image analysis component constructs a geometrical representation for the scene, stating the locations of the visible objects at consecutive points in time. The contents of the geometrical scene description, which is constructed incrementally, as new visual data arrive, are further interpreted by the processes on the cognitive level. This high-level scene analysis extracts spatial relations, interesting motion events, as well as presumed intentions, plans, and plan interactions of the observed agents. These conceptual structures bridge the gap between visual data and natural language concepts, such as spatial prepositions, motion verbs, temporal adverbs and purposive or causal clauses. They are passed on to the processes on the linguistic level which transform them into natural language

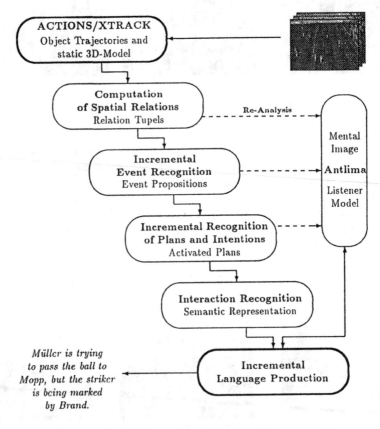

Fig. 3. Cascaded processing in VITRA.

utterances. In terms of reference semantics, explicit links between sensory data and natural language expressions are established.

VITRA provides a running report of the scene it is watching for a listener who cannot see the scene her/himself, but who is assumed to have prior knowledge about its static properties. In order to generate communicatively adequate descriptions, the system must anticipate the visual conceptualizations that the system's utterance elicits in the listener's mind (cf. Neumann 1989; Wahlster 1989). A peculiarity in VITRA is the existence of such a listener model. Depending on the current text plan the component ANTLIMA is able to construct a mental image corresponding to the (assumed) imagination of the listener. This mental image is re-analyzed and compared with the system's visual information. Possible discrepancies may lead to changes in the preliminary text plan.

3. INCREMENTAL HIGH-LEVEL SCENE ANALYSIS

Natural languages access systems like HAM-ANS (Wahlster *et al.* 1983) and NAOS (Neumann and Novak 1986) concentrate on an *a posteriori* analysis. Low level vision processing considers the entire image sequence for the recognition and cueing of moving objects; motion analysis happens afterwards, based on complete trajectories. Since only information about a past scene can be provided, these systems generate *retrospective* scene descriptions. In VITRA we favour an *incremental analysis*. Input data is supplied and processed simultaneously as the scene progresses. Information about the present scene is provided and immediate system reactions (like motor actions of a robot, *simultaneous* natural language utterances) are possible.

3.1. *Interpreting spatial relations and object movements*

The definition and representation of the semantics of spatial relations is an essential condition for the synthesis of spatial reference expressions in natural language. The computation and evaluation of spatial relations in VITRA is based on a multilevel semantic model, that clearly distinguishes between context specific conceptual knowledge and the basic meaning of a spatial relation (cf. Gapp 1994).

The detailed geometric knowledge, grounded in visual perception, can be exploited for the definition of a reference semantics, that does not assign simple truth values to spatial predications, but instead introduces a measure of degrees of applicability that expresses the extent to which a spatial relation is applicable (cf. André *et al.* 1989). Since different degrees of applicability can be expressed by linguistic hedges, such as '*directly*' or '*more or less*', more exact scene descriptions are possible. Furthermore, if an object configuration can be described by several spatial predications, the degree of applicability is used to select the most appropriate reference object(s) and relation(s) for verbalization.

In the context of the VITRA project, different classes of spatial relations have been examined in more detail. Wazinski (1993a, b) are concerned with topological relations. Orientation-dependent relations are treated in André *et al.* (1987a, 1989). Since the frame of reference is explicitly taken into account, the system is able to cope with the *intrinsic, extrinsic,* and *deictic* use of directional prepositions (cf. Retz-Schmidt 1988). Recently, the algorithms developed so far have been generalized for 3-dimensional geometric representations (cf. Gapp 1993, 1994). If a real-world image sequence is to be described simultaneously as it is perceived, one has to talk about object motions even while they are currently happening and not yet completed. Thus, motion events have to be recognized stepwise as they progress and event instances must be made available for further processing from the moment they are noticed first. Consider the examples given in Fig. 4, where a white station wagon is passing a pick-up truck, and in Fig. 1, where a player is transferring the ball to a team mate.

Fig. 4. A passing event in a traffic scene.

Since the distinction between events that have and those that have not occurred is insufficient, we have introduced the additional predicates start, proceed,and stop which can be used to characterize the progression of an event. The recognition of an occurrence can be thought of as traversing the course diagram, where the edge types are used for the definition of our basic event predicates. Course diagrams rely on a discrete model of time, which is induced by the underlying image sequence. They allow incremental event recognition, since exactly one edge per unit of time is traversed. Using constraint-based temporal reasoning, the course diagrams are constructed automaticly from interval-based concept definitions (cf. Herzog 1992a).

The event concepts are organized into an abstraction hierarchy, based on specialization (e.g., walking is a moving) and temporal decomposition (e.g., passing consists of swing-out, drive-beside, and swing-into-line). This conceptual hierarchy can be utilized in the language production process in order to guide the selection of the relevant propositions.

3.2. *Recognizing intentions, interactions, and causes of plan failures*

Human observers do not only pay attention to the spatio-temporal aspects of motion. They also make assumptions about intentional entities underlying the behaviour of other people (e.g., player A does not simply *approach* player B, but he *tackles* him).

One criterion for the choice of soccer as a domain of discourse in VITRA was the fact that the influence of the agents assumed intentions on the description is particularly obvious here. Given the position of players, their team membership and the distribution of roles in standard situations, stereotypical intentions can be assumed for each situation. As described in Retz-Schmidt (1991, 1992), the VITRA system is able to incrementally recognize intentions of and interactions between the agents as well as the causes of possible plan failures.

Partially instantiated plan hypotheses taken from a hierarchically organized plan library are successively instantiated according to the incrementally recognized events. The leaves of the plan hierarchy represent observable events and spatial relations. An inner node corresponds to an abstract action. An egde, that connects two nodes either represents a decomposition or a specialization relation. In addition, a node also contains information about necessary preconditions of the action it represents as well as information about its intended effect.

In a continually changing domain it would be computationally intractable to keep track of all agents that occur in the scene. Therefore, domain specific focussing heuristics are applied in order to reduce the number of agents whose actions have to be observed. In the soccer domain, for example, the system would focus on the agents that are near the goal or the player who has the ball.

Knowledge about the cooperative (e.g., double-pass) and antagonistic behaviour (e.g., offside-trap) of the players is represented in the interaction library. A successful plan triggers the activation of a corresponding interaction schema. Similar to the plan recognition process this interaction schema has to be fully instantiated before the particular interaction is recognized.

There are several possibilities for a plan failure that can be detected with respect to the underlying plan and interaction recognition component: (i) An agent might assume a precondition for a plan that is not given, (ii) an antagonistic plan can lead to a plan failure, or (iii) in case of an cooperative interaction the partner fails.

4. SIMULTANEOUS NATURAL LANGUAGE DESCRIPTION

Since an image sequence is not described *a posteriori* but rather as it progresses, the complete course of the scene is unknown at the moment of text generation. In addition, temporal aspects such as the time required for text generation and decoding time of the listener or reader have to be considered for the coordination of perception and language production. These peculiarities of the conversational setting lead to important consequences for the planning and realization of natural language utterances (cf. André *et al.* 1987). As the description should concentrate on what is currently happening, it is necessary to start talking about motion events and actions while they are still in progress and not yet completely recognized. In this case encoding has to start before the contents of an utterance have been planned in full detail. Other characteristics of simultaneous reporting besides incremental generation of utterances need to be dealt with. The description often lags behind with respect to the occurrences in the scene and unexpected topic shifts occur very frequently.

Language generation in VITRA includes processes that handle the selection, linearization and verbalization of propositions (cf. André *et al.* 1988). The listener model provides an imagination component, in order to anticipate the listener's visual conceptualizations of the described scene.

4.1. *Selection and linearization of propositions*

As the time-varying scene has to be described continuously, language generation underlies strong temporal restrictions. Hence, the system cannot talk about all events and actions which have been recognized, but instead it has to decide which propositions should be verbalized in order to enable the listener to follow the scene. According to the conversational maxims of Grice (1975), the listener should be informed about all relevant facts and redundancy should be avoided.

Relevance depends on factors like: (i) salience, which is determined by the frequency of occurrence and the complexity of the generic event or action concept, (ii) topicality, and (iii) current state, i.e., fully recognized occurrences are preferred. Topicality decreases for terminated movements and actions as the scene progresses and during recognition events and plans enter different states, i.e., relevance changes continually. To avoid redundancy, an occurrence will not be mentioned if it is implied by some other proposition already verbalized, e.g., a have-ball event following a pass will not be selected for verbalization.

Additional selection processes are used to determine deep cases and to choose descriptions for objects, locations, and time; in these choices the contents of the text memory and the listener model must also be considered.

The linearization process determines the order in which the selected propositions should be mentioned in the text. The temporal ordering of the corresponding events and actions is the primary consideration for linearization; secondarily, focusing criteria are used to maintain discourse coherence.

4.2. *Anticipating the listener's visual imagination*

After propositions are selected and ordered, they are passed on to the listener model ANTLIMA (cf. Schirra and Stopp 1993), which constructs a *"mental image"* corresponding to the visual conceptualizations that the system's utterance would elicit in the listener's mind. The (assumed) imagination is compared with the system's visual information and incompatibilities are fed back to the generation component in order to adjust the preliminary text plan. A similar *anticipation feedback loop*, has been proposed in Jameson and Wahlster (1982) for the generation of pronouns.

A plausible mental image is constructed by searching for a maximally typical representation of a situation described by the selected propositions. The typicality distribution corresponding to a certain proposition is encoded in a so-called *Typicality Potential Field* (TyPoF), a function mapping locations to typicality values. TyPoFs are instances of typicality schemas associated with spatial rela-

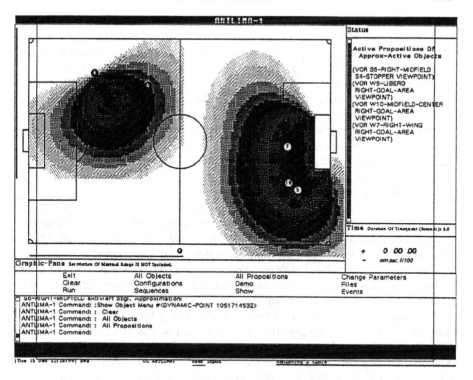

Fig 5. Examples of typicality distributions.

tions as well as event and action concepts. Each TyPoF takes into account the dimensionality, size, and shape of the objects involved. In Fig. 5, the TyPoFs for *'player A in front of player B'* and *'in front of the goal area'* are visualized. A typicality value associated with a spatial expression corresponds to the (degree of) applicability of a spatial relation for a given object configuration.

If several propositions impose restrictions on an object, the corresponding TyPoFs are combined by taking the average. In the case of incompatible restrictions the preliminary text plan has to be retracted. Hillclimbing is employed in order to find an interpretation with maximal typicality. Then the mental image is re-analyzed, i.e., the processes of high-level analysis are applied to it. The resulting set of propositions is compared to the propositions computed from the image sequence and detected misunderstandings may be dispeled by changing the preliminary text plan.

4.3. *Incremental verbalization*

The encoding of the selected propositions includes lexicalization, the determination of morphosyntactic information, and surface transformations.

In the process of transforming symbolic event descriptions into natural language utterances, first a verb is selected by accessing the concept lexicon, and the case-roles associated with the verb are instantiated. Control passes back to the selection component, which decides which information concerning the case-role fillers should be conveyed. The selected information is transformed into natural-language expressions referring to time, space or objects. Time is indicated by the verb tense and by temporal adverbs; spatial prepositions and appropriate objects of reference are selected to refer to spatial relations. Internal object identifiers are transformed into noun phrases by the selection of attributes that enable the listener to uniquely identify the intended referent. If an object cannot be characterized by attributes stored *a priori* in the partner model, it will be described by means of spatial relations, such as *'the left goal'*, or by means of occurrences already mentioned in which it was (is) involved, e.g., *'the player who attacked'*. Anaphoric expressions are generated if the referent is in focus and no ambiguity is possible.

Recognized intentions can be reflected in natural language descriptions in various ways. For instance, they can be expressed explicitly (*'She wants to do A'*) or be construed as expectations and formulated in the future tense. They can also be expressed implicitly, using verbs that imply intention (e.g., *'chase'*). In addition, relationships between intentions and actions or among several intentions of a single agent can be described, e.g., using purposive clauses (*'He did A in order to achieve B'*). Cooperative interactions can be summarized most easily, using a natural language expression describing the collective intention. Cooperative as well as antagonistic interactions can be described in more detail using temporal adverbs and conjunctions. Plan failures can also be stated explicitly, or they can be related to their causes by means of causal clauses. In our current implementation it is only possible to explicitly express intentions and relationships between intentions of a single agent.

To meet the requirements of simultaneous scene description, information concerning partly-recognized events and actions is also provided. Consequently, language generation cannot start from completely work-out conceptual contents; i.e., the need for an incremental generation strategy arises (see, e.g., Reithinger 1992). In the newest version of the VITRA system the incremental generation of surface structures is realized with the module described in Harbusch *et al.* (1991); Finkler and Schauder (1992), an incremental generator for German and English, which is based on *Tree Adjoining Grammars*.

5. CONCLUSION

VITRA is the first system that automatically generates natural language descriptions for recognized trajectories of objects in a real world image sequence. High-level scene analysis in VITRA is not restricted to the purely visual, i.e., spatio-temporal, properties of the scene, but also aims at the recognition of presumed goals and plans of the observed agents. In addition, the listener model in VITRA anticipates the (assumed) imagination of the listener for the generation of the most appropriate description.

Our approach towards *simultaneous* scene description emphasizes concurrent image sequence evaluation and natural language processing. The processing in all subcomponents is carried out on an *incremental* basis, and hence provides an important prerequisite for real-time performance.

Despite these promising results, we are still far away from a universally applicable AI system capable of describing an arbitrary sequence of images. Nonetheless, the VITRA system will serve as a workbench for the further investigation of problems arising in the field of integrated vision and natural language processing.

In order to improve the quality of text production in the VITRA prototype, the language generation component will be extended for the description of plan failures and interactions, i.e., information that can already be provided by the high-level scene analysis.

So far, we have only been concerned with a bottom-up analysis of image sequences, recorded with a stationary TV-camera. Future work will concentrate on expectation-driven scene analysis. Intermediate results of the high-level analysis shall support low-level vision in focussing on relevant objects and in providing parameters for the active control of the sensor adjustment. On the one hand, focussing techniques are necessary to compensate the computational complexity of the analysis in more advanced applications, on the other hand, interaction between low-level and high-level analysis is required if VITRA is to become robust for the difficulties caused by insufficient low-level image processing. These issues will be studied in the context of natural language interaction with an autonomous mobile robot, equipped with several sensors.

6. TECHNICAL NOTES

The current version of the VITRA system is written in Common Lisp and CLOS, with the graphical user interface implemented in CLIM. The system has been developed on Symbolics 36xx Lisp Machines, Symbolics UX1200S Lisp Coprocessors, and on Hewlett Packard 9720 and SPARC Workstations.

ACKNOWLEDGEMENTS

The work described here was partly supported by the Sonderforschungsbereich 314 der Deutschen Forschungsgemeinschaft, "Künstliche Intelligenz und wissensbasierte Systeme" Projekt N2: VITRA.

We would like to thank Paul Mc Kevitt and an anonymous reviewer for their helpful comments on an earlier version of this article.

REFERENCES

André, E., Bosch, G., Herzog, G. & Rist, T. (1987). Coping with the Intrinsic and the Deictic Uses of Spatial Prepositions. In Jorrand, K. & Sgurev, L. (eds.) *Artificial Intelligence II: Methodology, Systems, Applications*, 375–382. North-Holland: Amsterdam.
André, E., Rist, T. & Herzog, G. (1987). Generierung natürlichsprachlicher Äußerungen zur

simultanen Beschreibung zeitveränderlicher Szenen. In Morik, K. (Hrsg.) *GWAI-87*, 330–337. Springer: Berlin, Heidelberg.

André, E., Herzog, G. & Rist, T. (1988). On the Simultaneous Interpretation of Real World Image Sequences and their Natural Language Description: The System SOCCER. In Proceedings of *The Eighth ECAI*, 449–454. Munich.

André, E., Herzog, G. & Rist, T. (1989). *Natural Language Access to Visual Data: Dealing with Space and Movement*. Report 63, Universität des Saarlandes, SFB 314 (VITRA), Saarbrücken. Presented at the 1st Workshop on Logical Semantics of Time, Space and Movement in Natural Language, Toulouse, France.

Bajcsy, R., Joshi, A., Krotkov, E. & Zwarico, A. (1985). LandScan: A Natural Language and Computer Vision System for Analyzing Aerial Images. In Proceedings of *The Ninth IJCAI*, 919–921. Los Angeles, CA.

Finkler, W. & Schauder, A. (1992). Effects of Incremental Output on Incremental Natural Language Generation. In Proceedings of *The Tenth ECAI*, 505–507. Vienna.

Gapp, K.-P. (1993). *Berechnungsverfahren für räumliche Relationen in 3D-Szenen*. Memo 59, Universität des Saarlandes, SFB 314.

Gapp, K.-P. (1994). Basic Meanings of Spatial Relations; Computation and Evaluation in 3D Space. In Proceedings of *The AAAI-94*. Seattle, WA. (to appear).

Grice, H. P. (1975). Logic and Conversation. In Cole, P. & Morgan, J. L. (eds.) *Speech Acts*, 41–58. Academic Press: London.

Harbusch, K., Finkler, W. & Schauder, A. (1991). Incremental Syntax Generation with Tree Adjoining Grammars. In Brauer, W. & Hernandez, D. (eds.) *Verteilte Künstliche Intelligenz und kooperatives Arbeiten: 4. Int. GI-Kongreß Wisssensbasierte Systeme*, 363–374. Springer: Berlin, Heidelberg.

Herzog, G. (1986). *Ein Werkzeug zur Visualisierung und Generierung von geometrischen Bildfolgenbeschreibungen*. Memo 12, Universität des Saarlandes, SFB 314 (VITRA).

Herzog, G. (1992). Utilizing Interval-Based Event Representations for Incremental High-Level Scene Analysis. In Aurnague, M., Borillo, A., Borillo, M. & Bras M. (eds.). Proceedings of *The Fourth European Workshop on Semantics of Time, Space, and Movement and Spatio-Temporal Reasoning*, 425–435. Château de Bonas, France.

Herzog, G. (1992). *Visualization Methods for the VITRA Workbench*. Memo 53, Universität des Saarlandes, SFB 314 (VITRA).

Herzog, G., Sung, C.-K., André, E., Enkelmann, W., Nagel, H.-H., Rist, T., Wahlster, W. & Zimmermann, G. (1989). Incremental Natural Language Description of Dynamic Imagery. In Freksa, Ch. & Brauer, E. (eds.) *Wissensbasierte Systeme. 3. Int. GI-Kongreß*, 153–162. Springer: Berlin, Heidelberg.

Herzog, G., Maaß & Wazinski, P. (1993). VITRA GUIDE: Utilisation du langage Naturel et de Représentation Graphiques pour la Description d'Itinéraires. In *Colloque Interdisciplinaire du Comité National "Images et Langages: Multimodalité et Modélisation Cognitive*, 243–251. Paris.

Herzog, G., Schirra, J. & Wazinski, P. (1993). *Arbeitsbericht für den Zeitraum 1991–1993: VITRA – Kopplung bildverstehender und sprachverstehender Systeme*. Memo 58, Univesität des Saarlandes, SFB 314 (VITRA).

Jameson, A. & Wahlster, W. (1982). User Modelling in Anaphora Generation. In Proceedings of *The Fifth ECAI*, 222–227. Orsay, France.

Koller, D. (1992). *Detektion, Verfolgung und Klassifikation bewegter Objekte in monokularen Bildfolgen am Beispiel von Straßenverkehrsszenen*. Infix: St. Augustin.

Koller, D., Daniilidis, K., Thórhallson, T. & Nagel, H.-H. (1992a). Model-based Object Tracking in Traffic Scenes. In Sandini, G. (ed.). Proceedings of *The Second European Conf. on Computer Vision*, 437–452. Springer: Berlin, Heidelberg.

Koller, D., Heinze, N. & Nagel, H.-H. (1992b). Algorithmic Characterization of Vehicle Trajectories from Image Sequences by Motion Verbs. In Proceedings of *The IEEE Conf. on Computer Vision and Pattern Recognition*, 90–95. Maui, Hawaii.

Kollnig, H. & Nagel, H.-H. (1993). Ermittlung von begrifflichen Beschreibungen von Geschehen in Straßenverkehrsszenen mit Hilfe unscharfer Mengen. *Informatik Forschung und Entwicklung* 8(4): 186–196.

Lüth, T. C., Längle, Th., Herzog, G., Stopp, E. & Rembold, U. (1994). Human-Machine Interaction for Intelligent Robots Using Natural Language. In *Third IEEE Int.Workshop on Robot and Human Communication*, RO-MAN'94, Nagoya, Japan (to appear).

Maaß, W., Wazinski, P. & Herzog, G. (1993). VITRA GUIDE: Multi-modal Route Descriptions for Computer Assisted Vehicle Navigation. In Proceedings of *The Sixth Int. Conf. on Industrial and Engineering Applications of Artificial Intelligence and Expert Systems IEA/AIE-93*, 144–147. Edinburgh, Scotland.

Neumann, B. & Novak, H.-J. (1986). NAOS: Ein System zur natürlichsprachlichen Beschreibung zeitveränderlicher Szenen. *Informatik Forschung und Entwicklung* 1: 83–92.

Neumann, B. (1989). Natural Language Description of Time-Varying Scenes. In Waltz D. L. (ed.) *Semantic Structures*, 167–207. Lawrence Erlbaum: Hillsdale, NJ.

Niemann, J., Bunke, H., Hofmann, I., Sagerer, G., Wolf, F. & Feistel, H. (1985). A Knowledge Based System for Analysis of Gated Blood Pool Studies. *IEEE Transactions on Pattern Analysis and Machine Intelligence* 7: 246–259.

Reithinger, N. (1992). The Performance of an Incremental Generation Component for Multi-Modal Dialog Contributions. In Dale, R., Hovy, E., Rösner, D. & Stock, O. (eds.) *Aspects of Automated Natural Language Generation*: Proceedings of *The Sixth Int. Workshop on Natural Language Generation*, 263–276. Springer: Berlin, Heidelberg.

Retz-Schmidt, G. (1988). Various Views on Spatial Prepositions. *AI Magazine* 9(2): 95–105.

Retz-Schmidt, G. (1991). Recognizing Intentions, Interactions, and Causes of Plan Failures. *User Modeling and User-Adapted Interaction* 1: 173–202.

Retz-Schmidt, G. (1992). *Die Interpretation des Verhaltens mehrerer Akteure in Szenenfolgen*. Springer: Berlin, Heidelberg.

Rohr, K. (1994). Towards Model-based Recognition of Human Movements in Image Sequences. *Computer Vision, Graphics, and Image Processing (CVGIP): Image Understanding* 59(1): 94–115.

Schirra, J. R. J. & Stopp E. (1993). ANTLIMA – A Listener Model with Mental Images. In Proceedings of *The Thirteenth IJCAI*, 175–180. Chambery, France.

Schirra, J. R. J., Bosch, G., Sung, C.-K. & Zimmermann, G. (1987). From Image Sequences to Natural Language: A First Step Towards Automatic Perception and Description of Motions. *Applied Artificial Intelligence* 1: 287–305.

Sung, C.-K. & Zimmermann, G. (1986). Detektion und Verfolgung mehrerer Objekte in Bildfolgen. In Hartmann, G. (Hrsg.) *Mustererkennung*, 181–184. Springer: Berlin, Heidelberg.

Sung, C.-K. (1988). Extraktion von typischen und komplexen Vorgängen aus einer langen Bildfolge einer Verkehrsszene. In Bunke, H., Kübler, O. & Stucki, P. (Hrsg.) *Mustererkennung*, 90–96. Springer: Berlin, Heidelberg.

Tsotsos, J. K. (1985). Knowledge Organization and its Role in Representation and Interpretation for Time-Varying Data: the ALVEN System. *Computational Intelligence* 1: 16–32.

Wahlster, W., Marburger, H., Jameson, A. & Busemann, S. (1983), Over-answering Yes-No Questions: Extended Responses in a NL Interface to a Vision System. In Proceedings of *The Eighth IJCAI*, 643–646. Karlsruhe, FRG.

Wahlster, W. (1989). One Word Says More Than a Thousand Pictures. On the Automatic Verbalization of the Results of Image Sequence Analysis Systems. *Computers and Artifial Intelligence* 8: 470–492.

Walter, I., Lockemann, P. C. & Nagel, H.-H. (1988). Database Support for Knowledge-Based Image Evaluation. In Stocker, P. M., Kent, W. & Hammersley, R. (eds.) Proceedings of *The Thirteenth Conf. on Very Large Databases, Brighton, UK*, 3–11. Los Altos, CA: Morgan Kaufmann.

Wazinski, P. (1993a). *Graduated Topological Relations*. Memo 54, Universität des Saarlandes, SFB 314.

Wazinski, P. (1993b). Graduierte topologische Relationen. In Hernandez (ed.) *Hybride und integrierte Ansätze zur Raumrepräsentation und ihre Anwendung, Workshop auf der 17, KI-Fachtagung, Berlin*, 16–19. Technische Univ. München. Institut für Informatik. Forschungsberichte Künstliche Intelligenz, FKI-185-93.

Artificial Intelligence Review **8**: 189–214, 1994.
© 1994 *Kluwer Academic Publishers. Printed in the Netherlands.*

A Vision of 'Vision and Language' Comprises Action: An Example from Road Traffic

HANS-HELLMUT NAGEL

*Fraunhofer-Institut für Informations- und Datenverarbeitung (IITB),
Fraunhoferstr. 1, D-76131 Karlsruhe/Germany and Fakultät für Informatik der
Universität Karlsruhe (TH), Karlsruhe, E-mail address: hhn@iitb.fhg.de*

Abstract. This contribution is based on two previously published approaches one of which automatically extracts vehicle trajectories from image sequences of traffic scenes and associates these trajectories with motion verbs. The second approach exploits machine vision in order to maneuver autonomous road vehicles. The combination of these two approaches provides a link from the evaluation of video signals via an abstract representation at the level of natural language concepts to actuator devices in automatic closed loop control of road vehicles. Building on implemented representations for elementary motion verbs and for elementary road vehicle maneuvers, a grammar to represent a nontrivial subset of more complex driving activities on a highway is formulated. Driving on a highway can thereby be investigated not only at the level of control algorithms, but simultaneously at the level of natural language descriptions.

Key words: image sequence evaluation, autonomous driving, motion verbs.

1. INTRODUCTION

Attempts to algorithmically link conceptual descriptions in terms of natural language expressions to the results of image evaluation have already fascinated the Artificial Intelligence community a quarter of a century ago. Winograd (1972) described a program SHRDLU which 'understood' commands and questions typed in as natural language text about an admittedly limited discourse world of blocks. The computer-internal representation of this 'blocksworld' was employed to generate a line drawing which was then shown to the user of the program. This allowed to visualize manipulations applied to the blocks without actually operating a robot. The effect of a command would be shown as a new line drawing, depicting the blocksworld state following the execution of the desired manipulation. In this manner, the user could determine whether the program 'had understood' what the meant or he could demand an explanation of relations in the depicted blocksworld scene as a computer generated natural language text. Likewise, SHRDLU could request additional information if the typed-in text incompletely specified the desired manipulation.

Although this program appeared to demonstrate some kind of link between 'vision and language', one has to realize that it did not analyze the images shown, but merely employed images to visualize a computer-internal representation of the actual blocksworld state. On the other hand, it already emphasized the use of natural language text to not only communicate state descriptions, but in addition to give natural language commands specifying activities of an imaginary robot which purportedly manipulated the depicted blocksworld scene. It appears important to realize two implications: in addition to descriptions of objects of different types, their pose, their attributes like color, and relations between these objects, SHRDLU already comprised representations for state *changes*, i.e. a temporal aspect, and representations for activities which could bring about state changes. The series of images generated during a session can be treated as a special case of an image sequence, and the activities as concepts usually related to verbs in a natural language.

Why did it take so long to extend SHRDLU or analogous germs into approaches which evaluate image sequences in order to derive an estimate of the actual configuration of objects in a depicted real world scene and to represent the recorded activities of (certain) entities as agents by natural language concepts? A moment's reflection will immediately result in at least three components of an answer to this question:

(i)   the complexity of real world scenes;
(ii)   the sheer mass of data to be evaluated even in the simplest case of monocular gray value video sequences;
(iii) a lack of experience with the development and exploitation of programming tools to cope with the aforementioned problems.

In order to extract hints towards spatial gray value changes from an image sequence, one needs to convolve the image with at least a mask each for the x- and y-component of the gray value gradient. If we assume that a 5×7 mask (about 2^5 pixels) is necessary in order to avoid the introduction of distortions by inadequate derivative operators, we need 2^5 multiplications and the same number of additions, i.e. 2^7 operations in order to estimate both the x- and y-component of the gray value gradient at each image location. For a 512×512 digitized image, we end up with at least $2^{18} \times 2^7 = 2^{25}$ operations per frame – only for the convolution! With approximately 2^5 frames per second, the mere computation of the gray value gradient already requires a sustained computation rate of 2^{30} or about 1 billion operations per second. It has only been in the recent past that specialized processing boards for convolutions and sufficiently fast computers for further processing became available at reasonable cost, for example comparable with the cost of a middle class sedan, which facilitate experiments in this area by research groups in universities.

Apart from the pure number of instructions executed per second, there has been another hurdle to be overcome before experiments would become feasible enough to be actually performed, namely random access memory. Experience has shown that for every raw digitized pixel – stored as an 8 bit Byte – intermediate results require between 25 and 50 times the memory space of the original pixel, i.e. between 25 and 50 Bytes. Of course, one can cut corners and get away with a much smaller multiple, but only at the cost of not having available the inspection and tracing tools necessary to track down the true causes of inadequate processing results. If one wants to observe whether or not a car driving at a speed of about 50 km/h can stop in front of a suddenly appearing obstacle, about three seconds of observation time are required, assuming a deceleration of 5 m/s². In order to evaluate such an activity which extends through three seconds, an image sequence of 75 frames is needed which requires about 18 MByte of storage after digitization. Adding the storage requirement for intermediate data structures during the evaluation of such a short sequence, even generous swap space allocations will not do unless 16 to 64 MByte random access storage such as in a modern workstation are available. Without random access memory in the 10 MByte range, computational experiments tend to become prohibitively time-consuming and thus will not be undertaken sufficiently often to clearly understand the consequences of implicit or explicit assumptions, parameter settings, or to detect and track down bugs.

It should be no surprise, therefore, that only in the last few years, progress in the evaluation of image sequences can be observed which gradually enables the exploration of the multitude of problems related to the automatic extraction of descriptions of objects and their movements from video sequences. On the other hand, once these thresholds regarding random access memory and computing power have been overcome as it appears to be the case nowadays, experience with programming tools developed in the course of performing experiments often accelerate progress in research. The current contributions explores such a combination of experiences from the following areas:

* automatic detection of moving cars in image sequences recorded by a stationary black/white video camera from a road scene as well as the model-based extraction of vehicle trajectories for moving vehicles;
* association of natural language verbs with occurrences in the depicted scene, based on an analysis of vehicle trajectories extracted automatically from an image sequence (see Section 2);
* autonomous driving of road vehicles based on machine vision (see Section 3);
* transition diagrams as a means to formalize admissible sequences of driving maneuvers for regular road vehicles on a subset of public roads, namely on highways without intersections (see Sections 4 + 5).

The subsequent discussion provides initial evidence that a computer-internal representation of driving on a highway can be formulated by using concepts which are directly related to natural languages. These concepts are simultaneously suited for immediate linkage to the processing of digitized video signals from image sequences as well as to control algorithms for autonomous road vehicles which perform activities expressed as natural language verbs. In clear distinction to the work of *Winograd 72*, the 'understanding' of natural language descriptions is now based not only on the evaluation of real world image(sequence)s, but even on performing related actions!

2. DESCRIPTION – IN TERMS OF NATURAL LANGUAGE NOTIONS – OF VEHICLE MOVEMENTS EXTRACTED FROM IMAGE SEQUENCES OF ROAD SCENES

Our investigations with the goal of relating the results of image sequence evaluation to a description at the level of abstraction associated with natural language notions started more than a decade and a half ago, in late 1976. An intermediate summary of early efforts and of insights gained thereby as well as a survey of the relevant literature up to the fall of 1987 can be found in (Nagel 1988). The effort to present a coherent view of research extending throughout a decade resulted in a systematic approach to collect all relevant motion verbs of the German language suitable for the description of road vehicle activities which could possibly be determined by image sequence evaluation. A series of investigations to develop computer-internal representations for this set of verbs – comprising between 60 and 120 verbs, depending on the selection criteria – culminated in a first approach to an automatic association of motion verbs with vehicle trajectories reported by Heinze et al. (1991). In parallel to these investigations, efforts were intensified to improve the extraction of vehicle trajectories from image sequences, see Koller et al. (1991).

As it turned out, tracking object images purely in the picture domain as reported by Koller et al. (1991) began to exhibit systematic difficulties which were overcome by switching to a model-based tracking approach, the Xtrack system, using an Iterated Extended Kalman Filter (Koller 1992, Koller et al. 1993). This approach yielded trajectories which were much smoother and sampled more densely than the ones used in Heinze et al. (1991). As a consequence, the computational process which associated the resulting 3-D vehicle trajectories with motion verbs had to be redesigned. Using fuzzy sets facilitated the simultaneous treatment of uncertainties from the estimation process and vagueness caused by the abstraction process from the geometry of trajectory data to natural language notions for motion verbs. An example is shown in Figure 1.

In Figure 1b, the trajectory of the agent is indicated by ribbons of different gray shades, each ribbon referring to a particular verb. The width of a ribbon is related to the level of confidence – a number between 0 and 1 – with which the corresponding part of the trajectory is associated with a verb: the broader the ribbon, the larger the level of confidence. The part of the trajectory marked by a white stripe in Figure 1b has been accepted as a valid description for *to approach (location 1)*. The bright gray wedge is associated with the verb *to reach (location 1)*, the medium gray wedge with *to (begin to) leave (location 1)*, and the dark gray wedge with *to drive away (from location 1)*. The black back-to-back-wedge corresponds to *driving across (location 1)*: this shape exhibits the initial increase and, after passing location 1, the subsequent decrease in the strength of association between the verb *to drive across* and a point on the trajectory as a function of its spatial relation with respect to location 1.

Significant improvements of the Xtrack system have been realized during the past year and a half since the submission of Koller et al. (1993). A new automatic initialization of the tracking process, a new extraction approach for straight line image segments and additional modifications resulted in a more robust image sequence evaluation. This simplified investigations regarding the association of motion verbs with (parts of) vehicle trajectories. Moreover, the recognition automata for a subset of 67 motion verbs have been extended to recognize and generate English verbs – see Kollnig *et al.* (1994).

The following discussion thus proceeds on the basis of the working hypothesis that it is possible to extract vehicle trajectories from image sequences which have been recorded by a stationary video camera and to associate these trajectory segments with elementary natural language concepts such as motion verbs in an acceptable manner.

3. A SET OF ELEMENTARY DRIVING MANEUVERS OF AUTONOMOUS ROAD VEHICLES

So far, the discussion concentrated on the ability to link intermediate results from image sequence evaluation to natural language notions. Reference to the results of image sequence evaluation could be considered to provide computer-internal semantics for a restricted subset of natural language notions. It is one of the primary points of this contribution that such an observational or passive approach need not be the only one: it is now possible to associate a small subset of natural language notions to the results of image evaluation by the actual performance of the activities that denote the selected subset. The subsequent discussion will be restricted to natural language notions referring to certain maneuvers of an autonomous vehicle which are considered to be 'primitive' or 'elementary' in the following sense: given certain boundary conditions which define a discourse world, all other vehicle maneuvers admissible in this discourse world can be composed by concatenation of these primitive or elementary maneuvers. In order to prepare for an exemplary exposition of the concatenation approach, this set of elementary vehicle maneuvers (Nagel and Enkelmann 1991) is first enumerated. The asterisk preceding a maneuver indicates that control algorithms to perform such a maneuver based on machine vision have already been implemented and tested in at least one of the two autonomously operating road vehicles of our institute (IITB) – see, e.g. (Siegle *et al.* 1992, Struck *et al.* 1993, Nagel *et al.* 1994). Asterisks in parentheses point to maneuvers for which only preliminary results are available so far.

*   1) *Start_and_continue*;
*   2) *Follow_a_road* (includes the case where the road bends and the speed has to be adapted such that the lateral acceleration remains within acceptable limits);
(*)   3) *Approach_obstacle_ahead* (includes approaching a preceding car as special case; implies a transition from velocity control to distance control);
     4) *Overtake*;
*   5) *Stop_in_front_of_obstacle*;
(*)   6) *Pass_obstacle_to_the_left/right*;
     7) *Start_after_preceding_car* (differs from *Start_and_continue* by the

A00:01:07:24

Fig. 1a. A frame from the video image sequence 'Durlacher-Tor-Platz' in Karlsruhe, with super-imposed vehicle trajectories which have been estimated according to Koller *et al.* (1993) (from Kollnig and Nagel 1993).

requirement to synchronize the start with the start of the preceding car and by necessitating control over the distance to the preceding car during the motion phase);

8) *Follow_preceding_car*;

* 9) *Cross_intersection*;

* 10) *Merge_to_left/right_lane*;

* 11) *Turn_left/right*;

* 12) *Slowdown_to_right_road_edge_and_stop*;

13) *Back_up* (drive backwards without changing the orientation of the vehicle);

14) *U-turn_to_the_left/right*;

15) *Reverse_direction* (i.e. turn vehicle by 180 degrees and drive into the opposite direction as previously);

16) *Enter_parking_slot*;

17) *Leave_parking_slot*.

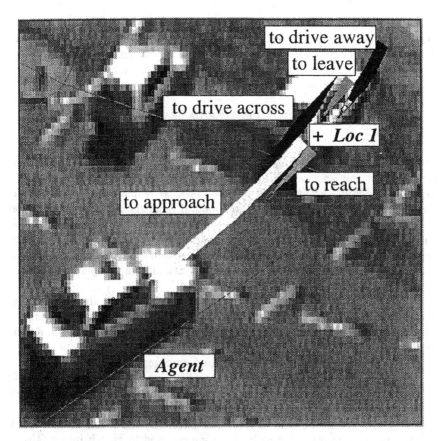

Fig. 1b. Section from Fig. 1a with the trajectory of the cab in the lower left of this section, denoted as 'Agent' (from Kollnig and Nagel 1993).

It is to be understood, however, that these are experimental versions of automatic maneuvers, executable under a restrictive set of precautionary conditions. Although it is certainly premature to claim that autonomous driving is routinely possible on public roads, this list may nevertheless serve as a justification to proceed with the attempt to investigate more complex maneuvers as concatenations of these elementary maneuvers.

The maneuvers in the above set are not claimed to be independent from each other: a U-turn, for example, can be considered to be composed by two consecutive 90 degree turns in the same direction. Entering and leaving a parking slot can be thought of as being inverse maneuvers with respect to each other. Entering and leaving a highway are considered special cases of *Merge_to_left* (through)/*right* (exit)_*lane.*

These maneuvers are considered to be generic in the sense that the distance to the reference line for lateral control, the speed, and other entities are parameters which have either to be chosen properly by some higher control level or have to be estimated based on the current state of the vehicle and the road. Moreover, the alternatives 'left' and 'right' for some maneuvers are explicitly indicated as parameters, i.e. they, too, represent a dimension with respect to which the corresponding maneuvers are understood to be generic.

4. BOUNDARY CONDITIONS FOR A CONCEPTUALIZATION OF DRIVING ON HIGHWAYS

The concepts referred to by natural language notions are abstractions from reality. One does not only encounter difficulties, however, associated with every attempt to algorithmically capture the abstraction process which takes place between the recorded signal and the appropriate natural language expression. A formalization of such an abstraction process must be prepared to be confronted with counterexamples which attempt to demonstrate that the abstraction process has been pushed too far, i.e. the algorithm is incapable of distinguishing between acceptable and unacceptable instances which associate a complex combination of signals and a natural language notion.

In order to prevent endless discussions about whether an algorithmic interpretation is correct or not, I suggested in (Nagel 1988) to restrict the range of admissible applications to a well delimited 'discourse world', for which it could be demanded, in turn, that
- the system should serve a clearly defined purpose;
- the system should be endowed with an exhaustive internal representation for all tasks and environmental conditions it is expected to handle in order to serve its purpose;
- the system should be able to recognize explicitly the limits of its capabilities, to indicate this state to its environment, and to switch into a fail-safe mode.

The subsequent remarks attempt to delimit the discourse world of 'driving on a high-way without intersections' in order to facilitate clear decisions about success or failure (Nagel 1993). Activities which can not be directly detected in a video recording of the road scene will be excluded from the discussion – for example 'to let a police or ambulance vehicle pass'. In addition, only activities executable by a road vehicle are admissible, i.e. all human activities are excluded initially. This comprises, for example, activities like resting or filling gas. Initially, only road vehicles will be admissible which can be described by a variant of the generic car model, see Figure 2, discussed by Koller (1992), Koller *et al.* (1993). Pedestrians and animals are excluded from the discourse world.

Moreover, it will be postulated that all traffic participants behave according to legal traffic code: it is assumed that rude or illegal behavior of a driver and the associated maneuvers of a road vehicle need not be taken into account. The density of cars on the road should be low enough to allow recognition of the actual lane structure of the highway by evaluation of recorded video image (sequence)s.

The admissible environment is restricted to approximately planar roads (no

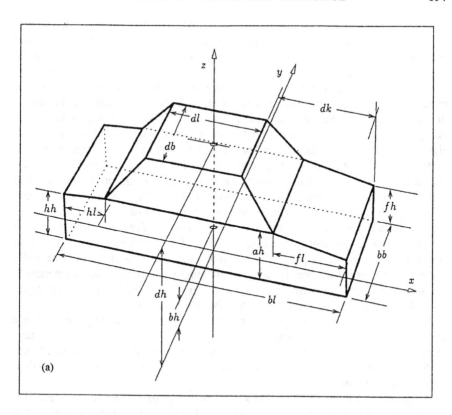

(a)

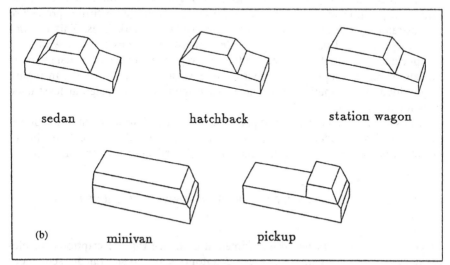

sedan   hatchback   station wagon

(b)   minivan   pickup

Fig. 2. Generic car model (a) and various specializations (b) obtained from it by appropriate choices for parameters such as length of hood, trunk, or roof, as discussed by Koller (1992). These figures have been taken from (Koller *et al.* 1993).

105

potholes or bumps) with well defined, but not necessarily well marked, borders. The topology of the relevant highway network is accessible through a digital road map. The lane structures of admissible highway segments should be compatible with those sketched in Figure 3.

At this point, the following remark regarding the notion of model-based vision with respect to the road appears useful. In order to facilitate automatic driving at higher speeds, for example in excess of 30 km/h, one aims at a short delay time between the recording of a scene and the derivation of correction signals for the steering, throttle, and brake actuators by the control algorithm (one tenth of a second or shorter). Otherwise, automatic control may become unstable. Given the limited computing power available today within an automatic road vehicle, one can not evaluate the entire video frame 25 times per second. Usually, only a small number of elements (between 2 and 16) of the right and/or left lane border are detected and tracked, based on a road border model which consists of a straight line segment in the simplest case. If curved roads have to be taken into account, a circle, a parabola, a spline, or a clothoid (a curve where the curvature changes as a linear function of arc length) are employed. These models are simple enough to be incorporated in the form of (partial) differential equations or piecewise integrals thereof into the control algorithm.

At intersections, such simple approaches may become inadequate. In these cases it can be advisable to incorporate explicit models of the intersection lane structure into the image evaluation subsystem as well as into the control subsystem. Figure 4 shows a complicated urban road intersection between two dual carriage, double and triple lane roads.

A simplified model of this intersection, made up from straight line segments, is superimposed on the intersection scene of Figure 4. The improvement of the estimated position of this model in space during an iterative fitting procedure is illustrated by the difference between the bright and dark lines. This demonstrates that a model-based approach offers plausible options to cope with even complicated lane structures. It should thus be no problem to accommodate various models of more complicated highway junctions such as those shown in Figure 3, provided the computing power to fit such models to an image at least once or twice a second is available.

Lanes are assumed to be free of potholes. Anything protruding out of the planar lane surface is considered to be an obstacle which should become amenable to detection based on an algorithm such as that described in Enkelmann (1991).

5. AN ATTEMPT TO FORMALIZE SEQUENCES OF DRIVING MANEUVERS ON HIGHWAYS

Preceding sections discussed experimental evidence that descriptions for elementary maneuvers can be *extracted* automatically from image sequences recorded by a stationary video camera as well as evidence for the *performance* of similar elementary maneuvers by automatic machine-vision-based control of road vehicles. In these cases, either a direct link from signals to abstractions at

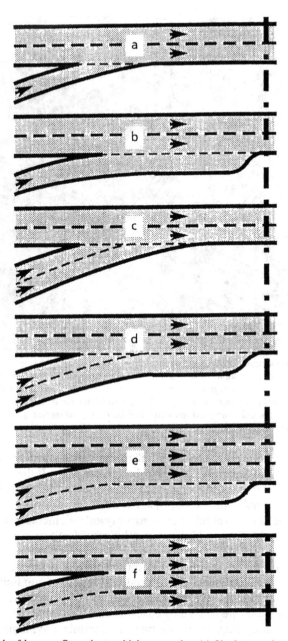

Fig. 3a-d. Sketch of lane configurations at highway entries. (a) Single entry lane without acceleration lane. (b) Single entry lane with acceleration lane. (c) Twin entry lanes without acceleration lane. (d) Twin entry lanes with acceleration lane. (e) Twin entry lanes including an acceleration lane which continues as additional regular lane. (f) Twin entry lanes with acceleration lanes both of which continue as additional regular lanes. Arrows indicate the driving direction. Reflection of lanes with respect to the bold-faced, interrupted vertical line at the right – retaining, however, the original arrow directions – results in corresponding lane configurations for highway exits.

Fig. 4. Urban intersection between two dual carriage, double and triple lane roads, taken from a video image sequence recording innercity traffic. The white lines indicate an approximate intersection model as projected into the image plane from an 'inital guess' position in space. The dark lines represent an analogous projection following an iterative fit of this model to the image line segments which have been extracted from road markings and borders (courtesy of T.-H. Osswald and H. Kollnig, Institut für Algorithmen und Kognitive Systeme der Universität Karlsruhe).

the level of natural language notions for elementary maneuvers or the inverse link from such notions to (control) signals has been established. It thus appears natural to investigate how one could extend such links to even higher levels of abstractions, i.e. more complicated driving maneuvers.

If we assume that a vehicle performs only one elementary maneuver at a time, driving a vehicle on a highway can be considered as a concatenation of elementary maneuvers. Although a very large number of maneuver sequences can be observed, driving according to the traffic code will not result in random sequences of elementary maneuvers. In order to represent admissible sequences of maneuvers, we attempt to treat such sequences of maneuvers as words in a formal language which are formed by concatenation of symbols according to some grammar. Elementary maneuvers are treated as terminal symbols (written subsequently in plain modern characters) of the grammar to be constructed. More complex maneuvers, which are considered to be subsequences constructed from elementary maneuvers, are treated as non-terminal symbols (written subsequently in boldface modern characters). The set of all admissible maneuver sequences is thus the set of all words which can be formed in this formal language according to its grammar.

The start symbol of the grammar to be constructed now is **Drive_a_road_ vehicle**. Its expansion is given in Figure 5. The non-terminals **Start_a_trip**, **Drive_to_highway**, **Drive_towards_destination**, and **Terminate_trip** will not be decomposed any further since the subsequent discussion will be restricted to the complex maneuver 'driving on a highway' for which, however, a non-terminal will not be introduced explicitly. It rather is decomposed immediately into a subsequence of three non-terminals **Enter_highway_system** (Figure 6), **Cruise_on_highway** (Figure 12), and **Leave_highway_system** (Figure 17). The further decomposition of these and subsequently introduced non-terminals can be easily tracked by following the references to the figures explaining each non-terminal.

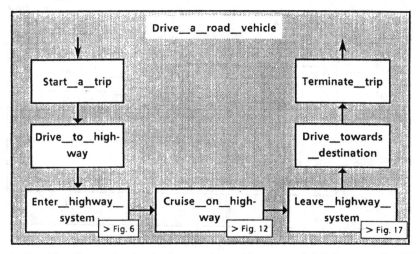

Fig. 5. Transition diagram showing the decomposition of the start symbol **Drive_a_road_vehicle**.

An analogous modeling of all reasonable vehicle maneuvers on the premises of a gas station with two petrol pumps has been discussed in (Nagel 1991), based essentially on a subset of the same set of terminals.

The terminals of this grammar will now be enumerated alphabetically, with reference numbers to the list of elementary maneuvers in Section 3 given in braces (see subsequent discussion regarding maneuvers with a question mark appended to the reference number):

  1) Accelerate_in_lane   {2}
  2) Approach_vehicle_preceding_in_same_lane   {3}
  3) Continue_in_deceleration-lane_to_junction_or_exit   {2}
  4) Cross_virtual_entrance_of_highway_system   {2}
  5) Decelerate_in_lane   {2}
  6) Drive_with_constant_speed   {2}
  7) Evade_obstacle_without_leaving_lane   {6}
  8) Follow_lane-deviation   {2}
  9) Follow_vehicle_beginning_to_move   {7}

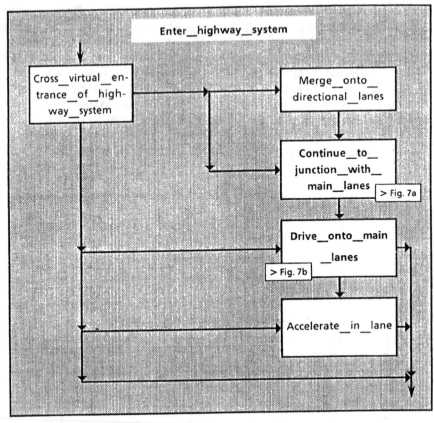

Fig. 6. Transition diagram for **Enter_highway_system**.

10)	Follow_vehicle_preceding_in_same_lane	{8}
11)	Leave_deceleration-lane	{11}
12)	Leave_virtual_exit_of_highway_system	{2}
13	Merge_into_deceleration_lane	{10}
14)	Merge_into_left_lane	{10}
15)	Merge_into_right_lane	{10}
16)	Merge_left_into_main_lane	{10}
17)	Merge_left_into_overtaking_lane	{10}
18)	Merge_onto_directional_lanes	{10}
19)	Merge_to_left	{10}
20)	Merge_to_right	{10}
21)	Overtake	{4}
22)	Pull_onto_emergency_lane	{10}
23)	Pull_up_to_left_curb	{10?}
24)	Pull_up_to_right_curb	{12}
25)	Start_driving	{1}

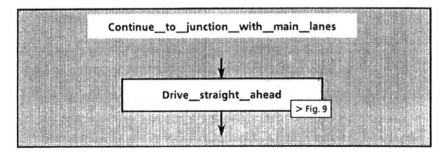

Fig. 7a. Transition diagram for **Continue_to_junction_with_main_lanes**.

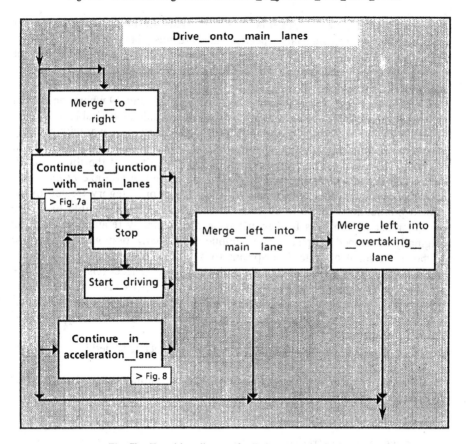

Fig. 7b. Transition diagram for **Drive_onto_main_lanes**.

26) Start_driving_on_emergency_lane {1}
27) Stop {12?}
28) Stop_in_front_of_obstacle {5}
29) Stop_on_emergency_lane {12?}

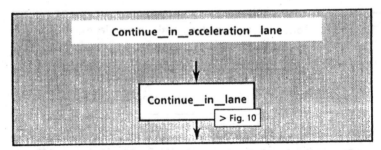

Fig. 8. Transition diagram for **Continue_in_acceleration_lane**.

Apparent multiplicities within this set of terminals are intended: whereas, for example, Merge_into_left_lane specifies the left(most) lane as the destination, Merge_to_left leaves the final lane open, it need only be to the left to the current one, but need not be the immediately adjacent left lane. It could possibly be some lane even further to the left!

It can be seen that – apart from the terminals 23, 27, and 29 where the quoted elementary maneuver is somewhat less generic than would be desirable – all other terminals can be understood as instances of an elementary maneuver with possibly some qualification regarding a lane or a location. These two qualifications, with respect to lane and to location, correspond exactly to two of the three qualification categories for elementary motion verbs treated in (Heinze *et al.* 1991) and (Kollnig and Nagel 1993). The third qualification category treated in the quoted publications refers to objects. Although it is easily possible to reduce the given set of terminals further, it has been deliberately retained in the form originally developed, emphasizing an implicit characterization, without recourse to the full arsenal of state descriptions to be obtained by model-based image evaluation of road traffic scenes. These and other imperfections (see e.g., the question marks behind some of the maneuver references given above within braces) should illustrate the continuing process of gradual refinement of representations for natural language abstractions which have been developed against different backgrounds:

* on the one hand, by the evaluation of image sequence recorded by a stationary video camera;
* on the other hand, by automatic control of autonomous vehicles based on machine vision, implying a moving camera.

6. DISCUSSION AND OUTLOOK

This contribution demonstrates that research on the interaction between vision and language begins to cross the border between exploration and systematic consolidation of an integrated approach towards a restricted, but by no means unrealistic, subsection of the real world, namely driving on a highway. An attempt has been made

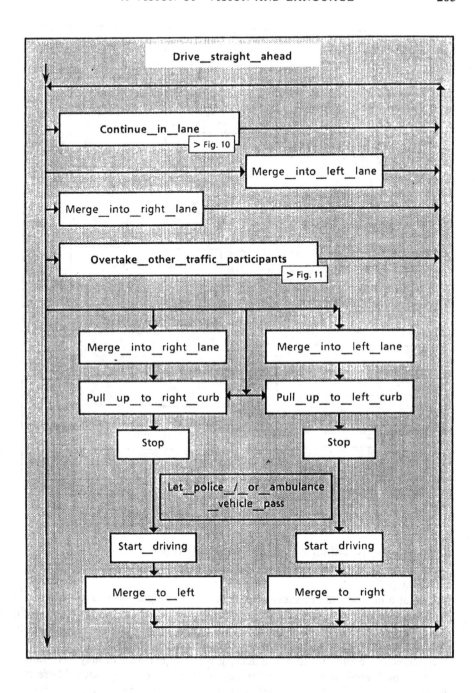

Fig. 9. Transition diagram for **Drive_straight_ahead**.

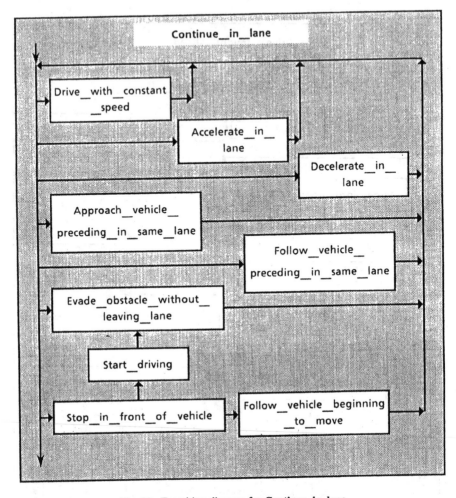

Fig. 10. Transition diagram for **Continue_in_lane**.

- to deliberately delimit the discourse world in order
- to strive for complete coverage of maneuver sequences within this discourse world

such that a decision about success or failure of the algorithmic approach under investigation becomes possible. The postulates which delimit the discourse world have to be refined in an iterative manner during further experimentation. Admitting this, even an incomplete enumeration of boundary conditions is considered to be superior to not indicating when an experiment may have failed.

It is considered to be a particular aspect of the research presented here that both the 'passive', observational, link between machine vision and natural language notions as well as the 'active' link in the form of control algorithms realizing a maneuver denoted by a natural language concept are taken into

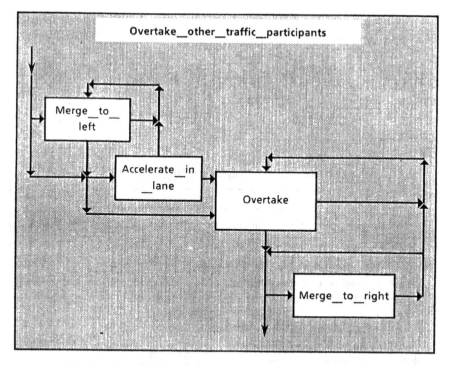

Fig. 11. Transition diagram for **Overtake_other_traffic_participants**.

account. So far, only one direction of the link between signals and symbols in this discourse world has been pursued.

The models for vehicles, roads, elementary maneuvers, and sequences of elementary maneuvers implementing more complex maneuvers have been outlined explicitly. In order to see the complexity with which this approach attempts to cope, the reader is invited to treat the nonterminal **Drive_straight_ahead** as the start symbol of a drastically reduced grammar and to visualize some of the maneuver sequences covered by this apparently simple abstraction! The larger set of driving activities covered by the grammar exposed in the appendix has been deliberately included in order to demonstrate that a significant subset of 'driving on a highway' becomes amenable to experimentation. The more encompassing this subset, the more realistic will be experiments and thus the more useful will be an analysis of the true causes of failure. An unrealistically small subset of real-world driving maneuvers may easily mask important aspects of the problem area and the associated methodological approach.

The research reported here has been restricted to express even complicated motion sequences as instances of a set of generic elementary occurrences expressed by natural language terms describing vehicle maneuvers. The approach implies that the algorithmic system 'knows' when one terminal or non-terminal begins to become relevant and when it stops being relevant. An approach which determines this has been presented by Kollnig & Nagel (1993) for the case of

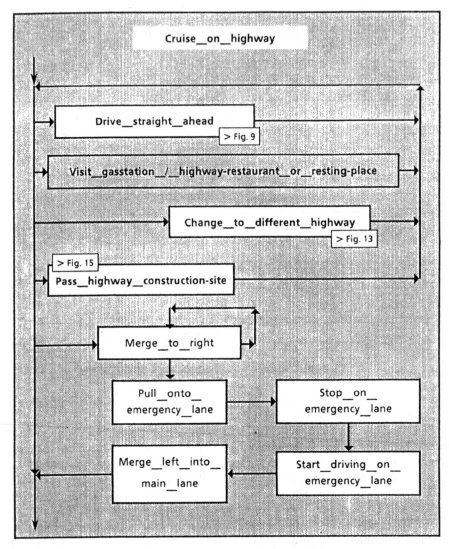

Fig. 12. Transition diagram for **Cruise_on_highway**.

associating motion verbs to vehicle trajectories extracted automatically from image sequences recorded by a stationary video camera – see, for example, the verb *to drive across location 1* in Figure 1b. In the case of an image sequence recorded by a camera moving with the autonomous road vehicle, knowledge about locations is not only determined from land marks or road signs which have to be detected within an image and subsequently have to be decoded. In addition, information about the actual location where an image has been recorded can be extracted from a navigation system such as the commercially available Travelpilot® of Robert-Bosch-GmbH, Stuttgart/Germany, provided the navigation

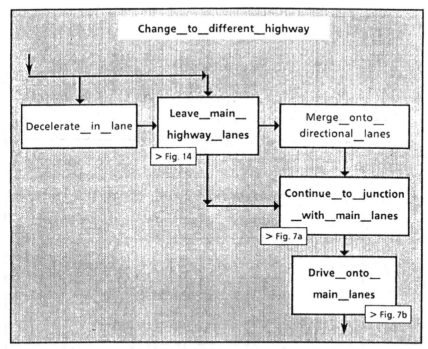

Fig. 13. Transition diagram for **Change_to_different_highway**.

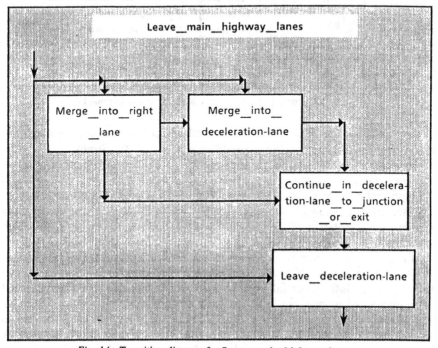

Fig. 14. Transition diagram for **Leave_main_highway_lanes**.

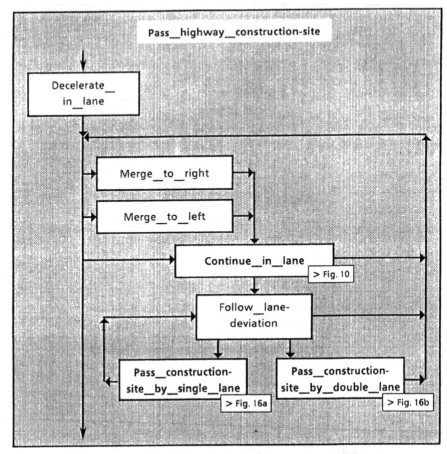

Fig. 15. Transition diagram for **Pass_highway_construction-site**.

system has been integrated into the overall control approach of a machine-vision-based autonomous vehicle, see (Siegle *et al.* 1992), (Struck *et al.* 1993).

Given a computer-internal representation for all admissible sequences of activities, one can arrange these into a hierarchical graph somewhat analogous to the representation of a context-free grammar for the concatenation of elementary maneuvers as shown in the appendix. Each node in such a graph incorporates a generic representation of the state of the agent and its environment for which the activity is considerable admissible. Finding a path through such a network of 'situation' nodes than corresponds to the task of instantiating a description of visual observations. Of course, once such a representation is available, it can also be used to infer potential plans of agents by attempting to match observed subsequences of maneuvers to initial parts of admissible maneuver sequences represented as paths in such a network. These ideas have been presented in more detail in (Nagel 1989 + 1991), see also (Retz-Schmidt 1991 + 1992). A formal description for situation graphs can be found in (Krüger 1991).

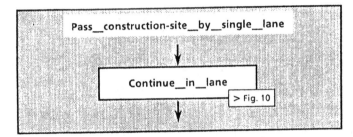

Fig. 16a. Transition diagram for **Pass_construction-site_by_single_lane**.

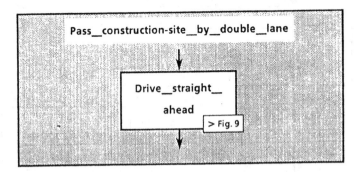

Fig. 16b. Transition diagram for **Pass_construction-site_by_double_lane**.

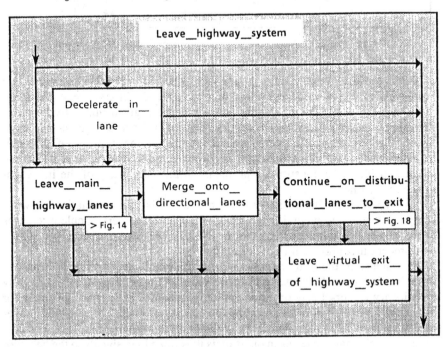

Fig. 17. Transition diagram for **Leave_highway_system**.

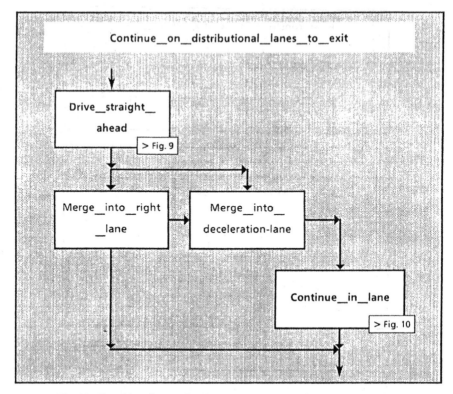

Fig. 18. Transition diagram for **Continue_on_distributional_lanes_to_exit**.

The algorithms linking natural language terms for vehicle movements and maneuvers to image sequences – and thus realizing the link between (machine) vision and (natural) language (concepts) – have been given implicitly by referring to previous publications where these algorithms have been treated in more detail. The transformation of computer-internal representations of (vehicle) trajectories into natural language text has been treated in (Herzog *et al.* 1989) and is not considered to constitute a problem within the context of the investigations reported here.

No survey regarding other approaches towards the association between computer vision and natural language has been included here: ample references to the earlier literature can be found in (Nagel 1988) and – with respect to the more recent literature – in (Kollnig *et al.* 1994).

In conclusion, then, the current contribution combines experience from two different backgrounds for using machine vision – image sequences recorded by a stationary camera for *description* and those recorded by a moving camera for *automatic control* – in order to refine the conditions under which object movements are associated algorithmically with natural language terms. The semantic of the natural language terms in question is thus linked via signals to the behavior of agents in the real world rather than merely to some system of logic definitions. The important point consists in that this link can be established in both directions, based on the same computer-internal representation of a hierarchy of abstractions for complex sets of driving maneuvers.

It will depend on the particular application whether the computer-internal representation for a complex series of driving maneuvers is related at the surface level to commands, warnings, a complete natural language sentence or even to an entire paragraph. Once this association between signals and computer-internal representations of natural language notions has been established as reliable, it can be exploited, e.g., for the design of powerful and flexible in-vehicle driver support as well as road traffic surveillance systems.

A significant number of the required algorithms have already been implemented and subjected to initial tests with real-world data. The taxing experiences when processing real world image data have taught us to abstain from any claims as to having solved all problems or at least all the problems touched upon in this contribution! Due to the same consideration, no additional research problems are outlined despite the fact that an entire gamut of extensions immediately springs to mind, for example extending the discourse world to include vehicle traffic on other road systems than highways.

ACKNOWLEDGEMENTS

The help of W. Enkelmann, N. Heinze, H. Kollnig, and T.-H. Osswald in obtaining Figure 4 and discussions with them as well as with W. Krüger and M. Otte are gratefully acknowledged. Carefully prepared, extensive comments by H. Kollnig and P. Mc Kevitt on a draft version of this contribution have been very helpful and are thoroughly appreciated.

REFERENCES

Enkelmann, W. (1991). Obstacle Detection by Evaluation of Optical Flow Fields from Image Sequences. *Image and Vision Computing* 9: 160–168.

Heinze, N., Krüger, W. & Nagel, H.-H. (1991). Berechnung von Bewegungsverben zur Beschreibung von aus Bildfolgen gewonnenen Fahrzeugtrajektorien in Straßenverkehrsszenen. *Informatik – Forschung und Entwicklung* 6: 51–61 (in German).

Herzog, G., Sung, C.-K., André, E., Enkelmann, W., Nagel, H.-H., Rist, T., Wahlster, W. & Zimmermann, G. (1989). Incremental Natural Language Description of Dynamic Imagery. In Brauer, W. & Freksa, C. (eds) In Proceedings of *Dritter Internationaler GI-Kongreß Wissensbasierte Systeme*, 153–162. Springer-Verlag: Berlin Heidelberg New York/NY, Informatik-Fachberichte 227.

Koller, D., Heinze, N. & Nagel, H.-H. (1991). Algorithmic Characterization of Vehicle Trajectories from Image Sequences by Motion Verbs. In Proceedings of *The IEEE Conference on Computer Vision and Pattern Recognition CVPR '91*, 90–95. Lahaina, Maui/Hawaii, 3–6 June 1991.

Koller, D. (1992). *Detektion, Verfolgung und Klassifikation bewegter Objekte in monokularen Bildfolgen am Beispiel von Straßenverkehrsszenen*. Dissertation, Fakultät für Informatik der Universität Karlsruhe (TH); appeared in the series 'Dissertationen zur Künstlichen Intelligenz' DISKI vol. 13. infix: Sankt Augustin/Germany (in German).

Koller, D., Daniilidis, K. & Nagel, H.-H. (1993). Model-Based Object Tracking in Monocular Image Sequences of Road Traffic Scenes. *International Journal of Computer Vision* 10: 257–281.

Kollnig, H. & Nagel, H.-H. (1993). Ermittlung von begrifflichen Beschreibungen von Geschehen in Straßenverkehrsszenen mit Hilfe unscharfer Mengen. *Informatik – Forschung und Entwicklung* 8: 186–196 (in German).

Kollnig, H., Nagel, H.-H. & Otte, M. (1994). Association of Motion Verbs with Vehicle Movements Extracted from Dense Optical Flow Fields. In Eklundh, J.-O. (ed.) In Proceedings of *The Third European Conference on Computer Vision ECCV '94*, Stockholm/Sweden, vol. II, 338–347. Springer-Verlag: Berlin Heidelberg New York/NY, Lecture Notes in Computer Science vol. 801.

Krüger, W. (1991). *Begriffsgraphen zur Situationsmodellierung in der Bildfolgenauswertung.* Dissertation, Fakultät für Informatik der Universität Karlsruhe (TH), Karlsruhe/Germany. A revised version appeared as *Situationsmodellierung in der Bildfolgenauswertung.* Springer-Verlag: Berlin Heidelberg (1992), Informatik-Fachberichte vol. 311 (in German).

Nagel, H.-H. (1988). From Image Sequences towards Conceptual Descriptions. *Image and Vision Computing* 6: 59–74.

Nagel, H.-H. (1989). Zur Erkennung von Situationen durch Auswertung von Bildfolgen. *FhG-Berichte* 1(89): 25–33.

Nagel, H.-H. (1991). The Representation of Situations and Their Recognition from Image Sequences. In Proceedings of *AFCET 8ᵉ Congrès Reconnaissance des Formes et Intelligence Artificielle*, 1221–1229. Lyon-Villeurbanne/France, 25–29 November.

Nagel, H.-H. (1993). *Überlegungen zur Formalisierung der sichtsystemgestützten Straßenfahrzeugführung.* Internal report, Fraunhofer-Institut für Informations- und Datenverarbeitung (IITB), Karlsruhe/Germany (in German).

Nagel, H.-H. & Enkelmann, W. (1991). Generic Road Traffic Situations and Driver Support Systems. In Proceedings of the *Fifth PROMETHEUS Workshop*, 76–85. Munich/Germany, 15–16 October 1991.

Nagel, H.-H., Enkelmann, W. & Struck, G. (1994). *FhG-Co-Driver: From Map-Guided Automatic Driving by Machine Vision to a Cooperative Driving Support.* Computers and Mathematics with Applications, Special Issue on "Network, Control, Communication and Computing Technologies for Intelligent Vehicle Highway Systems" (in press).

Retz-Schmidt, G. (1991). Recognizing Intentions, Interactions, and Causes of Plan Failures. *User-Modelling and User-Adapted Interaction* 1: 173–202.

Retz-Schmidt, G. (1992). *Die Interpretation des Verhaltens mehrerer Akteure in Szenenfolgen.* Springer-Verlag: Berlin Heidelberg, Informatik-Fachberichte vol. 308 (in German).

Siegle, G., Geisler, J., Laubenstein, F., Nagel, H.-H. & Struck, G. (1992). Autonomous Driving on a Road Network. In Proceedings of *Intelligent Vehicles '92 Symposium*, 403–408. Detroit/MI: 29 June–1 July 1992.

Struck, G., Geisler, J., Laubenstein, F., Nagel, H.-H. & Siegle, G. (1993). Interaction between Digital Road Map Systems and Trinocular Autonomous Driving. In Proceedings of *Intelligent Vehicles '93 Symposium*, 461–466. Tokyo/Japan: 14–16 July 1993.

Winograd, T. (1972). *Understanding Natural Language.* Academic Press, Inc.: New York, NY. For a synopsis, see: Winograd, T. (1973) A Procedural Model of Language Understanding. In Schank, R. C. & Colby, K. M. (eds.) *Computer Models of Thought and Language.* W.H. Freeman and Company: San Francisco/CA.

Artificial Intelligence Review **8**: 215–234, 1994.

What You Say is What You See – Interactive Generation, Manipulation and Modification of 3-D Shapes Based on Verbal Descriptions

YURI A. TIJERINO, SHINJI ABE, TSUTOMU MIYASATO and FUMIO KISHINO

ATR Communication Systems Research Laboratories, 2-2 Hikaridai, Seikacho, Sorakugun, Kyoto 619-02 Japan, E-mail address: yuri@atr-sw.atr.co.jp

Abstract. The advent of virtual reality (VR) introduced a paradigm for human-to-human communication in which 3-D shapes can be manipulated in real time in a new kind of computer supported cooperative workspace (CSCW) (Takemura and Kishino 1992). However, mere manipulation – either with 3-D input devices (e.g., the DataGlove™ [1]) or with spoken language (Mochizuki and Kishino 1991) – does not do justice to this new paradigm, which could prove to be revolutionary for human-to-human and human-to-machine – communication. This paper discusses the possibility of providing the means for VR-based CSCW participants not only to interactively manipulate, but also to generate and modify 3-D shapes using verbal descriptions, along with simple hand gestures. To this end, the paper also proposes a framework for interactive indexing of knowledge-level descriptions (Newell 1982, Tijerino and Mizoguchi 1993) of human intentions to a symbol-level representation based on deformable superquadrics (Pentland 1986; Horikoshi and Kasahara 1990, Terzopoulos 1991). This framework, at least, breaks ground in integration of natural language with interactive computer graphics.

Key words: virtual reality, 3-D visual ontology, superquadrics.

1. INTRODUCTION

Computers provide a nice medium for simulating 2-D and 3-D spaces, which people may employ to communicate with one another. Although, 2-D representations have achieved an advanced state-of-the-art – which currently may be multimedia-based representations – so far real-time communication in 3-D representations has not been exploited as one might expect. Recently, virtual reality (VR) has captured the imagination of researchers as well as of the mass media, in part, because it promises to add that one more dimension of which we all seem to be so enamored of – i.e., depth – to human-to-human and human-to-machine communication. Nevertheless, research on VR environments has predominantly focused on manipulation of 3-D shapes or interactive playback of scripts, and has essentially ignored more important aspects – i.e., real-time generation and modification of those shapes – which are fundamental for VR-based communication of thoughts and ideas.

At ATR we have been developing a Virtual Teleconferencing System (Kishino 1990) that brings participants together in a computer-generated virtual conference room, even though they might be at distant locations (see Figure 1). Recently, Takemura and Kishino (1992), acknowledged the importance of this type of virtual environment for computer-supported cooperative workspaces (CSCW). However, most research efforts currently focus on issues such as real-time reconstruction of facial expressions, hand gestures of participants, manipulation of virtual objects and so on.

Though Mochizuki and Kishino (1991) recognized the need for integrating natural language commands with hand gestures for manipulation of 3-D shapes, only recently the authors have embarked on efforts to provide interactive generation or modification of such shapes (Tijerino *et al.* 1993). This paper further helps to break ground in this direction, by proposing a framework for interactive indexing of knowledge-level descriptions (Newell 1982, Tijerino and Mizoguchi 1993) of human intentions to a symbol-level representation based on deformable superquadrics (Pentland 1986, Horikoshi and Kasahara 1990, Terzopoulos 1991). Where a superquadrics is a mathematical function of volumetric ellipsoids easily modified with a small set of parameters (Gardiner 1965).

This framework promises to create a means in which we can communicate our intentions or thoughts to the computer with natural language and simple hand gestures to generate, manipulate and modify 3-D shapes in real time so that we can "see" what we really want to "say." We coined the term WYSIWYS (What You Say Is What You See) for these types of interactions. Though WYSIWYS has numerous applications in fields such as design, art and computer imagery, it is specially helpful for virtual space teleconferencing and CSCW, because it serves to enhance human-to-human communication.

Fig. 1. A virtual teleconferencing room. Participants take part in a conference, with very realistic sensations, even when they may be at different distant locations.

This paper is organized in the following manner. Section 2 proposes the existence of a two-level ontology – that is, a knowledge level and a symbol level – for 3-D visual knowledge. Section 3 presents some preliminary results in an experiment to acquire knowledge-level 3-D visual concepts. Section 4 introduces a candidate symbol-level representation for symbol-level 3-D shape ontologies. Section 5 discusses the implications and applications of the framework for WYSIWYS interactions and describes an implementation effort taking place at ATR Communication Systems Research Laboratories. Section 6, addresses some problems and provides some concluding remarks.

2. A TWO-LEVEL ONTOLOGY FOR 3-D VISUAL KNOWLEDGE

The word ontology means the study of existence in philosophy, but in artificial intelligence (AI) it usually means the set of most primitive terms or concepts that canonically describe some particular field of knowledge. In this section, a two-level ontology for 3-D visual knowledge is proposed to help bridge the gap between the knowledge level and the symbol level (Newell 1982, Tijerino and Mizoguchi 1993). The knowledge level corresponds to concepts humans apply when describing 3-D visual knowledge. The symbol level corresponds to the symbolic representation or mechanism that operationalizes the descriptions in a visual manner, in this case, 3-D shapes.

The existence of a knowledge level was first proposed by Newell (1982), but was meant to explain how knowledge engineers interpret a particular domain expert's knowledge and translate it to a symbolic level in which a computer might make use of that knowledge to accomplish some task. However, only recently the knowledge-based systems research community has benefited from knowledge-level ontologies for knowledge-based system construction (e.g.; Neches *et al.* 1991, Gruber 1992, Steels 1992, Tijerino and Mizoguchi 1993). In addition, Mizoguchi *et al.* (1992) recently proposed an interactive translation approach in which it is the end-user, and not some intermediary such as a knowledge-engineer, who interactively translates the knowledge level to the symbol level which the computer understands. In this section, we propose the existence of a knowledge-level 3-D visual ontology, that can be useful for modeling 3-D shapes via verbal descriptions, and a symbol-level 3-D shape ontology, that provides operationalization of shape concepts and modification of those shapes. Figure 2 illustrates the relation of the knowledge-level ontologies to symbol level representations. Notice that there are several levels of representation which one could choose for representing visual knowledge, i.e., from machine language to high level representations provided by CAD (Computer Aided Design) software. This figure does not intend to capture the whole spectrum of representation, but only intends to give an idea of the relation of where ontologies are in relation to symbol level representations.

The knowledge-level 3-D visual ontology which we propose consists of simple 3-D visual concepts and their combinations, which in most cases might be hierarchical, repetitious, or both. Early work on various fields has demonstrated

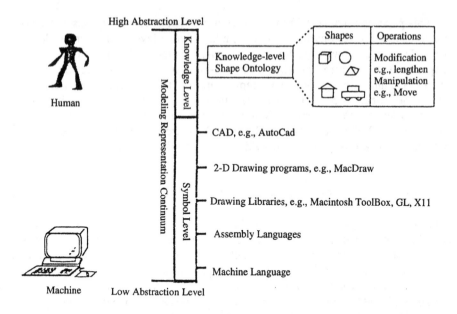

Fig. 2. The knowledge-level 3-D visual ontology taxonomizes concepts that are intuitive to humans because of their high level of abstraction, while the symbol-level 3-D shape ontology presents a computer representation of those concepts and an operationalization of modifications to shapes.

that these visual concepts do exist in nature and in perceptual forms (Wertheimer 1923, Thompson 1942, Johansson 1950, Rosch 1973, Stevens 1974). What we perceive as basic shapes – i.e., cubes, cylinders, spheres, cones, prisms, pyramids and so on – constitute the basic shape concepts for our knowledge-level 3-D visual ontology. It is not difficult to demonstrate that most shapes in nature,[2] animate or inanimate, can be broken down into these basic shapes. Nishihara (1981) noticed that these types of volumetric primitives seemed to be enough to decompose more complex shapes. Figure 3, illustrates how one may combine these basic shapes to assemble shapes that one perceives as different concepts. Biederman (1987), proposed 36 geons (i.e., geometrical ions) or primitives in his famous RBC (Recognition-by-components) theory and demonstrated that those 36 primitives were enough to represent all 30,000 categories of objects that an adult person might know.

These basic shapes are not useful enough for our knowledge-level 3-D visual ontology if we cannot perform operations on and with them. That is, our ontology also embraces concepts such as bending, twisting, tapering, rounding, swelling, sharpening, and so on. There are also, descriptors that help to specify states and features of shapes. Where features may be geometrical (e.g., round), visual (e.g., color), functional (e.g., for sitting down) quantitative (e.g., measure of size) or qualitative (e.g., large). Similarly, states may be quantitative positional (e.g., 50 cm to the left) or qualitative positional (e.g., to the left of A).

There seems to be some intricate relation in how we organize these basic shapes to generate more complex ones. Figure 4, illustrates this point. First, Figure 4-a

Fig. 3. Combination of basic shapes such as cubes, cylinders, spheres, cones, prisms, pyramids can be arranged to produce more complex ones as this figure illustrates.

presents some primitive shapes in a random pattern. Then, in Figure 4-b the same shapes are organized in an specific pattern that we recognize as a car. It was not necessary to give detailed attributes to the car – such as an engine, doors, windows and so on – to recognize that it has the basic shape of car. Yet, we still insist on recognizing it as a car. Changing the primitive shapes of our car, we can represent more complex concepts – such as that of a sports car – without major effort (see Figure 4-c).

These basic shape organization relations seem to be canonical, but are not easily described just in geometric terms. That is, we may be able to recognize Figures 4-b and 4-c as a car and a sports car respectively, because at some point in our lives we have seen what a car and a racing car look like. However, someone who has never seen a car in his/her life might still recognize the primitive shapes of Figure 4-a. Interestingly enough, Rosch (1973) found that even primitive New Guinea tribesmen also used primitive shapes to describe more complex shapes unknown to them. Therefore, there seems to be some kind of background knowledge implicit in the recognition process. Moreover, there also seems to be some boundary conditions as to what we recognize as the shape for something. For instance, consider that the tires of the car represented with the four cylinders in Figure 4-b were not placed at the same height in relation to the body or too close together. Would that still be considered a car?

The knowledge-level 3-D visual ontology that we have proposed above lends itself to all sorts of criticisms. For instance, one can argue that it does not provide any kind of insight, since the shapes that we perceive daily are far too complex and, therefore, cannot be captured in any useful way, even with primitive shapes. However, there are numerous techniques that can be employed to analytically and statistically classify concepts with computer assistance. For

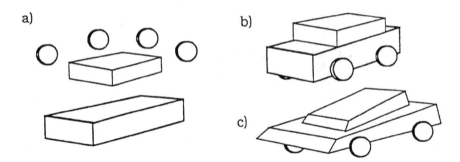

Fig. 4. Basic shapes can describe more complex ones: (a) presents some basic shapes in random order without any particular meaning, (b) organizes the shapes into the simple form of a car, and (c) shows how deformations can represent the more complex concept of a sports car.

instance, machine learning has had great success in learning from examples with techniques such as those for induction (Quinlan 1986) and explanation-based learning (DeJong 1986), which could be adapted for common sense visual knowledge. In Section 3, we will present results on an experiment which adapted personal construct psychology [PCP] (Kelly 1955), a technique that has had great success in knowledge-acquisition for knowledge-based systems (Boose 1986, Boose and Bradshaw 1987, Bradshaw *et al.* 1993, Diederich *et al.* 1987, Ford *et al.* 1990, Garg-Janardan and Salvendy 1987, Shaw and Gaines 1987), to the acquisition of 3-D visual concepts.

Another criticism that may arise of this type of knowledge-level 3-D shape ontology is that it is only an approximation, and a relatively poor one on many occasions. Newell (1982) calls it a radically incomplete approximation, but explains that such incompleteness can be tolerated because it leads to unstructured descriptions that can be translated to implementable symbol levels. In this paper, we present an approach in our framework for WYSIWYS which takes advantage of knowledge-level unstructured descriptions and interactively translates them to the symbol level.

A third criticism that may arise is that this ontology is in no way at the knowledge level. However, Chandrasekaran and Narayanan propose that it is necessary to also provide a theory of common sense visual reasoning (1990). This aroused interest in different research circles and resulted in a field of research known as diagrammatic reasoning (Chandrasekaran *et al.* 1993). Nonetheless, most work in this area focuses on 2-D diagrams. To this end, we believe that 3-D shapes should also be included in visual reasoning research and that the type of ontology we propose above makes a significant contribution towards this direction. This type of ontology could make even a larger contribution to knowledge sharing and large common sense knowledge base research, if some adaptations or translations – to accommodate 3-D visual representations – are made to symbolic knowledge sharing languages such as Ontolingua (Gruber 1992) or CycL (Lenat and Goha 1990).

In short, our knowledge-level 3-D visual ontology consists of verbal concepts of basic shapes plus operators and descriptors of those shapes that people perceive as common sense. Though very recent experiments support the existence of these concepts (Lass *et al.* 1993), these concepts are not useful for our purposes if no means for machine interpretation is provided. To this end, a symbol level 3-D shape ontology is necessary to which a translation can be performed in order to operationalize the generation, manipulation and modification of computer-simulated 3-D shapes from verbal description.

We define a symbol-level ontology as the set of algorithms or mechanisms that operationalize canonical concepts in a particular task. Consequently, what we need for our symbol-level 3-D shape ontology is: (1) a symbolic representational language that supports feature and state descriptions of the basic and complex shapes, and (2) a set of mechanisms that operationalize transformations of those features and states.

Commercially available CAD applications, such as AutoCAD, WaveFront, Alias and so on, partially fulfill both requirements. CAD applications provide, in most cases, primitives such as cubes and spheres plus a set of menu- or command-driven mechanisms that help modify those primitives. Nonetheless, interaction between the users and CAD applications occurs at a very low level, because CAD applications only provide a set of primitives and a set of tools, which may or may not be the most appropriate. That is, although the basic shape primitives are available (e.g., cubes, spheres, lines, faces, etc.), their combinations into complex shapes have no particular meaning to the application (e.g., the two blocks and four cylinders of Figure 3a will never be a car to the computer, no matter how they are combined), but only to the user. Also, the tools for modification provide only low level modification of the primitives (e.g., extruding, twisting, etc.) and it is left up to the user to combine the tools in some particular sequence to achieve higher level modifications (e.g., a longer car), which may not be intuitive at all.

What is needed to overcome these insufficiencies is a kind of language that can represent higher level concepts (e.g., cars, cups, chairs, etc) and that at the same time provides higher level mechanisms for modification. In Section 4 we will introduce a candidate representation, deformable superquadrics, that fulfills both requirements to a higher degree than current CAD applications.

3. AN EXPERIMENT ON VISUAL CONCEPT ACQUISITION

The basic primitives of an ontology are the concepts from which it is formed. It is extremely difficult to create an ontology that contains all common sense concepts, especially when dealing with visual concepts. Though there is actual research taking place in that direction (Lenat and Goha 1990), it is useful to constrain the context of the concepts to some specific domain or task (Mizoguchi *et al.* 1992). This section reports preliminary results of an experiment on visual concept acquisition for description of cars (Umamichi and Tijerino 1993).

The basic question that we wanted to answer before performing the experiment was: Are there any primitive concepts behind peoples' verbal descriptions of cars? The reason for choosing cars as the object of our experiment was more arbitrary, than anything else. The fact that more than 200 3-D CG models of cars were already available in a 3-D dead set catalog, courtesy of Viewpoint Datalabs,[3] was a determining factor.

We used Personal Construct Psychology (Kelly 1955) to acquire visual descriptive concepts for cars from a total of 8 subjects, 4 males and 4 females. To insure that the concepts being acquired were of common sense nature, none of the subjects were car designers. To restrain the scope of the concepts, the information shown visually was constrained to 2-D wireframe snapshots of the 3-D models exhibited from random perspectives. That is, with these simplified models, we could guarantee that only descriptive concepts about shape could be acquired.

We begun the experiment by randomly choosing 20 models of cars from a stack of 85. Then for each of the 8 subjects the following experiment steps were followed:

1) Randomly choose 3 cards from the stack of 20 and put them in front of the subject.
2) Ask the subject to select two models with a similar feature which the third model does not have.
3) Ask the subject to shortly describe what is similar in the two models and what makes the third one different from the first two. These two opposite descriptions constitute a so-called dichotomy.
4) Repeat steps 1 through 3 until it becomes difficult to describe new dichotomies.
5) For every dichotomy, draw a straight line showing the features at opposite ends of the line.
6) Ask the subject to identify where, on each of the lines, every one of the 20 models can be placed. That is, for every car how would each of the features identified in step 3 best fit.
7) Divide each dichotomy line in 10 equal segments and label each dividing marker from 0 to 10.
8) For each model on each dichotomy line select the closest numeric label as its rating on the dichotomy.

For all dichotomies identified by each subject, we created rating grids showing the name of the subject on the left-most column, each concept of the dichotomy on the next two columns and the names of the models on the top line. Then we rated each model on the dichotomy according to the data gathered on step 8. Table 4 shows the ratings obtained from one subject.

Careful analysis of data obtained from all subjects revealed that some concepts, though differently labeled, showed a very similar pattern of the ratings. We assumed this concepts to be the same. We attributed reason for this concept duplication to the lack of data (i.e., not enough car models) or bias towards one concept. To overcome this difficulty we chose three car models from the ones in each duplicate dichotomy and performed steps 2 through 8 above for each subject. This time the subjects were asked to think of concepts different from the ones already identified. Only a few new concepts were identified with this second run of the experiment.

Then, we selected dichotomies with similar labels, or that we thought to have the same meaning, and normalized the ratings for all subjects, by taking their average. We then entered the results into a grid that contained the normalized dichotomies (see Table 1).

From this simple experiment we could learn that it is possible to acquire common sense visual concepts by applying psychological techniques such as PCP. Though the experiment is very simple, there are still many other techniques in PCP that we didn't explore. However, the fact that we could identify, with simple visual analysis, that some of the concepts seem to be canonical among the subjects, makes PCP an appropriate tool for visual concept acquisition. The results of the experiments could also serve to provide numeric ratings of concepts for easy database retrieval.

Figure 5 shows some of the 2-D snapshots of the 3-D wireframe models of cars used for our experiment. The simplicity of the models makes them ideal for acquiring visual concepts about shapes; this explains the small number of concepts acquired with the experiment. It may be that attaching textures and color to the models helps the subjects identify other types of concepts (i.e., perhaps descriptive concepts that do not relate to shape).

We are currently implementing a VR-based program for concept acquisition which allows subjects to handle colored 3-D models with 6 degrees of freedom. This way, the subjects are able to see the models from different perspectives as they wish. We hope that this will result in the subjects identifying more concepts that have to do with the 3-dimensional shape of the models. Results on this experiment will be presented in later papers. In the mean time we have constructed a preliminary knowledge-level ontology with concepts shown in Table 5. Notice the entry about "bad mileage"/"good mileage" which is the result of one of the subject's being knowledgeable about cars, thus, associating this dichotomy with a priori knowledge about the recognized cars.

4. A CANDIDATE REPRESENTATION FOR SYMBOL-LEVEL 3-D SHAPE ONTOLOGY

It is now appropriate to describe a candidate representation for our symbol-level 3-D shape ontology. The representation we present here is only a candidate because, as explained in previous sections, the only requirements for our representation are that it allows us symbolically to represent feature and state descriptions of basic and complex shapes. Superquadrics comply with this requirement and we have, therefore, chosen it for representation of our symbol-level 3-D shape ontology. This section describes the representation as well as how it fulfills our requirements.

Though superquadrics, which were first discovered by Hein (see Gardiner 1965), has recently gathered much attention as a representation useful for shape reconstruction from 2-D and 3-D data (Pentland 1986, Horikoshi 1990, Terzopolous 1991), they have also been recognized as a powerful representation for intuitively building 3-D models.

Superquadrics can be defined by the following vector:

Table 1. Rating grid for normalized ratings of all 8 subjects.

| CDichonomy | | Car Type | | | | | | | | | | | | | | | | | | | | |
Concept (0-Rat)	Concept (10-Rat)	A	B	C	D	E	F	G	H	I	J	K	L	M	N	O	P	Q	R	S	T
Slow	Fast	6	6	4	6	5	6	2	2	5	7	5	2	5	5	7	6	6	4	9	8
Cheap	Expensive	5	4	5	5	4	6	3	5	4	8	4	3	4	5	6	5	6	4	6	5
Narrow bag co.	Wide bag comp.	4	4	6	5	6	7	10	1	6	8	6	4	8	8	3	6	6	5	1	6
Light weight	Heavy weight	8	4	9	7		5	5	4	7	9	3	1	5	6	7	8	7	3	2	2
Old style	New style	7	7	3	4	6	7	3	1	4	2	4	1	7	5	6	6	7	7	4	6
Squarish	Roundish	6	6	4	3	5	3	1	10	2	1	3	2	5	5	6	5	6	4	8	2
Sedan	Sports car	5	4	3	4	4	5	2	4	3	3	4	3	4	4	4	4	6	4	8	7
Small	Big	7	6	6	6	4	7	6	2	8	6	4	1	6	9	7	9	6	3	6	4
Short	Long	5	4	6	7	5	3	9	0	5	9	3	3	5	5	5	5	4	5	2	6
Straight lined	Round lined	5	6	3	3	4	3	1	10	5	1	1	2	6	4	5	4	8	5	10	1
Bad mileage	Good mileage	4	5	4	3	5	4	2	6	4	4	7	4	5	4	5	4	4	6	6	6
Cold style	Warm style	6	5	5	4	5	3	3	8	5	2	5	6	5	4	3	3	5	5	6	2
Japanese style	Western style	2	2	7	6	2	3	7	10	6	8	4	8	3	5	5	2	5	2	8	4

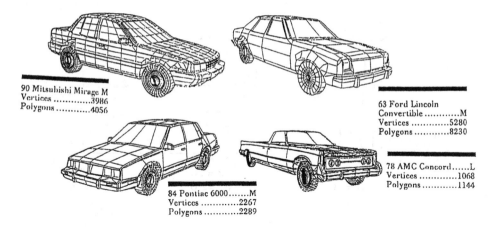

90 Mitsubishi Mirage M
Vertices 3986
Polygons 4056

63 Ford Lincoln
Convertible ....M
Vertices 5280
Polygons 8230

84 Pontiac 6000.......M
Vertices 2267
Polygons 2289

78 AMC Concord......L
Vertices 1068
Polygons 1144

Fig. 5. Some examples of 2-D snapshots of car 3-D wireframe models.

$$(1) \qquad x = a1 \cos^{\varepsilon 1} \alpha \cos^{\varepsilon 2} \omega$$
$$y = a2 \cos^{\varepsilon 1} \alpha \sin^{\varepsilon 2} \omega$$
$$z = a3 \sin^{\varepsilon 1} \alpha$$

where x, y and z are the coordinates of a surface point on a superquadrics ellipsoid. The parameters $a1$, $a2$ and $a3$ define the scale in the x, y and z directions respectively. The angles α and ω each represent the degrees of latitude and longitude respectively on the superellipsoid. Finally, $\varepsilon 1$ represents the squareness parameter along the z-y plane and $\varepsilon 2$ the squareness parameter along the x-y and x-z planes. Though by just changing the squareness and scale parameters we can represent a few basic shapes such as those illustrated in Figure 6, these shapes are only allowed to be symmetrical.

We can substitute the scale parameters $a1$ and $a2$ with modifying functions $f(z)$ and $g(z)$ to yield:

$$(2) \qquad x = f(z) \cos^{\varepsilon 1} \alpha \cos^{\varepsilon 2} \omega$$
$$y = g(z) \cos^{\varepsilon 1} \alpha \sin^{\varepsilon 2} \omega$$
$$z = a3 \sin^{\varepsilon 1} \alpha$$

which will in turn allow us to bend, taper or twist the basic shapes into non-symmetrical ones.

Pentland (1986) demonstrates superquadrics' utility in building 3-D models through a system called SuperSketch, a Symbollics-3600-based 3-D modeling application (recently ported to Sun machines and renamed ThingWorld). In this system, users create "lumps," change their squareness/roundness, stretch, bend, taper them, and make Boolean combinations of them in real time by moving the mouse through the relevant parameter space, controlling which parameter is being varied by using the mouse buttons. Pentland noticed that because primitives, operations and combining rules used by the computer are well matched to those of the human operator, the interactions described above were surprisa)

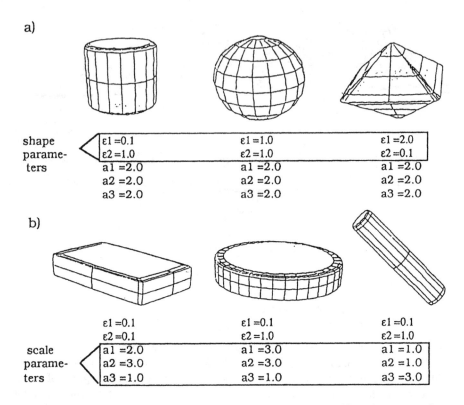

shape parame- ters	ε1 =0.1 ε2 =1.0 a1 =2.0 a2 =2.0 a3 =2.0	ε1 =1.0 ε2 =1.0 a1 =2.0 a2 =2.0 a3 =2.0	ε1 =2.0 ε2 =0.1 a1 =2.0 a2 =2.0 a3 =2.0

b)

	ε1 =0.1 ε2 =0.1	ε1 =0.1 ε2 =1.0	ε1 =0.1 ε2 =1.0
scale parame- ters	a1 =2.0 a2 =3.0 a3 =1.0	a1 =3.0 a2 =3.0 a3 =1.0	a1 =1.0 a2 =1.0 a3 =3.0

Fig. 6. 6 symmetrical shapes that can be represented with simple superquadrics: (a) represents shape modification through squareness parameters and (b) represents changes through scale parameters (adapted from Horikoshi and Kasahara 1990).

ingly effortless. Pentland further states that descriptions couched in this representation are similar to peoples' (naive) verbal descriptions and appear to match peoples' (naive) perceptual notion of "a part", and that this correspondence is strong evidence that the descriptions we form will be good spatial primitives for a theory of common-sense reasoning. However, he noticed that domains experts formed descriptions differently from naive observers, reflecting their understanding of the domain-specific formative processes and their more specific, limited purposes, and that accounting for expert descriptions will require additional, more specialized models. It is with respect to this last point where we believe that the two-level ontology can be the most helpful, because abstract and specialized descriptions at the knowledge level can be indexed to descriptions at the symbol level which provide proper operationalization.

On a separate research effort, Horikoshi and Kasahara (1990) proposed superquadrics as a multiple purpose indexing language for 3-D models. They demonstrated that superquadrics parameters can be easily mapped to descriptive words of shape and transformations of shapes. They also employ superquadrics parameters to index and search in a database of 3-D objects with the help of two orthogonal free-hand sketches. They further claim that this is an unified 3-D indexing language that can interconnect descriptive words or 2-D images with 3-D information. The power of their approach becomes clear with the fact that simple words such as cube, sphere, cone and pyramid can be indexed to shapes with small variations but that can be considered to fall into those categories. Also, simple words such as pinching, collapsing, denting, sharpening, etc. can be used to represent transformations on the shapes. Figure 7 shows an example of how these types of words can be indexed to these type of transformations.

Later on, Terzopolous makes further contribution by introducing deformable superquadrics (1991) which incorporate the global shape parameters of conventional superquadrics with the local degrees of freedom of a spline. This combination of local and global deformation parameters make superquadrics particularly useful to provide both global salient part descriptors for efficient indexing into a database of stored models and to reconstruct the local details of complex shapes that the global abstraction misses. Terzopolous applies equations of motion to govern the behavior of deformable superquadrics by employing local finite element basis functions because they provide greater shape flexibility for local deformations.

Superquadrics allows us to index numerous 3-D shape classes, with both global

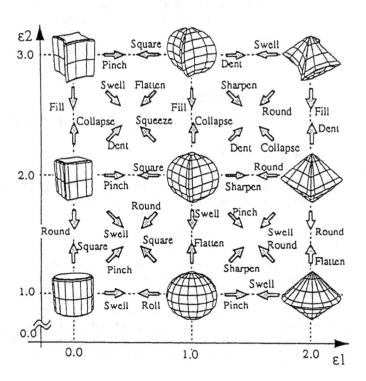

Fig. 7. The relation between shape parameters and words (from Horikoshi and Kasahara 1990).

and local variations. Thus, superquadrics are appropriate for representing symbol-level 3-D shape ontologies, because the number of parameters involved is very small and also have been proven to map very intuitively to words which describe objects and their transformations. However, a one-to-one mapping from words to arrangement of parameters or transformation is not desirable for our WYSIWYS framework, because it doesn't take into consideration the vagueness in natural language. For this reason, it is necessary to make the mapping between concepts of the knowledge-level 3-D visual ontology described in a previous section. This way, the vagueness in natural language can be managed to some extent by indexing concepts with one or more labels (i.e., words).

5. THE WYSIWYS FRAMEWORK

People tend to picture in their minds what an object might look like after reading or listening to its description (Anderson 1978). If the object is known, we would automatically retrieve from our memory a prototype of the object (Lass *et al.* 1993). When it is not known, then we try to imagine what it looks like by relating it to known objects (Rosch 1973). With the WYSIWYS framework we could actually see what someone is describing as the description progresses. This framework allows people to verbally describe 3-D objects and transformations performed on those objects as the objects are being displayed by the computer. If the framework is implemented taking advantage of natural language processing and virtual reality technologies, it promises to revolutionize human-to-human and human-to-machine communication.

5.1. *Characteristics of the WYSIWYS framework*

A system based on the WYSIWYS framework requires at least the following characteristics:
1) flexibility in interpretation of vagueness in verbal descriptions,
2) real-time visual simulation of verbal descriptions,
3) accessibility of simulated shapes through some intuitive input device, and
4) flexibility in selection and assignment of spatial attributes.

Flexibility in interpretation of vagueness in verbal descriptions
In our two-level ontology approach, words-to-concept mapping permits the flexibility required by verbal descriptive vagueness when describing objects. Take for instance the concept of a "cube," the labels cube, box and block are all indexed into it; this allows us to refer to the same object in three different manners. Correspondingly, we could define a fuzzy set that takes into account the square-ness parameters range to prescribe the meaning of "cube" in a superquadrics representation (Horikoshi and Kasahara 1990), which are necessary to, among other things, index the concept of "cube" at the symbol level and to display the object.

The indexing of words to concepts and concepts to symbolic representations should be interactive. In the case of words to concepts mapping, interactiveness of mappings allows customizing. Interactive indexing can be accomplished by allowing a familiarization period for the user and the system, in which – for instance – the system gets acquainted with how the user calls its primitive shapes and primitive operators. This is simple to attain because – considering that the number of primitives remains small – all the system has to do is show the basic shapes or animate the primitive operations and request the user to label them. The system could then keep an active glossary (Klinker *et al.* 1992) of the labels for the concepts. In the other case – indexing of concepts to symbolic representation – interactivity provides easy expandability of the scope of the two-level ontology. That is, when a person wants to define a new concept, all that is needed for that person to do is to define what the concept means in terms of the symbolic representation. With deformable superquadrics, for instance, if the concept of a new shape is to be defined, the person has only to provide the range of values of the global and local parameters that define the new shape. Because in both cases, instantaneous visual feedback can be obtained, the need for a more complex natural language processing sub-system can then be avoided.

Real-time visual simulation of verbal descriptions
It is very important to provide real-time visual feedback in the form of perspective monoscopic or stereoscopic display of 3-D shapes and operations being performed on the shapes. This is the essence of the "see" part in the WYSIWYS framework. A system based on this framework should be able to match the intentions of the verbal descriptions, i.e., the "say" part of the WYSIWYS framework, with adequate changes to the visual display environment. This makes possible for a WYSIWYS-based system to avoid dependance solely on natural language processing. Instantaneous visual feedback allows the user to "see" what the system "interprets."

Accessibility of simulated shapes through some intuitive input device
A WYSIWYS-based system should also support some kind of pointing device, preferably a DataGlove™ or similar device, that at least permits actions such as moving in the 3-D space, pointing or selecting objects, identifying a point in space, etc.

Flexibility in selection and assignment of spatial attributes
When we verbally describe objects, we tend to make gestures with our hands which may or may not aid a listener to better understand what we are describing. We often employ simple hand gestures that describe rough position, direction and orientation. Concepts such as here, there, in this direction and so on, depend on abstract hand gestures, which do not have to be precise as long as they convey the intention. Superquadrics allows us to adjust scale parameters to hand positions – provided that a DataGlove™-like input device is being used – for concepts such as enlarging or reducing the size of an object. In a similar manner, direction and proportion of movement of our hands can also help to adjust position or orientation vectors.

5.2. *OVO-Genesys: a system that implements the WYSIWYS framework*

We are currently developing an Ontology-based Virtual Object GENerating SYStem: OVO-GENESYS (Tijerino *et al.* 1993), which implements the WYSIWYS framework described above. The architecture is illustrated in Figure 8 and is composed of the following:

Concept database

This consists of a knowledge-level 3-D visual ontology about cars. Concepts may or may not be hierarchical. Each concept may be associated with one or more labels. Concepts are classified in four major groups: state descriptors, feature descriptors, state operators and feature operators. Features may be of geometrical (e.g., round, square), visual (e.g., color), functional (e.g., for sitting down) quantitative (e.g., size) or qualitative (e.g., large) nature. Similarly, states may be quantitative positional (e.g., 50 cm to the left), qualitative positional (e.g., to the left of A).

Object database

A database that contains 3-D models of cars along with indexing to relevant concepts.

Natural language parser

This uses labels associated with concepts in the concept database as its basic vocabulary.

Gesture understanding module

This interprets simple hand gestures – such as extended hand and pointing with one finger –, translation and rotation.

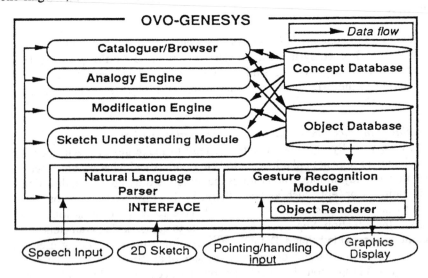

Fig. 8. OVO-GENESYS's general architecture.

Object cataloguer/browser
This permits interactive indexing of labels to concepts to deformable superquadrics representations.

Object analogy engine
This module parses a natural language phrase and searches in the concept database
for an adequate state or feature descriptor/operator.

Object modification engine
This module parses natural language phrases and maps concepts which express
object modification in terms of feature or state operators to specific actions on
the objects. The operators are coupled with hand gestures for modification.

2-D Sketch understanding module
The 2-D sketch understanding module allows the user to input 2-D sketches of
objects directly into the computer with help of position tracking sensors attached
to the hand. The objects are then transformed into 3-D representations with
help of verbal descriptions of the object. The 2-D sketch serves as the rough
representation of the object, its spatial characteristics and its proportional
geometry. The verbal description of the object is mapped to state and feature
descriptions and coupled with hand gestures in a similar manner to the Object
Modification Engine. Because this is not in the scope of this paper, a more
extensive description of how we accomplish this will be reported in a later
paper as it is not trivial to transform a 2-D sketch into a volumetric representation.

As this paper is being written. Ovo-Genesys is still in an early development
stage, therefore it is still difficult to say how accurate conceptual descriptions can
be. The system is being implemented on a Onyx RE^2 graphics super computer
in both C++ and CLOS. Currently we are working with a database of auto-
mobiles but plan to extend it to include more general types of objects. A later
paper will report on experiments with Ovo-genesys to test for accuracy of
mappings from verbal descriptions to visual display.

6. DISCUSSION

The WYSIWYS framework proposed here has numerous implications to human-
to-human and human-to-machine communications. It enables people to "show"
to each other what they mean in a computer simulated 3-D medium which can
be manipulated in a very intuitive manner through verbal descriptions and simple
hand gestures. This in itself, has many applications to such fields as CAI, CG
art, CSCW, VR, virtual space teleconferencing, and so on. Another implication
for human-to-human communication, is that it provides guidelines for research
in common sense 3-D visual knowledge and reasoning that are essential for
building very large 3-D visual knowledge bases and also for allowing 3-D visual
knowledge sharing.

For human-to-machine, on the other hand, the implications of the WYSIWYS framework are not less important. For instance, CAD applications could incorporate support for knowledge-level 3-D visual ontologies on top of their existing symbol level representations and thus allow intuitive verbal interactions. This is, of course, just one of the many applications that can benefit from the WYSIWYS framework. Other include but are not limited to, intelligent 3-D database search through verbal instructions and 2-D sketches (Horikoshi and Kasahara 1990), 3-D scientific simulations, machine learning and so on.

A very important contribution of the framework is in the integration of natural language and computer graphics. It provides guidelines on how to avoid too much dependance on natural language processing and take advantage of real time computer graphics interpretations. This way, the people can "see" what the computer is "interpreting" from natural language. This instantaneous feedback allows people to interactively guide the interpretation process. The framework also makes an important contribution to VR technology by providing an alternative means for interactive generation, manipulation and modification of 3-D models, an area in which not much research has been focused (Mochizuki and Kishino 1991, and Butterworth *et al.* 1992).

There are many problems that have to be solved before the WYSIWYS framework can be widely applied. Probably, the most important problem is the generation of adequate knowledge- and symbol-level 3-D shape ontologies for various domains. The domain chosen in this paper was for cars, but there are numerous domains that can be more useful, not only for common sense 3-D knowledge, but also for 3-D visual knowledge sharing. For instance, human anatomy, architecture, sculpture, and so on. Likewise, natural language understanding is another problem; it also has to be improved. Though simple hand gestures might help towards this end (Mochizuki and Kishino 1991), there is still much to be expected from speech understanding. Additionally, there remains the problem of resolving segmentation of shapes to support common sense 3-D visual knowledge. That is, we must answer the question of whether everyone segments all shapes in a consistent manner (e.g., can the shape of a house always be segmented in a prism for the roof and a block for the body?).

In this paper, we proposed the existence of a two-level ontology – that is, a knowledge level and a symbol level – for 3-D visual knowledge that supports a WYSIWYS framework. We also presented some preliminary results in an experiment to acquire knowledge-level 3-D visual concepts to prove the feasibility of the framework. We introduced a candidate symbol-level representation, deformable superquadrics, for symbol-level 3-D shape ontologies. In addition, we described the essential characteristics of the framework for WYSIWYS interactions and described an implementation effort taking place at ATR CSRL. This paper at least, makes an initial contribution for the WYSIWYS framework for human-to-human and human-to-machine communication.

7. CONCLUDING REMARKS

Virtual reality technology has been revolutionizing fields that benefit from computer visualization. However, interactions have been limited to input devices, such as the DataGlove™, the SpaceBall, Joysticks and so on. Although in a few cases there has also been incorporation of voice input, the WYSIWYS framework outlines guidelines for more intuitive verbal interactions. The two-level 3-D visual ontology conception introduced in this paper supports the framework so that intentions are better captured from verbal descriptions. In other words, it makes it possible for a word to be worth a million pictures.

NOTES

[1] The DataGlove™ is a trademark of VPL Corp.
[2] In this paper we consider only concrete objects with specified boundaries, that is, those objects that can be quantified easily. For instance, we consider objects such as a "chair", but not objects such as "water" or "sand". The former can be counted while the two later can not. Biederman (1987), differentiates them as count entities versus mass entities.
[3] Viewpoint Datalabs specializes on custom design of 3-D CG data and is based in Orem, Utah.

REFERENCES

Anderson, J. R. (1978). Arguments Concerning Representations for Mental Images. *Psychological Review* 85: 249–277.

Biederman, I. (1987). Recognition-by-Components: A Theory of Human Image Understanding. *Psychological Review* 94(2): 115–147.

Boose, J. H. (1986). *Expertise Transfer for Expert Systems*. Elsevier: Amsterdam.

Boose, J. H. & Bradshaw, J. M. (1987). Expertise Transfer and Complex Problems: Using AQUINAS as a Knowledge Acquisition Workbench for Knowledge-Based Systems. *International Journal of Man-Machine Studies* 26: 3–28.

Bradshaw, J. M., Ford, K. M., Adams-Webber, J. R. & Boose, J. H. (1993). Beyond the Repertory Grid: New Approaches to Constructivist Knowledge Acquisition Tool Development. *International Journal of Intelligent Systems* 8(2): 287–333.

Butterworth, J., Davison, A., Hench, S. & March Olano, T. (1992). 3DM: A Three Dimensional Modeler Using a Head-Mounted Display. ACM 0-89791-471-6/92/0003/0135.

Chandrasekaran, B. & Narayanan, N. H. (1990). Towards a Theory of Commonsense Visual Reasoning. In Nori, K. V. & Veni Madhavan, C. E. (eds.) *Lecture Notes in Computer Science* 472, 388–409. Springer-Verlag: Berlin.

Chandrasekaran, B., Narayanan, N. H. & Iwasaki, Y. (1993). Reasoning with Diagrammatic Representations – A Report on the Spring Symposium –. *AI Magazine*, 49–56.

Dejong, G. F. (1986). Explanation-Based Learning. In Michalski, R. S., Carbonell, J. G. & Mitchell, T. M. (eds.) *Machine Learning: An Artificial Intelligence Approach*. Volume II. Morgan Kaufmann: Los Altos, CA.

Diederich, J., Ruhmann & May M. (1987). KRITON: A Knowledge Acquisition Tool for Expert Systems. *International Journal of Man-Machine Studies* 26(1): 29–40.

Ford, K. M., Cañas, A., Jones, J., Stahl, H., Novak, J. & Adams-Webber, J. (1990). ICONKAT: An Integrated Constructivist Knowledge Acquisition Tool. *Knowledge Acquisition* 3(2): 215–236.

Gard-Jarnadan, C. & Salvendy, G. (1987). A Conceptual Framework for Knowledge Elicitation. *International Journal of Man-Machine Studies* 26(4): 521–531.

Gardiner, M. (1965). The Superellipse: A Curve Between the Ellipse and the Rectangle. *Scientific America* 213: 222–234.

Gruber, T. (1992). A Translation Approach to Portable Ontology Specifications. Stanford University KSL Technical Report KSL 92-72.

Horikoshi, T. & Kasahara, H. (1990). 3-D Shape Indexing Language. In Proceedings of *The 1990 International Conference on Computers and Communications*, 493–499.

Johansson, G. (1950). *Configurations in Event Perception*. Almqvist and Wiksell: Stockholm.

Kelly, G. A. (1955). *The Psychology of Personal Constructs*. Norton: New York.

Kishino, F. Communication with realistic sensations (1990). *3-D Image*, 4, 2 (in Japanese).

Klinker, G., Marques, D., McDermott, J., Marsereau, T. & Stintson, L. (1992). The Active Glossary: Taking Integration Seriously. In Proceedings of *The Seventh Knowledge Acquisition for Knowledge-Based Systems Workshop*, 14-1 to 14-19. Banff, Canada.

Lass, U., Lüer, G., Ulrich, M. & Werner, S. (1993). Access to Analog Representations in Memory for Visually Perceived Forms: The Facilitating Effect of Declarative Knowledge. In Strube, G. & Wender, K. F. (eds) *The Cognitive Psychology of Knowledge*, 75–96. Elsevier Science Publishers B.V.: The Netherlands.

Lenat, D. B. & Guha, R. V. (1990). Cyc: Toward Programs with Common Sense. *Communications of the ACM* 33(8): 30–49.

Mizoguchi, R., Tijerino, Y. A. & Ikeda, M. (1992). Two-Level Mediating Representation for a Task Analysis Interview System. In Proceedings of *AAAI-92 Workshop for Knowledge Representation Aspects of Knowledge Acquisition*, 107–114. San Jose, Ca.

Mochizuki, K. & Kishino, F. (1991). A 3-D Scene Access Interface Considering an Individual Variations of Spatial Indication Concepts. In Proceedings of *The Seventh Symp. on Human Interface*, 51–54. Kyoto, Japan.

Neches, R., Fikes, R., Finin, T., Gruber, T., Patil, T., Snator, T. & Swartout, W. R. (1991). Enabling Technology for Knowledge Sharing. *AI Magazine* 12(3): 36–56.

Newell, A. (1982). The Knowledge Level. *Artificial Intelligence* 18(1): 87–127.

Nishihara, H. K. (1981). Intensity, Visible-Surface, and Volumetric Representations. *Artificial Intelligence* 28: 293–331.

Pentland, A. P. (1986). Perceptual Organization and the Representation of Form. *Artificial Intelligence* 28: 292–331.

Quinlan, R. (1986). Induction of Decision Trees. *Machine Learning* 1(1): 81–106.

Rosch, E. (1973). On the Internal Structure of Perceptual and Semantic Categories. In Moore, T. E. (ed.) *Cognitive Development and the Acquisition of Language*. Academic Press: New York.

Shaw, M. L. G. & Gaines, B. R. (1987). KITTEN: Knowledge Initiation and Transfer Tools for Experts and Novices. *International Journal of Man-Machine Studies* 27(3): 251–280.

Steels, J. (1992). End-User Configuration of Applications. In Proceedings of *The Second Japanese Knowledge Acquisition for Knowledge-Based Systems Workshop*, 47–64. Kobe, Japan.

Stevens, S. (1974). *Patterns in Nature*. Atlantic-Little, Brown Books: Boston, MA.

Takemura, H. & Kishino, F. (1992). Cooperative Work Environment Using Virtual Workspace. In Proceedings of *ACM Conf. on CSCW'92*, 226–232. Toronto, Canada.

Terzopoulos, D. (1991). Dynamic 3D Models with Local and Global Deformations: Deformable Superquadrics. *IEEE Transactions on Pattern Analysis and Machine Intelligence* 13(7): 703–714.

Thompson, D-A. (1942). *On Growth and Form*. University Press: Cambridge, U.K., 2nd ed.

Tijerino, Y. A., Abe, S. Miyasato, T. & Kishino F. (1993). In Proceedings of *The 47th National Conference of the Information Processing Society of Japan*, 385–386. Tottori, Japan. Vol. 2.

Tijerino, Y. A. & Mizoguchi, R. (1993). MULTIS II: Enabling End-Users to Design Problem-Solving Engines via Two-Level Task Ontologies. In Aussenac, N., Boy, G., Gaines, B., Linster, M., Ganascia, J. G. & Kodratoff, Y. (eds.) *Lecture Notes in Artificial Intelligence 723 – Knowledge Acquisition for Knowledge-Based Systems –*, 340–359. Springer-Verlag.

Umamichi, T. & Tijerino, Y. A. (1993). A Report on the Acquireability of Descriptive Concepts for Cars Based on Personal Construct Psychology. ATR Technical Report TR-C-0092 (in Japanese).

Wertheimer, M. (1923). Laws of Organization in Perceptual Forms. In Ellis, W. D. (ed.) *A Source Book of Gestalt Psychology*. Harcourt Brace: New York.

Artificial Intelligence Review **8**: 235–253, 1994.
© *1994 Kluwer Academic Publishers. Printed in the Netherlands.*

Towards an American Sign Language Interface

BRIGITTE DORNER AND ELI HAGEN

*School of Computing Science, Simon Fraser University, Burnaby, B.C., Canada,
V5A 1S6, E-mail: {dorner,hagen}@cs.sfu.ca.*

Abstract. In this paper, we present two major parts of an interface for American Sign Language (ASL) to computer applications currently under work; a hand tracker and an ASL-parser. The hand tracker extracts information about handshape, position and motion from image sequences. As an aid in this process, the signer wears a pair of gloves with colour-coded markers on joints and finger tips. We also present a computational model of American Sign Language. This model is realized in an ASL-parser which consists of a DCG-grammar and a non-lexical component that records non-manual and spatial information over an ASL-discourse.

Key words: American Sign Language, ASL-interface, visual interface, visual hand tracking, manual languages, parsing, natural language understanding

1. INTRODUCTION

In recent years, American Sign Language (ASL) has received increasing recognition as the official language of the deaf in North America. This alone would warrant the effort to design an ASL-interface to allow more natural communication with computers and electronic media for the deaf and hearing-impaired. Due to the differences in modes of communication (i.e., manual vs. spoken) native ASL-speakers find it difficult to learn a spoken language and that their expressive capacity is limited in a spoken language. ASL is also a formalized version of body language, with a ready-made descriptive apparatus for classification and differentiation of non-verbal expressions. Thus, it makes an ideal object of study to get a better understanding of body language, a necessary prerequisite for integration of non-verbal communication and language processing.

Unlike previous efforts (e.g., Davis and Shah 1993; Charayphan and Marble, 1992) we are not aiming at merely 'recognizing ASL-signs' but rather at a system that can understand ASL as a language. Our proposed system is illustrated in Figure 1. It consists of three main modules: a visual interface, a sign interpreter and a parser, where the parser is divided into two sub-modules; one for lexical items, i.e., signs produced manually[1] and processed by an ASL-grammar and one for non-lexical information, i.e., non-manual signals and spatial indexing (see section 2), which is processed by our non-lexical parsing routine. From a sequence of images representing an ASL-sentence, the system produces a semantic representation of this sentence.

A typical sequence of events proceeds as follows. The visual interface extracts

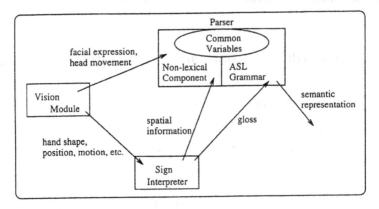

Fig. 1. An ASL front end.

information about hand-shape, position, motion, head motion, facial expressions, etc. from the visual input. It transmits the non-manual information to the non-lexical component of the parser, while information about handshape, motion, position, etc. is transmitted to the sign interpreter. The sign interpreter translates its input into a sequence of English glosses and spatial information, which serves as the input to the parser. The non-lexical parsing routine records its input in variables accessible by the ASL-grammar. When this task is completed, the ASL-grammar proceeds to produce a semantic representation of the ASL-sentence.

Since we do not have an implementation of the sign interpreter yet we will mainly describe our research on the visual interface and the parser here. The reminder of this paper is structured as follows: after a short introduction of ASL (section 2), we present our hand tracker (section 3) and parser (section 4), followed by a short summary and an outlook on further work (section 5).

2. AMERICAN SIGN LANGAUGE

This section provides a crude overview of the linguistic structure of ASL (Friedman 1975; Isenhath 1990; Klima and Bellugi 1979; Lucas 1990; Wilbur 1987).

2.1. *The sign*

A sign is defined by the following four parameters: *hand shape* – ASL has 36 distinct hand shapes, *hand position* – relative to the body, *hand movement* – path specification, local movement (e.g., opening or closing hand, flicking a finger) and speed of delivery, and *palm direction.*

2.2. *Basic sentence structures*

It takes roughly twice as long to produce a single ASL-sign as an average English word, yet the information transmission rate is the same for both languages. Consequently, ASL must use many fewer words than English. The basic technique is to eliminate redundant words and phrases; **articles, interjections, dummy subjects, idle chatter** and **linking verbs** (e.g., any form of 'to be') are always deleted. ASL uses **conjunctions** and **prepositions** only if they supply additional information or represent an idea that cannot be determined by context alone.

Sign order in ASL is still a topic of much discussion; some linguists argue that the underlying sign order is Subject-Verb-Object, while others argue for free sign order (for different analyses see, for example, Fisher 1975; Friedman 1975; Friedman 1976; Isenhath 1990). From a computational point of view, sign order is largely an implementation issue. We quite arbitrarily choose to follow Isenhath's analysis (Isenhath 1990), i.e., Subject-Verb-Object.

2.2.1. Declarative sentences

The simplest sentence patterns in ASL are: subject + verb (+ object), e.g., DOG BITE MAN ('The dog bit the man.') and subject + complement, e.g., CAR FLAT TIRE. ('The car has a flat tire.') However, ASL-speakers tend to structure a sentence such that information that is new (topic), with respect to the current discourse, is presented first, and what is already known follows. In addition to being moved to the beginning of the sentence, the topic is marked: 1. It lasts longer than if the same element were in a non-topicalized position. 2. It is accompanied by a non-manual signal; the head is titled up and back as the eyebrows are raised. In printing, topics are separated from the rest of the sentence with a comma. E.g., SWIM, HE. ('He is swimming.') HAIRCUT, TINA GIVE ERIC ('Tina gave Eric a haircut.').[2]

2.2.2. Non-manual signals; questions and negated sentences

Non-manual signals are signals that are produced simultaneously with the sequence of signs by body parts different from the hands (mainly face and head) and that carry grammatical functions.

In addition to topicalized sentences (see section 2.2.1), questions and negated sentences are marked by non-manual signals. Both questions and negated sentences assume the same basic sign order as declarative sentences and they are distinguished by the presence or absence of certain facial expressions. A wh-question also includes a (manual) interrogative sign as *the last* sign of a sequence. In printing, non-manual signals are written on a line above the sentence; q for question and **n** for negation. E.g., WOMAN $\overline{\text{BUY DOG}}^{\text{n}}$. ('The woman didn't buy the dog.'), $\overline{\text{DIANA HERE?}}^{\text{q}}$ ('Is Diana here?') $\overline{\text{WASH DISH WHO}}^{\text{q}}$ ('Who is going to wash the dishes?').

ASL also has negating signs (e.g., NOT, CAN'T, NEVER, NONE) but the non-manual signal is the fundamental way of negating a sentence and it is always present even if the signer chooses to include a negating sign. The sign NONE is used to express the absence of something/somebody. NONE follows its target sign, e.g., $\overline{\text{CHANGE NONE}}^{\text{p}}$, ME HAVE ('I have no change.').

145

2.3. *Verbs and pronominal references in ASL*

Verbs are divided into two main groups: 1) non-directional, and 2) multi-directional. Non-directional verbs (e.g., EAT, LIKE, LOVE, WANT, WRITE) have all four parameters (hand shape, movement, position, palm direction) completely specified and they are always performed the same way, regardless of discourse. Pronominal references in sentences with non-directional verbs are achieved by *indexing*. If a referent is actually present, the pronominal reference is made by making an indexing motion directly towards the referent. If the referent is not present, the signer must establish a contextual reference; the signer introduces the noun and establishes a reference point (rather area) in space for that person/object. (There are several ways of introducing referents and corresponding reference points into the discourse, for example, by giving the sign for, or spelling the name of the referent at the particular location. Figure 2 illustrates a possible arrangement of spatial reference points). All later reference to that person/object is made by an indexing motion in the direction of this point. Consider the following discourse, DIANA (establ) CALL. INDEX(DIANA) PLAN LATE. ('Diana called. She will be late.') In the first sentence, the signer may establish a reference point for Diana at *LOC3* (see Figure 2), while in the second sentence she would make an indexing motion in the direction of *LOC3*. A signer may have 4–5 active reference points at a time.

Multi-directional verbs (e.g., ASK, GIVE, MEET) have only the hand shape and location parameters completely specified. The verb's movement and/or palm direction parameters are not determined until the verb is put in context. Multi-directional verbs use spatial loci and linear movement to differentiate between the subject and the object of a sentence. As with non-directional verbs, the signer must establish contextual reference points in space. But instead of indexing the point, pronominal reference is achieved by incorporating the reference points into the verb's movement; the starting point represents the subject and the end point represents the object.[3] Consider the following situation where spatial references for Diana and Alicja are established say, to the left and the right of the signer respectively. The sentence 'Diana asked Alicja.' would be signed by starting ASK at the left and moving it over to the right. Some multi-directional verbs (e.g., tease) use palm direction to distinguish between the subject and the object of a sentence; the back of the hand faces the subject, while the palm faces the object.

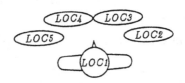

Fig.2. A possible arrangement of spatial references.

2.4. *Surface structure in discourse*

If the subject of a sentence is the same as the subject of the previous sentence, the signer can delete it without any change in meaning. If the first verb in a discourse appears without a subject, first person is assumed. This kind of subject deletion is optional and the signer may choose to use both overt and deleted subjects in the same discourse. One can use this technique with non-directional verbs.

In a situation where first person reference is not relevant, the signer can use her body to refer to a third person, and an index motion towards the body is interpreted as a third person reference, and similarly, for multi-directional verbs, a start/end point near the signers body is interpreted as third person.

A variation of the above can be used with multi-directional verbs; the signer 'takes on' the 'roles' of two other referents. At the beginning of the discourse, the signer gives the nominal signs for the referents and establishes a body orientation (left/right) for each. When giving the sign for the verb, the signer conveys subject reference by turning her head in the direction established for the subject referent.

ASL does not use verb tense or verb inflection to indicate time. A base time frame is established at the beginning of a discourse and – until the signer deliberately changes the time frame – all further references to time are made with respect to this time frame.

ASL includes a mechanism to temporarily switch time frame. If the signer tilts the body slightly forward/backward, neutral space no longer represents the initial time frame but future/past. This remains in effect until the body is returned to an upright position.

3. THE VISION MODULE

The vision module extracts the information necessary for ASL-understanding from the stream of input images and converts this information into a form suitable for further interpretation. The first question that has to be answered on this level is therefore "what kind of information do we need from the images?" The most important factor for sign-language-understanding are the hands and their motion, though facial expressions play an important role as well. So far, our vision module consists only of a hand tracker, but there are several prototype studies that can track and analyze facial expressions sufficiently well to meet the requirements of sign-language-understanding (see e.g., Pentland *et al.* 1993; Ralescu and Iwamoto 1993).

3.1. *Design requirements*

Sign language recognition can be seen as speech recognition with visual input data. As such, it faces most of the problems of traditional speech recognition: segmentation of continuous sign stream into sign descriptors and signs, influence of context and spatial referencing on the execution of a sign, and factors such as emphasis, position in the sentence, personal style and signing dialect, etc. While all these problems are mainly problems pertaining to sign interpretation and need not directly affect the hand tracking system as such, they do imply requirements for its design: we cannot assume that the hand is always in the process of making a regular sign; there will be transitions and irregularities, and the tracker must be able follow these since it will be impossible to say a priori when exactly the next sign begins.

The large variation in sign execution makes it difficult to describe the characteristics of a sign in terms of 2D images. The essence of a sign can only be conveyed in terms of the $3+1D^4$ properties: handshape, position, and orientation, and their change during the execution of the sign. Thus, signing is essentially a 3+1D process, and any sign interpreter will need this kind of 3+1D input (which, of course, implies that the hand tracker will have to provide it somehow).

The analysis of the visual input data itself, i.e., the computer vision aspect of the tracker poses another set of problems and requirements. The human hand is difficult to track: it does not have a simple geometrical shape, it can change its shape quickly and drastically, and it can move very fast. Hand motion, and human motion in general, is also complicated, in the sense that it is muscle controlled and thus neither describable by a simple physical model nor predictable over more than a few frames.

Another problem one has to overcome when tracking the shape of a human hand is partial or complete occlusion of hand and fingers, often for prolonged periods. From the standpoint of sign language interpretation this is not a serious issue. After all, signs – as well as other gestures – are executed to communicate with other humans who cannot see more of the occluded body parts than the camera. The exact shape of occluded fingers therefore will never be crucial for the correct interpretation of a sign. However, most visual tracking systems – just as our hand tracker – use motion continuity over a series of frames to constrain their search space and therefore rely on being 'close' to the actual handshape at any time. Hence, an 'information gap' due to occlusion could create serious problems.

Instead of aiming for a perfect system, we though it more realistic to go for general robustness and good ability to recover from failures, and to achieve *graceful degradation* when the system has to deal with difficult, fast shape changes; massive, prolonged occlusion; and/or poor image quality: low resolution of the hand itself as part of an upper body image, motion blur, etc.

3.2. *The hand model and other design choices*

There are several prototype implementations of hand trackers and/or sign language understanding systems that are based on 2D interpretation of images and typically use 2D trajectory information and some kind of silhouette comparison (Tamura and Kawasaki 1998, Charayphan and Marble 1992, Davis and Shah 1993, Darell and Pentland 1993). These 2D approaches are fast and relatively straightforward, but it has yet to be shown whether they can be made to work for a realistic number of signs and natural, continuous signing.

3.2.1. *A 3+1D approach to hand tracking*

Our hand tracking system uses a simple skeleton-like 3D model of the hand to perform 3D interpretation of the image data. Even though it was designed with an application to sign language in mind, it is a general-purpose hand tracker. Its output is a description of hand position, palm orientation, and 3D handshape in terms of joint angles, similar to the information provided by a data glove. The tracker does not require knowledge about the sign that is currently performed and thus avoids dragging along segmentation problems of sign interpretation onto the vision level.

To fit our model to the image data we follow a 3-step iterative scheme to recover the pose of the hand: the model is projected into 2D; the projection is compared to the image data; based of this comparison the model is then adjusted towards a pose that better matches the image data, and the process is repeated until the match is close enough.

In order to do direct matching to hand contours one either has to build a very realistic and detailed model of the hand or do some serious preprocessing of the image data. Unfortunately, a realistic model is difficult to build and might need major adaptations for new users. Keeping the model simple also means one can do fast and easy projection, a feature that is very important considering the large amount of possible handshapes. Even with the knowledge of the previous handshape to constrain the range of possible handshapes for a new image it might still take many adaptation steps before a good correspondence with the image is reached.

For these reasons our hand model is kept to the bare essentials needed to represent the relevant characteristics of the hand. Its skeleton-like structure only contains joints – their location and range of possible motion – and a mathematical representation of joint-angle interdependencies that are determined by the hand's physiology.[5] There is no representation of surface skin, nor any volumetric representation of the hand's body. The only additional ingredient is the '+1D', the time component. The model 'remembers' its motion during the previous image frames, and this motion information is used to predict the handshape for the next frame. In the fitting process, preference is given to handshapes that are close to this prediction. This effectively imposes a motion-continuity constraint.

The features used for matching are the joint positions and finger tips. They are made more salient in the image by attaching colour-coded markers to them – or, more precisely, making the user wear painted cotton gloves.[6,7] Since the fingers and finger joints may appear from any viewpoint during signing it would be difficult to place small square or circle-shaped markers in a way that they always indicate the center of the joint they are attached to. To avoid this problem we chose ring-shaped markers wherever possible.

As the straight-forward encoding of one colour per marker would need too many distinct colours we use a scheme in which a marker is uniquely described by a combination of two colours: a 'joint' colour and a 'finger' colour. Each marker consists of three stacked rings: the middle ring, the center of which is taken as the position of the joint, indicates the finger. On each side of this central ring is another ring indicating the joint type or a finger tip. Thus, our encoding schemes requires 10 distinct colours, 5 for the fingers, four for the three joints and the finger tips, and one for the wrist marker (see Figure 3 and Figures 5 and 6).

Figure 4 shows an overview of the hand tracking module. First, the 2D marker locations are extracted form the image (box A). This extraction process is not always reliable, however. Due to background noise, partial occlusion, irregular-

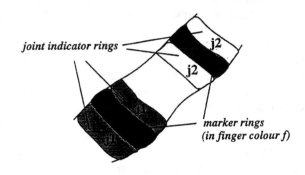

Fig. 3. Marker encoding scheme.

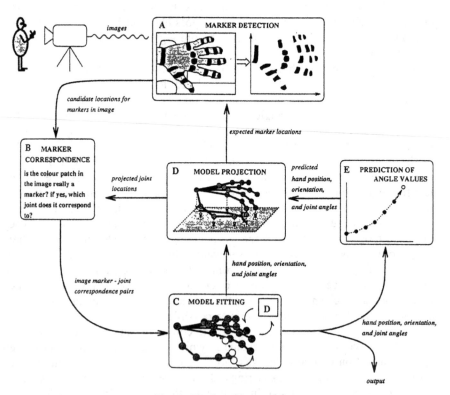

Fig. 4. Hand tracking module.

ities in glove painting, folds in the gloves' fabric etc., the marker detection module sometimes finds more than one patch in the image that answers the description of a particular marker. Thus, we need to detect and eliminate false markers (box B) before the model can be fitted to the marker locations.

The first criterion for the detection of false markers is the distance between the marker as it is found in the image and its expected location as predicted from the current shape of the hand model and recent motion. As a physical object the hand has to obey Newton's law of inertia. Thus, the region in which a marker may show up in the image is limited around its predicted position, and markers that are too far away can be rejected.

If there is more than one candidate marker for a particular joint, the correct one will usually be the one nearer to the predicted joint location. Sometimes this criterion does not give a clear decision, though. In these difficult cases we make use of the knowledge about the hand – its possible shapes and movement – embedded in the hand model, by doing a tentative fit for each doubtful marker assignment and selecting the candidate to which the model can best adapt. Because of the motion-continuity constraint incorporated in the hand model, tentative fitting also subsumes the 'nearest-to-prediction' criterion.

Once we have identified the correct markers, we can start to recover the pose of the hand (box C). The actual fitting of the model to the image is done by nonlinear, continuous optimization, minimizing the Euclidean distance between the projections of the joints in the hand model and the markers found in the image. We use a Newton-style algorithm, but we expect qualitatively similar results from other optimization methods (e.g., a neural-net approach; for details, see Dorner 1994). Since the predicted handshape provides a good initial point for the optimization process (i.e., an initial point that is near to the final solution) convergence is usually fast (30–40 iterations per frame), and there is little danger that the routine converges to a false minimum.

Once the model has been adapted to fit the image data we need to update the prediction for the next frame (box E). From what has been said about hand motion this can only be a rather imprecise short-term prediction. We are using an estimate of whole-hand motion and joint-rotation, averaged over the last two frames, to extrapolate hand position and joint angles and thus obtain the expected hand position and handshape for the next frame. The hand model in this predicted pose in then projected back onto the image plane to provide estimates for marker locations that can be compared to the markers detected in the next frame, completing the cycle.

The tracker delivers as its output the 3D location of the wrist, the orientation of the palm, and 20 joint angles. Currently it does not work in real time, but with some special equipment to allow real time detection of colour markers this goal might not be out of reach.

3.3. *Tracking examples*

Figures 5 and 6 show the hand tracker in action, the original image frame compared to a 3D wireframe representation of the hand model (grey joints or

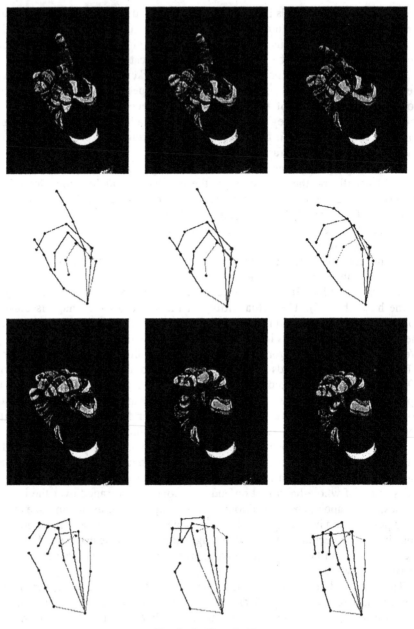

Fig. 5. Spelling 'D–E'.

tips in the model indicate that the corresponding marker could not be found in the image).[8] Figure 5 shows an excerpt of a fingerspelling sequence, the transition from 'D' to 'E'. As an example of ASL-signing, Figure 6 shows an excerpt of a sign roughly corresponding to 'time' or 'what's the time?' Since we did

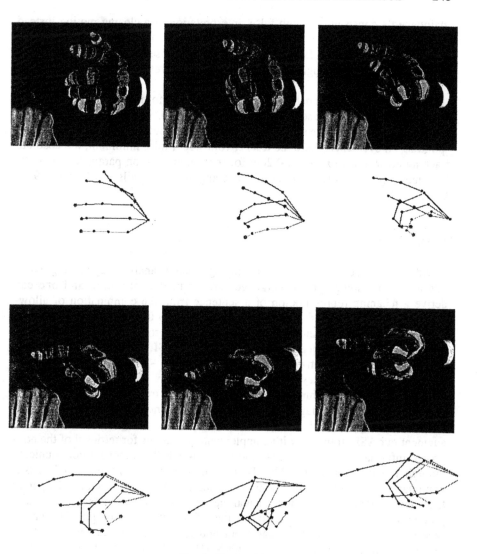

Fig. 6. Signing 'time'.

not have real time capturing equipment available the image sequences shown here consist of stills taken with a video board.

The tracker was tested on more than 20 such sequences, ranging in length from 5 to 10 frames. In general, tracking proved to be stable and robust with regard to occlusion, inexact marker locations, and errors in marker detection. The only difficult cases for the tracker were gestures where the palm or back of the hand is directly facing the camera, since bending of fingers in this situation results in a very similar pattern of marker motion as pointing the extended finger(s) towards or away from the camera. In such a situation the tracker in some cases maintained a consistent, though false, interpretation of a closing motion instead of a pointing motion or vice versa. As soon as the handshape becomes unambiguous again the tracker falls back into the correct pose. Luckily such dangerous situations are easily recognized, and the sign interpreter can be warned of the pending danger.

To obtain quantitative data about the tracker's performance, we also tested it on model-generated input sequences where we had a 3D description of the original handshape available. Except for some of the sequences containing ambiguous 'pointing'-movements where the tracker followed a false minimum, the absolute tracking error never exceeded 0.2cm for recovered location parameters and 10° for recovered palm orientation and joint angles (for details see Dorner 1993; Dorner 1994).

4. AN ASL-PARSER

A wide range of sentences in spoken languages can be analyzed by parsing words one at a time, since spoken languages are sequential of nature and one can derive a meaning representation of a sentence from the combination of allowable sentence patterns (as defined by a grammar) and individual lexical features (number, person, case, etc). However, sequential processing of lexical items (signs) in an ASL-sentence is not sufficient since ASL uses non-manual signals and spatial information in parallel with lexical items – instead of inflection and sign order – to convey several grammatical functions.

We propose an algorithm that expands the scope of traditional natural language parsers to manual languages by adding a component that records spatial and non-manual signals. This component is external to the grammar. Hence we augment our ASL-grammar with complementary routines for retrieval of the non-lexical information. The grammar and the non-lexical component communicate through a set of common variables. Both the non-lexical component and the ASL-grammar were developed in a logic programming framework. Our ASL-parser takes lexical items (signs), non-manual and spatial information as its input, and produces a semantic representation of the ASL-sentence as output. Out prototype is part of a natural language front end to a deductive database, and the semantic representation we use is called LM (Hagen 1993; Hagen and Dahl 1994).

In order to put the remainder of this section into context, we provide a top level view of the parser (see also Figure 1). A startup routine initializes the variables in the interface between the grammar and the non-lexical parsing routine. After having executed the initialization routine, the parser enters a loop in which it successively retrieves and processes the input to the non-lexical parsing routine and the ASL-grammar. It is important to ensure that the non-lexical parsing routine is completely finished before the ASL-grammar starts, since the grammar uses the non-lexical information to build a semantic representation of the ASL-query. The semantic representation is finally passed to a query evaluation module and the interface is ready to process the next query.

4.1. *The interface between the grammar and non-lexical component*

The lexical and the non-lexical parsing routines communicate through a set of common variables:

> *Topic, Question, Negation, Loc1, Loc2, Loc3, Loc4, Loc5, Left, Right, First-Referent, Second-Referent, Third-Referent, Fourth-Referent, First-location, Time-Frame, Old-Time-Frame, Last-Subject*

Topic, Question and Negation are boolean variables that record of non-manual information in a sentence. *Loc1, Loc2, Loc3, Loc4,* and *Loc5* record the referents of the spatial reference points as established by the signer (i.e., *LOC2–LOC4* in Figure 2). If, for example, the signer in Figure 2 establishes a spatial reference point for, say Pepe, at location LOC2 and, say David, at location LOC4, the variables *Loc2* and *Loc4* would be assigned the values Pepe and David respectively. One of these variables is reserved for the signer, say *Loc1*, and must be initialized to the signer at the beginning of a conversation. *left* and *Right* store the referents of role play, e.g., if the signer establishes a reference for Pepe to her left and a reference for David to her right, the variables *Left* and *Right* are assigned the values Pepe and David respectively.

    First-Referent, Second-Referent, Third-Referent, and *Fourth-Referent* record the referents of spatial references made by the signer during a conversation (The term 'spatial reference' includes indexing, role play, and incorporation of spatial locations into verb movement.), and implicitly keep track of the order in which the references are made. E.g., if *Loc2, Loc4, Left,* and *Right* are assigned referents as in the above examples, and the signer indexes LOC2 first and LOC4 second or if the first reference is made by turning the head left and the second by turning the head right, then *First-Referent* would have the value Pepe and *Second-Referent* would have the value David. The variables *Loc1–Loc5, Left, Right* are valid over a whole discourse, while the *First-Reference–Fourth-Reference* change with every new sentence.

    First-location records the first *location* that the signer references, and this variable is used by the ASL-grammar in situations where the signer *establishes* new referents. *Time-Frame* records the current time frame, e.g., if the signer is telling a story that happened yesterday, the value of *Time-Frame* is 'yesterday'. What 'yesterday' really means is up to the user to decide (could be the date, for example). *Old-Time-Frame* records the time frame that is effective before the signer temporarily switches to a new time frame by shifting her body backward or forward. *Last-Subject* records the last articulated subject reference.

4.2. *The non-lexical parsing routine*

The interpretation of the non-lexical input through the non-lexical parsing routine is straight forward. For example, if the sentence includes a non-manual signal for questioning, the value PRESENT is assigned to the variable *Question*; if the first spatial reference was LOC2, the current value of *Loc2* is assigned to *First-Referent*; if the signer temporarily changes the time frame by leaning forward, the current time frame is stored in *Old-Time-Frame* and the value of

Time-Frame is modified to "after"-current time frame; if the signer establishes a new referent in position LOC4, the new referent is assigned to *Loc4*, etc. See (Hagen 1993) for a more complete description.

4.3. *ASL-grammar*

We describe how our prototype grammar interacts with the non-lexical component through the interface variables described in the previous sections.

4.3.1. *Basic sentences*

We consider as basic sentences those that do not include non-manual signals, role play or indexing, i.e., ASL-sentences as they appear in isolation outside a discourse. Since there is no non-lexical information present, a meaning representation of these sentences is obtained in the same way as for spoken languages; simple parsing of lexical items by a grammar. We illustrate the grammar:

```
sent(S) —> np(Subj),
               non__dir__vp(Subj, S).
sent(S) —> multi__dir__vp(Subj, Vp).
non__dir__vp(Subj, Vp) —> intrans__non__dir__verb(Subj, Vp).
non__dir__vp(Subj, Vp) —> trans__non__dir__verb(Subj, Obj, Vp),
                  np(Obj).
multi__dir__vp(Vp) —> ditrans__multi__dir__vp(Dobj, Vp),
                  np(Dobj).
ditrans__multi__dir__vp(Dobj, Vp) —>
                      np(Subj),
                      ditrans__multi__dir__verb(Subj, Iobj, Dobj, Vp)
                      np(Iobj).
np(NP) —> noun(Noun).
```

```
% nouns
noun(diana) —> [diana].
noun(sergio) —> [sergio].
noun(book) —> [book].
% verbs
intrans__non__dir__verb(Subj, swim(Subj)) —> [swim].
trans__non__dir__verb(Subj, Obj, love(Subj, Obj)) —> [love].
ditrans__multi__dir__verb(Subj, Iobj, Dobj, give(Subj, Iobj, Dobj)) —> [give].
```

Below we show the input to the parser and the resulting semantic representation for some sample sentences.

Sentence	Grammar input	Grammar output
Sergio loves diana	[sergio, love, diana]	love(sergio, diana)
Sergio is swimming	[sergio, swim]	swim(sergio)

4.3.2. *Establishment of spatial references and roles*

There are two types of references: *spatial references*, which are referenced through indexing, and *roles*, which are referenced by turning the head left or right. We assume that establishment of both spatial references and roles are processed one by one.

When the signer establishes a new reference, she must supply both a spatial location and a referent. The referent is naturally lexical, while the location is spatial, so the two pieces of information are separated in the visual interface and must 'meet up' again in the parser: The referent must be a single noun phrase, and since no other ASL-"sentence" consists of a single noun phrase it is easy for the grammar to recognize when the signer establishes a new referent. The non-lexical routine stores the location indexed by the signer in the interface variable *First-location*. Once the grammar has parsed the referent, it retrieves the spatial location from *First-location* and by combining the two pieces of information it assigns the referent to one of the interface variables *Loc2–Loc5, Left* or *Right*. For example, if the referent noun phrase is Pepe and the value of First-Location is LOC2, the interface variable *Loc2* is assigned the referent Pepe. We illustrate:

$$sent(\_) \longrightarrow establish\text{-}reference(\_).$$
$$establish\text{-}reference(\_) \longrightarrow np(Np)$$
$$\{get\text{-}first\text{-}location(Location)\},$$
$$\{establish\text{-}reference(Np, Location)\}.$$

get-first-location() retrieves the value stored in *First-location* and *establish-reference()* assigns *NP* to *Location*. The following example shows the state of the interface before and after the signer establishes a spatial reference for Diana at location LOC2. Suppose the old referent at location LOC2 was Alicja.[9]

Input: 1. Non-lexical: Assume Location = *LOC2* after *get-first-location (Location)* has been executed.
2. Grammar: [**diana**]

Interface before	Interface after	Grammar output
Loc2 = alicja	Loc2 = diana	
First-location = LOC2	First-location = LOC2	

(There is no output since establishing a new reference point is not a real sentence, and only updates the interface.)

4.3.3. *Indexing and role play*

When a signer uses indexing or role play, the grammar must access the previously established spatial information in order to build a semantic representation of the sentence. Recall from Section 4.2 that the references have already been interpreted, so the grammar obtains the necessary referents by simply reading off the value of the interface variables *First-ref, Second-ref, Third-ref,* or *Fourth-ref.* Consider the following grammar fragment:

$$ditrans\_multi\_dir\_vp(Dobj, Vp) \longrightarrow$$
$$\{get\text{-}first\text{-}ref(Subj)\},$$
$$ditrans\_multi\_dir\_verb(Subj, Iobj, Dobj, Vp),$$
$$\{get\text{-}second\text{-}ref(Iobj)\}.$$
$$non\_dir\_vp \longrightarrow \{get\text{-}first\text{-}ref(Subj)\},$$
$$trans\_non\_dir\_verb(Subj, Obj, Vp)$$
$$\{get\text{-}second\text{-}ref(Obj)\}.$$

get-first-ref() and *get-second-ref()* retrieve the values stored in *First-Referent* and *Second-Referent* respectively. The following example shows how the grammar retrieves the proper referents for the sentence $_{LOC2}GIVE_{LOC3}$ BOOK ("Sergio gave Diana a book."), where spatial reference points for Sergio and Diana have previously been established in locations LOC2 and LOC3.

Input: 1. Non-lexical: Assume Subj = Sergio and Iobj = Diana after the routines *get-first-ref(Subj)* and *get-second-ref(Iobj)* have been executed.

2. Grammar: [**give, book**]

Interface	Grammar output
Loc2 = sergio	give(sergio, diana, book)
Loc3 = diana	
First-referent = sergio	
Second-referent = diana	

4.3.4. *Question, negation, and topicalization*

The grammar accesses the non-manual information stored in the interface variables *Question, Topic* and*Negation* through the routines *non-manual-topic(), non-manual-question()* and *non-manual-negated().* Yes-no questions and negated sentences use the same sentence patterns as the declarative sentences so only two new clauses, which check for the presence of the appropriate non-manual signal, are needed to parse these sentences. We illustrate:

```
% Yes-no questions
sentence(S) --> {non-manual-question(present)},
                sent(S).
% Negated sentences
sentence(S) --> {non-manual-negation(present)},
                sent(S).
```

The goals *non-manual-question()* and *non-manual-negation()* succeed if the value of *Question* and *Negates* is PRESENT.

An interrogative question is posed by deleting some part of speech and by including an interrogative sign at the end of a sentence. Topicalization affects the order in which signs are produced and since both objects and verb phrases can be topicalized the complexity of the grammar will increase considerably. We don't include any of these grammar rules since they are only concerned with sign order.

4.3.5. Subject deletion

In order to obtain a subject referent when the signer uses this technique, the grammar must record every articulated subject that it encounters. An example:

di_trans__multi_dir__vp(Dobj, Vp) —>
        {get-first-ref(Subj)},
        di_trans__multi_dir__verb(Subj, Iobj, Dobj, Vp),
        {get-second-ref(Iobj)},
        {store-last-subject}.

store-last-subject() records every articulated subject in *last-subject*.

Later, when the grammar parses a subjectless sentence, it reads off the value of *Last-subject* and uses it as the subject referent. An example:

sent(S) —> missing __subject(Vp).
missing_subject__vp(Vp) —> trans__non__dir__verb(Subj, Obj, Vp),
        {get-first-ref(Obj)}
        {get-last-subject(Subj)}.

get-last-subject() retrieves the value stored in *Last-Subject*. For example, if the last subject mentioned was Diana. Then the missing__ subject__vp(Vp) clause would produce **swim(diana)** from the grammar input SWIM(= 'Diana is swimming').

For a more complete grammar that for instance accounts for how ASL deals with time, see (Hagen 1993).

5. CONCLUSION

We have presented a general-purpose hand tracker and a computational model of ASL, two essential steps towards the building of an ASL-interface to computer applications. What remains to be done is to gather the necessary non-manual information from the images and to implement a sign interpreter to link the two presented modules.

As suggested in section 3, there are vision systems available that can provide adequate face tracking and interpretation of facial expressions (Pentland *et al.* 1993; Ralescu and Iwamoto 1993). The same cannot necessarily be said for the sign interpreter, but studies like the one by Fels (Fels 1990) offer interesting insights into the problems one has to solve. We have to build a module that takes a continuous stream of handshape-descriptors (as computed by our hand tracker), segments this stream into ASL-signs, and identifies these signs. These two functions need not be performed in strictly sequential order; the beginning of a sign might be identifiable only a posteriori after the interpretation process is already halfway through the sign.

One possible approach would be to represent signs in terms of raw shape-descriptor sequences and try to match the current sequence (the matching process would have to contain some form of time-warping). The difficulty with this method is the size of the sign-dictionary we will eventually have to handle. Hence, it might be useful to use a two-layer classification scheme: in the first layer, the three basic parameters handshape, palm orientation, and hand position are classified by means of the 36 ASL-handshapes and a crude subdivision of signer-space. This could be done relatively fast, independent of the size of the actual ASL-vocabulary by using, e.g. Hidden Markov Models. The second layer could then use these three components to determine the fourth – hand movement – and to identify the sign by these four basic sign-components, checking out different hypotheses over time.

ACKNOWLEDGMENTS

B. Dorner thanks David Lowe for encouragement and helpful discussions. Both authors thank Veronica Dahl, Brian Funt, Jörg Überla, and Allan Bennet-Brown for helpful comments on earlier drafts of this paper. Last but not least, our thanks go to the editor, Paul Mc Kevitt, and the anonymous referee who patiently corrected errors in the manuscript and suggested some important improvements. This research was supported by NSERC grant no. #31-611024, the Centre for Systems Science, and Simon Fraser University.

NOTES

[1] In this article, *manually* means 'produced by the hands' and a *non-manual signal* is a grammatical signal not produced by the hands.

[2] We will not discuss the ASL tense system in detail here. Please see section 2.4 and/or one of the ASL source texts for details.

[3] Some verbs reverse the direction, e.g., TAKE.

[4] 3D space + time component.

[5] For example, the last two segments of a finger do not move independently.

[6] Markers are a convenient way to identify key points of motion. Joint markers in the form of simple reflectors are commonly used in studies of human whole-body-motion. Joints, as fixed points of angular limb motion, could also be identified by analyzing 2D image motion, however.

[7] As an interesting aside the reader may note in this context that the human face shows a natural colour coding scheme that emphasizes the most relevant features: red for the lips, black for the eyebrows and white eyeballs that allow easy tracking of eye motion and gaze direction.

[8] The tracker does not need a specific initial handshape or position; it can start from any open handshape.

[9] We only show the relevant variables.

REFERENCES

Charayphan, C. & Marble A. E. (1992). Image Processing System for Interpreting Motion in ASL. *Journal of Biomedical Engineering* **14**(5): 419–425.

Darell, T. & Pentland, A. P. (1993). Space-time Gestures. In *'Looking at People: Recognition and Interpretation of Human Action', Workshop WS26 at the International Joint Conference on Artificial Intelligence (IJCAI-93)*, Chambery: France.

Davis, J. & Shah, M. (1993). *Gesture Recognition*. Technical Report CS-TR-93-11, University of Central Florida.

Dorner, B. (1993). Hand Shape Identification and Tracking for Sign Language Interpretation. In *'Looking at People: Recognition and Interpretation of Human Action', Workshop WS26 at the International Joint Conference on Artificial Intelligence (IJCAI-93)*, Chambery: France.

Dorner, B. (1994). *Chasing the Colour Glove: Visual Hand Tracking*. Master's Thesis, School of Computing Science, Simon Fraser University, Burnaby, Canada.

Fels, S. S. (1990). *Building Adaptive Interfaces with Neural Networks: The Glove-talk Pilot Study*. Technical Report CRG-TR-90-1, University of Toronto, Toronto, Canada.

Fisher, S. (1975). Influences on Word Order Change in American Sign Language. In Li, C. N. (ed.) *Word Order and Word Order Change*, 1–25. University of Texas Press.

Friedman, L. A. (1975). Space, Time, and Person Reference in American Sign Language. *Language* **51**(4): 940–961.

Friedman, L. A. (1976). The Manifestation of Subject, Object, and Topic in the American Sign Language. In Li, C. N. (ed.) *Subject and Topic*, 125–148. Academic Press.

Hagen, E. & Dahl, V. (1994). On Multiple-Valued Deductive Databases. In Proceedings of *The 10th Canadian Conference on Artificial Intelligence (AI94)*, 31–38.

Hagen, E. (1993). *A Flexible American Sign Language Interface to Deductive Databases*. Master's thesis, School of Computer Science, Simon Fraser University, Burnaby, Canada.

Isenhath, J. O. (1990). *The Linguistics of American Sign Language*. McFarland & Company, Inc., Publishers: Jefferson, N.C.

Klima, E. S. & Bellugi, U. (1979). *The Signs of Language*. Harvard University Press: Cambridge, Mass.

Lucas, C. (ed.) (1990). *Sign Language Research: Theoretical Issues*. Gallaudet Press: Washington, D.C.

Pentland, A., Starner, T., Etcoff, N., Masiou, A., Oliyide, O. & Turk, M. (1993). Experiments with eigenfaces. In *'Looking at People: Recognition and Interpretation of Human Action', Workshop WS26 at the International Joint Conference on Artificial Intelligence (IJCAI-93)*, Chambery: France.

Ralescu, A. & Iwamoto, H. (1993). Reading Faces: A Fuzzy Logic Approach to Representation, Recognition and Description of Facial Expressions. In *'Looking at People: Recognition and Interpretation of Human Action', Workshop WS26 at the International Joint Conference on Artificial Intelligence (IJCAI-93)*, Chambery: France.

Tamura, S. & Kawasaki, S. (1988). Recognition of Sign Language Motion Images. *Pattern Recognition* **21**(4): 343–353.

Wilbur, R. B. (1987). *American Sign Language: Linguistic and Applied dimensions*. College Hill Press, A division of Little, Brown and company (Inc.): Boston, second edition.

Artificial Intelligence Review **8**: 255–276, 1994.
© 1994 *Kluwer Academic Publishers. Printed in the Netherlands.*

Integrating Natural Language Understanding with Document Structure Analysis

SUZANNE LIEBOWITZ TAYLOR, DEBORAH A. DAHL,
MARK LIPSHUTZ, CARL WEIR, LEWIS M. NORTON,
ROSLYN WEIDNER NILSON and MARCIA C. LINEBARGER

Unisys Corporation, 70 E. Swedesford Road, Paoli, Pennsylvania 19301,
E-mail address: {suzanne,dahl,mark,weir,norton,roslyn,marcia}@vfl.paramax.com

Abstract. Document understanding, the interpretation of a document from its image form, is a technology area which benefits greatly from the integration of natural language processing with image processing. We have developed a prototype of an Intelligent Document Understanding System (IDUS) which employs several technologies: image processing, optical character recognition, document structure analysis and text understanding in a cooperative fashion. This paper discusses those areas of research during development of IDUS where we have found the most benefit from the integration of natural language processing and image processing: document structure analysis, optical character recognition (OCR) correction, and text analysis. We also discuss two applications which are supported by IDUS: text retrieval and automatic generation of hypertext links

Key words: document analysis, natural language processing, image processing, vision, optical character recognition.

1. INTRODUCTION

Document understanding is a technology area which benefits greatly from the integration of natural language processing with image processing. Given a document in image form, the ultimate goal of a document understanding system is to reverse-engineer the authoring process, with the final output being a conceptual representation of the document. Natural language understanding serves two functions in document interpretation. First it is important if the text of the document must be interpreted and processed in some way, for example, to fill a database. In addition, natural language understanding technology can be used to improve the accuracy of optical character recognition (OCR) output, whether the ultimate goal is to interpret the text, to find textual clues, or simply to obtain accurate character recognition. Many OCR errors result in output which is meaningless, either because the output words are not legitimate words of the language, or because the output sentences do not make sense. If facts about the linguistic context could be used during OCR error correction, the error rate could be further reduced, thereby greatly improving the results.

Since the input to the document understanding system is an image of the document, image processing is essential to convert the image from bits to a meaningful representation. Typical document image processing includes image skew correction, noise removal, segmentation, and OCR. A key component of document understanding is document structure analysis: the determination of the *physical, logical, functional* and *topical* organization of a document. Document image processing is required for the physical decomposition of the document. However, image processing is not sufficient enough to determine the logical, functional and topical organization of the document. Although, features derived from the document image are used as input to determine the logical and functional organization of the document, we feel it is necessary to incorporate textual information (i.e., information obtained from the ASCII content) for a comprehensive document representation.

The goal of a document understanding system is to develop this robust representation of the document which can support a variety of applications such as routing, retrieval, reuse and reconstitution. All these applications require some level of natural language understanding of the document's textual components. However, in all cases, it is also critical to discover the document layout structure for two reasons: (1) document layout attributes such as position of text and font specifications are key clues into the relative importance of textual content on a page and (2) understanding the layout puts the text in the correct reading order for OCR conversion to ASCII/machine-readable text. If the text is not in an appropriate reading order, the natural language system will fail to interpret the text. The key to a successful document understanding system is the appropriate integration of document structure analysis and natural language understanding.

Our document understanding technology is implemented in a system called IDUS (Intelligent Document Understanding System), which creates the data for a text retrieval (Taylor *et al.* 1993) and a hypertext application (Lipshutz and Taylor 1994a). This system employs several technologies – Image Understanding, Optical Character Recognition (OCR), Document Structural Analysis and Text Understanding – in a knowledge-based cooperative fashion (Taylor *et al.* 1992). The current implementation is on a SPARCstation™ II with the UNIX™ operating system using the 'C' and Prolog programming languages. OCR is performed with the Xerox Imaging Systems ScanWorX™ Application Programmer's Interface toolkit. All features are accessible via an X-Windows™/Motif™ user interface.

After scanning the document page(s), IDUS works page-by-page, performing image-based segmentation to initially locate the primitive regions of text and nontext which are manipulated during the logical and functional analysis of the document. Each text unit's content is internally homogeneous in physical attributes such as font size and spacing style.

The ASCII text associated with each block is found through OCR and a set of features based both on text attributes (e.g., number of text lines, font size and type) and geometric attributes (e.g., location on page, size of block) is used to refine the segmentation and organize the blocks into proper logical groupings, i.e., "articles". The ASCII text for each "article" is assembled in a proper reading order. During this process the column structure of the document is determined, and noise and nontext blocks are eliminated. Each "article" text is saved as part of the document corpus.

A text processing component consists of a part-of-speech tagger, a parser and a case-frame generator. The goal of the text processing component is to extract the key ideas from each text block and then represent them by case frames. A text retrieval interface allows the user to pose a query in natural language. Each word in the query is assigned a part-of-speech tag, and then the tagged query is matched against the tagged corpus. The results are displayed as a menu of retrievable articles from which the user may select to peruse the text and/or image.

The emphasis on the remainder of this paper will be to detail the areas of research during IDUS development where we have found the most benefit from the integration of image processing with natural language/text processing: Document structure analysis (Section 2), OCR correction (Section 3), Text analysis (Section 4), and two applications: generation of information for retrieval (Section 5.1) and automatic generation of hypertext links for presentation (Section 5.2).

2. DOCUMENT STRUCTURE ANALYSIS

As stated in the introduction, document structure analysis includes the determination of the *physical, logical, functional* and *topical* organization of a document. This involves finding the primitive components on each page of the document and connecting them both within and among the pages. Much of the existing body of work in document structure analysis has emphasized image-based approaches (operating on a single page of a document) which have limitations, particularly in the logical and functional areas. We first describe the various aspects of structure analysis and then in the following subsections, describe our implementation of the three we have been emphasizing (physical, logical and functional analysis).

Physical analysis of the document determines the primitive segments that make up each page and their attributes. Primitives include both text and non-text segments (photographs, graphics, rule lines, etc.). Attributes may include chromatic features (color or gray scale) and typesetting features (margins, point size and face style). Physical analysis is achieved through geometric page segmentation of the the bit map (or image) of each page of the document and optical character recognition (also an image-based process).

Logical analysis groups the primitive regions into units (both within and among pages) which are part of the same functional unit (Tsujimoto and Asada 1990) and determines the reading order of the text units through manipulation of both image-based features and text-based features. Logical analysis is first done on a page level and then on a document level.

Functional analysis labels each unit (as determined through logical analysis) by role or function within the document. For example, a popular journal article will have a title, author reference, body text and photos. Functional analysis combines image-based and text-based features.

Topical analysis includes referential links among components, such as from the body of a text to a photograph it mentions. Examples of references include both explicit references (e.g., "see Figure 1.5") and implicit references (e.g., "following the definition described in the introduction"). The topical organization could also accommodate text summary templates or other interpretive notes. Linguistic processing should play a key role in determining the topical organization.

The current implementation of the document layout analysis module of IDUS consists of physical analysis, logical analysis, and a rudimentary functional component. We are currently developing a more sophisticated functional analysis. These three structure organizing principles are described below.

2.1. *Physical analysis*

Physical organization of the document is predicated on geometric page segementation. Geometric page segmentation starts with a binary image of a document page and partitions it into fundamental units of text or non-text. A desirable segmentation will form text units by merging adjacent portions of text with similar physical attributes, such as font size and spacing, within the framework of the physical layout of the document. The final output of the geometric analysis is a list of polygonal blocks, their locations on the page, and the locations of horizontal rule lines on the page.

Our segmentation technique combines a top-down analysis (X-Y segmentation) with a bottom-up analysis (run-length smoothing with connected component analysis) of the image. X-Y tree segmentation produces a coarse segmentation of the image by slicing through the white space of the image (Lam and Niyogi 1988). Segmentation is obtained by successively detecting white gaps between text blocks using either a vertical or horizontal projection of the data, as appropriate. Each node in the tree corresponds to a segmented block. The successors of each node correspond to a set of rectangles obtained by horizontal or vertical partitioning of the parent rectangle. The number of levels that the X-Y tree contains is controlled by a fixed set of parameter values which corresponds to a text column or portion of a text column. The final layer of the X-Y tree output, which contains the smallest rectangles segmented, is used as input to the run-length smoothing/connected components analysis along with the image, specifically to adaptively determine the parameters needed for the run-length smoothing. The output of X-Y partitioning is represented as a set of nested rectangular blocks in tree form.

This list of rectangular regions and the image are inputs to the run-length smoothing algorithm (RLSA) (Wong *et al.* 1982). Non-background (ink) pixels are merged together into words, paragraphs, columns, and continuous picture elements. This blurring process is implemented in four stages: a vertical smoothing, a horizontal smoothing, a logical AND of the two smoothing results, and a final smoothing in the horizontal direction (Hinds *et al.* 1990). Horizontal smoothing connects adjacent black pixels along a scan line. If the number of consecutive white (non-ink) pixels between the two black (ink) pixels is less than a threshold value, all the white pixels between the two black pixels are changed to black. Similarly, vertical smoothing is obtained by connecting adjacent black pixels along a vertical line. The final output is a single smoothed image.

The connected component analysis (Ronse and Devijver 1984) uses the output from the RLSA algorithm and finds all the connected components in the region. A connected component is a region where every non-background pixel has at least one other non-background pixel as its neighbor. Each connected component is represented by a bounding box (four coordinates which represent an enclosing rectangle). The end product of the connected component analysis is a list of bounding boxes of the connected regions in the page image.

Even though the run-length smoothing applied before the connected component analysis forces some merging of pixel regions into words, lines, paragraphs, and columns of text, there are usually some residual characters or words that may be isolated from the paragraphs or columns they belong to. Accordingly, we incorporate a final step of merging overlapping connected component bounding boxes where all overlapping bounding boxes are merged into a single bounding box. These resulting bounding boxes are used as input to the logical page analysis.

Each portion of the document image which corresponds to a text region (as determined from the geometric segmentation) is fed to an optical character recognizer. As a result, we have the ASCII characters, as well as text attributes such as face style, point size, and indentation within each region. These attributes are used as input to the logical page organization, along with the image-based feature output from the geometric segmentation. We have found that the controlled application of the OCR engine to the blocks found by segmentation yields much more reasonable results (i.e., reading order is better preserved) than trying to have the OCR "digest" an entire page at once, especially on complicated layouts.

Besides the locations of text and on-text regions, rule lines are an important image-based feature which indicate boundaries between functional components in a document. They are found by detecting large consecutive ink pixel runs in the image. The locations of the horizontal rule lines (represented by a start coordinate and an end coordinate) are recorded for subsequent input to the logical analysis.

2.2. *Logical analysis*

The emphasis of the current logical analysis module has been at the page level. The objective of logical page analysis is to group appropriately (e.g., into articles in the case of a newspaper page) the text components which comprise a document page, sequence them in the correct reading order and establish the dominance pattern (e.g., find the lead article). A list of text region locations, rule line locations, associated ASCII text (as found from an OCR) for the text blocks, and a list of text attributes (such as face style and point size) are input to logical page analysis.

Transforming the blocks produced by the geometric segmentation into a logical structure is accomplished via the methods developed by Tsujimoto and Asada (Tsujimoto and Asada 1990), who provided a set of rules for this purpose. In addition to the location and size of the blocks, their rules employ a gross functional classification as to whether a block is a *head* or a *body*. *Head* blocks are defined as those which serve in some way as labels or pointers, such as headlines and captions; *body* blocks are those which are referenced by head blocks and which have substantive content. Our head/body classification relies on features calculated for each block and for the page as a whole. The inputs to the feature calculations are the outputs of geometric segmentation and optical character recognition.

Construction of the geometric structure tree is predicated on the way that head blocks are positioned relative to their associated body blocks. In English, for example, we read top-down, left-to-right and it is usually the case that a headline horizontally spans the text and graphic material it "owns", and that it precedes that material.

The Tsujimoto and Asada method for building the geometric structure tree assumes that the layout is well behaved in terms of uniformity of column configurations and placement of blocks along column boundaries. By finding ways of creating the geometric structure tree when the layout does not behave in the above manner, we have broadened the applicability of their approach. Key to both the basic method and the enhancements is the determination of a page's underlying column structure, since it plays so strong a role in logical page organization for so many document classes.

We compute column boundaries by applying area-based criteria to the set of all page-spanning column chains, where neighboring links represent contiguous blocks. Details are given in (Taylor *et al.* 1992). The method is independent of the width of individual columns.

To discover the underlying structure of a document with multiple sets of column bounds we look for consistent column patterns in subregions of the document. This means that the page can be viewed as a composition of horizontal bands, each of which has internal column consistency. Thus, a geometric structure tree can be constructed within each band, after which the individual trees can be merged, by treating each as a child of "root", to form a single tree for the page. To find these bands or zones, we use the results of the X-Y tree segmentation (described in Section 2.1).

Especially with the advent of computer-aided publishing, layouts increasingly include phenomena like inset blocks which interrupt straight column flows. We deal with these objects by "peeling them off" into an overlay plane, constructing separate trees for this plane and the base plane, and then merging them so that an inset block is placed in the context of, but logically subordinate to, its surrounding article.

The logical transformation applies layout rules which associate blocks into "article" groupings and determines the reading order. A result of this analysis can be seen in Figure 1. One of the three articles found on the page is highlighted, and its text is available in the correct reading order.

Text processing enhances logical analysis particularly in the area of determining

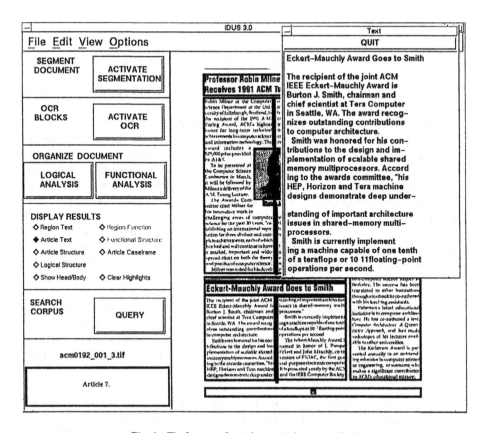

Fig. 1. Final output from document layout analysis.

the reading order. Continuity of articles in a document may be very simple or very complex (Lipshutz and Taylor 1994b). An article may require many pages, but flow through the document in a linear fashion. In this case continuity may be determined by proximity. Popular periodicals, though, often have multiple articles per page with continuations separated by many pages. In fact, continuations may occur on pages which precede the initial text, as well as the more typical case of those which succeed the initial text.

To determine where an article continues, it may be sufficient to look for text such as "continued from page 13" or "continued on next page". However, there are several cases where a deeper linguistic interpretation will be necessary to find the article flow. Consider the scenario of multiple articles per page. If reading order is determined solely from geometric and typesetting attributes, then it is possible that some text components will be grouped incorrectly. If the reading order in this case must be verified, it may be necessary to incorporate more sophisticated linguistic processing, for example, comparing the last sentence fragment of one text region and verifying that is consistent with the sentence fragment of the candidate following region (either syntactically or semantically).

2.3. *Functional analysis*

Functional labeling of regions, first at a high level to discriminate between head and body or text and non-text, and ultimately to determine the particular role a region plays, can be enhanced through the use of textual clues. Often these clues would be used in conjunction with format clues and clues derived from pixel-level features (Fisher 1991).

The simplest type of textual clue is string-based pattern matching or basic keyword search (such as looking for "Fig." or "Figure" to identify a non-text region). Since OCR systems tend to be overeager in recognizing regions as text, a reasonable clue combination would have the system look for the presence of a left-justified or centered figure tag between a region with a high number of character recognition errors. If both conditions are met, there is strong support for designating that region as non-text.

While much can be gained from simple string-based pattern matching, there are other information retrieval techniques of varying kinds and degrees of complexity which can be applied to advantage. We mention a few below, using informal descriptions.

String-based pattern matching with boolean operators and positional constraints. The "Figure" example above falls in this category. As another example, we might classify a block as an affiliation block (hence giving evidence that the document is a scholarly article) if it contains "College" or "University" within two lines of a (U.S.) state name or abbreviation.

Adherence to a simple grammar. The section headings for scholarly articles can be characterized by a grammar which specifies a sequence of digits and dots followed by an alpha-numeric string. As another example, newspaper headlines and captions may conform to a certain style which has a syntactic basis, such as noun phrase followed by present participle for a picture caption: "Heroic firefighter rescuing cat from tree".

Frequency of string occurrences. In government *Requests for Proposals* (RFPs), phrases of the form *the offerer* shall and *the contractor shall* occur with much higher frequency than in other types of documents. This frequency information can be used to infer document type.

Frequency of syntactic structure occurrences. Newspaper articles typically contain a higher frequency of appositive constructions than other types of prose. Using syntactic analysis to detect the presence or absence of appositive constructions would license the inference that a newspaper writing style was present in a given text block, and therefore that a newspaper document type should be expected.

3. OCR CORRECTION

Aside from the general need for producing the most accurate possible ASCII text in a document understanding system, OCR accuracy is important within our current scope for finding textual clues to assist in document structural analysis. Although commercial OCR systems have improved significantly in recent years, the accuracy level is not always sufficient for our applications. Accordingly, we are making an effort towards improving word accuracy through the post-processing of OCR output (Dahl *et al.* 1993).

Many instances of character misinterpretation can be resolved by the use of a *spelling corrector*.[1] Such programs are available from a variety of sources; we have prototyped a spelling corrector with features designed specifically for the OCR context. However, even with spelling correction, there is some residue of errors for which spelling information alone is not sufficient. These errors result in legitimate words of the language which are nevertheless syntactically or semantically inappropriate for their context. We address these through natural language processing techniques.

Our method for using linguistic context to improve OCR output is based on extending work previously done in spoken language understanding (Dahl *et al.* 1990, Norton *et al.* 1991), where a natural language system is used to constrain the output of a speech recognizer. OCR output resembles the output from speech recognition systems in that both outputs contain errors which are essentially due to indeterminacy in the input signal. That is, acoustic events in speech waveforms do not map deterministically to the phonetic events that make up words. Scanning and OCR technology provide similar indeterminacy with respect to character input.

3.1. *Pundit natural language system*

We have applied linguistic constraints to the OCR with the natural language processing system, PUNDIT, developed at Unisys. PUNDIT is a large, domain-independent natural language processing system. It is modular in design, and includes distinct syntactic, semantic and application components.

PUNDIT's syntactic component is based on the string grammar formalism described in (Sager 1981). The Unisys implementation is described in (Hirschman and Dowding 1990). The syntactic component includes a large grammar which covers a wide variety of linguistic constructions. Parsing accuracy is improved by checking parsed constituents during parsing against compiled semantic patterns (Lang and Hirschman 1988).

Completed parses are regularized and sent to the semantic component for further processing. Semantic analysis in PUNDIT is based on the interpreter described in (Palmer 1990). Verbs and other predicates are interpreted using declarative rules and are represented in the output of the system with a case-frame representation as described in (Fillmore 1980). PUNDIT also includes a component for determining the reference of pronouns (Dahl and Ball 1990) as well as a dialog manager (Norton *et al.* 1990). An application module (Ball *et al.* 1989) formats the output from the natural language processing system for the end application.

3.2. *Applying natural language to OCR correction*

In current spoken language understanding research, linguistic constraints are being used to improve the accuracy of speech recognizers by restricting the output to meaningful sentences comprised of legitimate words. One typical architecture for achieving this goal is the N-best strategy. In the N-best strategy, a speech recognizer outputs a list of candidate utterances, ordered from one to N on the basis of their acoustic probability (Schwartz and Austin 1990, Soong and Huang 1990). The natural language component examines each candidate in order and selects the first one that makes sense (Zue *et al.* 1990, Dahl *et al.* 1990).

We have applied linguistic constraints to the OCR problem using a variation of the N-best interface with the PUNDIT system. The architecture of the sub-system we have implemented is shown in Figure 2.

The data used for this experiment were obtained from processing facsimile output, since optical character recognition for these documents typically results in a high error rate. Because we wished to determine the maximum potential benefit of using natural language understanding to correct OCR output, we selected a domain of input texts on which the natural language system was already

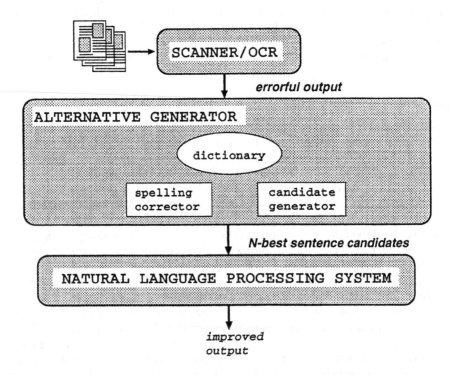

Fig. 2. This architecture illustrates the OCR/natural language interaction for error correction.

known to perform well. The texts used are from a domain of air travel planning information, previously used for the development of spoken language understanding systems (Price 1990). The OCR output is sent to the *Alternative Generator*, which consults with a lexicon of allowable words and a spelling corrector, developed as part of this project. The output of the spelling corrector is used to generate an ordered list of N-best alternative sentences for each input. These sentences are sent to PUNDIT, which selects the first meaningful alternative sentence.

3.2.1. *Spelling correction*

The spelling corrector implemented for improving OCR performance differs from spelling correctors commonly available in at least three ways:

- It outputs not just an unordered set of possible corrections, but a list of candidates ranked by score.
- It considers two-character transformations;
- It does not attempt transformations which corresponds to errors which OCR is unlikely to make, such as transpositions and transformations based on phonetic properties of words.

The output of this spelling corrector is used to generate a list of N-best candidates to be input to the natural language system. Figure 3 gives an overall picture of the spelling correction and N-best generation processes. We now describe the operation of the spelling corrector.

The spelling corrector uses two data files when trying to correct a word. The first is a dictionary and the second contains tables of one- and two-character

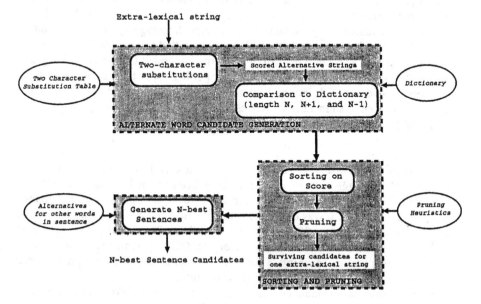

Fig. 3. Alternatives for words not in the lexicon are generated, scored, and used to create a list of N-best sentence alternates.

confusion possibilities. Penalties are associated with the confusion possibilities and are used in the calculation of scores for possible corrections. The dictionary that we currently use is a domain-specific one, with about 2000 entries. The sentences that we have been processing are all in the domain of air travel planning.

The main design ideas behind the operation of the spelling corrector are:

- Given an unknown character string, variations of it are generated on the basis of two-character substitution transformations corresponding to known OCR performance errors;
- Given an unknown character string, a score is assigned to each word in the dictionary of the same or nearly same character length. This score is intended to measure how likely the word is to be the proper correction. Easily modifiable pruning heuristics can then restrict consideration to those words with the best scores. The scores involve examination of single character substitutions.

Thus, two-character transformations are attempted when suggested by experience with the OCR system, while one-character transformations are attempted when suggested by potential candidates for the correct word from the dictionary.

3.2.2. N-best candidate generation and selection

The spelling corrector, by itself, successfully corrects many OCR errors. In addition, it produces output which can be easily used to generate N-best sentence candidates to process using the natural language system. In particular, the generation of an N-best list of sentence candidates is a simple matter of taking a "cross-product" of all word alternatives across the words of a given sentence. The score of each candidate sentence is the product of the scores of the words in it; words without multiple alternatives are assigned a score of 1.0. N-best sentence candidates are presented to the natural language system in ascending order of score. The sentence with the lowest score that is accepted by the natural language system is taken to be the output of the integrated OCR-natural language recognition system. Thus "mistakes" by the spelling corrector, i.e., lower-scoring sentence candidates with incorrect words, may be detected and discarded if the natural language system fails to process the sentence. In this way the recognition output is further improved.

3.2.3. Evaluation

The system was tested with 120 sentences of air travel planning data on which the natural language system had previously been trained. A known text was formatted in LATEX in both roman and italic fonts, and printed on an Imagen 8/300™ laser printer. It was then sent through a Fujitsu dex9™ facsimile machine and received by a Lanier 2000™ facsimile machine. The faxed output was used as input to a Xerox ScanWorX™ scanner and OCR system. Figure 4 shows a typical sentence after scanning, after spelling correction (with N-best sentence candidates), and after natural language correction.

Performance was evaluated using word error as a metric. Word error rate refers to the percent of words in the output which differ from the word that was input to the scanner. It was measured using software originally designed to evaluate

```
Uncorrected OCR Output:
      What is the latest fgght fiom Phaadelphi& to Boston

After Spelling Correction:
                         ⎧ eight  ⎫
                         | flight |
      What is the latest ⎨ night  ⎬ from Philadelphia to Boston
                         ⎩ right  ⎭

After Natural Language Correction:
      What is the latest flight from Philadelphia to Boston
```

Fig. 4. Successive improvement in OCR output occurs with spelling and natural language correction.

speech recognizers, distributed by the National Institute of Standards and Technology (Pallett 1991).

As shown in Figure 5, the word error rate for output directly from the OCR was 14.9% for the roman font and 11.3% for the italic font. After the output was sent through the alternative generator, it was scored on the basis of the first candidate of the N-best set of alternatives. The error rate was reduced to 6% for the roman font and to 3.2% for the italic font. Finally, the output from the natural language system was scored, resulting in a final error rate of 5.2% for the roman font and 3.1% for the italic font.

Most of the improvement seen in these results is the effect of the spelling corrector, although there is also a small but consistent improvement in word accuracy due to natural language correction. Spelling correction and natural language correction have a much bigger effect on *application accuracy*. In this domain, application accuracy measures how well the natural language processing system did in formulating a correct query to the database. The National Institute

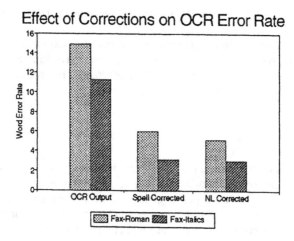

Fig. 5. Spelling correction and natural language correction decrease the word error rate.

of Standards and Technology and the research community in spoken language systems have defined a standard for measuring application accuracy in the air travel planning domain (Pallett 1991). For each database query, the system will either produce an answer or not, and the answer can be correct (T) or incorrect (F). If the system produces no answer the result for the query is NA (no answer). The standard metric for application error rate has been defined as:

$$(2 * \%F) + \%NA.$$

Sending the uncorrected OCR output directly into the natural language system for processing without correction leads to a 73% average weighted error rate. This high error rate is due to the fact that the entire sentence must be nearly correct in order to correctly perform the database task. Spelling correction improves the error rate to 33%. Finally, with natural language correction, the application error rate improves to 28%. These results are shown in Figure 6.

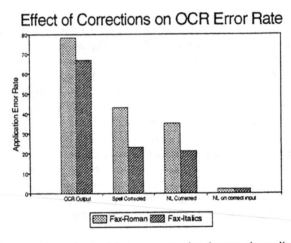

Fig. 6. Spelling correction and natural language correction decrease the application error rate.

These results are similar to the pattern seen in previous experiments with speech recognizers. In one previous test, natural language correction reduced the word error rate of a speech recognizer from 31.1 to 26.1%, but reduced the application error rate from 78 to 54% (Dahl *et al.* 1990).

4. TEXT UNDERSTANDING

Once the OCR is corrected and the ASCII text is assembled in the correct reading order, we can employ text understanding to support a document application. Towards this goal, we developed a generic, fast, robust, domain-independent text understanding module. The text understanding module is a natural language processing system consisting of components for syntactic and semantic processing. The syntactic component includes a statistical part-of-speech tagger developed at the University of Pennsylvania (Church 1988) and a robust Prolog parser developed at New York University (Strzalkowski and Vauthey 1992). The semantic component is a case frame interpreter developed at Unisys.

The part-of-speech tagger uses trigram and unigram probabilities to assign parts of speech to words in a corpus. It was trained on the 1M word Brown corpus of general English (Kucera and Francis 1967). The part-of-speech tagger includes models for part-of-speech assignment for unknown words and heuristics for recognizing proper nouns. Thus, unknown words resulting from OCR errors, new proper names, and unusual technical terminology can be correctly tagged, and will not cause problems downstream.

The tagged articles are input to the parser, which uses a grammar consisting of 400 productions to derive regularized parses which reflect each sentence's logical structure. The parser achieves domain independence by using an 40,000 word lexicon, and by using time-outs and a skip-and-fit mechanism to partially parse sentences for which it lacks appropriate productions. Thus, no sentence will be left completely unanalyzed; the system will extract as much information as it can from every sentence. Average parsing time is approximately 0.5 sec/sentence.

The semantic component represents the meaning of the sentence in the form of a *case frame*, a data structure which includes a *frame*, representing a situation and typically corresponding to a verb, as well as its *case roles*, which represent the participants in the situation and which typically correspond to the subjects and objects of verbs (Fillmore 1977). The semantic component of IDUS takes the parsed output and maps it into case frames reflecting each sentence's semantic content. For example, it lists each action mentioned in the sentence, the entity that performed the action, the object of the action, and other information such as the time or location of the action. If the system is unable to determine what action the entity participates in, the entity is simply represented on its own, as an entity that was mentioned in the text.

The case-frame generator uses unigram frequencies of case frame mappings based on training data obtained from a corpus in the Air Travel Planning domain to select the most probable case frame mappings for the arguments of verbs (Hemphill *et al.* 1990, Norton *et al.* 1991). The case frame generator is an extension of work described in (Dahl 1993). For example, the most frequent mapping of the subject of a sentence in this data is to the *actor* role; thus, the system will guess that the subject of a completely novel verb will likely fill the actor role. This training data is supplemented by additional mapping rules based on the semantics of prepositions occurring in the University of Pennsylvania Treebank (a database of parse trees) (Marcus 1990). Because the Treebank is based largely on very general texts from the *Wall Street Journal*, these supplementary prepositions allow the semantic component to function domain-independently. For example the prepositions "approaching" and "toward" are mapped into the concept of "motion in the direction of".

Figure 7A–D show the different stages of the text understanding component. In tagging (Figure 7B), each word is associated with a part of speech, selected from the set of parts of speech used in the Treebank. The sentence is correctly

177

parsed (Figure 7C), with *recognize* as the main verb, with *the award* as the subject and *outstanding contributions* as the direct object. Finally, the case frame (Figure 7D) shows the semantic relationships between the action *recognize*, its actor *award*, its theme *contribution*, and its goal *architecture*.

Figure 8 shows the actual IDUS output. The tagged and parsed text are available for examination, along with the case frame output.

```
The award recognizes outstanding contributions to computer architecture.
```

A. Original text.

```
[[the,dt],[award,nn],[recognizes,vbz],[outstanding,jj],
[contributions,nns],[to,to],[computer,nn],[architecture,nn], [perS,perS]].
```

B. Tagged text.

```
[[assert,
  [[verb,
     [[recognize,
        [tense,prs3]]]],
   [subject,
     [np,
       [n,
         [award,sg]],
       [t_pos,the]]],
   [object,
     [np,
       [n,
         [contribution,pl]],
       [adj,[outstanding]]]],
   [to,
     [np,
       [n,
         [architecture,sg]],
       [n_pos,
         [np,
           [n,
             [computer,sg]]]]]]]],
```

C. Parsed text.

```
Action:  recognize
  Actor:  award singular
  Theme:  contribution plural
    Adj:  outstanding
   Goal:  architecture singular
    Noun_modifier:  computer singular
```

D. Case frame.

Fig. 7. Example of the different components of the text processing module.

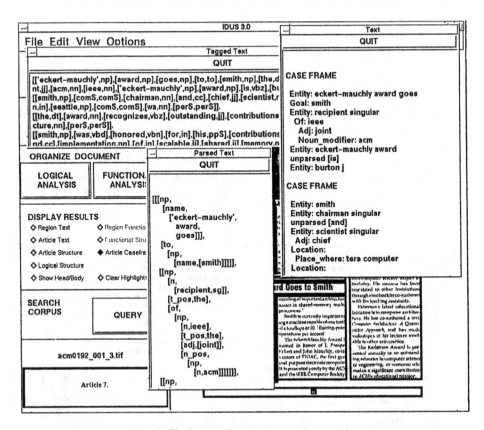

Fig. 8. Final output from text processing module.

5. APPLICATIONS

5.1. *Text retrieval*

We have developed a small text retrieval application to demonstrate the utility of document understanding from hardcopy materials. Each "article" found during the logical page analysis is stored in a corpus of documents along with a pointer to the original image from which it came. A natural language query is made and a search for matches in the tagged corpus is performed based on part-of-speech tagging of the query. Every sentence (i) in the tagged corpus receives a score S_i, where

$$S_i = \frac{M_i}{W_i}.$$

M_i is the total number of words and associated parts-of-speech in sentence i that match the words and their associated parts-of-speech in the query. W_i is the total number of words in the sentence. Grammatical function words such as prepositions, conjunctions, and pronouns are ignored during the matching process.

The score of an entire article S is

$$S = \max\{S_i\}.$$

By basing the comparison on tagged words rather than raw words, fewer irrelevant articles are retrieval because parts-of-speech corresponding to grammatical function words can be ignored and because words in the query and corpus must have the same part of speech in order to count as a match. After articles have been retrieved, a menu pops up with a list of hits. The user then has an option to examine the ASCII text associated with the article and/or the image from which the article came, which affords the user the full richness of context. An example of the text retrieval application is shown in Figure 9.

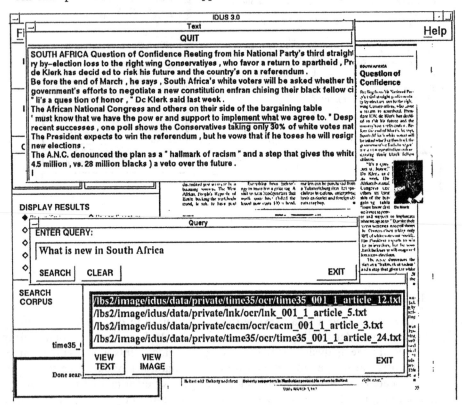

Fig. 9. Text retrieval application for the IDUS prototype system.

5.2. Hypertext

We have also developed a hypertext generation module which converts the output of the IDUS system to a hypertext representation (Lipshutz and Taylor 1994a). The target of this application was legacy technical manuals.

An initial prototype system was developed that generated Standard Generalized Markup Language (SGML) (van Herwijnin 1990) and Hypertext (Nielsen 1990) links from raw OCR output. The output of this prototype was provided directly as input to the Unisys hypertext system IDE/AS,™, which encodes hypertext links as SGML tags. The main steps are the classification of the individual text lines, the grouping of them into functional units, the labeling of these units and the embedding the corresponding SGML tags.

We employed a two-stage fuzzy grammar to classify and group lines into logical units regardless of physical page boundaries in the original document. The first stage was to tokenize each line, recognizing key character sequences, such as integers separated by periods, which would be useful downstream in determining line type, in this case some level of (sub)section. This method allowed us to overcome certain kinds of OCR errors. The second stage found a best match of the sequence of tokens representing each line against a dictionary of token sequences to arrive at a line classification. Classifications include page header, page footer, blank line, ordinary line, four levels of section indicator lines and list item lines. The validity of the individual line classifications was then checked in context. If a line type did not seem to fit with respect to its neighboring lines, it was reclassified.

A further set of rules was then applied to group lines together into functional units, label the units and choose titles for them. With this preparation, the SGML tags upon which the IDE/AS™ hypertext system relies could be generated and inserted.

From the unit labels and titles an active index was generated where a click on any entry would take the reader directly to the corresponding frame. Additional processing of each line searched for cross-references to paragraphs (e.g., "See paragraph 1.2"), tables and figures in order to insert tags which would transform the references into "hotspots". Paragraph and table cross-references were implemented and work was begun on creating links to figures, each of which constitutes a separate image file when output by IDUS, requiring a different type of linking mechanism from text-to-text links. Text blocks are fed to the hypertext generation module from IDUS as lines of ASCII characters.

6. CONCLUSIONS

We have described our progress towards developing a document understanding system with an emphasis on those components which benefit from the interaction of natural language processing with image processing. The current system has been used with a diverse set of document types including: technical and popular journals, newspapers, business correspondence, legal briefs, newsletters and a pizza menu.

In the next few years, we plan to bolster the robustness of the current IDUS prototype by both improving its existing capabilities and adding new functionality. Our primary research goal is to organize the information we obtain from processing both the document image and its ASCII text into a comprehensive document representation. Towards this goal, we are focusing on system development, technology integration, document structure analysis and document representation. We intend to incorporate the results of other researchers and even commercial products where appropriate. Immediate plans include adding the OCR post-processing correction based on linguistic analysis to the IDUS system and linking articles across pages.

NOTE

[1] A spelling *corrector*, which both flags words outside of its dictionary and offers alternative spellings to the user, should be distinguished from a spelling *checker*, which only flags words outside of its lexicon. An example of a spelling checker is the Unix utility *spell*; the Unix utility *ispell* is an example of a spelling corrector.

REFERENCES

Ball, C. N., Dahl, D., Norton, L. M., Hirschman, L., Weir, C. & Linebarger, M. (1989). Answers and Questions: Processing Messages and Queries. Proceedings of *The DARPA Speech and Language Workshop*, 60–66. Morgan Kaufman Publishers (San Mateo, CA): Cape Cod, MA.

Church, K. W. (1988). A Stochastic Parts Program and Noun Phrase Parser for Unrestricted Text. Proceedings of *the Second Conference on Applied Natural Language Processing*, 136–143. Association for Computational Linguistics: Austin.

Dahl, D. A. (1993). Hypothesizing Case Frames for Unknown Verbs. *A Festschrift for Gerald Sanders*, John Benjamins: Philadelphia. Edited by Gregory Iverson and Mushira Eid.

Dahl, D. A. & Ball, C. N. (1990). Reference Resolution in PUNDIT. In Saint-Dizier, P. and Szpakowicz, S. (eds.) *Logic and Logic Grammars for Language Processing*. Ellis Horwood Limited: London.

Dahl, D. A., Hirschman, L., Norton, L. M., Linebarger, M. C., Magerman, D. & Ball, C. N. (1990). Training and Evaluation of a Spoken Language Understanding System. Proceedings of *The DARPA Speech and Language Workshop*, 212–218. Morgan Kaufman Publishers (San Mateo, CA): Hidden Valley, PA.

Dahl, D. A., Norton, L. M. & Taylor, S. L. (1993). Improving OCR Accuracy with Linguistic Knowledge. In *Second Symposium on Document Analysis and Retrieval*, 169–177. University of Las Vegas, Nevada: Las Vegas, Nevada.

Fillmore, C. (1977). The Case for Case Reported. In Cole, P. and Sadock, J. (eds.) *Syntax and Semantics*. Volume 8: Grammatical Relations. Academic Press: New York.

Fillmore, C. (1980). The Case for Case. In Bach and Harms (eds.) *Universals in Linguistic Theory*, 1–88. Holt, Reinhart, and Winston: New York.

Fisher, J. (1991). Logical Structure Descriptions of Segmented Document Images. In Proceedings of *The First International Conference on Document Analysis and Recognition*, 302–310. AFCET-IRISA/INRIA, Saint-Malo, France.

Hemphill, C. T., Godfrey, J. J. & Doddington, G. R. (1990). The ATIS Spoken Language System Pilot Corpus. Proceedings of *The DARPA Speech and Language Workshop*. Morgan Kaufman Publishers (San Mateo, CA): Hidden Valley, PA.

Hinds, S. C., Fisher, J. L. & D'Amato, D. P. (1990). A Document Skew Detection Method Using Run-Length Encoding and the Hough Transform. In Proceedings of *The Tenth International Conference on Pattern Recognition*, 464–468. IEEE Computer Society Press (Los Alamitos, CA): Atlantic City, NJ.

Hirschman, L. & Dowding, J. (1990). Restriction Grammar: A Logic Grammar. In Saint-Dizier,

P. and Szpakowicz, S. (eds.) *Logic and Logic Grammars for Language Processing*, 141–167. Ellis Horwood: London.

Kucera, H. & Francis, W. (1968). Computational Analysis of Present-Day American English. *Technical Report*. Brown University: Providence, Rhode, Island.

Lam, W. & Niyogi, D. (1988). Block Segmentation of Document Images Using the X-Y Tree Approach. *Technical Report TR 88-14*, Dept. of CS, SUNY/Buffalo.

Lang, F.-M. & Hirschman, L. (1988). Improved Portability and Parsing Through Interactive Acquisition of Semantic Information. Proceedings of *The Second Conference on Applied Natural Language Processing*, 49–57. Association for Computational Linguistics: Austin, TX.

Lipshutz, M. & Taylor, S. L. (1994a). Automatic Generation of Hypertext from Legacy Documents. Accepted to the *RIAO Conference on Intelligent Multimedia Information Retrieval Systems and Management*: New York, NY.

Lipshutz, M. & Taylor, S. L. (1994b). Comprehensive Document Representation. Accepted for publication in *Mathematical and Computer Modelling*.

Marcus, M. (1990). Very Large Annotated Database of American English. Proceedings of *The DARPA Speech and Language Workshop*, 428. Morgan Kaufman Publishers (San Mateo, CA): Hidden Valley, PA.

Nielsen, J. (1990). *Hypertext and Hypermedia*. Academic Press, Inc., San Diego, CA.

Norton, L. M., Dahl, D. A., McKay, D. P., Hirschman, L., Linebarger, M. C. Magerman, D. & Ball, C. N. (1990). Management and Evaluation of Interactive Dialog in the Air Travel Domain. Proceedings of *The DARPA Speech and Language Workshop*, 141–146. Morgan Kaufman Publishers (San Mateo, CA): Hidden Valley, PA.

Norton, L. M., Linebarger, M. C., Dahl, D. A. & Nguyen, N. (1991). Augmented Role Filling Capabilities for Semantic Interpretation of Natural Language. Proceedings of *The DARPA Speech and Language Workshop*, 125–133. Morgan Kaufman Publishers (San Mateo, CA): Pacific Grove, CA.

Pallett, D. S. (1991). DARPA Resource Management and ATIS Benchmark Poster Session. Proceedings of *The DARPA Speech and Language Workshop*, 49–58. Morgan Kaufman Publishers (San Mateo, CA): Pacific Grove, CA.

Palmer, M. (1990). *Semantic Processing for Finite Domains*. Cambridge University Press, Cambridge, England.

Price, P. (1990). Evaluation of Spoken Language Systems: The ATIS Domain. Proceedings of the *DARPA Speech and Language Workshop*, 91–95. Morgan Kaufman Publishers (San Mateo, CA): Hidden Valley, PA.

Ronse, C. & Devijver, P. A. (1984). *Connected Components in Binary Images: The Detection Problem*. John Wiley and Sons, Inc., New York.

Sager, N. (1981). *Natural Language Information Processing: A Computer Grammar of English and Its Applications*, Addison-Wesley: Reading, Mass.

Schwartz, R. & Austin, S. (1990). Efficient, High-Performance Algorithms for N-Best Search. Proceedings of *The DARPA Speech and Language Workshop*, 6–11. Morgan Kaufman Publishers (San Mateo, CA): Hidden Valley, PA.

Soong, F. K. & Huang, E.-F. (1990). A Tree-Trellis Based Fast Search for Finding the N-Best Sentence Hypotheses in Continuous Speech Recognition. Proceedings of *The DARPA Speech and Natural Language Workshop*, 12–19. Morgan Kaufman Publishers (San Mateo, CA): Hidden Valley, PA.

Strzalkowski, T. & Vauthey, B. (1992). Information Retrieval Using Robust Natural Language Processing. Proceedings of *The Thirteenth Annual Meeting of the Association for Computational Linguistics*, 104–111. Association for Computational Linguistics: Newark, DE.

Taylor, S. L., Lipshutz, M. & Weir, C. (1992). Document Structure Interpretation by Integrating Multiple Knowledge Sources. *Symposium on Document Analysis and Information Retrieval*, 58–76. University of Las Vegas, Nevada: Las Vegas, Nevada.

Taylor, S. L., Lipshutz, M., Dahl, D. A. & Weir, C. (1993). An Intelligent Document Understanding System. Proceedings of *The Second International Conference on Document Analysis and Recognition*, 107–110. IEEE Computer Society Press (Los Alamitos, CA): Tsukuba City, Japan.

Tsujimoto, S. & Asada, H. (1990). Understanding Multi-Articled Documents. Proceedings of *The*

Tenth International Conference on Pattern Recognition, 551–556. IEEE Computer Society Press (Los Alamitos, CA): Atlantic City, NJ.

van Herwijnin, E. (1990). *Practical SGML*. Kluwer Academic Publishers, Norwell, MA.

Wong, K., Casey, R. & Wahl, F. (1982). Document Analysis System. *IBM J. Research and Development* **26**(6): 647–656.

Zue, V., Glass, J., Goodine, D., Leung, H., McCandless, M., Phillips, M., Polifroni, J. & Seneff, S. (1990). Recent Progress in the Voyager System. Proceedings of *The DARPA Speech and Language Workshop*, 206–211. Morgan Kaufman Publishers (San Mateo, CA): Hidden Valley, PA.

Artificial Intelligence Review **8**: 349–369, 1994–5.
© 1995 *Kluwer Academic Publishers. Printed in the Netherlands.*

Computational Models for Integrating Linguistic and Visual Information: A Survey

ROHINI K. SRIHARI

*Center of Excellence for Document Analysis and Recognition (CEDAR), and
Department of Computer Science, State University of New York at Buffalo, UB
Commons, 520 Lee Entrance – Suite 202, Buffalo, NY 14228-2567, U.S.A.; E-mail:
rohini@cs.buffalo.edu*

Abstract. This paper surveys research in developing computational models for integrating linguistic and visual information. It begins with a discussion of systems which have been actually implemented and continues with computationally motivated theories of human cognition. Since existing research spans several disciplines (e.g., natural language understanding, computer vision, knowledge representation), as well as several application areas, an important contribution of this paper is to categorize existing research based on inputs and objectives. Finally, some key issues related to integrating information from two such diverse sources are outlined and related to existing research. Throughout, the key issue addressed is the correspondence problem, namely how to associate visual events with words and vice versa.

Key words: natural language understanding, computer vision, diagram understanding, spatial reasoning, multimedia

1. INTRODUCTION

Much has been said about the necessity of linking language and vision in order for a system to exhibit intelligent behaviour (Winograd 1973, Waltz 1981). A complete natural-language understanding system should be able to understand references to the visual world, especially if it is engaged in discourse or conversation or even reading narratives. Without the ability to visualise, a discourse-understanding system does not have access to a major source of information that speakers may refer to, explicitly or implicitly. Thus, full understanding may not be possible. The same can be said about single-reader situations such as captioned photographs where the ability to 'see' the photograph is crucial in understanding the overall scenario and may in fact be useful in clarifying otherwise ambiguous text. Thus, the integration of language and vision is of great relevance to the task of natural-language understanding.

Integrating language and vision also has implications for knowledge-based vision, since linguistic input (in the form of text or speech) accompanying pictures can be used to dynamically construct scene descriptions. Such a situation could arise in robotics, where a robot is being guided through a visual field by a human who is viewing the same scene on a monitor. These scene descriptions can then be used by an image-processing system to guide the interpretation of the associated picture.

To date there has been little activity in developing computational models for integrating language and vision. Computer vision has traditionally been viewed as one of the most difficult AI problems; the very modest successes of vision research over the years is a testament to this. The perceived complexity of integrating two intrinsically difficult sub-disciplines, natural language understanding and vision, has kept researchers away from this area. In actuality, the integration of information from these two diverse sources can often simplify the individual tasks (as in collateral text based vision and resolving ambiguous sentences through the use of visual input).

Due to the advent of multimedia processing, there has been an increased focus in this area. There are several applications which can immediately benefit from this new technology. These range from natural language assisted graphics to information retrieval from integrated text/picture databases. Several of these are discussed in this paper.

Whatever be the motivation of the research, the central issue is the *correspondence problem*, namely, how to correlate visual information with words. It is not a simple matter of correlating pictures with words (e.g., nouns); it is necessary to associate visual information with events, phrases or entire sentences thus making the indexing problem very difficult.

Figure 1 depicts the various components of a computational model for integrating linguistic and pictorial information. Depending on the task being attempted, various processing paths may be followed. Each of these tasks involves a mapping of information from a given modality (e.g., text, image, line-drawing) into the appropriate representation in another modality. In cases where multimodal input is present, the task involves consolidating information into a single, unified representation. An example of the latter is the co-referencing task which will be discussed in later sections. What is common to all these tasks is the need for knowledge bases consisting of language models and visual models. These models, combined with domain specific knowledge, enable the mapping of information from one modality into another. Language models may consist of lexicons, grammars and statistical models of language. Visual knowledge consists of the information required to generate and/or recognize objects from line-drawings, raster images or moving image sequences (e.g., video). This could include object schemas (for vision), descriptions of graphical primitives (such as lines, curves and icons) as well as the processing modules associated with these representations.

We organize this survey into three major sections. The first section examines computational models for integrating linguistic and visual information and spans a variety of tasks. This is followed by a computationally motivated discussion of the human cognitive system, one which successfully integrates perceptual information (from the various senses) as well as linguistic information. Finally, the major research issues which arise in the task of integrating visual and linguistic information are discussed.

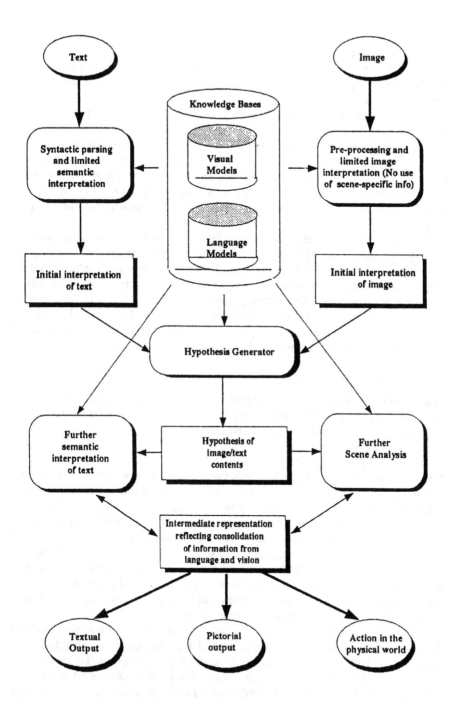

Fig. 1. Computational model for integrating linguistic and pictorial information. Ovals indicate input/output; rounded boxes indicate computational steps; regular boxes indicate derived data.

2. COMPUTATIONAL MODELS

We have classified existing work into two broad areas based on the input types used by these systems as well as their functionality. They are (i) systems that accept either language or visual input but not both, and (ii) systems that deal with both linguistic and pictorial inputs.

Before presenting research in these areas, we mention two systems which are noteworthy since they represent the historical background of this area from two different perspectives. Kirsch (1964) is significant, since he pointed out that in many cases (such as diagrams), text and pictures need to be considered as a whole when it comes to understanding. He described the need for a computer system which could deal with both types of input using uniform methods. The paper is now best known for introducing the idea of syntactic pattern recognition.

Winograd (1973) describes one of the first systems to attempt an integration of language and vision, by accepting block-manipulation instructions in English and displaying the results visually. The ultimate goal was to develop a system for natural-language conversation which could incorporate visual information about the physical world and actually make changes to this world. The system did not have a true vision component however, and relied on symbolic descriptions of objects comprising the physical world. Changes to the world resulted in changes to the configuration of these symbolic descriptions.

2.1. *Language or Visual Input*

The following sections deal with research where either language or visual inputs are used, but not both. However, they rely on integrated visual/language knowledge bases in performing the given task.

2.1.1. *Natural Language Assisted Graphics*
Natural language assisted graphics has been the topic of several recent papers. In such systems, a natural-language sentence is parsed and semantically interpreted, resulting in a picture depicting the information in the sentence. It should be noted that there may be several pictures (in fact, an infinite number) that can be associated with a single sentence. The objective is to produce the most representative picture without generating unintended detail. The key issue that researchers face is understanding spatial language as is illustrated in Figure 2. Understanding this sentence involves correctly interpreting the prepositional phrase 'on the ladder'. The latter implies that the man is on a rung of the ladder and that the ladder is supported by some surface.

In the case of Waltz (1981), the ultimate goal was the ability to reason about the plausibility of utterances. Waltz argued that the ability to visualise both static scenes and events helps us in the understanding process. He proposed a computer model to do this, namely 'event simulations'. An event simulation uses vast amounts of world knowledge and qualitative reasoning in an attempt to visualise (i.e., construct a picture of) a scene based on natural-language input.

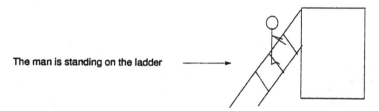

The man is standing on the ladder   ——————➤

Fig. 2. Illustration of natural language assisted graphics. It is important to infer that the ladder must rest on some surface.

Examples were provided which took simple phrases as input and resulted in line-drawings as output. This was one of the first research endeavours to generate pictures corresponding to an entire sentence.

Where Waltz's work described in general terms a scheme to handle all types of physical events, Adorni *et al.* (1984) describes a specific method of visual-ising spatial events. The examples in this system were sentences containing prepositional phrases, such as 'the wine is on the table'. Qualitative reasoning suggests that the wine must be in a container (such as a bottle) which is in fact on the table. More recently, Olivier *et al.* (1994) present WIP (Words Into Pictures), a system which automatically generates depictions of spatial descrip-tions. The focus of this work is on capturing the inherently fuzzy meaning of spatial language. The authors present a method which combines quantitative models as well as a new qualitative model (potential fields) in deriving the semantics of spatial language.

Geller and Shapiro (1987) discuss machine drafting of circuit boards based on natural-language input. The authors describe 'Graphical Deep Knowledge', which is declarative knowledge that can be used for both display and reasoning purposes.

2.2. *Natural-Language Descriptions of Pictorial Information*

Figure 3 illustrates the task of generating a natural-language description of results obtained from a vision system. The problem is to generate a coherent text describing relevant objects, relationships between objects and events which are implicit in the output of the vision system. McDonald and Conklin (1981) describes a system which takes as input a high-level description of the output of a vision system; i.e., a scene is described in terms of the objects present and 3D spatial relationships between them. The objective of the system is to generate coherent text which describes this output. Visual salience is used as a key heuristic in deciding the order of mention of objects. The focus here is entirely on the natural-language generation process, and the visual information is used only as interesting data for this process.

Maddox and Pustejovsky (1987) and Neumann and Novak (1983) describe both systems which deal with time-varying data. They address the problem of recognising events based on intermediate-level visual percepts obtained at

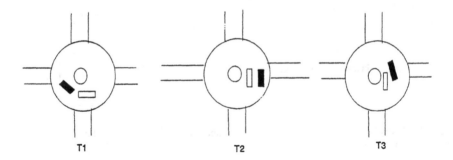

T3-Black car is overtaking white car

Fig. 3. Generating a natural language description of visual data comprising of moving images; assume that the image sequence was obtained from a camera viewing traffic at a roundabout.

different instances of time. The former uses simulated data and focuses on 'dynamic learning', whereby the system is able to construct or refine event schemata based on an interactive critic's comments. The latter is part of a comprehensive system which uses the output of a motion sequence analyser. The focus is on generating a continuous commentary about events taking place at a busy traffic intersection, which simulates what a human observer might report.

More recently, Howarth and Buxton (1993) discuss the task of selective attention in dynamic vision. The application domain here is once again road traffic. The task is to take as input a temporally ordered stream of 3D pose updates representing traffic movement and (i) identify areas/objects to focus on as well as (ii) determine relationships such as overtaking, and following. The authors conjecture that by limiting the focus of attention, the computational load of interpretation is reduced since it is no longer necessary to consider the interactions of all objects.

2.2.1. *Optical Character Recognition (OCR)*

We have more or less assumed that linguistic input is in the form of text (already separated into words and sentences). In the case of machine-printed and handwritten OCR, the task is to convert spatial data (word images) into a symbolic form, namely, ASCII text. This task also involves the integration of linguistic and visual information. The word images constitute visual input; linguistic information is in the form of statistical models of language which are employed in order to improve the performance of a word recognizer. Khoubyari and Hull (1993) discusses a system which combines visual word-spotting techniques with statistical language models in order to recognize keywords in machine-printed text. Srihari and Baltus (1993) discuss the use of statistical language models in recognizing handwritten text. In Figure 4, it is possible to use syntactic knowledge such as part-of-speech transition probabilities in order to recover the correct sentence from the available word choices.

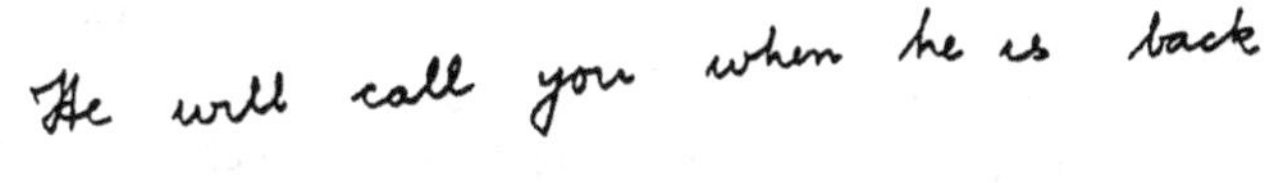

He will call you when he is back

| he | with | call | pen | when | he | us | back |
| she | will | will | you | were | be | is | bank |

Fig. 4. Digitized image of sentence 'He will call you when he is back' along with the top two word choices for each word image.

2.3. *Incorporating both Linguistic and Pictorial Inputs*

These systems are categorized by their use of both pictorial information as well as language as inputs. They can be classified into four distinct areas: (i) diagram understanding, (ii) map understanding, (iii) computer vision systems, and (iv) multimedia systems. Many of these are within the scope of *document image understanding*. Document image understanding is the task of making a computer understand messages conveyed by printed documents such as newspapers and journals.

2.3.1. *Diagram Understanding*

A simplistic view of diagram understanding is the conversion of a raster representation to a vector representation: i.e., to convert a binary pixel representation of line-work into a connected set of segments and nodes. Segments are typically primitives such as straight lines, parametric curves, domain-specific graphical icons and text. In addition, (i) portions of the drawing containing text must be converted to ASCII and (ii) graphical icons must be recognized and converted to their symbolic representation. Line segments have parameters such as start positions, extent, orientation, line width, pattern etc. associated with them. Similar features are associated with parametric curves. The connections between segments represent logical (typically, spatial) relationships.

A deeper level of understanding can be attained if groups of primitives (lines, curves, text, icons) are combined to produce an integrated meaning. Consider a dotted line appearing between two words representing city names in a map. If the legend block associates a dotted line with a two-lane highway, one should infer that a two-lane highway exists between the two cities. It is possible to define meanings for documents such as maps, weather maps, engineering drawings, flow-charts, etc. The definition of meaning is somewhat ambiguous in diagrams such as those found in a physics textbook.

Montalvo (1985) introduces the notion of *diagrammatic conversations* between a user and a system, which allows both parties to communicate about different aspects of a diagram using a common language. In order to achieve this, a mapping between symbolic descriptions and visual properties is necessary. The paper discusses how a rich set of visual primitives may be discovered. Examples are presented in the domain of business graphics.

In many diagram understanding applications, the task is to determine the pictorial referent of the entity being described in the text, in other words, the task of *co-referencing*. In Novak and Bulko (1990), the pictorial input consists of symbolic descriptions of lines, circles and rectangles, which, when combined, depict a diagram involving pulleys and ropes. The authors point out that an image pre-processor could easily be trained to recognize basic geometrical shapes. Accompanying the diagram (see Figure 5) is some English text giving further information about the diagram (e.g., the value for theta, an angle depicted in the diagram). A picture parser is able to infer the presence of higher-level entities in the picture such as angles, pulleys, and ropes. This research is interesting, since the parsing of the picture sets up expectations for the parsing of the text. For example, the detection of an angle in the picture may set up an expectation for the value of the angle to be specified in the text. Thus, in some sense, the picture parsing guides the parsing of the text.

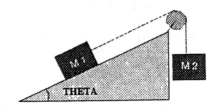

Test Problem

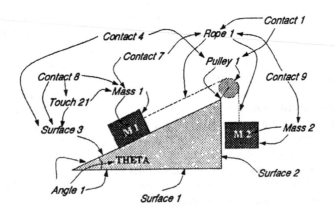

Interpretation after Diagram Parsing

Fig. 5. Example illustrating the use of text in diagram understanding. The text accompanying this figure reads: 'Two masses are connected by a light string as shown in the figure. The incline and peg are smooth. Find the acceleration of the masses and the tension in the string for theta = 30 degrees and m1 = m2 = 5 KG.' Example taken from Novak and Bulko (1990).

Rajagopalan (1994) also discusses the co-referencing task with respect to diagrammatic reasoning. The focus of the work is on integrating qualitative spatial and dynamic reasoning for physical systems.

2.3.2. Map Understanding

Yokota *et al.* (1984) illustrates the importance of a common intermediate representation in an application which synthesises information from textual weather reports and accompanying weather charts. The system demonstrates its consolidation of the information by presenting visual information verbally and linguistic information pictorially. The latter is illustrated by the generation of a weather chart based on natural-language input from the user. In the case of weather charts, it is possible to derive a straightforward correlation between words and pictures, since every weather concept has a corresponding pictorial symbol.

Reiter and Mackworth (1987) use the domain of geographic maps to illustrate the need for a formal framework for interpretation. The paper defines axioms relating to image-domain knowledge, scene-domain knowledge, and the depiction mapping between the image and scene domains. The authors take an existing map-understanding program, Mapsee, and show how it can be formally defined using these axioms. The claim is that such a formal specification can not only be used in other domains, but is necessary in order to ensure correct performance. The emphasis in this research is on formalising correspondences (once they are known), rather than deriving new ones.

2.3.3. Computer Vision Systems

The systems described in this section consider situations where pictures are accompanied by some descriptive text. They illustrate the use of language in constraining the image interpretation task or the use of visual input in constraining the language understanding task.

Abe *et al.* (1981) implement a story-understanding system in which both visual and natural-language input are used to describe the plot. Although the visual processing is relatively simple (line-drawings of a few objects), the system is noteworthy since it attempts to use language to constrain image interpretation *and* visual input to eliminate ambiguities arising in understanding language. Information from language is used initially to guide the search for objects. An example is shown in which an ambiguity in the text is clarified by the detection of a certain object in the picture, thus illustrating the flow of control from the picture to the text.

Truve and Richards (1987) describe an attempt to bridge language and vision through an alternate method of modelling objects. They describe a scheme for transforming image-based descriptions of objects (3D skeleton) into language-based descriptions and vice-versa. Two intemediate representations are described, namely an Object Description Language (ODL) and Connection Tables. ODL is a convenient and formal method of describing how objects are created by the connection of different parts and has the advantage that it is easily translated into English. Thus, ODL serves as an intermediate stage between language and high-level symbolic descriptions of objects. At a lower level, Connection

Tables are an intermediate stage between the ODL representation and the 3D skeleton derived from the image itself. Algorithms are presented in order to convert ODL representations into Connection Tables, thus completing the link between language and vision. The highlight of this work is the establishment of a strong, formal (as opposed to traditionally ad-hoc) method of modelling objects. However, their ideas for transforming language-based descriptions to image-based descriptions extend only to single objects (manufactured, as opposed to natural) rather than a collection of objects (as in a picture).

Srihari (1991), Srihari and Burhans (1994), Srihari (1994) present a computational model whereby textual captions are used as collateral information in the interpretation of the corresponding photographs. The final understanding of the picture and caption reflects a consolidation of the information obtained from each of the two sources and can thus be used in intelligent information retrieval tasks. Although the concept of using collateral information in scene understanding has been explored in systems that use general scene context in the task of object identification, the work described here extends this notion by incorporating picture specific information. A multi-stage system *PICTION* which uses captions to identify humans in an accompanying photograph is described. The author states that this provides a computationally less expensive alternative to traditional methods of face recognition since it does not require a pre-stored database of face models for all people to be identified. A key component of the system is the utilisation of spatial and characteristic constraints (derived from the caption) in labelling face candidates (generated by a face locator). The principal contributions of this work are (i) a theory of systematically extracting visual information from text and representing it as a set of visual constraints, and (ii) an efficient top-down method whereby these constraints can be exploited by an image understanding module engaged in the task of scene interpretation. Step (i) involves the dynamic generation of object and scene *schema*, and employs visual information associated with words in a semantic lexicon.

Finally, Zernik and Vivier (1988) describe a system which, when given scenes of military installations, is able to locate individual objects in the scene (e.g., a tank), based on English sentences containing identifying information (*directive semantics*). An example of the latter is 'The tank is between the hangar and the fueling-depot'. This system uses line-drawings of scenes, rather than digitised images of actual scenes thus simplifying the task of image interpretation.

2.3.4. *Multimedia systems*
Multimedia systems (see Maybury 1993) are those which integrate data from various media (e.g., paper, electronic, audio, video) as well as various modalities (e.g., text, tables, diagrams, photographs) in order to present information more effectively to a user. This is illustrated in Figure 6.

Kobsa *et al.* (1986), Neal *et al.* (1988) and Moore and Swartout (1990) discuss work in the area of intelligent user interfaces. Kobsa *et al.* (1986) describe a system which accepts as input both deictic gestures (i.e., pointing) in reference to a tax form as well as English sentences, and returns as output the exact field in the tax form which the user pointed to. An example input sequence would

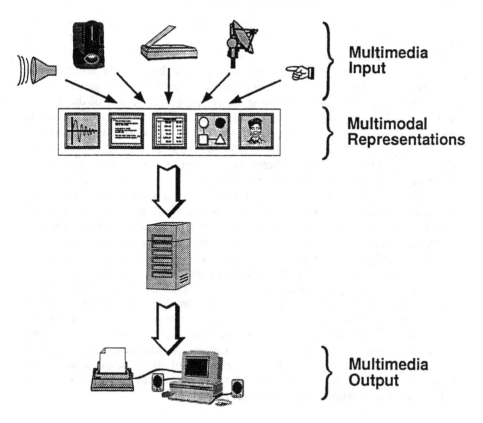

Fig. 6. Multimedia systems deal with different media (paper, audio, video) encompassing several modalities of information (text, diagrams, images).

be the sentence 'Can I add my ACL dues to these membership fees?' combined with the user touching the area of the screen representing some field in the tax form. The challenge is to determine the referent of the pronoun 'these', that is, to determine the field being pointed to. The type of deixis being used in this situation, known as *demonstratio ad oculus*, is distinguished by the fact that the objects on display are visually observable (i.e., have already been introduced) and that the user and the system share a common visual field. This eliminates the need for image interpretation systems. The challenge is to determine which of these pre-identified objects is being referred to, based on simple spatial information (i.e., place on screen which was touched) as well as the linguistic information. Neal *et al.* (1988) describe a system which integrates speech, natural-language text, graphics, and pointing gestures for a human-computer dialogue in the domain of military tactical air control. Moore and Swartout (1990) also address the problem of determining the correct referent but extend the work to generating explanations.

Feiner and McKeown (1991) describe a system in which text and graphics are to be jointly employed in generating helpful explanations for tasks involving equipment maintenance and repair. For example, the task of clearing a display is explained through a picture of the device in question with the 'CLR' button highlighted (and indicated by an arrow), along with the sentence 'Press the CLR button'. It is assumed that some other process has already generated the content of the explanation and, furthermore, that both the text generator and the graphics generator use the same input. An interesting aspect of this project is the idea of annotating the explanations. If the graphics generator decides to make a knob red (rather than highlighting it), it will record this information. This subsequently causes the text generator to output the phrase 'the red knob'. Thus, we have the notion of bi-directional interaction, an important element of integrating linguistic and pictorial information.

Finally, there has been some recent work in using photograph captions for the purpose of information retrieval. Specifically, Rowe and Guglielmo (1993) discuss a system whereby photographs taken at a naval airbase are entered into a database along with their corresponding captions. Natural language understanding techniques are employed to extract information from the caption which can be later used in retrieving photographs corresponding to user's queries. This avoids the manual step of annotating each photograph such that the relevant 'keys' have the appropriate values. Furthermore, more intelligent querying is enabled by considering the deeper semantics of a caption as opposed to matching against a set of keys. Given the need to convert large collections of photographs to digital format, this technique could be used to catalogue photographs automatically. It should be noted that in cases where captions do not already exist, a user could be asked to input some relevant text. This is more natural than asking users to fill in a form requesting values for all keys.

3. COGNITIVE MODELS LINKING HUMAN PERCEPTION AND LANGUAGE

Since this is a survey of computational models for integrating linguistic and visual information, it is useful to examine theories of how the most efficient computational device, namely the human mind, performs this task. In fact, it is the ease with which humans perform this task that makes it intriguing to attempt a computational model for the same task. Although the word 'perception' could involve any of the five senses as input, for the purpose of the discussion here, it is assumed to be visual perception. There are several viewpoints with regard to this topic and consequently an abundance of literature, but only a few have been discussed here since they attempt to address the correspondence problem form a computational point of view rather than philosophically. We begin with mental imagery since it provides some precedence for attempting the task of integrating visual and linguistic information. This is followed by a discussion of cognitive theories of language understanding and generation.

3.1. *Mental Imagery*

Mental imagery is defined as the human ability to visualise (or construct mental pictures) of various concepts, where the concept can be a simple object (e.g., a dog) or as complex as an entire sentence. Pinker says that 'unlike (object) recognition, direct inputs and outputs of the imagery system are not known beforehand and must be discovered' (Pinker 1984 p. 37). Although there is agreement among philosophers and cognitive scientists regarding the existence of mental imagery, controversy remains regarding the mechanisms in the brain which support this function.

Kosslyn (1990), gives a convincing argument for the existence of visual imagery and suggests the mechanism by which it operates. He proposes two classes of abilities which mental imagery possesses. The first of these is the ability to use images to retrieve information about the visible (and incidental rather than important) properties of objects (e.g., does a donkey have pointed ears?). The second is the ability to use visual imagery in the course of thinking or reasoning (e.g., imagining how a garden will look after the flowers bloom).

Kosslyn proposes the existence of special hardware in the human brain dedicated to mental imagery, including a special medium in short-term memory (STM) for displaying mental images (known as a visual buffer). This visual buffer has a spatial or array-like structure on which shapes are displayed. He suggests that the long-term memory (LTM) representation of shapes and surface properties used in imagery are the same as those used by our perceptual system in object recognition. More specifically, LTM contains propositional information about the appearance of an object (e.g., a table has four legs) as well as information describing the literal appearance of that object. The former is an object-centred representation, whereas the latter is viewer-centred information. Finally, Kosslyn describes a set of processing modules which operate on the information in STM, LTM, and the visual buffer. Of special interest is the processing module, which can 'produce new combinations of previously viewed objects, including those evoked by verbal descriptions of novel scenes' Kosslyn et al. (1984 p. 201).

The work on mental imagery provides some cognitive basis for researchers working in natural language assisted graphics as well as collateral text-based vision.

3.2. Language Understanding and Generation

Miller and Johnson-Laird (1976) approach the correspondence problem from a psycholinguistic perspective and attempt to give algorithmic-like descriptions of processes whenever possible. They assume that the perceptual system can make judgments about concepts such as objects, space, time, change, and causation. The output of the perceptual system is input to the conceptual system which attempts to link language and perception.

The authors outline a conceptual theory which is based on (but not limited to) a procedural theory of meaning rather than a verification theory. In the latter, verification is viewed as the fundamental source of evidence for determining linguistic meaning. They state that the conceptual system consists of two parts, a translator and an executor. The translator takes a word or a sentence and produces the procedures which are subsequently executed. These instructions may necessitate a search through perceptual, short-term, or long-term memory. An augmented transition network is presented as a model for the behaviour of the translator. Some of the instructions include *find* (to search long-term memory), *store* (to affect long-term memory), *generate* (for visual imagery), and *identify* (which references both long-term memory as well as perceptual memory).

As a first step, the authors examine how objects are related to the words that name them. They adopt the view that a label is associated with a perceptual 'paradigm' rather than with an object or class. A perceptual paradigm consists of information which is necessary in order to identify an object (this is known as an 'object model' in computer vision). Additionally, there is also functional information associated with a label. These two types of information are combined together into a 'schema' which incorporates different sets of perceptual paradigms. This type of information is represented in long-term memory.

In summary, the authors recognise that integration is performed at a common intermediate level, namely, the conceptual level. Second, the representation of lexical concepts makes it plain that both functional information as well as information relating to perception must be associated with a word. This could be taken as a guideline for constructing integrated language/vision lexicons.

Jackendoff (1987) describes a theory for correlating words and images on a lower level. In particular, he outlines a method whereby an intermediate representation (referred to as 'conceptual semantics') provides the link between language and Marr's computational theory of vision (Marr 1982). He suggests that the human ability to categorise objects and recognise individuals is due to the conceptual primitives 'TOKEN' and 'TYPE', where the first is used to label an individual object and the second is used to recognise and label categories of objects. In order to recognise objects, Jackendoff suggests that object descriptions similar to Marr's 3D models are associated with classes of objects, thus providing a link between the perceptual system and the conceptual level. Furthermore, both visual imagery and object recognition share the same 3D representation of objects.

He suggests an extension to Marr's 3D representation of objects which would include path information (helpful in describing the motion of objects) and would extend object-internal coordinate axes to the space exterior to an object. The latter would prove helpful in spatial reasoning. The ideas he expresses are powerful, since his method would establish a correlation between language and pictures at the conceptual level. Implementation of these ideas, however, requires a very sophisticated vision system which can disambiguate among models at very detailed levels of description.

Jackendoff deals with the correspondence problem mainly at the single-word level (both nouns and verbs) but does not extend the discussion to establishing a correspondence between a sentence/phrase and the complex scene which it may evoke.

4. RESEARCH ISSUES IN INTEGRATING LINGUISTIC AND VISUAL INFORMATION

There are several areas in which further research is necessary if truly integrated systems are to be realized. Some of these have already been encountered earlier but are elaborated on here.

4.1. Integrated Language/Vision Knowledge Bases

The development of large scale linguistic knowledge bases has been the focus of recent research. Wordnet (see Beckwith *et al.* 1991) is a large ontology of words based on psycholinguistic principles and is frequently used in natural language applications. Unfortunately, such a large scale ontology of visual object descriptions has not been investigated although preliminary work is reported in Srihari and Burhans (1994). If available, a visual ontology would permit (i) objects to be detected at various resolutions, (ii) objects sharing several visual properties to be grouped, and (iii) new objects to be classified based on their visual properties (i.e., visual learning).

It is not sufficient to develop independent ontologies corresponding to language and vision. In order for language understanding systems and vision systems to interact, the knowledge bases they use must be integrated. Integrated knowledge bases when combined with world knowledge as well as spatial and qualitative reasoning modules, would facilitate:

- Language understanding systems to access visual knowledge thereby allowing the generation of visual analogues corresponding to sentences or phrases. The latter could be used by diagrammatic reasoning systems.
- Vision systems to access linguistic knowledge thereby allowing natural language descriptions of visual data.
- Enforcing uniform word meanings across language processing and vision systems.

Integrated language/vision knowledge bases would also facilitate automatic learning of new linguistic concepts (i.e., words) and new visual concepts (i.e., object schemas). Siskind (1990) reports on preliminary attempts to design a system which learns the meaning of new words. It takes as input both linguistic input, expressed as a set of sentences, and visual input, expressed as a sequence of conceptual structures describing visual scenes. The system produces a lexicon as output which reflects its 'learning' of unknown words. It would be interesting to see if such a system could be extended to use line-drawings or raster images as its visual input rather than higher-level conceptual structures.

A major issue is the modelling of dynamic events. If one is to describe action in the world, or moving sequences of images, it is necessary to represent dynamic events such as running, overtaking, and jumping. This requires the matching of low-level dynamic visual percepts with intermediate concepts in event frames.

Although some work has been reported in creating integrated knowledge bases for certain specialized domains (e.g., weather maps, traffic scenes), in general this remains an open problem.

4.2. *Visual Semantics: Extracting and Interpreting Visual Information in Language*

One of the key problems arising in tasks such as co-referencing, collateral text-based vision and language assisted graphics is deriving visual semantics from the text. Visual semantics refers to information present in textual input which is useful in understanding an accompanying picture or in generating a visual analogue. Deriving visual semantics involves lexical, syntactic and semantic processing of text. A significant portion of visual semantics involves the interpretation of spatial prepositions, a topic which has been actively investigated and discussed later in this paper. However, there has been little work in the spatial interpretation of open class words (e.g., wearing, holding) which convey a wealth of visual information.

4.3. *Mapping Visual Data Into Symbolic Representations*

Computer vision systems deal with the problem of image interpretation, that is, deriving the meaning of a scene in terms of the objects present and their inter-relationships. Although such a high-level symbolic representation is the ultimate goal for picture processing systems, achieving it is extremely difficult due to the noise present in the input as well as the enormous size of the search space. For many applications however, it is sufficient to derive more modest symbolic representations of visual data. Examples of this include colour histograms, texture measures as well as skeletons (see Chang 1989). Nakatani and Itoh (1994) report on an image retrieval system based on colour indexing where users communicate their queries in English. Words such as 'darker' are interpreted based on the colour model being employed. Significant work is being conducted in deriving such representations by the image database research community.

4.4. *Spatial Reasoning*

The semantic interpretation of prepositional phrases constitutes a formalism for establishing correspondence between language and pictures and is the focus of much research. It is discussed extensively in Herskovits (1986) and Talmy (1983) from the point of view of understanding language.

An intelligent spatial reasoning module must allow for arbitrary shape representations. Many have expressed the viewpoint that it is difficult to formulate a general purpose qualitative spatial model since it would require knowledge of exact shapes of objects. However, recent work in qualitative spatial reasoning has focused on approximating shapes of objects. Abella and Kender (1993) present a method for 'fuzzifying' qualitative spatial prepositions such as 'near' and 'along'. The proposed method works for irregular shaped objects and uses a shape representation based on the center and elongation axes of the object. Rajagopalan (1994) discusses a model for integrating qualitative spatial and dynamic reasoning about physical systems; it extends current methods by allowing for effects of translational or rotational motion on the spatial state. Generalising these models sufficiently to enable their use in a natural language understanding system still remains a challenge.

4.5. *Control structures for Integrating Language and Vision*

In tasks involving back and forth processing both language and visual data, sophisticated control structures are required which are able to exploit constraints obtained from one modality in the processing of the other. This may entail redesign of existing NLP and vision systems such that:

- the system is modularized thereby permitting an external control mechanism to call on low-level processes;
- lower-level processes can exploit contextual (top-down) constraints by instantiation of appropriate parameters and other mechanisms;
- costs and weights are associated with individual processes thereby allowing an external control mechanism to evaluate the various control choices at any given time;
- processing can be suspended and reactivated when useful information is obtained.

General purpose control models such as constraint satisfaction may be appropriate for such tasks. However, issues such as adding and retracting constraints, utility and costs associated with satisfying constraints and effectively integrating top-down and bottom-up control must all be explored. More importantly, it should be feasible to derive the required constraints from the input and exploit them efficiently at the appropriate time. Other control structures such as blackboard systems have previously been used in applications (such as speech recognition) where it is necessary to integrate information from diverse sources.

4.6. *Knowledge Representation*

One of the issues to be considered is whether the intermediate representation is flexible enough to handle both visual and linguistic information. This applies primarily to those systems that employ both pictorial and linguistic input.

Allen in Allen (1987) mentions three types of knowledge which are used in natural-language processing, namely syntactic knowledge, word-sense knowledge, and world knowledge. Syntactic knowledge refers to the permissible structures of sentences. Word-sense knowledge (which is a type of semantic knowledge) refers to the meanings of words (in given situations) and the associations between words. When combined, the above three types of knowledge permit a representation of the initial meaning of the sentence to be constructed.

The most commonly used knowledge representation (KR) formalisms for representing semantic knowledge are logic and semantic networks (Sowa 1991). Logic programming languages such as Prolog have been successfully employed in natural language understanding systems. SNePS (see Shapiro and Rapaport 1990) is a fully intensional, propositional semantic-network processing system in which every node represents a unique concept. Especially noteworthy is the natural-language parsing and generating facility which is part of SNePS (Shapiro 1982). A vital component of a KR scheme is the inference system that operates on the knowledge base. Rule-based systems such as Prolog employ a knowledge base of axioms and rules and use resolution or natural deduction to carry out reasoning. The majority of existing semantic networks use path-based infer-

ence (or 'inheritance'), where the presence of a specified path of arcs is used
to infer facts. SNePS, on the other hand, allows both rule-based inference (called
'node-based inference') as well as path-based inference.

Knowledge representation in vision refers to the process of modelling physical
constraints of the real world such that this information can be used by a computer
vision system in 'understanding' a scene. In Ballard and Brown (1982), the
authors specify several criteria which are essential to a knowledge base to be used
in computer vision: (i) represent analogical, propositional, and procedural structures, (ii) allow quick access to information, (iii) be easily and gracefully exten-
sible, (iv) support inquiries to the analogical structures, (v) associate and convert
between structures, and (vi) support belief maintenance, inference, and planning.

One of the earliest knowledge-representation schemes proposed for computer
vision was the idea of 'frames' Minsky (1975). More recently, *schemas*, which
are based on frames, have been used widely in the vision community. A schema
is 'a collection of information about an object, including the relations between
parts of the object, a description of the geometric structure of the object and strategies for recognition of the object' (see Weymouth 1986). Information such as
size, colour, and sub-components is typically declarative information, whereas
the description of an object's shape is often expressed procedurally. There is
also the need for a schema hierarchy, where components of objects may be
object schemas themselves. Finally, schema networks are collections of schemas
capturing relations among individual objects and expected contents.

Semantic networks such as KL-ONE have also been successfully used in
computer vision systems to represent schemas. LOOM (see MacGregor 1991)
is a semantic network system which has been employed in natural language applications such as machine translation, computer vision applications, and applications
requiring both natural language processing as well as visual processing (see Srihari
1994). LOOM is a high level programming language and environment for constructing knowledge based systems which is based on the KL/1 family of semantic
networks. It provides an object-oriented model specification language, classification based inference and multiple programming paradigms in a framework of
query based assertion and retrieval.

We have discussed the need for a rich knowledge representation formalism
which could effectively model knowledge from either modality as well as represent the consolidated knowledge. Such representations are required if the objective
is to build systems which reason with both language and visual data. However,
such powerful representation schemes have considerable overhead associated with
them and thus may not be practical (or required) for use in applications such
as information retrieval. It may be necessary to condense the information and
use data models suited for database systems. The next section discusses such types
of representations.

4.7. *Consolidating Linguistic and Visual Information*

In order to enhance the presentation of information to a user, multimedia systems
require information pertaining to a query to be presented in various modalities

and media. Significant research has focused on (i) linking semantically related information from various modalities, (ii) developing methods for effectively presenting the information to a user and (iii) developing techniques for automatically deriving the links in (i). We have already discussed how systems which perform co-referencing as well as collateral based vision systems assist in task (iii) above. There are many issues which remain pertaining to how the information should be consolidated to permit efficient access. Multimedia data modelling (see Ishikawa *et al.* 1993) continues to be an actively researched area.

5. SUMMARY

In this paper, we have presented research on computational models for integrating language and vision. Both implemented systems as well as computationally motivated research in human cognition have been presented. Some of the key issues in integrating knowledge from such diverse sources have been outlined and related to existing research.

Although the ultimate goal of developing an intelligent agent which has both language and perceptual abilities remains elusive, progress has been made towards integrated language/vision systems in restricted domains and tasks. The advent of multimedia processing has given some impetus for continuing research in this field since several applications can immediately benefit from this technology. In that respect, there has been recent interest in developing systems which correlate visual data with linguistic data at a very high-level (e.g., using natural language to describe picture attributes in a text/image retrieval system). In order to develop truly intelligent systems however, the difficult problem of relating language and visual abilities at the basic levels of cognition must be investigated. For the latter, insight offered by cognitive scientists may prove to be useful.

The nature of this research is such that it spans many subfields of artificial intelligence, including natural-language processing, computer vision, spatial reasoning and knowledge representation and inference. Based on a survey of existing research, it is apparent that a new area of research is emerging, one which attempts to link the above subfields in a cohesive manner.

REFERENCES

Abella A. & Kender R. (1993). Qualitatively Describing Objects Using Spatial Prepositions. In Proceedings of *The Eleventh National Conference on Artificial Intelligent (AAAI-93)*, 536–540. Washington, DC.

Allen, J. (1987). *Natural Language Understanding*. Benjamin/Cummings: Menlo Park, CA.

Adorni, G., Di Manzo, M. & Giunchiglia, F. (1984). Natural Language Driven Image Generation. In Proceedings of *COLING*, 495–500.

Abe, N., Soga, I. & Tsuji, S. (1981). A Plot Understanding System on Reference to Both Image and Language. In Proceedings of *IJCAI-81*, 77–84.

Ballard, D. H. & Brown, C. *Computer Vision*. Prentice Hall: New Jersey.

Beckwith, R., Fellbaum, C., Gross, D. & Miller, G. A. (1991). WordNet: A Lexical Database Organized on Psycholinguistic Principles. In *Lexicons: Using On-line Resources to Build a Lexicon*. Lawrence Erlbaum: Hillsdale, NJ.

Chang, Shi-Kuo (1989) *Principles of Pictorial Information Systems Design*. Prentice-Hall.

Feiner, S. K. & McKeown, K. R. (1991). Automating the Generation of Coordinated Multimedia Explanations. *IEEE Computer* 24(10): 33–41.

Geller, J. & Shapiro, C. (1987). Graphical Deep Knowledge for Intelligent Machine Drafting. In *Proceedings of The Tenth International Joint Conference on Artificial Intelligence (IJCAI-87)*, 545–551. Morgan Kaufmann: Los Angeles, CA.

Hearth, R. & Burton H. (1993). Selective Attention in Dynamic Vision. In Proceedings of *The 13th International Joint Conference on Artificial Intelligence (IJCAI-93)*, 1579–1584.

Herskovits, A. (1986) *Language and Spatial Cognition*. Cambridge University Press.

Ishikawa, H., Suzuke, F., Kozakura, F., Makinouchi, A., Miyagishima, M., Izumida, Y., Aoshima, M. & Yamane, Y. (1993). The Model, Language, and Implementation of an Object-Oriented Multimedia Knowledge Base Management System. *ACM Transactions on Database Systems.* 18(1): 1–50.

Jackendoff, R. (1987). On Beyond Zebra: The Relation of Linguistic and Visual Information. *Cognition*, 26(2): 89–114.

Kosslyn, S. M., Brunn, J., Cave, K. & Wallach, R. (1984). Mental Imagery Ability. In Pinker, S. (ed.) *Visual Cognition*, 1–63. MIT Press: Cambridge Mass.

Khoubyari, S. & Hull, J. (1993). Keyword Location in Noisy Document Images. In Proceedings of *The Second Annual Symposium on Document Analysis and Information Retrieval*, 217–231.

Kirsch, R. A. (1964). Computer Interpretation of English Text and Picture Patterns. *IEEE Transactions on Electronic Computers* 13: 363–376.

Kobsa, A. *et al.* (1986). Combining Deictic Gestures and Natural Language for Referent Identification. In Proceedings of *COLING*, 356–361.

Kosslyn, S. M. (1990). Mental Imagery. In Osherson, D. A. *et al.* (eds.), *Visual Cognition and Action*, 73–97. MIT Press: Cambridge Mass.

MacGregor, R. (1991). The Evolving Technology of Classification-Based Knowledge Representation Systems. In *Principles of Semantic Netwerks: Exploration in the Representation of Knowledge*, 385–400. Morgan Kaufmann: Los Angeles, CA.

Marr, D. (1982). *Vision*. W. H. Freeman: San Francisco.

Maybury, T. (ed.). (1993). *Intelligent MultiMedia Interfaces*. AAAI Press/The MIT Press.

McDonald, D. & Conklin, E. J. (1981). Salience as a Simplifying Metaphor for Natural Language Generation. In Proceedings of *AAAI-81*, 49–51.

Minsky, M. (1975). A Framework for Representing Knowledge. In Winston, P. H. (ed.), *The Psychology of Computer Vision*, 211–277. McGraw-Hill Book Company: New York, NY.

Miller, G. A. & Johnson-Laird, P. N. (1976). *Language and Perception*. The Belknap Press of Harvard University Press: Cambridge, MA.

Montalvo, S. F. (1985). Diagram Understanding: The Intersection of Computer Vision and Graphics. A.I. Memo 873, Massachusetts Institute of Technology.

Maddox, A. B. & Pustejovsky, J. (1987). Linguistic Descriptions of Visual Event Perceptions. In Proceedings of *The Ninth Annual Cognitive Science Society Conference*, 442–454, Seattle.

Moore, J. D. & Swartout, W. R. (1990). Pointing: A Way Toward Explanation Dialogue. In Proceedings of *The Eighth National Conference on Artificial Intelligence (AAAI-90)*, 457–464.

Novak, G. S. & Bulko, W. C. (1990). Understanding Natural Language with Diagrams. In Proceedings of *The Eighth National Conference on Artificial Intelligence (AAAI-90)*, 465–470, Boston.

Neal, J. G., Dobes, Z., Bettinger, K. E. & Byoun J. S. (1988). Multi-Modal References in Human-Computer Dialogue. In Proceedings of *AAAI-88*, 819–823. Morgan Kaufmann.

Nakatani, H. & Itoh, Y. (1994). An Image Retrieval System that Accepts Natural Language. In *Working Notes of the AAAI-94 Workshop on Integration of Natural Language and Vision Processing*, 7–13.

Neumann, B. & Nova, H. (1983). Event Models for Recognition and Natural Language Description of Events in Real-World Image Sequences. In Proceedings of *IJCAI 1983*, 724–726.

Olivier, P., Maeda, T. & Tsujii, J. ichi (1994). Automatic Depiction of Spatial Descriptions. In Proceedings of *AAAI-94*, 1405–1410. Seattle, WA.

Pinker, S. (ed.). (1984). *Visual Cognition*. MIT Press: Cambridge Mass.

Rajagopalan, R. (1994). A Model for Integrated Qualitative Spatial and Dynamic Reasoning about Physical System. In Proceedings of *AAAI-94*, 1411–1417. Seattle, WA.

Rowe, N. & Gugliemo, E. (1993). Exploiting Captions in Retrieval of Multimedia Data. *Information Processing and Management* 29(4): 453–461.

Reiter, R. & Mackworth, A. K. (1987). A Logical Framework for Depiction and Image Interpretation. Technical Report 88-17. The University of British Columbia.

Shapiro, S. C. (1982). Generalized Augmented Transition Network Grammars for Generation from Semantic Networks. *The American Journal for Computational Linguistics* 8(2): 12–25.

Shapiro, S. C. & Rapaport, W. J. (1990). The SNePS Family. CS Technical Report 90-21, SUNY at Buffalo.

Siskind, J. M. (1990). Acquiring Core Meanings of Words, Represented as Jackendoff-Style Conceptual Structures, from Correlated Streams of Linguistic and Non-Linguistic Input. In Proceedings of *The 28th Annual Meeting of the Association for Computational Linguistics*, 143–156.

Sowa, J. F. (1991). *Principles of Semantic Networks: Exploration in the Representation of Knowledge*. Morgan Kaufmann: Los Angeles, CA.

Srihari, R. K. (1991). PICTION: A System that Uses Captions to Label Human Faces in Newspaper Photographs. In Proceedings of *The 9th National Conference on Artificial Intelligence (AAAI-91)*, 80–85. Anaheim, CA.

Srihari, R. K. & Baltus, M. (1993). Incorporating Syntactic Constraints in Recognizing Handwritten Sentences. In Proceedings of *The International Joint Conference on Artificial Intelligence (IJCAI-93)*, 1262–1267.

Srihari, R. K. & Burhans, D. T. (1994). Visual Semantics: Extracting Visual Information from Text Accompanying Pictures. In Proceedings of *AAAI-94*, 793–798. Seattle, WA.

Srihari, R. K. (1994). Use of Collateral Text in Understanding Photos. *Artificial Intelligence Review (special issue on integration of NLP and Vision)*, (this volume).

Talmy, L. (1983). How Language Structures Space. In Pick, H. & Acreolo, L. (eds.) *Spatial Orientation: Theory, Research, and Application*, 225–282. Plenum: New York.

Truve, S. & Richards, W. (1987). From Waltz to Winston (via the Connection Table). In Proceedings of *The First International conference on Computer Vision*, 393–404. Computer Society Press.

Waltz, D. L. (1981) Generating and Understanding Scene Descriptions. In Webber, Bonnie & Sag, Ivan (eds.) *Elements of Discourse Understanding*, 266–282. Cambridge University Press: New York, NY.

Weymouth, T. E. (1986). Using Object Descriptions in a Schema Network for Machine Vision. PhD thesis, University of Masschussetts at Amherst.

Winograd, T. (1973). A Procedural Model of Language Understanding. In *Computer Models of thought and Language*, 152–186. W. H. Freeman and Company: San Francisco.

Yokota, M., Taniguchi, R. & Kawaguchi, E. (1984). Language-Picture Question-Answering Through Common Semantic Representation and its Application to the World of Weather Report. In Bolc, Leonard (ed.) *Natural Language Communication with Pictorial Information Systems*. Springer-Verlag.

Zernik, U. & Vivier, B. J. (1988), How Near Is Too Far? Talking about Visual Images. In Proceedings of *The Tenth Annual Conference of the Cognitive Science Society*, 202–208. Lawrence Erlbaum Associates.

Artificial Intelligence Review **8**: 371–391, 1994–5.
© 1995 *Kluwer Academic Publishers. Printed in the Netherlands.*

Grounding Language in Perception

JEFFREY MARK SISKIND

*Department of Computer Science, University of Toronto, Toronto,
Ontario M5S 1A4, Canada; E-mail: qobi@cs.toronto.edu*

Abstract. This paper describes an implemented computer program that recognizes
the occurrence of simple spatial motion events in simulated video input. The program
receives an animated line-drawing as input and produces as output a semantic
representation of the events occurring in that animation. This paper suggests that the
notions of *support, contact,* and *attachment* are crucial to specifying many simple
spatial motion event types and presents a logical notation for describing classes of
events that incorporates such notions as primitives. It then suggests that the truth values
of such primitives can be recovered from perceptual input by a process of counterfactual simulation, predicting the effect of hypothetical changes to the world on the
immediate future. Finally, it suggests that such counterfactual simulation is performed using knowledge of naive physical constraints such as *substantiality, continuity,
gravity,* and *ground plane.* This paper describes the algorithms that incorporate these
ideas in the program and illustrates the operation of the program on sample input.

Key words: visual event perception, lexical semantics, motion analysis

1. INTRODUCTION

People can describe what they see. Not only can they describe the objects that
they see, they can also describe the events in which those objects participate.
For example, when seeing a man throw a ball to a woman, a person might say
The man threw the ball to the woman. In this paper I present an implemented
computer program called ABIGAIL that tries to mimic the human ability to describe
visually observed events. In contrast to most prior work on visual recognition that
attempts to segment a static image into distinct *objects* and classify those objects
into distinct object types, this work instead focuses on segmenting a motion
picture into distinct *events* and classifying those events into event types.

My long-term goal is to apply the techniques described in this paper to actual
video input. Since that is a monumental task, this paper describes a much more
limited implementation. ABIGAIL watches a computer-generated stick-figure
animation. Each frame in this animation is constructed out of figures, namely line
segments and circles. ABIGAIL receives as input the positions, orientations, shapes,
and sizes of these figures for each frame of the movie. From this input, ABIGAIL
segments sequences of adjacent frames into distinct events and classifies those
events into event types such as dropping, throwing, picking up, and putting down.
In segmenting and classifying events, ABIGAIL makes use of a library of event-

type descriptions. These descriptions are analogous to the models used for model-based object recognition in machine vision. I believe that the techniques described in this paper can be generalized to deal with real video.

The version of ABIGAIL described in this paper does not perform object segmentation or classification. Such informataion is provided as input to ABIGAIL. Siskind (1992) described an automatic object segmentation technique that utilizes the same underlying mechanisms that are discussed in this paper. No object models are needed to use that technique. I will not, however, discuss that object segmentation technique in this paper.

This paper advances three central claims. First, I claim that the notions of *support*, *contact*, and *attachment* are crucial to specifying the truth conditions for classifying a given event as an occurrence of some event type as described by a simple spatial motion verb. For example, part of the standard meaning of the verb *throw* is the requirement that the object thrown be in unsupported motion after it leaves the hand of the thrower. Second, I claim that support relations between objects can be recovered by a process of *counterfactual simulation*, the ability to imagine the immediate future of the perceived world under the effect of forces such as gravity and to project the effect of hypothetical changes to the world on the simulated outcome. For example, one can determine that an object is unsupported by predicting that it will fall immediately. Likewise, one can determine that an object *A* supports another object *B* if *B* is in fact supported but ceases to be supported when *A* is removed. I refer to this ability to perform counterfactual simulations as the *imagination capacity*. Finally, I claim that the human imagination capacity – if it exists – operates in a very different fashion from traditional kinematic simulators used to simulate the behavior of mechanisms under the effect of applied forces. Such simulators take physical accuracy to be primary – by performing numerical integration on Newton's laws – and thus must take collision detection to be secondary. I propose a novel simulator that reverses these priorities. It is based instead on the naive physical notions of *substantiality, continuity, gravity*, and *ground plane* (cf. Hayes 1984). The substantiality constraint states that solid objects cannot pass through one another. The continuity constraint states that if an object first appears in one location – and later appears at a different location – then it must have moved along a continuous path between those two locations. In other words, objects do not disappear and then reappear elsewhere later. The gravity constraint states that unsupported objects fall. Finally, the ground plane constraint states that the ground acts as universal support for all objects. I argue that a simulation strategy based on these naive physical notions is better suited to the event-recognition task.

The remainder of this paper is organized as follows. Section 2 describes the ontology that ABIGAIL projects onto the world. Section 3 addresses the first claim, namely that the notions of support, contact, and attachment are crucial to specifying the truth conditions for simple spatial motion verbs, by presenting an event logic for representing such truth conditions for a number of verbs. Section 4 addresses the second claim, namely that support relations between objects can be recovered using counterfactual simulation, by demonstrating the procedure used to recover such relations. Section 5 addresses the third claim, namely that counterfactual simulation should be based on naive physical notions, by discussing the simulation algorithms embodied in the imagination capacity and how they facilitate the recovery of support relations. Section 6 gives an example of ABIGAIL in operation. Section 7 discuss some related work. Finally, Section 8 concludes with a discussion of the overall goals of this work.

2. ABIGAIL'S ONTOLOGY OF THE WORLD

Figure 1 shows several frames from a typical movie that ABIGAIL can process. This movie depicts a man picking up a ball from the table, bouncing it on the floor, catching it, and placing it back on a table. I have written a general facility for producing such movies from *scripts*. Figure 2 illustrates the script used to produce the movie in Figure 1. ABIGAIL has no access to the script when processing the movie, for such access would be tantamount to providing the desired output as input. ABIGAIL attempts to produce a description analogous to the script by tracking the changing position and orientation of the line segments

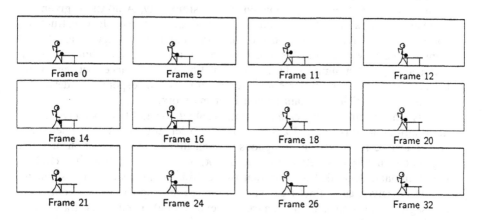

Fig. 1. Several key frames from a typical movie presented as input to ABIGAIL.

```
(define-movie a-ball-of-fun
    ((table (make-instance 'table :name 'table :x 16.0 :y 0.0))
     (ball (make-instance 'ball :name 'ball :x 14.0 :y 3.0))
     (john (make-instance 'man :name 'john :x 12.5 :y 0.0)))
  (pick-up (left-hand john) ball)
  (bounce john (x (left-hand john)) 0.5)
  (put-down (left-hand john)
            14.0
            (+ (y (p (top table))) (size (surface ball)))))
```

Fig. 2. The script used to produce the movie depicted in Figure 1.

and circles that constitute the frames of the movie and comparing those changes to a library of event types.

2.1. *The Input to* ABIGAIL

The input to ABIGAIL consists of a sequence of *frames*, each being a collection of *figures*. Figures have one of two *shapes*: line segment or circle. Each frame of the movie specifies the *position, orientation, shape,* and *size* of each figure. *Objects* such as table, balls, and people are aggregate entities constructed out of connected collections of figures.

ABIGAIL imposes certain restrictions on the input movie. First, figures are always visible. They never appear or disappear. This implies that objects never enter or leave the field of view and are never occluded. Second, figures do not change shape or size during the course of the movie. Only their position and orientation can change. This implies that figures cannot bend, break into pieces, or fuse together. While figures as atomic entities cannot change shape or size, bend, break into pieces, or fuse together, objects – which are constructed out of collections of figures – can nonetheless undergo such changes in form.

The above constraints imply that it is possible to place the figures in adjacent frames in a one-to-one correspondence. For simplicity, ABIGAIL is given this correspondence as input. It would not be difficult, however, to construct this correspondence given just the position and orientation of the figures in adjacent frames. One way of doing this would be to use a greedy algorithm to find the correspondence that minimized some cost function of the distances between paired figures. I refrain from implementing such automatic correspondence derivation as it is orthogonal to the main emphasis of my work.

I also make some simplifying assumptions about the ability to perceive figures in certain situations. First, I assume that the orientation of line segments and circles can be perceived unambiguously, even though the orientation of a line segment is ambiguous between θ and $\theta + \pi$, and the orientation of a circle is indeterminate. Second, I assume that two collinear intersecting line segments can be perceived as distinct figures, even though they appear as one contiguous line segment. This means, for instance, that even though an elbow is straightened, the forearm and upper arm are perceived as distinct line segments. Finally, I assume that two circles that have the same center and radius can be perceived as distinct figures, even though they appear to be a single circle due to the fact that they precisely overlap. These assumptions simplify the perceptual mechanisms to be described later.

2.2. *Layer and Joint Models*

The position and orientation of figures are directly perceivable quantities. Beyond these perceivable quantities, the perceptual mechanisms used by ABIGAIL project a particular ontology onto the world in order to help recover information that is not directly perceivable. First, ABIGAIL's ontology allows pairs of figures to be connected by *joints*. Such joints may be independently rigid or flexible along each of the three relative degrees of freedom between the two joined figures. I refer to such degrees of freedom as *joint parameters*. The rigidity of joint parameters may change over time. For example, observing someone bend their elbow implies that the elbow joint has a flexible rotation parameter. A later observation of that same arm supporting some grasped object requires the adoption of the belief that the elbow-joint rotation-parameter is now rigid in order to offer the necessary support to the grasped object. Similarly, the existence of joints may change over time. For example, the process of grasping an object when picking it up is modeled by the formation of a new joint between one's hand and the object. Likewise, the process of releasing an object when putting it down is modeled by the dissolution of that joint. The set of joints and their parameters collectively constitutes a *joint model*. Since joints are not directly perceivable, ABIGAIL must construct and maintain a joint model that is consistent with the observed world.

Second, ABIGAIL's ontology projects a third dimension onto the two-dimensional observed world. This is necessary since most movies depict events that would require objects to pass through one another if the world were two dimensional. For example, in Figure 1 the ball might appear to pass through the table as it bounces. Humans are strongly biased against event interpretations that require one object to pass through another object. Such interpretations constitute violations of the substantiality constraint. A human observer would conjecture instead that the ball passed either in front of, or behind, the table during its bounce. To model such phenomena, ABIGAIL does not need a full third dimension – an impoverished one will do. ABIGAIL's ontology assigns each figure to a *layer*. Layers are unordered. There is no notion of one layer being in front of, or behind, another. Furthermore, there is no notion of one layer being adjacent to another. ABIGAIL's ontology allows only for the knowledge that two figures lie on the same, or on different, layers. Such knowledge is represented by *layer assertions* that specify whether or not two figures are known to be on the same layer. The collection of layer assertions constitutes a *layer model*. This layer model is an equivalence relation, i.e. it is reflexive, symmetric, and transitive. Furthermore, it must be consistent. Two figures cannot simultaneously be on the same, and on different, layers.

Just as the joint model might need to change over time, the layer model too might need to change to remain consistent with the movie. For example, in Figure 1 the ball must initially be on the same layer as the table top to account for the fact that the table top supports the ball, preventing it from falling. Later, as the ball bounces, it must be on a different layer than the table top to avoid a substantiality violation. Finally, as the ball comes to rest again on the table top at the end of the movie, they must again be on the same layer.

Joints and layer assertions are not directly perceivable quantities. Accordingly, ABIGAIL must construct and maintain joint and layer models that are consistent with the observed world. These models can change over time as the movie progresses. Siskind (1992) presents a mechanism whereby ABIGAIL can construct and update both the joint and layer model automatically, solely from the position and orientation of the figures in each frame. Joint-model construction is currently not a robust process however. Thus, the version of ABIGAIL described in this paper incorporates only automatic layer-model construction. Accordingly, ABIGAIL is presented with an initial joint-model for the first frame as input, along with incremental changes to that model as the movie progresses.

3. REPRESENTATION OF EVENT TYPES

In order to recognize the occurrence of events in the world, we need some way of representing the truth conditions on occurrences of those events. Since we typically use verbs to name events, the truth conditions on event occurrence will constitute the definitions of the verbs used to name such events. I am not the first to attempt to construct formal verb definitions. Previous attempts include those of Leech (1969), Miller (1972), Schank (1973), Jackendoff (1983, 1990), Borchardt (1985), and Pinker (1989). With the exception of Borchardt's, these prior efforts did not attempt to ground the proposed verb definitions in perceptual input, i.e. they did not offer a procedure for determining whether some perceived event meets the truth conditions specified by some verb definition. In this section, I present my *event logic*, a formal language for specifying the truth conditions on event types. I subsequently define several verbs using expressions in this event logic. I limit my consideration to simple spatial motion verbs in nonmetaphoric uses, verbs like *throw, fall, drop, bounce, jump, put, pick up, carry, raise, slide, roll, step,* and *walk*. In subsequent sections, I discuss how these definitions are grounded.

3.1. *Epistemological Issues*

The task of formulating the necessary and sufficient truth conditions on the use of a verb to describe an event is immensely difficult. Many have argued that it is in-principle impossible to formulate definitions that clearly delineate occurrences from nonoccurrences of an event. The problem arises in part because of the fuzzy nature of event classes. For any event type there will be events that are clear instances of that event type, those that clearly aren't instances, and those whose membership in that class of events is unclear. Philosophers often debate whether or not some instance really is in some class. I circumvent such epistemological issues of absolute truth and attempt only to construct a cognitive model of truth. More specifically, I require my definitions to label an event as an instance or noninstance of a given class precisely when humans would unequivocally make the same judgment. If humans would be unsure as to whether a given event was an instance of some class I do not care whether or not my definition classifies the event as a member of the class, or whether it too indicates somehow that it is unsure.

Using the above criteria, one can assess the adequacy of a set of verb definitions only by experiment. Such experiments would rely crucially on the ability to compare human judgments with an impartial procedure for evaluating the truth values of those definitions. I have not yet performed the experiments necessary to test the adequacy of my definitions. My definitions currently exhibit too many false positives and false negatives for such experiments to be meaningful. For example, when processing the movie from Figure 1, ABIGAIL fails to recognize the picking up event and spuriously conjectures several raising and carrying events that do not occur. These errors are discussed further in Section 6. I do however, believe that my representations admit fewer false positives and negatives than those of my predecessors. I further believe that the goal of research in lexical semantics should be to strive for ever more robust definitions according to the aforementioned criteria.

3.2. Event Logic

I represent verb definitions as event-logic expressions. The truth value of an event-logic expression is relative to a particular interval of a particular movie. I write $M \models \Phi@i$ to denote the proposition that an event of the type described by the event description Φ occurred during interval i of the movie M. As the designated movie is usually invariant, I often write $\Phi@i$ when the movie is clear from context. Note that I use the notation $\Phi@i$ to specify that an event of type Φ started at the beginning of i and terminated at the end of i. The proposition $\Phi@i$ would not be true, for instance, if Φ occurred during some subinterval or superinterval of i but not precisely during i. I will shortly introduce a mechanism for specifying alternative commencement and termination requirements.

3.2.1. Event-Logic Perceptual Primitives
My event logic has two components: a set of *perceptual primitives* that denote primitive event types and a set of forms for combining event types into more complex aggregate event types. Table I lists the perceptual primitives that I currently use. I make no claim that these primitives are *sufficient* for defining all simple spatial motion verbs. I do however, believe that they are *necessary* for accurately specifying the truth conditions of the verbs that I discuss in this paper, in the context of animated line-drawings.

The intuitive meaning of most of the perceptual primitives given in Table I should be clear from their names. But such an intuitive interpretation does not

Table I
The event-logic perceptual primitives

EXISTS(x)	MOVINGPART(x)	$x = y$
PROMINENT(x)	ROTATING(x)	PART(x, y)
SUPPORTED(x)	ROTATINGCLOCKWISE(x)	DISJOINT(x, y)
SUPPORTS(x, y)	ROTATINGCOUNTERCLOCKWISE(x)	
CONTACTS(x, y)	TRANSLATING(x)	
ATTACHED(x, y)	TRANSLATINGUP(x)	
AT(x, y)	TRANSLATINGDOWN(x)	
	TRANSLATINGTOWARDS(x, y)	
	TRANSLATINGAWAYFROM(x, y)	
	FLIPPING(x)	
	SLIDINGAGAINST(x, y)	

suffice for defining their formal semantics. A significant limitation of the formal verb definitions given by Leech (1969), Miller (1972), Schank (1973), Jackendoff (1983, 1990), Borchardt (1985), and Pinker (1989) is that they never precisely specify the semantics of the primitives they use to formulate those definitions. By grounding my primitives in the perceptual processes described in Section 4, I give them a formal semantics, at least for the restricted domain of animated line-drawings. While perceptual grounding is not the only way one can precisely delineate the meaning of a calculus used to represent verb meaning, the desire to give a formal semantics for my event logic is a prime motivating force behind my attempt to provide such grounding. Lack of space limits my ability to present the definitions of all of my primitives in this paper. A future paper will contain such definitions.

The perceptual primitives from Table I fall into three classes. The primitives in the right-hand column are time independent. Their truth values can be determined once for the whole movie. The truth values of those in the left-hand column can be determined from an individual frame in isolation. The truth values of these primitives are determined on a frame-by-frame basis. The truth values of the motion primitives in the central column cannot be determined from a single frame. The truth values of these primitive depend on an appropriate change between adjacent frames. By definition, when a requisite change happens between frame i and $i + 1$, I say that the appropriate motion primitive is true both during frames i and $i + 1$. Thus a motion primitive will be true during frame i if the requisite change happens either between frames $i - 1$ and i or between i and $i + 1$. This introduces a slight anomaly that arises when an object moves between all pairs of adjacent frames in $i, \ldots, j$ and in $j + 1, \ldots, k$ but is immobile for the single transition between frame j and $j + 1$. In this situation, the motion primitive will be true for all frames i through k, filtering out the momentary immobility.

3.2.2. Event-Logic Combining Forms

More complex event expressions can be composed out of simpler event expressions using the combining forms listed in Table II. The semantics of these combining forms is defined as follows. The proposition $(\neg\Phi)@i$ is true if and only if $\Phi@i$ is false. Note that $(\neg\Phi)@i$ could be true even if Φ occurred during some subinterval or superinterval of i, just so long as no instance of Φ started precisely at the beginning of i and terminated precisely at the end of i. Similarly,

Table II
The event-logic combining forms

$\neg\Phi$	
$\Phi \vee \Psi$	
$\forall x\ \Phi$	
$\exists x\ \Phi$	
$\Phi \wedge_R \Psi$	Where $R \subseteq \{=, <, >, \text{m, mi, o, oi, s, si, f, fi, d, di}\}$
$\diamond_R \Phi$	Where $R \subseteq \{=, <, >, \text{m, mi, o, oi, s, si, f, fi, d, di}\}$
Φ^+	

$(\Phi \vee \Psi)@i$ is true if and only if either $\Phi@i$ is true or $\Psi@i$ is true. Event-logic expressions can contain variables. The formula $(\forall x\, \Phi)@i$, where x is a variable, is true if and only if $\Phi[x := o]@i$ is true for all objects o that have been seen so far. I use $\Phi[x := o]$ to designate the expression derived by substituting o for all free occurrences of x in Φ. Similarly, $(\exists x\, \Phi)@i$ is true if and only if $\Phi[x :=o]@i$ is true for some object o that has been so far. Note that $\forall$ and $\exists$ denote bounded quantification over only those objects (connected collections of figures) that have been observed.

The next three combining forms utilize a subscript R that ranges over subsets of the thirteen possible relations between two intervals as proposed by Allen (1983), namely $\{=, <, >, \text{m}, \text{mi}, \text{o}, \text{oi}, \text{s}, \text{si}, \text{f}, \text{fi}, \text{d}, \text{di}\}$.[1] The proposition $(\Phi \wedge_R \Psi)@i$ is true if and only if there exist two intervals j and k such that the relations $j$si and $k$fi both hold, the propositions $\Phi@j$ and $\Psi@k$ are both true, and jrk for some $r \in R$. I abbreviate the special cases $\Phi \wedge_{\{=\}} \Psi$ and $\Phi \wedge_{\{\text{m}\}} \Psi$ as $\Phi \wedge \Psi$ and $\Phi;\Psi$ respectively. Thus $\Phi \wedge \Psi$ describes an aggregate event where both Φ and Ψ happen simultaneously, starting and finishing at the same time, while $\Phi;\Psi$ describes an aggregate event of Φ immediately followed by Ψ. Similarly, $(\diamondsuit_R\Phi)@i$ is true if and only if there exists an interval j such that $\Phi@j$ and jri for some $r \in R$. The $\diamondsuit_R$ combining form can act as a tense operator. Expressions such as $\diamondsuit_{\{<\}}\Phi$, $\diamondsuit_{\{>\}}\Phi$, $\diamondsuit_{\{\text{m}\}}\Phi$, and $\diamondsuit_{\{\text{mi}\}}\Phi$ specify that Φ happened in the distant past, distant future, immediate past, or immediate future respectively. I abbreviate the special case $\diamondsuit_{\{=, \text{o}, \text{oi}, \text{s}, \text{si}, \text{f}, \text{fi}, \text{d}, \text{di}\}}\Phi$ simply as $\diamondsuit\Phi$. The utility of this abbreviation will be described shortly. Finally $\Phi^+@i$ is true if and only if there exists some set of intervals $\{i_1, \ldots, i_n\}$ such that $\Phi@i_k$ for all $1 \leq k \leq n$ and $i_k\text{mi}_{k+1}$ for all $1 \leq k < n$. The expression Φ^+ denotes contiguous repeated occurrence of Φ.

Note that an expression such as $(\neg\Phi)@i$, does *not* mean that Φ *never* occurs during i. It means that no instance of Φ occurs beginning precisely at the beginning of i and ending precisely at the end of i. Thus an expression such as $\neg$TRANSLATING(y) would be true of an interval if y were stationary for part of that interval but nonetheless moving for some other part. The proposition $(\diamondsuit\Phi)@i$ can be used to express the statement that some part of some occurrence of Φ occurs sometime during some part of i, i.e. that an occurrence of Φ occurred during some subinterval or some superinterval of i, or during some other interval that overlaps with i. Similarly, the proposition $(\neg\diamondsuit\Phi)@i$ can be used to express the statement that no part of Φ occurs during a part of i. This allows one to use $(\neg\diamondsuit$TRANSLATING$(y))@i$ to mean that y was stationary throughout i.

3.3. *Sample Verb Definitions*

Table III illustrates some sample verb definitions formulated in my event logic. For example, the definition for *throw* states that x throws y if y is not a part of x and there is some z that is a part of x, typically x's hand, such that for some interval, z is attached to y, is touching y, and is moving with y, while in the immediate subsequent interval, z no longer is attached to y, no longer touches y, and y is in unsupported motion. Likewise, the definition for *fall* states that x falls if

Table III
Some verb definitions formulated in my event logic

$$\text{Throw}(x,y) \triangleq \neg\Diamond\,\text{Part}(y,x) \land \exists z \left(\left[\begin{pmatrix} \text{Part}(z,x)\land \\ \text{Translating}(z)\land \\ \text{Contacts}(z,y)\land \\ \text{Attached}(z,y) \end{pmatrix} ; \begin{pmatrix} \neg\Diamond\,\text{Contacts}(z,y)\land \\ \neg\Diamond\,\text{Attached}(z,y)\land \\ \neg\Diamond\,\text{Supported}(y) \end{pmatrix} \right] \land \atop \text{Translating}(y) \right)$$

$$\text{Fall}(x) \triangleq \neg\Diamond\,\text{Supported}(x) \land \text{TranslatingDown}(x)$$

$$\text{Drop}(x,y) \triangleq \exists z \left(\left[\begin{pmatrix} \text{Part}(z,x)\land \\ \text{Contacts}(z,y)\land \\ \text{Attached}(z,y)\land \\ \text{Supports}(x,y)\land \\ \text{Supported}(y) \end{pmatrix} ; \begin{pmatrix} \neg\Diamond\,\text{Contacts}(z,y)\land \\ \neg\Diamond\,\text{Attached}(z,y)\land \\ \neg\Diamond\,\text{Supports}(x,y)\land \\ \neg\Diamond\,\text{Supported}(y) \end{pmatrix} \right] \right)$$

$$\text{Bounce}(x) \triangleq \left(\begin{array}{c} \text{Translating}(x)\land \\ \exists y[\neg\Diamond\,\text{Contacts}(x,y); \text{Contacts}(x,y); \neg\Diamond\,\text{Contacts}(x,y)] \end{array} \right)$$

$$\text{Jump}(x) \triangleq \text{Supported}(x); \left(\begin{array}{c} \neg\Diamond\,\text{Supported}(x)\land \\ \text{TranslatingUp}(x) \end{array} \right)$$

$$\text{Put}(x,y) \triangleq \exists w \left(\left[\begin{pmatrix} \text{Part}(w,x)\land \\ \text{Translating}(w)\land \\ \text{Contacts}(w,y)\land \\ \text{Attached}(w,y)\land \\ \text{Supports}(x,y)\land \\ \text{Translating}(y) \end{pmatrix} ; \exists z \begin{pmatrix} \text{Disjoint}(z,w)\land \\ \neg\Diamond\,\text{Translating}(y)\land \\ \text{Supported}(y)\land \\ \text{Supports}(z,y) \end{pmatrix} \right] \right)$$

$$\text{PickUp}(x,y) \triangleq \exists w \left(\left[\exists z \begin{pmatrix} \text{Part}(w,x)\land \\ \text{Disjoint}(z,w)\land \\ \text{Supported}(y)\land \\ \text{Supports}(z,y)\land \\ \text{Contacts}(z,y) \end{pmatrix} ; \begin{pmatrix} \text{Translating}(w)\land \\ \text{Contacts}(w,y)\land \\ \text{Attached}(w,y)\land \\ \text{Supports}(x,y)\land \\ \text{Translating}(y) \end{pmatrix} \right] \right)$$

$$\text{Carry}(x,y) \triangleq \text{Translating}(x) \land \text{Translating}(y) \land \text{Supports}(x,y)$$

$$\text{Raise}(x,y) \triangleq \neg\Diamond\,\text{Part}(y,x) \land \text{Supports}(x,y) \land \text{TranslatingUp}(y)$$

$$\text{Slide}(x) \triangleq \exists y\,\text{SlidingAgainst}(x,y)$$

$$\text{Roll}(x) \triangleq \exists y \left(\begin{array}{c} \neg\Diamond\,\text{SlidingAgainst}(x,y)\land \\ [\text{RotatingClockwise}(x) \lor \text{RotatingCounterClockwise}(x)]\land \\ \text{Contacts}(x,y) \end{array} \right)$$

$$\text{Step}(x) \triangleq \exists y \left(\begin{array}{c} \text{Part}(y,x)\land \\ [\text{Contacts}(y,\text{ground}); \neg\Diamond\,\text{Contacts}(y,\text{ground}); \text{Contacts}(y,\text{ground})] \end{array} \right)$$

$$\text{Walk}(x) \triangleq \left(\begin{array}{c} \text{Step}(x)^+\land \\ (\exists y[\text{Part}(y,x) \land \text{Contacts}(y,\text{ground})])^+\land \\ \neg\Diamond\,\exists y[\text{Part}(y,x) \land \text{SlidingAgainst}(y,\text{ground})] \end{array} \right)$$

it is in unsupported downward motion. Similarly, the definition for *drop* states that x drops y if there is some z that is a part of x, typically x's hand, such that for some interval, z initially supports y by way of being attached to it, while in the immediate subsequent interval, z no longer supports, touches, or is attached to y, and y is unsupported.

Note that the notion of support plays a crucial role in these definitions. It is not sufficient for an object to be in motion after it leaves one's hand for one to have thrown that object. Rolling a ball does not constitute throwing. The object must be in unsupported motion after it leaves one's hand. Likewise, not all downward object motion constitutes falling. Airplanes (hopefully) are not falling when they descend to land. Objects must be in unsupported downward motion to be classified as falling.[2] Similarly, dropping too, requires that the dropped object be unsupported. One is not dropping a teacup when one places it gently in its saucer. Such a distinction between supported and unsupported motion plays a role in delineating the difference between the verbs *drop* and *put*. Siskind (1992) argues this case more extensively.

I do not claim that the definitions given in Table III fully specify the necessary and sufficient truth conditions for the indicated event types. Nor do I claim that my current formulation of event logic is sufficiently expressive to formulate such truth conditions. For instance, there is no way to specify the default expectation that an agent's hand is the part of the agent typically involved in throwing. Likewise, there is no model of prototypical classes, radial categories, or focus of attention.

When classifying events, prior researchers (Vendler 1967, Dowty 1979, Verkuyl 1989, Krifka 1992) have noted that some event types have the following two properties. First, if they are true during an interval i then they are also true during any subinterval of i. Second, if they are true during two intervals i and j such that $i\mathbf{m}j$ then they are also true during the encompassing interval that begins at the beginning of i and ends at the end of j. Events with these properties are termed *liquid*, following Shoham (1987). All of the event types denoted by perceptual primitives are liquid. Not all compound events are liquid however. Some compound events such as FALL, CARRY, RAISE, SLIDE, and ROLL are liquid, while others such as THROW, DROP, BOUNCE, JUMP, PUT, PICKUP, STEP, and WALK are not.

Note that one cannot use $\neg$TRANSLATING(y) in the definition of PUT to specify that y be at rest after leaving the agent's hand, since as discussed previously, such a definition would admit events where the object continued to move for a while after it left the agent's hand but before it eventually came to rest. To circumvent this problem the proposition $\neg\Diamond$TRANSLATING(y) is used to denote an interval during which y did not move at all. This $\neg\Diamond$ cliché is used is many of the verb definitions in Table III.

4. RECOVERING SUPPORT RELATIONS

ABIGAIL processes the movie a frame at a time. For each frame, ABIGAIL performs the following operations in sequence. First, ABIGAIL constructs a layer model consistent with the current frame.[3] For the first frame, the layer model must be computed from scratch. In subsequent frames, the layer model is updated incrementally from the layer model for the previous frame. Next, ABIGAIL performs object segmentation, partitioning collections of figures in the frame into distinct objects. Then, ABIGAIL computes the support relationships between the objects just segmented. Finally, ABIGAIL determines the truth values of the perceptual primitives enumerated in Table I for the current frame. ABIGAIL tracks these changing truth values so that the truth values of the event types given in Table III can be computed at the end of the movie.

4.1. *Computing and Updating the Layer Model*

The layer model is computed by the following process. At all times ABIGAIL maintains a layer model L. This layer model is initially empty. ABIGAIL uses the layer model from the previous frame to construct the layer model for the current frame. When processing each frame, ABIGAIL first collects all pairs of figures that overlap and forms a set D of different-layer assertions between such figures. Such assertions are needed because the substantiality constraint would be violated if those figures were on the same layer. For example, when processing frame 0 of the movie shown in Figure 1, ABIGAIL would form a different-layer assertion between the man's left forearm and his torso. ABIGAIL then collects all pairs of figures that touch but don't overlap as the set S of candidate same-layer assertions. For example, when processing frame 0, ABIGAIL would form a candidate same-layer assertion between the surface of the ball and the table top. Note that $D \cup S$ may be inconsistent. For example, when processing frame 0, ABIGAIL would form candidate same-layer assertions between the man's left forearm and upper arm, and between his left upper-arm and torso. Since same-layer assertions are transitive, these two candidates would imply that his left forearm was on the same layer as his torso, which is inconsistent with the different-layer assertion just formed. Also note that $D \cup S \cup L$ may be inconsistent – even if $D \cup S$ was consistent – since objects may change layers during the course of the movie. For example, in the movie shown in Figure 1, while the surface of the ball must be on the same layer as the table top in frame 0, later on it must be on a different layer to avoid a substantiality violation as the ball falls. Thus, current different-layer assertions must take priority over both candidate and previously-adopted same-layer assertions. Furthermore, it is desirable to give previously-adopted same-layer assertions priority over newer candidate same-layer assertions. Let $C(D, S, L)$ denote a maximal consistent subset of $D \cup S \cup L$ where elements of D are given priority over elements of S, and elements of D and S are given priority over those elements of L that are not in either D or S. ABIGAIL then uses the kinematic simulator described in Section 5, with $C(D, S, L)$ as the layer model, to imagine the future and predict which figures fall and which do not. ABIGAIL forms the set F of figures that did not fall and then selects a minimal subset S' of S such that no figure from F falls when imagining the future using $C(D, S', L)$ as the layer model instead of $C(D, S, L)$. ABIGAIL then adopts $C(D, S', L)$ as the new layer model L for the current frame. In this way, ABIGAIL decides that two figures are on the same layer only when necessary to generate a support relationship, and furthermore gives priority to previously-adopted same-layer assertions over newer candidate same-layer assertions when both generate the same support relationships.

Figure 3 gives an example of the layer-model construction performed when analyzing frame 0 of the movie shown in Figure 1. Here, ABIGAIL will adopt the same-layer assertion between the surface of the ball and the table top since the ball will fall without such an assertion but will remain supported with that assertion.

The layer-model construction algorithm appears overly complicated. One may wonder why it is necessary to compute the set F and not simply compute a minimal subset S' of S such that no figure falls at all with $C(D, S', L)$ as the layer model. Figure 3 illustrates why this simpler algorithm will not work. In this example, since the eye is unsupported[4] no subset of S' will succeed in preventing all of the figures in the image from falling. Thus one can only find a minimal subset of S' that prevents those figures that could be supported from falling.

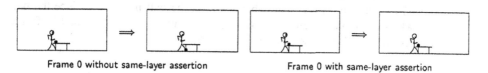

Frame 0 without same-layer assertion   Frame 0 with same-layer assertion

Fig. 3. The use of counterfactual simulation during layer-model construction.

4.2. *Object Segmentation*

Object segmentation is performed by a very simple procedure. ABIGAIL finds the connected components in the graph whose vertices are figures and whose edges are joints that are rigid along all three joint parameters. Each such connected component is added to the list of objects. Objects are never removed from this list, even though in subsequent frames they may no longer be connected components as just defined. Nonetheless, objects may cease to exist and later come back into existence. An object *exists* if it is connected. For an object to exist, it need not be a connected component. It could be a part of a new object comprising a larger connected component. Also, for an object to exist, the joint parameters need not be rigid. It can consist of flexibly connected parts. The stronger connected-component and rigid-joint criteria are used only for determining the initial existence of newly detected objects and not for tracking their continued existence.

The perceptual primitive EXISTS(x) can be used to formulate definitions of verbs that depend on changes in the state of an object's existence. For example, *break* might be modeled as a change to nonexistence. Likewise, *make* might be modeled as a change to existence. Similarly, *fix* might be modeled as a change to nonexistence followed by a change to existence.

Once model construction and object segmentation have been completed, the support relationships between objects can be computed. Such support relationships are also computed using counterfactual simulation. An object is supported in the current frame if it does not fall when imagining the immediate future of that frame. Similarly, an object A supports another object B in the current frame if B is supported but ceases to be supported when imagining the immediate future of an image that is identical to the one in the current frame except that the figures comprising A have been removed. A single run of the simulator can be used to determine the truth value of the SUPPORTED(x) primitive for all of the objects x in the movie. Those objects that fall during this single simulation are unsupported while those that remain stable are supported. Computing the truth value of the SUPPORTS(x, y) primitive for all pairs of objects x and y can be done with n calls to the simulator where n is the number of objects in the image. One calls the simulator once for each object x, removing that object from the image, and determining which other objects y fall or remain supported.

Figure 4 illustrates the use of counterfactual simulation to recover support relations when processing the movie shown in Figure 1. The ball is supported in both frames 0 and 11 because it does not fall. The ball is unsupported in frame 14 since it does fall. The table supports the ball in frame 0 since the ball falls when the table is removed. Similarly the man supports the ball in frame 11 since the ball falls when the man is removed.

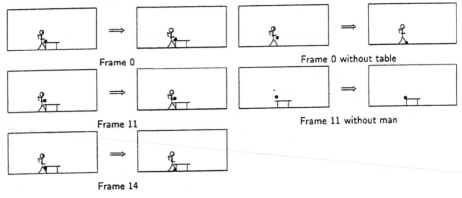

Fig. 4. The use of counterfactual simulation during the recovery of support relations.

5. THE IMAGINATION CAPACITY

Much of my event-recognition procedure relies on counterfactual simulation, the ability to predict the immediate future subject to hypothetical changes to the world. This imagination capacity is used both for layer-model construction and to recover support relationships. Nominally, it would appear that such simulation could be performed by a kinematic simulator of the type typically used by mechanical engineers, since in ABIGAIL's world ontology, objects correspond essentially to mechanisms and figures correspond to the links comprising such mechanisms. Figure 5 illustrates a problem with such a view. Conventional kinematic simulators use numerical integration to solve the differential equations obtained by applying Newton's laws to the mechanism being simulated.

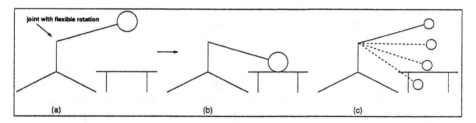

Fig. 5. A comparison between ABIGAIL's imagination capacity (a) and (b) with one based on numerical integration (c).

Numerical integration requires the use of a nonzero step size. Collision detection is performed after each step to determine whether or not to allow the state change entailed by that step. If this step size is large, there is the possibility that one object will pass totally through another object in the transition from one step to the next allowing a substantiality violation to go undetected. There is no way, in principle, to use a numerical integration procedure as a simulator that soundly avoids substantiality violations. If the step size is reduced as a practical attempt to mitigate this unsoundness, the numerical integration process becomes much slower. The simulation time becomes dependent on the distance that objects must move until they come to rest. This is illustrated in Figure 5(c). Classical kinematic simulators based on numerical integration would repeatedly vary the joint angle by a small step size until the ball collides with the table. If the step size is too small, the simulation is slow. If the step size is too large, the collision might not be detected, resulting in a simulation that violates the substantiality and continuity constraints.

People appear to use a different process when projecting the future. First, from early infancy humans are very strongly biased against visualizing substantiality violations (Spelke 1988, though see Leslie 1988 for some exceptions). Second, from early infancy humans also are very strongly biased against imagining objects disappearing and later reappearing elsewhere. People appear to enforce a continuity constraint on object motion that is incompatible with the quantized motion of numerical simulators. Finally, people appear to be able to quickly predict that the joint in Figure 5 will pivot precisely the amount needed to bring the ball in contact with the table, no more and no less. The simulator incorporated into ABIGAIL's imagination capacity can make the prediction illustrated in Figure 5(a) and 5(b) in a single precise step, never producing the anomalous prediction shown in Figure 5(c). Such a capacity appears incompatible with numerical simulation.

The simulator used by ABIGAIL is therefore based on very different principles. It directly incorporates the notions of substantiality and continuity, in addition to gravity – the fact that unsupported objects fall – and ground plane – the fact that the ground can support all objects. The simulator operates by examining all rigid collections of figures and considering all motions that such collections can exhibit as a result of gravity. Qualitatively, objects can exhibit four kinds of motion.

1. They can fall straight downward.
2. They can slide down an inclined surface.
3. They can fall over, pivoting about a contact point between a corner and a surface.
4. A part of an object can move along the degree of freedom of a flexible joint.

ABIGAIL considers each such case separately and can calculate how much objects can move under these cases until they collide with other objects. Such calculation is performed analytically. The simulator consists simply of a loop that chooses an object to move – along with a type of motion – and moves that object the analytically defined amount in a single step.

ABIGAIL's simulator suffers from numerous limitations. It cannot accurately predict the time course of events since it does not model velocity, momentum, or kinetic energy. Thus it can incorrectly predict the outcome of a situation exhibiting simultaneous motion of interacting objects. Furthermore, the analytical calculations can only be done for objects moving along linear or circular paths. Thus this technique is not suitable for simulating mechanisms with closed loop kinematic chains, for such mechanisms exhibit more complex motion.

Humans however, appear to exhibit the same limitations as ABIGAIL. Furthermore, despite the limitations of ABIGAIL's simulator, it is nonetheless capable of sufficient accuracy for its intended uses: constructing layer models and determining support relationships. A kinematic simulator based on the notions of substantiality, continuity, gravity, and ground plane is well suited to this task since these naive physical notions are intimately intertwined with the notions of support, contact, and attachment. Furthermore, the latter notions form the basis of event perception as discussed in Section 3. I conjecture that the human imagination capacity is designed the way it is precisely because an imagination capacity based on naive physics is better matched to the task of event perception than one based on Newtonian physics.

6. AN EXAMPLE

Figure 6 shows the output generated by ABIGAIL when processing the movie from Figure 1. Each line indicates a detected event from the event definitions given in Table III. Notation such as [BALL] denotes collections of figures that constitute objects that partake in the detected events. Since ABIGAIL does not perform object classification, these names are given as input. They are used solely to make the output more readable and are not accessed in any other way during the event perception process. The notation $[i : j, k : l]\Phi$ specifies that an occurrence of the event type Φ was detected for all intervals starting in frames between i and j and ending in frames between k and l. I call such a concise representation of numerous intervals a *spanning interval*. The abbreviations $[i : j, k]\Phi$, $[i, k : l]\Phi$, $[i : k]\Phi$, $[i, k]\Phi$, and $[i]\Phi$ are shorthand for $[i : j, k : k]\Phi$, $[i : i, k : l]\Phi$, $[i : k, i : k]\Phi$, $[i : i, k : k]\Phi$, and $[i : i, i : i]\Phi$ respectively. The algorithm used by ABIGAIL for evaluating the truth value of event-logic expressions computes directly with spanning intervals. This affords a substan-

```
[20:21](RAISE [(LEFT-FOREARM JOHN)] [BALL])
[7:11](RAISE [(LEFT-FOREARM JOHN)] [BALL])
[27:32](RAISE [(LEFT-UPPER-ARM JOHN)] [(LEFT-FOREARM JOHN)])
[20:21](RAISE [(LEFT-UPPER-ARM JOHN)] [(LEFT-FOREARM JOHN)])
[6:11](RAISE [(LEFT-UPPER-ARM JOHN)] [(LEFT-FOREARM JOHN)])
[20:21](RAISE [(LEFT-UPPER-ARM JOHN)] [BALL])
[6:11](RAISE [(LEFT-UPPER-ARM JOHN)] [BALL])
[27:32](RAISE [JOHN-part 5] [(LEFT-FOREARM JOHN)])
[20:21](RAISE [JOHN-part 5] [(LEFT-FOREARM JOHN)])
[6:11](RAISE [JOHN-part 5] [(LEFT-FOREARM JOHN)])
[28:32](RAISE [JOHN-part 5] [(LEFT-UPPER-ARM JOHN)])
[25:26](RAISE [JOHN-part 5] [(LEFT-UPPER-ARM JOHN)])
[7:12](RAISE [JOHN-part 5] [(LEFT-UPPER-ARM JOHN)])
[4:5](RAISE [JOHN-part 5] [(LEFT-UPPER-ARM JOHN)])
[20:21](RAISE [JOHN-part 5] [BALL])
[6:11](RAISE [JOHN-part 5] [BALL])
[20:21](RAISE [JOHN-part 3] [BALL])
[7:11](RAISE [JOHN-part 3] [BALL])
[20:26](CARRY [(LEFT-FOREARM JOHN)] [BALL])
[7:12](CARRY [(LEFT-FOREARM JOHN)] [BALL])
[27:32](CARRY [(LEFT-UPPER-ARM JOHN)] [(LEFT-FOREARM JOHN)])
[20:26](CARRY [(LEFT-UPPER-ARM JOHN)] [(LEFT-FOREARM JOHN)])
[6:12](CARRY [(LEFT-UPPER-ARM JOHN)] [(LEFT-FOREARM JOHN)])
[1:5](CARRY [(LEFT-UPPER-ARM JOHN)] [(LEFT-FOREARM JOHN)])
[20:26](CARRY [(LEFT-UPPER-ARM JOHN)] [BALL])
[6:12](CARRY [(LEFT-UPPER-ARM JOHN)] [BALL])
[26](CARRY [JOHN-part 3] [BALL])
[20:21](CARRY [JOHN-part 3] [BALL])
[12](CARRY [JOHN-part 3] [BALL])
[7](CARRY [JOHN-part 3] [BALL])
[20:26,27](PUT [JOHN-part 3] [BALL])
[16,17:19](JUMP [BALL])
[6:15,17:26](BOUNCE [BALL])
[7:12,13:15](DROP [JOHN-part 3] [BALL])
[13:15](FALL [BALL])
[6:12,13:15](THROW [JOHN-part 3] [BALL])
```

Fig. 6. The events recognized by ABIGAIL when processing the movie from Figure 1.

tial savings in both the space and time needed for event recognition. This algorithm will be discussed in a future paper.

Note that ABIGAIL successfully recognizes occurrences of the putting down,
bouncing, dropping, falling, and throwing events, and places them at the correct
points in time. The event recognition process, however, suffers from a number
of false positives and negatives. ABIGAIL fails to recognize the picking up event.
This is because the definition of PICKUP consists primarily of an expression of
the form $\Phi;\Psi$, and Φ is true during the interval ending in frame 5 while Ψ is
true during the interval beginning in frame 7, but these intervals do not
precisely meet. There are also numerous spurious recognitions of raising and
carrying events, as well as a spurious jumping event. This is because the current
definitions of *raise*, *carry*, and *jump* are too loose and admit many false posi-

tives. Much work remains to be done to more accurately characterize the necessary and sufficient truth conditions on the use of simple spatial motion verbs. I believe however, that the methodology presented in this paper offers an appropriate framework for continuing that work.

7. RELATED WORK

The work described in this paper sits in the context of much prior work. Leech (1969), Miller (1972), Schank (1973), Jackendoff (1983, 1990), and Pinker (1989) all present alternative representations for simple spatial motion verbs. None of this prior work perceptually grounds the presented representations. Thibadeau (1986) describes a system that processes the movie created by Heider and Simmel (1944) and determines when events occur. The Heider and Simmel movie depicts two-dimensional geometric objects moving in a plane. When viewing that movie, most people project an elaborate story onto the motion of abstract objects. Thibadeau's system does not classify event types. It just produces a single binary function over time delineating when an 'event' is said to have occurred. Badler (1975), Adler (1977), Tsotsos (1977), Tsuji et al. (1977), Tsotsos and Mylopoulos (1979), Tsuji et al. (1979), Okada (1979), Abe et al. (1981), and Borchardt (1985) all describe various implemented and unimplemented strategies for grounding the non-metaphoric meanings of simple spatial motion verbs in animated line-drawings, though only Borchardt's system utilizes changing support, contact, and attachment relations as a central part of the definition of event types. Borchardt's system receives support and contact information as input, in contrast to my system, which calculates such information using counterfactual simulation. Herskovits (1986) describes an unimplemented theory of the truth conditions underlying English spatial prepositions. Regier (1992) describes an implemented system that can learn the truth conditions on the use of spatial terms in a variety of languages in a language-independent fashion. Funt (1980) describes a counterfactual simulator for determining support relationship between objects in a static image. His system operates on a concentric retinotopic bitmap representation of the image rather than on line drawings. Cremer (1989) and Kramer (1990a, b) describe more conventional kinematic simulators that take physical accuracy to be primary and collision detection to be secondary. Freyd et al. (1988) presents experimental evidence that humans subconsciously imagine things falling when their source of support is removed.

8. CONCLUSION

I have described a computer program that recognizes the occurrence of simple spatial motion events in animated line drawings. I presented an event logic for describing classes of event types and used that logic to define a number of simple spatial motion verbs. I argued that the truth conditions of such verbs depend crucially on the notions of support, contact, and attachment. I showed how the truth values of such primitives can be recovered from perceptual input by a process of counterfactual simulation, predicting the effect of hypothetical changes to the world on the immediate future. Finally, I argued that such counterfactual simulation should be based on naive physical constraints such as substantiality, continuity, gravity, and ground plane, and not on Newtonian physics.

The main goal of this work is to develop a sound methodology for formalizing the meanings of verbs and studying the relationship between verb meaning and perception. This paper however, offers only an initial attempt at developing such a methodology. I do not claim that the verb definitions I give in Table III are correct in their current form. They clearly suffer from numerous deficiencies. I also do not claim that the perceptual primitives given in Table I or the combining forms given in Table II are adequate for constructing the ultimate necessary and sufficient truth conditions for all verbs, or even the ones discussed in this paper. I nonetheless do claim that the methodology that I employ in this paper – of precisely defining the semantics of the verb meaning representation language via perceptual grounding and experimentally verifying that the representation language combined with the definitions phrased in that language accurately collectively reflect the truth conditions on verb use – is the only methodology that will yield quality lexical semantic representations. Future work will attempt to remove the deficiencies of the current system within this methodological framework.

ACKNOWLEDGEMENTS

This research was supported in part by an AT&T Bell Laboratories Ph.D. scholarship to the author, by a Presidential Young Investigator Award to Professor Robert C. Berwick under National Science Foundation Grant DCR-85552543, by a grant from the Siemens Corporation, and by the Kapor Family Foundation. This research was also supported in part by ARO grant DAAL 03-89-C-0031, by DARPA grant N00014-90-J-1863, by NSF grant IRI 90-16592, by Ben Franklin grant 91S.3078C-1, and by the Canadian Natural Sciences and Engineering Research Council. Part of this research was performed while the author was visiting Xerox PARC as a research intern and as a consultant. I wish to thank Stuart Russell for pointing me to Shoham (1987), and Martha Palmer, Philip Resnik, Michael White, and the two anonymous referees for reading and commenting on earlier drafts of this paper. Any remaining errors are, of course, my own. This paper previously appeared in the Proceedings of SPIE-93.

NOTES

[1] The relation $i = j$ is true if and only if i and j start and end at the same time. The relation $i < j$ is true if and only if i ends before j begins. The relation imj is true if and only if i ends precisely when j begins. The relation ioj is true if and only if i starts before j starts and ends after j starts but before j ends. The relation isj is true if and only if i and j start at the same time but j ends after i does. The relation ifj is true if and only if i and j end at the same time but j starts before i

does. The relation idj is true if and only if i starts after j does and ends before j does. The relations $>$, mi, oi, si, fi, and di denote variants of the relations $<$, m, o, s, f, and d with reversed argument order.

[2] Appropriate cognitive modeling of the physical processes that constitute the support relationship for airplanes is beyond the scope of this paper.

[3] Recall that in the implementation discussed here, the joint model is given as input to ABIGAIL on a per-frame basis. In the implementation discussed in Siskind (1992), the joint model is computed from the image simultaneously with the layer model for each frame.

[4] The fact that there is no way to prevent the eye from falling during counterfactual simulation and also no way to have the eye be part of the man is a limitation of the world ontology currently incorporated into ABIGAIL.

REFERENCES

Abe, N., Soga, I. & Tsuji, S. (1981). A Plot Understanding System on Reference to Both Image and Language. In Proceedings of *The Seventh International Joint Conference on Artificial Intelligence*, 77–84, Vancouver, BC.

Adler, M. R. (1977). Computer Interpretation of Peanuts Cartoons. In Proceedings of *The Fifth International Joint Conference on Artificial Intelligence*, 608, Cambridge, MA.

Allen, J. F. (1983). Maintaining Knowledge About Temporal Intervals. *Communications of the ACM* **26**(11): 832–843.

Badler, N. I. (1975). Temporal Scene Analysis: Conceptual Descriptions of Object Movements. Technical Report 80, University of Toronto Department of Computer Science.

Borchardt, G. C. (1985). Event Calculus. In Proceedings of *The Ninth International Joint Conference on Artificial Intelligence*, 524–527, Los Angeles, CA.

Cremer, J. F. (1989). *An Architecture for General Purpose Physical System Simulation – Integrating Geometry, Dynamics, and Control*. PhD thesis, Cornell University. Available as TR 89-987.

Dowty, D. R. (1979). *Word Meaning and Montague Grammar*. D. Reidel Pub. Co.: Boston, MA.

Freyd, J. J., Pantzer, T. M. & Cheng, J. L. (1988). Representing Statics as Forces in Equilibrium. *Journal of Experimental Psychology, General* **117**(4): 395–407.

Funt, B. V. (1980). Problem-Solving with Diagrammatic Representations. *Artificial Intelligence* **13**(3): 201–230.

Hayes, P. J. (1984). The Second Naive Physics Manifesto. In Hobbs, J. & Moore, R. C. (eds.) *Formal Theories of The Commonsense World*. Ablex: Norwood, NJ.

Heider, F. & Simmel, M. (1944). An Experimental Study of Apparent Behavior. *American Journal of Psychology* **57**: 243–259.

Herskovits, A. (1986). *Language and Spatial Cognition: An Interdisciplinary Study of the Prepositions in English*. Cambridge University Press: New York, NY.

Jackendoff, R. (1983). *Semantics and Cognition*. The MIT Press: Cambridge, MA.

Jackendoff, R. (1990). *Semantic Structures*. The MIT Press: Cambridge, MA.

Kramer, G. A. (1990a). Geometric Reasoning in the Kinematic Analysis of Mechanisms. Technical Report TR-91-02, Schlumberger Laboratory for Computer Science.

Kramer, G. A. (1990b). Solving Geometric Constraint Systems. In Proceedings of *The Eighth National Conference on Artificial Intelligence*, 708–714. Boston, MA.

Krifka, M. (1992). Thematic Relations as Links Between Nominal Reference and Temporal Constitution. In Sag, I. A. & Szabolcsi, A. (eds.) *Lexical Matters*. CSLI.

Leech, G. N. (1969). *Towards a Semantic Description of English*. Indiana University Press.

Leslie, A. M. (1988). The Necessity of Illusion: Perception and Thought in Infancy. In Weiskrantz, L. (ed.), *Thought without Language*, Chapter 8, 185–210. Oxford University Press: New York, NY.

Miller, G. A. (1972). English Verbs of Motion: A Case Study in Semantics and Lexical Memory. In Melton, A. W. & Martin, E. (eds.) *Coding Processes in Human Memory*, Chapter 14, 335–372. V. H. Winston and Sons Inc.: Washington, DC.

Okada, N. (1979). SUPP: Understanding Moving Picture Patterns Based on Linguistic Knowledge. In Proceedings of *The Sixth International Joint Conference on Artificial Intelligence*, 690–692, Tokyo.

Pinker, S. (1989). *Learnability and Cognition*. The MIT Press: Cambridge, MA.

Regier, T. P. (1992). *The Acquisition of Lexical Semantics for Spatial Terms: A Connectionist Model of Perceptual Categorization*. Ph.D. thesis, University of California at Berkeley.

Schank, R. C. (1973). The Fourteen Primitive Actions and Their Inferences. Memo AIM-183, Stanford Artificial Intelligence Laboratory.

Shoham, Y. (1987). Temporal Logics in AI: Semantical and Ontological Considerations. *Artificial Intelligence* 33(1): 89–104.

Siskind, J. M. (1992). *Naive Physics, Event Perception, Lexical Semantics, and Language Acquisition*. Ph.D. thesis, Massachusetts Institute of Technology, Cambridge, MA.

Spelke, E. S. (1988). The Origins of Physical Knowledge. In Weiskrantz, L. (ed.), *Thought Without Language*, Chapter 7, 168–184. Oxford University Press: New York, NY.

Thibadeau, R. (1986). Artificial Perception of Actions. *Cognitive Science*. 10(2): 117–149.

Tsotsos, J. K. (1977). Some Notes on Motion Understanding. In Proceedings of *The Fifth International Joint Conference on Artificial Intelligence*, 611, Cambridge, MA.

Tsotsos, J. K. & Mylopoulos, J. (1979). ALVEN: A Study on Motion Understanding by Computer. In Proceedings of *The Sixth International Joint Conference on Artificial Intelligence*, 890–892, Tokyo.

Tsuji, S., Morizono, A. & Kuroda, S. (1977). Understanding a Simple Cartoon Film by a Computer Vision System. In Proceedings of *The Fifth International Joint Conference on Artificial Intelligence*, 609–610, Cambridge, MA.

Tsuji, S., Osada, M. & Yachida, M. (1979). Three Dimensional Movement Analysis of Dynamic Line Images. In Proceedings of *The Sixth International Joint Conference on Artificial Intelligence*, 896–901, Tokyo.

Vendler, Z. (1967). *Linguistics in Philosophy*. Cornell University Press, Ithaca, NY.

Verkuyl, H. J. (1989). Aspectual Classes and Aspectual Composition. *Linguistics and Philosophy* 12(1): 39–94.

Artificial Intelligence Review **8**: 393–408, 1994–5.

Connectionist Visualisation of Tonal Structure

NIALL GRIFFITH

Department of Computer Science, University of Exeter, Prince of Wales Road, Exeter, EX4 4PT, England; E-mail: ngr@dcs.exeter.ac.uk

Abstract. Some forms of artificial neural network models develop representations that have a high visual information content. An example of this kind of network is the Kohonen Feature Map (KFM). This paper describes how a KFM can be used in a model that categorises memorised sequential patterns of notes into representations of key and degrees of a musical scale. These patterns are derived from abstractions of musical sounds identified with pitch and interval. Both key and degree are important musical structures in the cognitive organisation of tonality. The acquisition of tonal organisation for music is analogous to the acquisition of language. The representations developed within the KFM form a map that can be seen to correspond directly with the images used by musicians to represent key relations.

Key words: music, images, tonality, pitch use, interval use, sequence categorisation, Kohonen Feature Maps.

1. INTRODUCTION

This paper describes the use of a particular form of self-organising artificial neural network in the context of a model that represents and classifies pitch use in melodies. The artificial neural network (ANN) described is the Kohonen Feature Map (KFM) (Kohonen 1989), which has been used to visualise two musical structures – key and degree – in the context of a model of key identification and pitch abstraction. This model uses various ANN paradigms in a modular fashion (Griffith 1993b). The recognition of the similarities between many aspects of language and music – not least their use of sound – and the many linguistic and visual analogies that are used by musicians make the visual representation of musical structure particularly interesting. The paper first describes the architecture and processing of a simple two dimensional KFM. The two musical concepts are then introduced and the use of the KFM in the development of maps that reflect the organisation of key and degree. The motivation for this work is the fact that the geometrical properties of ANN models are usually only accessible through analysis of the network after a simulation has been run. However, in the case of the KFM the geometrical properties of the representations and their relations are explicitly represented in a visual form as a surface. This arises as a property of the computations in the network, that is a specific form of Competitive Learning. The KFM is outlined below in the overall context of ANN's.

229

2. SELF-ORGANISING TOPOLOGICAL MAPS

An artificial neural network (ANN) is a configuration of idealised computational *units* that models networks of *neurons* in a brain. The analogy is generally conceived to be functional rather than physiologically plausible. Any ANN can be defined in outline as (i) a set or sets of units, (ii) a set or sets of links (called weights or connections) between these units, and (iii) a function or set of functions which defines the computations over the units and their connections.

Competitive Learning (von der Malsburg 1973, Rumelhart and Zipser 1986, Carpenter and Grossberg 1987, Kohonen 1989) is a self-organising network that is used to cluster sets of instances into *categories*. The representation of each category exemplifies the instances associated with it. Each potential category is associated with a set of receptive weights. The arrangement of such a network can be seen in Figure 1a. The process of classification proceeds by each instance in the data set 'stimulating' the weights of each of the units.[1] The differences between an input and the network's units results in different levels of activation across the units. These then compete, each unit inhibiting other units while exciting itself. Eventually, the net settles into a stable state with one active unit.[2] The chosen unit's weights are then modified by decreasing the distance between the unit's weights and the instance's values according to the following rule:

$$(1) \qquad \mathbf{w}_{i,j}(t + 1) = \mathbf{w}_{i,j}(t) + \eta(\mathbf{x}_j(t) - \mathbf{w}_{i,j}(t))$$

where $\mathbf{w}_{i,j}$ is the weight value and $\mathbf{x}_j$ is the instance value and η is the rate of charge $-0 < \eta < 1$.

The result of classifying a data set using Competitive Learning is the creation of a set of discrete exemplars, see Figure 1b, each one being associated with a network unit. The representation developed at each unit approximates the point that lies at the geometrical centre of the set of instances mapped into it (Hinton 1989).

In a standard Competitive Learning network the unit values, or exemplars, each reflect a set of instances that does not overlap with any other set. An exemplar

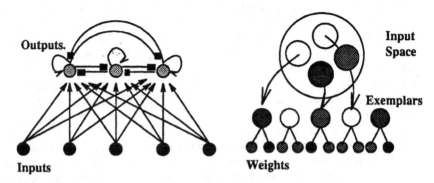

Fig. 1. (a) A Competitive Learning network showing its competitive links. Positive links are arrows, and negative links are filled boxes. (b) An input space mapped into discrete partitions.

is in effect like a bucket. Once an instance has been placed in the bucket it has no influence outside of it. However, a standard Competitive Learning network can be adapted so that the organisation of the representations it forms are not discrete, but continuous. The principle adaptation is to associate learning across a number of units in a Kohonen Feature Map (KFM) (Kohonen 1989). Before describing the KFM's usefulness in integrating representations and visualisation we will outline its architecture and learning algorithm. Figure 2 shows the arrangement of elements in a two dimensional KFM.

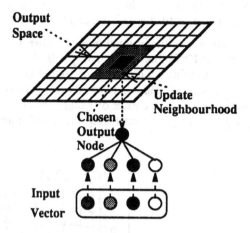

Fig. 2. A single layered, two-dimensional Kohonen feature map.

The KFM architecture consists of a set of output units **O**, each associated with a weight vector $\mathbf{W}_j$. The KFM takes as input normalised vectors. As has been said, the most significant difference between Competitive Learning and the KFM is the use of a mechanism that distributes learning over an area associated with a chosen unit. For example, in a two dimensional KFM learning takes place in a group around the chosen unit. This is shown in Figure 2. During learning the size of this area is reduced from its initial setting, which is usually a large fraction of the network's total area. The important network functions in a KFM are the calculation of the distance between an input and the output weights – Equation (2), choosing the nearest unit – Equation (3), and the updating of the weights – Equation (4).

$$(2) \qquad \mathbf{d}_j = \sum_{i=1}^{N-1} \mathbf{x}_i(t) - \mathbf{w}_{i,j}(t))^2$$

$$(3) \qquad \mathbf{w}_c = \min\{\mathbf{d}: j = 0 \dots N - 1\}$$

$$(4) \qquad \text{if} \quad j \in \mathbf{N}_* \quad \mathbf{w}_{i,j}(t+1) = \mathbf{w}_{i,j}(t) + \eta(t)(\mathbf{x}_j(t) - \mathbf{w}_{i,j}(t))$$

where $\mathbf{w}_{i,j}$ is the i'th weight of j'th output unit, $\mathbf{x}_i$ is the i'th weight of the input vector $\mathbf{X}$, t is the time, $\mathbf{d}_j$ is the distance between input and the j'th output unit, $\eta(t)$ is the learning rate at time $t = \eta(0) (1 - t/\mathbf{T})$. N is the number of units in the output layer, c is the subscript of the output unit nearest to the input. $\mathbf{N_*}$ is the neighbourhood associated with $\mathbf{w}_c$.

The learning algorithm for the *standard* KFM can be summarised as follows:

Step 0: Initialise the weights and define the update area.
Step 1: Normalise a chosen instance.
Step 2: Present the chosen instance to the network.
Step 3: Find the unit whose weights are nearest to this instance.
Step 4: Move this unit's weights and its neighbours towards the input vector.
Step 5: Adjust the learning rate and the size of the update neighbourhood.
Step 6: Repeat steps 1 to 5 until the update neighbour is reduced to 0.

The result of training a two dimensional map is shown in Figure 3. The first graph plots the initialised weights ($0.45 < \mathbf{w}_{i,j} < 0.55$) on a 10 by 10, two dimensional, KFM. The training set consisted of 10,000 vectors each containing two randomly generated pairs of values between 0 and 1. The second graph shows how, after training, the initial tight cluster of weights has been transformed into a grid of roughly equidistant points reflecting the distribution of points in the input set.

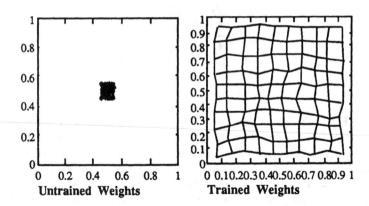

Fig. 3. Plots of an initialised KFM and after 10,000 cycles of training with an η value of 0.3 and an update neighbourhood set to 9.

KFM's are used to organise and compress data and reduce high dimensional descriptions (Ritter 1990, Tattershall 1989). It is a general model of topographic, or topological maps that have been observed in the brains of various species. For the simulations described below it is the relations that emerge upon the surface of the map that are of most interest. The network that will be used is a two dimensional map, and it reflects the geometrical relationships between the instances mapped onto it. Areas of the surface become associated with particular groups of instances and these areas are adjacent to other, similar, areas. The size of these areas reflects the relative frequency of different classes of instance, and the distance that separates different areas of the map reflects the similarity between the representations in these areas. The change between categories is continuous, change across the surface of the map is gradual, and the map can therefore be said to preserve the topology of the input space.

The simplicity of the KFM algorithm belies its computational power as a mechanism for ordering sets of data. The integration of representations that emerge on the surface of such maps is useful because it models directly, and moreover allows us to view, the geometry of the representational space that is created. The power of the KFM as a mechanism and as a visualisation will be used in a model that constructs representations of musical structures. This domain is appropriate because the use of visualisations in music is very broad, The printed score uses the rise and fall of printed notes on the stave to reflect the rise and fall of actual pitches. Pitches are described as high or low, cadences drop, instrumentation colours, and pieces are often described as a journey through musical space, with a leaving and a return. Structural concepts in music, some of which are quite abstract, for example the relationship between keys and degrees, are represented via spatial ideas and images. Before describing the use of the model we will outline these two musical structures emphasising the role of visualisation in their representation.

3. IMAGES OF KEY AND DEGREE

In Western tonal music *keys* are seen as a family of scales that are more and less distantly related to each other. The image that represents most directly this family is called the *The Circle Of Fifths* and it is shown in Figure 4.

On this circle the representation of distance is seen in terms of the length of the arc between two points (keys) on the circumference of the circle. Keys are maximally distant when they lie at opposite ends of a diameter of the circle.

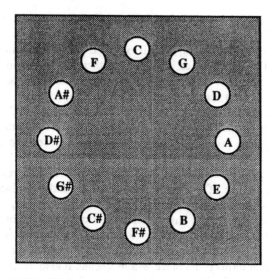

Fig. 4. The Circle of Fifths. The order of the keys is shown round the circumference of the circle.

The actual relations that it represents arise from the use that Western tonal music makes of a subset of seven out of twelve pitch classes, the Chromatic Set. Each key uses a different subset, or scale, of seven pitches, and each scale overlaps with other scales. The number of pitches shared by two keys determines the baseline of how closely the keys are related. The pitch membership of the Major scales is shown in Table I.

Table I

The pattern of pitch classes used within the twelve major scales. Each pitch class is identified by the scale position that pitch occupies within a scale

Pitch Membership of Major Scales

Pitch Classes

Keys	c	c#	d	d#	e	f	f#	g	g#	a	a#	b
C	1		2		3	(4)		5		6		7
G	4		5		6		(7)	1		2		3
D		7	1		2		3	4		5		6
A		3	4		5		6		7	1		2
E		6		7	1		2		3	4		5
B		2		3	4		5		6		7	1
F#		5		6		7	1		2		3	4
C#	7	1		2		3	4		5		6	
G#	3	4		5		6		7	1		2	
D#	6		7	1		2		3	4		5	
A#	2		3	4		5		6		7	1	
F	5		6		7	1		2		3	4	
C	1		2		3	4		5		6		7

For example, the keys of **C** and **G** share all but one pitch and are adjacent on the circle. The pitch that differs between the two scales is the fourth and seventh positions of the scales. A pair of these pitches are shown enclosed in parentheses in Table I. The scale whose fourth pitch is moved one step up, or *sharpened*, by a semitone becomes a scale in which the sharpened pitch occupies the seventh position in the new scale. The new key is based upon the pitch a fifth above the original scale. Thus, if the pitch **f** in the scale of **C** major is changed to **f#** the scale becomes **G** major. Table I shows the set of transformations that form the key system in tabular form. The circle is closed when the rotational transformations return to the key of **C**.

The changes in scale membership is associated with changes in the position and relative importance of pitches within the scale, and this also can be seen in Table I. The change from **C** to **G** major may involve changing the membership of the scale by only one pitch, but the scale positions of all the unchanged pitches are different. Thus, **c** moves from position 1 in **C** to position 4 in **G**, etc..

The position of a pitch in a scale is important for two reasons. It not only describes a pitch in terms of its place within a scale. It also describes a scale independently of any particular scale. This form of representation is significant because we remember melodies, at least in part, in terms of an abstract scale (Dowling 1984, 1988).

The description of the abstract scale comes in various forms. One type of scale that is used in teaching is the tonic sol-fa, in which pitches are identified by a mnemonic: **Doh Ray Me Fah Soh Lah Te**. Another system is that of scale degrees in which scale positions are described by accented arabic numerals: î 2̂ 3̂ 4̂ 5̂ 6̂ 7̂. The relationship between pitch height, pitch class and scale position is shown in Figure 5. Although these (and other) schemas are used for varying purposes, they share three characteristics. (i) The scale they describe is independent of pitch class, (ii) it describes the span of one octave and (iii) that octave is not specified.

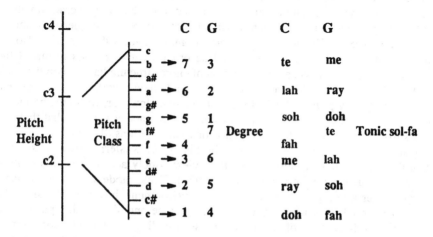

Fig. 5. The relationship between pitch, pitch class and degree of the scale.

The use of the circle to signify the key relations we hear is part of a more general set of relations and equivalences between vision and audition (Bregman 1990). For example the two modalities can be transformed in similar ways (Shepard 1984, 1987, 1982), e.g. by rotation and transposition. The implications of these connections will not be discussed further here. However, the similarities between the abstract manipulations that we can perform on pitches and images suggests comparisons between the processing and representation of the two modalities that was recognised as long ago as Aristotle in his idea of a common-sense (Barnes 1989). What is of interest in this context is that the geometrical properties of neural networks can used to develop a *structural analogy* in which the geometrical composition of the complete representational space can be seen to conform directly to a commonly used image of tonal structure. In this case this involves using a model that develops topological relationships between representations within an ANN mechanism to visualise the musical structures of key and degree.

Over the last 30 or so years various models of the way that people are able to recognise the key of a pieces of music have been proposed (Simon 1986,

Winograd 1968, Longuet-Higgins and Steedman 1970, Holtzmann 1977, Ulrich 1977, Krumhansl 1990a and Huron and Parncutt 1993). The mechanisms defined within these models have always assumed a fully developed sense of key, and little attention has been paid to how our sense of tonality develops. Interestingly, the work of Longuet-Higgins and Steedman (1970) included a visualisation of tonal coherence based upon intervals of a 3rd and 5th. However, this map played no part in the actual model itself, which used an algorithm based upon set membership, and explicit musical rules mainly relevant to a brief period of musical development (see also Holtzmann 1977). The algorithm also involved backtracking in its search strategy – which limits its plausibility as a cognitive model. The development of artificial neural network (ANN) models has allowed the development of tonality to be approached for the first time. ANN's are inductive mechanisms, and as such can be used to model the processes involved in *learning* about musical structure via simulated exposure to pieces of music (Bharucha 1987). The work of Leman (Leman 1990, 1992) should also be mentioned in this context as the model he proposes uses KFM's to model the organisation of chords via a representation of chord structure based upon the work of Parncutt (1989) and (Terhardt *et al.* 1982b, a). Leman's work is a good example of a more strictly psychophysical view of tonality. However, while the harmonic constituents of musical pitches are obviously necessary, it appears that they are not sufficient to explain the emergence of tonal relations. The variety of tonal organisation in different musics and the history of western music all suggest that the tonality has no absolute value, a view widely accepted in this century by major musical thinkers (Stravinsky 1970). Thus, models such as Leman's cannot offer a complete picture of tonal development, however plausible the images of tonal structure they present. The scope and size of this paper does not allow a discussion of all the issues surrounding what might constitute a convincing psychoacoustic representation, or what representational transforma-tions occur in the processes involved in deriving and using concepts such as categorical pitch and pitch class (to name but a few), or whether these concepts are only analytical descriptions or functioning constituents of tonal understanding. Given the relativity of tonality the approach adopted here has been to look at the possible influence of the way that pitches[3] are used. Can fundamental tonal structures be derived from patterns of pitch use? Initially, the approach taken to investigating pitch use has been through the statistics associated with it, and the clearest way of describing these statistics is at the level of categorical pitch class identity.

4. A MODEL OF KEY AND DEGREE

The context in which the visualisation of key and degree takes place is a self-organising model that abstracts key and degree identities from nursery rhyme melodies. The identities emerge from two connected processes, outlined in Figure 6, exploiting two streams of information. Key identities are developed from a stream of pitch identities, while abstract pitch or degree is identified from a stream

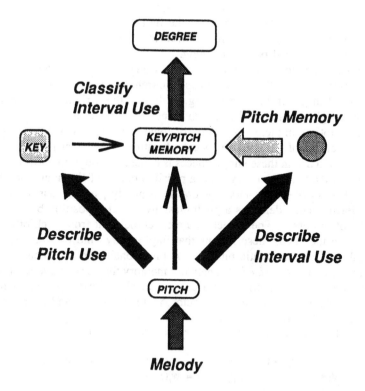

Fig. 6. An outline of the model used to classify memories of pitch use into key and memories of interval use into degree. Identified key is used to focus the process categorising interval use through pitch-in-key memories. When these memories are categorised exemplars representing degrees of the scale emerge.

of interval identities associated with pitches. The model uses the keys identified from pitch use to define the categorical reference of the process classifying the use of intervals.

The identification of keys as simple pitch sets, outlined in Section 3 above, is in fact quite difficult because of the overlap between the scales (Griffith 1993a). With only one pitch difference between nearest neighbour scales, the absence of some pitches, or the inclusion of accidentals, will make clear identification difficult. This is in fact a problem that beset the model proposed by Longuet-Higgins and Steedman (1970), which required the invocation of various genre specific rules. However, the way in which pitches are used by different scales varies, and so all pitches are not of equal importance. The simplest descriptor of pitch use in different scales is the frequency with which pitches occur. The frequency of occurrence of states in descriptions of the world is well known to be a property that nervous systems are sensitive to (Deutsch 1975, 1978, Krumhansl 1990b), and in the case of tonality there are persuasive arguments why the statistics of pitch use play a part in the definition of tonal structure (Griffith 1993b, Krumhansl 1990a). The purpose of this model is not to specify a neuro-psychologically plausible mechanism, but to show that the frequency of occurrence of pitch is a sufficiently stable source of information to allow categorisation in a functional model of musical pattern learning.

The input to the model is a set of nursery rhyme melodies represented in vectors of 1's and 0's. A set of 60 rhymes was used in training the networks, and a further 25 were used in generalisation testing. Although these rhymes can hardly be seen as a complete basis from which to induce tonal relations, just as the Circle of Fifths is not a complete description of tonal relations, such rhymes form an important element of children's musical education. What is at issue is whether patterns of pitch use in these simple pieces is coherent enough to allow categories to emerge. If they are then they offer a possible model of the induction of tonal relations that is potentially more general than purely psychoacoustic or formal models. Each vector identifies a pitch class by a vector position being set to 1 while the others are 0. These vectors are all equidistant from each other, there is nothing in the vector descriptions that implies any kind of structure except membership of the chromatic pitch set. A tune consists of a sequence of these vectors, which are *memorised* by a network memory that is sensitive to the occurrence of pitches. This memory is a process of slow learning implemented as follows. Where values in the input vector X are between 0 and n, the learning in the memory, where x_i is the input value, w_i is the memory value, initialised to zero, and the response of the memory is determined by η:

$$\text{if} \quad x_i(t) > 0 : \quad w_i(t + 1) = w_i(t) + \eta(x_i(t))(1 - w_i(t))$$
$$\text{else} \qquad\qquad : \quad w_i(t + 1) = w_i(t)$$

This learning causes the memory to reflect the frequency of occurrence of different pitches. The contents of the memory is categorised in an ART2[4] (Carpenter and Grossberg 1987) at the end of a song – with 93%–98% success and then mapped on a KFM. The use of the KFM to visualise keys will be described in Section 5. The classes developed in the ART2 network are quite clear and allow, for example, the identification of the key of a piece as it progresses with over 90% accuracy. The representations developed within the model are discrete. The model is fully described in (Griffith 1993a, 1993b, Griffith, in press).

The relations between pitches within scales is slightly more complex to model. Interval is the first order difference between pitches. However, intervals are not unique to particular pitch pairs, and the major scale is as much a pattern of intervals as it is particular pitches. This pattern of intervals involves single steps or semi-tones (s), or double steps or tones (T). Table II shows the pattern of

Table II
The pattern of pitch classes and intervals in the scale of C

Pitch and interval pattern for C Major													
Pitches	c		d		e		f		g		a		b	
Intervals		T		T		S		T		T		T		S

intervals laid next to the major scale of **C**. The pattern is the same whatever major scale is being used.

The use of interval allows direct comparison of pitch use in different scales. To compare the use of intervals associated with pitches in different keys the pattern of intervals were memorised in a set of memories associated with the different pitch classes in different keys. The process involved in identifying degree is otherwise very similar to that used for key. A stream of vectors representing the intervals associated with the pitches in the melodies was memorised firstly, in an echoic memory (Grossberg 1978, Gjerdingen 1989a, 1990), that traced the order of intervals over a short time window, and secondly the contents of this window was memorised in a memory similar to that used to tract the frequency of occurrence of ptich – see above. The pattern presented to the network reflects the frequency of occurrence of intervals associated with different pitch classes in different keys. When these patterns of interval are classified the units that emerge in the ART2 network are identified with the degrees of the scale.

The model is more fully described in (Griffith 1993b). However, it should be noted that the model uses the keys identified from pitch use to direct the reference of the memories learning from the second stream of interval information. It is in a crude sense an attentional mechanism based upon categorical reference. This strategy allows the model to develop patterns of intervals over a wider (hence longer term) reference than is possible if it were limited to developing patterns over a single song. By using this kind of focus the model is able to derive representations of the associations between pitch and interval that clearly distinguish the scale position of pitches in different scales. The model derives a functional description of pitch in a totally unsupervised manner.

5. VISUALISING KEYS AND DEGREES

Figure 7 shows the results for a single simulation in which the representations developed within the key units of the ART2 network are learned by a KFM. The keys are arranged over the surface of the map such that the keys are adjacent to each other, as on the Circle of Fifths. The KFM arranges the set of discrete representations that have been categorised in a 12 dimensioned pitch space so that the geometrical relations can be seen directly. The map does not show the actual pattern of value stores in each exemplar. These values are in fact rotations within the twelve dimensional pitch space that reflects directly what musicians know about the relative frequency and importance of pitches in different key contexts. The circle of keys on the map directly reflects this rotation through pitch space quite well, albeit that the order is reversed.

Also, the distance between the different keys on the surface of the map reflects the similarity and dissimilarity of the keys they represent. Figure 8 shows the response of different key units to the developing memory for two songs – *Ding Dong Bell* and *Little Bo Peep* – presented to the trained network in the key of C major. The illustration shows the units arranged with C in the centre of the illustration. The key activations fall away from to either side as the keys become

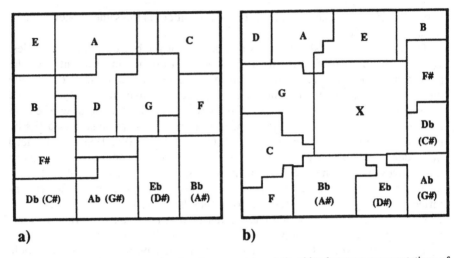

Fig. 7. Kohonen feature map showing the geometric relationships between representations of pitch use of major scales developed from a set of nursery rhymes. (a) shows the net trained with a set of key representations developed from the frequency of occurence of pitch. (b) shows the net trained with the same representations as used in (a) plus the complete set of chromatic pitches.

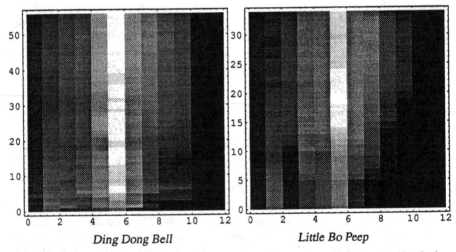

Fig. 8. The activation of the different identified key units in response to the memory developing through Ding Dong Bell and Little Bo Peep. The unit for **C** is placed in the middle of the figure to illustrate the decrease in activation of increasingly distant key units. The order of the key units across the figure is **C# G# D# A# F C G D A E B F#**.

more distant. The key is more quickly established in *Ding Dong Bell*. Once established the activation response of the C unit remains high for the rest of these simple nursery rhymes. The most distant key of **F#** is the least activated of all.

What the KFM allows us to see directly is the structural rotation through the set of keys as a circular arrangement on the surface of the map. The KFM makes explicit the geometrical relations between the key categories, and these can be seen to approximate the circle of fifths. However, the circle is not a perfect circle. Although the sequence of the keys round the map is circular, there is a kink where D and G occupy positions towards the centre of the map. This is because the network fills all its available space. The representations can be centred by including in the training set the representation of pitch use developed over all keys. This assumes the existence of a memory that attends to the occurrences of all pitches irrespective of key or song. The inclusion of this basic representation establishes the full pitch set of which the discrete key representations are subsets. Figure 7b shows the KFM surface trained in this way. The circle has a centre and the keys lie around the periphery, as visualised in the Circle of Fifths.

A similar visualisation of degrees of the scale can be shown with the degrees classified from patterns of interval. When these units are mapped to a KFM they show relations that are remarkably consistent. As in the visualisation of key relations the units are arranged on the surface of the KFM in a way that reflects the functional similarity of the degrees within the scale. This can also be seen in a cluster analysis of the exemplars in Figure 10. Degrees 1, 5 and 4 are the most similar, 2 and 6 are reasonably similar but dissimilar to 1, 5 and 4, while 3 and 7 are also similar but very dissimilar to the others. The areas on the KFM reflect the relative importance of the degree within the scale.

6. DISCUSSION

The images developed on the KFM map allows us to visualise a set of relations that exist only as sequential relationships between pitch and interval

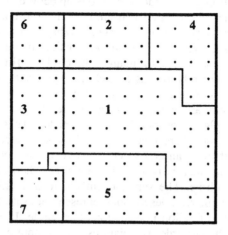

Fig. 9. A Kohonen feature map showing the areas associated with particular degrees of the scale, and the prototypical unit for each degree.

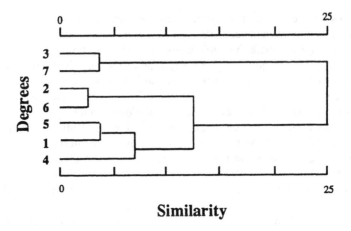

Fig. 10. Cluster analysis of the representations of degrees of the scale.

identities, which are themselves abstractions of real pitches. The visualisation of key categories that emerge from classifying these sequential patterns shows a set of relationships that approximates very well the Circle of Fifths, and while this is not the only structure recognised to organise tonality, it is nevertheless fundamental to the overall organisation of pitch space. Their obvious usefulness as visualisations of the simulation is based upon sound geometrical principles, although one is seen in the geometry of 2D space and the other is represented in a numerical 12D vector space. The process of categorisation in the KFM provides us with an image of key relationships that is directly comparable with the image of the circle, and the overall correctness of the relations in the map is immediately apparent.

However, establishing just what the relationship between the model that derives the map and the mental processes that are conceived to underly the conception of key and degree, is strewn with dangers. What is not advocated here is a notion of the mind's eye in which we *see* music; an image is not a musical structure. However, our ability to imagine the circle of fifths, that is to see the representation of these relations as a circle is appropriate presumably, because there are at some level structural analogies between vision and audition. It may well be that such similarities are based upon underlying processual similarities (Todd and Brown 1994) or sensory integration (Radeau 1994, Stein and Meredith 1993). The fact that we can recognise the analogy and speculate about its origin also implies that there is an equivalence between the mechanism that understands pitch relations, that derives the key map, and the mechanism underlying our conception of circle. The surrogate mechanism in this case is the KFM network, and the geometrical describable representations it constructs. We understand that a complete rotation is analogous to a circle. It is of course possible to speculate about higher order correlations across representational spaces, and the structural similarities that we can conceive between internal representations. While not approaching in this case anything like the complexity of such processes in a real brain, mechanisms such as the KFM are useful, in as much as they integrate processes and representation in a way that delineates the analogical processes they model, and hint about the kind of steps that need to be taken to unravel them. The most important issue that such analogies pose, but cannot answer, is whether there is a common internal representation at some level of abstraction, to which all modalities contribute; or whether there is only cross-modal feedback and correlation that mediates between discrete modalities.

NOTES

[1] The inner product is often used, or inversely, the dissimilarity of the instance and the exemplar is measured by calculating Euclidean Distance between them – Pythagoras' theorem generalised to n dimensions.
[2] Usually, this process is simplified by choosing the unit that is closest to the input.
[3] The generic term pitch is used here rather than 'tone'.
[4] Adaptive Resonance Theory networks are based upon Competitive Learning, which is described in Section 2. The difference between ART and a standard Competitive Learning network lies in the addition of a search mechanism that utilises a vigilance parameter to maintain the stability of acquired categories while maintaining the plasticity of the system when confronted with novel instances.

REFERENCES

Barnes, J. (1989). Aristotle. In Gregory, R. (ed.) *The Oxford Companion to the Mind*, 38–40 Oxford University Press: Oxford.

Bharucha, J. (1987). Music Cognition and Perceptual Facilitation: A Connectionist Framework. *Music Perception* 5(1): 1–30.

Bregman, A. (1990). *Auditory Scene Analysis*, MIT Press: Cambridge, MA.

Carpenter, G. & Grossberg, S. (1987). ART2: Self-Organization of Stable Category Recognition Codes for Analog Input Patterns. *Applied Optics* 26(23), 4919–4930.

Deutsch, D. (1975). Facilitation by Repetition in Recognition Memory for Tonal Pitch. *Memory and Cognition* 3: 263–266.

Deutsch, D. (1978). Delayed Pitch Comparisons and the Principle of Proximity. *Perception and Psychophysics* 23: 227–230.

Dowling, W. (1984). Assimilation and Tonal Structure: Comment on Castellano, Bharucha, and Krumhansl. *Journal of Experimental Psychology* 113(3): 417–420.

Dowling, W. (1988). Tonal Structure and Children's Early Learning of Music. In Sloboda, J. (ed.) *Generative Processes in Music*. Oxford University Press.

Gjerdingen, R. (1989a). Using Connectionist Models to Explore Complex Musical Pattern. *Computer Music Journal* 13(3): 67–75.

Gjerdingen, R. (1990). Categorisation of Musical Patterns by Self-Organizing Neuronlike Network. *Music Perception* 7(4): 339–370.

Griffith, N. (1993a). Modelling the Acquisition and Representation of Musical Tonality as a Function Of Pitch-Use through Self-Organising Artificial Neural Networks. PhD thesis, University of Exeter, Department of Computer Science. Unpublished.

Griffith, N. (1993b). Representing the Tonality of Musical Sequences Using Neural Nets. In Proceedings of The *First International Conference on Cognitive Musicology*, 109–132. Jyväskylä, Finland.

Griffith, N. (1994). The Development of Tonal Centres and Abstract Pitch as Categorisations of Pitch-Use. *Connection Science* 6(3&4): 155–176.

Grossberg, S. (1978). Behavioral Contrast in Short Term Memory: Serial Binary Memory Models or Parallel Continuous Memory Models. *Journal of Mathematical Psychology* 17: 199–219.

Hinton, G. E. (1989), Connectionist Learning Procedures. *Artificial Intelligence* 40: 185–234.

Holtzmann, S. R. (1977). A Program for Key Determination. *Interface*.

Huron, D. & Parncutt, R. (1993). An Improved Key-Tracking Method Encorporating Pitch Salience and Echoing Memory. *Psychomusicology*.

Kohonen, T. (1989). *Self-Organization and Associative Memory*. Springer Verlag: Berlin.

Krumhansl, C. (1990a), *Cognitive Foundations of Musical Pitch*. Oxford University Press: Oxford.

Krumhansl, C. (1990b). Tonal Hierarchies and Rate Intervals in Music Cognition. *Music Perception* 7: 309–324.

Leman, M. (1990). Emergent Properties of Tonality Functions by Self-Organization. *Interface* 19: 85–106.

Leman, M. (1992). The Theory of Tone Semantics: Concept, Foundation, and Application. *Minds and Machines* 2(4): 345–363.

Longuet-Higgins, H. & Steedman, M. (1970). On Interpreting Bach. *Machine Intelligence* 6: 221–239.

Parncutt, R. (1989). *Harmony: Psychoacoustic Approach*. Springer Verlag: Berlin.

Radeau, M. 91994). Auditory-Visual Spatial Interaction and Modularity. *International Journal of Psychology*.

Ritter, H. (1990). Self-Organizing Maps for Internal Representations. *Psychological Research* 52: 128–136.

Rumelhart, D. & Zipser, D. (1986). Feature Discovery by Competitive Learning. In Rumelhart, D. & McClelland, J. (eds.) *Parallel Distributed Processing: Explorations in the Microstructure of Cognition*, Vol. 1, Foundations, MIT Press: Cambridge, MA.

Shepard, R. (1982). Geometric Approximations to the Structure of Musical Pitch. *Psychological Review* 89(4): 305–333.

Shepard, R. (1984). Ecological Constraints on Internal Representation: Resonant Kinematics of Perceiving, Imagining, Thinking, and Dreaming. *Psychological Review* 91: 417–447.

Shepard, R. (1987). Toward a Universal Law of Generalisation for Psychological Science. *Science* 237: 1317–1323.

Simon, H. A. (1968). Perception du pattern musical par auditeur. *Science de l' art* V(2): 28–34.

Stein, B. & Meredith, M. (1993). *The Merging of the Senses*, MIT Press: Cambridge, MA.

Stravinsky, I. (1970). *The Poetics of Music*. Harvard Press. Translated by Arthur Knodel and Ingolf Dahl.

Tattershall, G. (1989). Neural Map Applications. In Alexander I. (ed.) *Neural Computing Architectures*, Chapter 4. MIT Press: Cambridge, MA.

Terhardt, E., Stoll, G. & Seewann, M. (1982a). Algorithm for Extraction of Pitch and Pitch Salience from Complex Tonal Signals. *The Journal of the Acoustical Society of America* 73(3): 679–688.

Terhardt, E., Stoll, G. & Seewann, M. (1982b). Pitch of Complex Signals According to Virtual-pitch Theory: Test, Examples, and Predictions. *The Journal of the Acoustical Society of America* 71(3): 671–678.

Todd, N. P. M. & Brown, G. (in press), Visualization of Rhythmic Structure. *Artificial Intelligence Review*, special issue on *Integration of Natural Language and Vision Processing*, ed. Paul Mc Kevitt.

Ulrich, W. (1977). The Analysis and Synthesis of Jazz by Computer. In Proceedings of *The 5th. IJCAI*, 865–872.

Von der Malsburg, C. (1973). Self-Organizing of Orientation Sensitive Cells in the Striate Cortex. *Kybernetic* 14: 85–100.

Winograd, T. (1968). Linguistics and the Computer Analysis of Tonal Harmony. *Journal of Music Theory* 12(3): 2–49.

Artificial Intelligence Review **8**: 409–430, 1994–5.
© 1995 *Kluwer Academic Publishers. Printed in the Netherlands.*

Use of Captions and Other Collateral Text in Understanding Photographs[1]

ROHINI K. SRIHARI

Center of Excellence for Document Analysis and Recognition (CEDAR), and Department of Computer Science, State University of New York at Buffalo, UB Commons, 520 Lee Entrance – Suite 202, Buffalo, NY 14228–2567, U.S.A.; e-mail: rohini@cs.buffalo.edu

Abstract. This research explores the interaction of textual and photographic information in image understanding. Specifically, it presents a computational model whereby textual captions are used as collateral information in the interpretation of the corresponding photographs. The final understanding of the picture and caption reflects a consolidation of the information obtained from each of the two sources and can thus be used in intelligent information retrieval tasks. The problem of building a general-purpose computer vision system without *a priori* knowledge is very difficult at best. The concept of using collateral information in scene understanding has been explored in systems that use general scene context in the task of object identification. The work described here extends this notion by incorporating picture specific information. A multi-stage system *PICTION* which uses captions to identify humans in an accompanying photograph is described. This provides a computationally less expensive alternative to traditional methods of face recognition. A key component of the system is the utilisation of spatial and characteristic constraints (derived from the caption) in labeling face candidates (generated by a face locator).

Key words: image understanding, natural-language processing, knowledge-based vision, information retrieval, face identification, constraint satisfaction.

1. INTRODUCTION

This paper describes a computational model for 'understanding' pictures based on accompanying, descriptive text. Understanding a picture can be informally defined as the process of identifying relevant people and objects. Several current vision systems (Weymouth 1986) employ the idea of top-down control in picture understanding, by providing the general context of the picture (e.g., airport scene, typical suburban street scene). The theory being presented in this paper carries the notion of top-down control one step further since not only the general context but the actual picture is being described.

At issue in the present research is the problem of identifying useful information (for picture understanding) in the text, extracting and representing this information, and, finally, using it to direct a computer vision system in the task of picture understanding. A system, *PICTION*, based on this model is described which uses information obtained from parsing a natural-language caption of a newspaper photograph to direct the interpretation of the associated photograph.

The computational model hinges on a systematic procedure for constructing a detailed prediction about the structure of a scene based on some descriptive text pertaining to the scene. We can test whether the system has predicted correctly by using a computer vision system to verify the predictions in the associated photographs. This part of the research has implications for knowledge-based vision, since the proposed method will dynamically construct scene descriptions based on information provided to it about the structure of the scene (i.e., when the system is told 'what it is seeing'). These scene descriptions can then be used by an image-processing system to guide the interpretation of the associated picture. We present a control paradigm where top-down collateral information can be efficiently exploited. We show how traditional image understanding architectures can be easily incorporated into this overall system.

This research is most relevant in the context of document image understanding. Pictures with captions are ubiquitous in documents, newspapers and magazines. The information contained in both pictures and captions enhances overall understanding of the accompanying text, and often contributes additional information not contained specifically in the text. This information could subsequently be incorporated into an integrated (text and picture) database as part of a larger information retrieval system which permits *content-based retrieval. Keyword* matching techniques have been used extensively; these keywords are either added manually or correspond to content words in the caption. Image-based techniques such as similarity-based and sketch-based retrieval are also being employed in this task (SPIE 1994).

This research improves upon current technology in several ways. By integrating image and text information in a uniform representation, content-based querying is enabled and the precision and recall of query processing is increased. First, by understanding the caption, more sophisticated retrieval is enabled. For example, if a user wished to retrieve pictures of Hillary Clinton, the photograph bearing the caption 'The President with his wife at a . . .' would be retrieved even though the name 'Hillary Clinton' did not occur in the caption. Second, the automatic tagging of pictures with relevant information (including who, what, where, when as well as general scene classification such as indoor/outdoor) is enabled. Finally, this research permits automatic cropping and labeling of people appearing in the picture through image understanding techniques which efficiently exploit collateral information.

2. PICTION: A CAPTION-BASED FACE IDENTIFICATION SYSTEM

The computational model to be presented in the next section is comprehensive and can be generalised to any situation where photos are accompanied by descriptive text. In describing the model however, it is useful to present working examples based on this model. For this reason, we refer to the system *PICTION* (Srihari 1993, 1991a, b) that identifies human faces in newspaper photographs based on information contained in the associated caption. More specifically, when given a text file corresponding to a newspaper caption and a digitised version of the associated photograph (referred to as an image), the system is able to locate, label, and give information about objects which are relevant to the communicative unit. A common representation for the information content form both the picture and the caption is employed.

PICTION has undergone numerous changes over the past two years, most notably, the development and use of a large-scale language/vision knowledge base, improved parsing abilities, formulation of the entire structure as a constraint satisfaction problem, and improved visual processing. Finally, the system has been re-implemented in LOOM and employs classification-based inference.

Most front-page newspaper photographs tend to have captions that are factual and descriptive, qualities required for this task. PICTION is noteworthy since it provides a computationally less expensive alternative to traditional methods of face recognition in situations where pictures are accompanied by descriptive text. Traditional methods (Weymouth 1986) employ model-matching techniques and thus require that face models be present for all people to be identified by the system; our system does not require this. It will be shown that spatial constraints obtained from the caption, along with a few discriminating visual characteristics (e.g., male/female) are sufficient for eliminating false candidates and correctly identifying faces.

Figure 1 is an example of a digitised newspaper photograph and accompanying caption that the system can handle. The system attempts to isolate and label those parts of the image that correspond to the faces of Mayor Coleman, Michael Illitch and his wife Marian. It should be noted that in this example, the caption assumes that the reader can distinguish between Michael and his wife, and hence they are not identified explicitly. Furthermore, there are two other people in the picture who are not identified in the caption and it is a challenge for the system to select the correct three people. The processing of this example is discussed in later sections.

3. A COMPUTATIONAL MODEL FOR COLLATERAL-BASED VISION

Figure 2 shows the overall control structure of a computer model for solving the state problem. As the diagram illustrates, the four main components of the model are as follows:
- a natural-language processing (NLP) module
- an image understanding (IU) module
- a control module
- an integrated language/vision knowledge base

All four modules employ a common intermediate knowledge representation scheme.

The NLP module is called on only once to parse the caption, extract visual semantics and produce a representation which includes both factual information in the caption as well as a description of the picture in terms of a set of *constraints*.

The Control module subsequently uses the visual constraints in order to direct

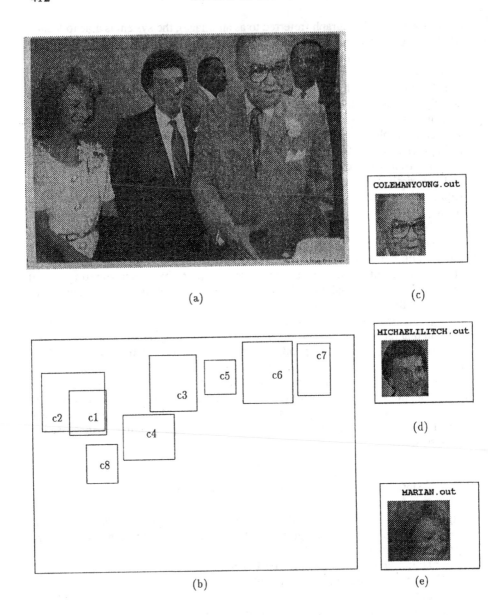

(a)

(c)

(b)

(d)

(e)

Fig. 1. (a) Digitised photograph whose caption is 'Mayor Coleman Young of Detroit, right, at an N.A.A.C.P. dinner last wek. With the Mayor were Michael Illitch, owner of the Detroit Red Wings, and his wife, Marian' (*The New York Times*, May 1, 1989). (b) face candidates; the false candidates c_4 and c_8 were generated due to edges along the shoulder and arm contours being mistakenly interpreted as part of the facial contours. (c)–(e) output of *PICTION*.

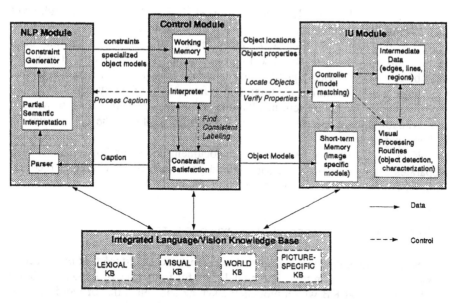

Fig. 2. Computational Model for Collateral-Based Vision. The NLP, IU and Control modules operate on a common knowledge base. Dotted boxes reflect the fact that knowledge bases are interconnected.

the IU module in the interpretation of the picture. The process of satisfying various constraints, spatial and otherwise, results in repeated calls to the IU module. The IU module which is required for this task must have several features which enable it to efficiently exploit collateral information. Some of these specialised features are: constrained search, ability to characterise objects, crude and refined object-location procedures, ability to change parameters and repeat actions, output compatibility with intermediate representation, and the ability to perform bottom-up interpretation when necessary.

3.1. *Intermediate Knowledge Representation*

The model calls for an intermediate knowledge representation suitable for both NLP as well as vision. In particular, the knowledge representation required for this task must provide the following capabilities (or possess the following properties as the case may be): (i) model both declarative and procedural knowledge, (ii) inference mechanisms (such as classification based inference), (iii) easy and fast access to information in the knowledge base, and (iv) access/operate on data outside of the knowledge base when necessary. The last condition may be dropped if the knowledge representation scheme includes analogical representations of data (such as images). Semantic networks have been successfully used for both natural language processing as well as vision since they provide the above capabilities.

PICTION has been implemented in LOOM (ISX 1991) which is a high level programming language and environment for constructing knowledge based systems. It is based on the KL/1 family of semantic networks and has been extensively used in NLP and also to an extent in low level vision. It provides an object-oriented model specification language, classification based inference and multiple programming paradigms in a framework of query based assertion and retrieval. The visual routines have been implemented in C and provisions are available for the interface between C and LISP/LOOM. The system runs on a Sun Sparcstation.

PICTION is interfaced with a larger document understanding system which separates the picture from the caption and performs optical character recognition on the caption before passing it as input to PICTION.

4. INTEGRATED LANGUAGE/VISION KNOWLEDGE BASE

As integrated language/vision knowledge base is essential in the task of extracting visual information from text. The model calls for four types of knowledge bases (KB): (i) a lexical KB which models the syntax and semantics of words as well as their interconnections, (ii) a visual KB which contains *object schemas* (declarative and procedural modeling of an object's shape designed to facilitate object detection) along with a hierarchy of these schemas, (iii) a world KB which contains facts about people, places, events and general domain constraints, and (iv) a picture-specific KB which contains facts specific to previously processed pictures and captions. The latter is used in information retrieval but is not necessary for the processing of a picture and caption.

4.1. *Linguistic Knowledge*

PICTION uses a syntactic/semantic lexical database which has been constructed from the following sources: (i) Longman's Dictionary of Contemporary English (LDOCE), (ii) Oxford Advanced Learner's Dictionary (OALD), (iii) WordNet (Beckwith *et al.* 1991) and (iv) manual augmentation (ontological information and visual semantics). A similar effort in integrating machine-readable sources has been reported in (Knight and Luk 1994). The entire lexicon is represented as a LOOM knowledge base. In the final step (ongoing), further ontological information and visual semantics has been manually added to a subset of words (nouns and verbs). This uses and extends the *Naive Semantics* model (Dahlgren *et al.* 1989) which is a theory of associating commonsense knowledge with words. It is necessary to represent fixed properties of objects such as size and colour, as well as procedural information for certain words and phrases. For example, a recent caption identified one of the people in the corresponding photograph as 'the person wearing the hat'. This should generate a call to an object finder with the location 'above head', and the scalar and shape properties of the object (hat).

In Figure 3 |HAT| is the name of the lexical instance for the word 'hat'. It

```
(tellm (:about |HAT|
 :is-primitive LDOCEconcept
 (WNsynset WNN0206338)
 (vis-info V0438)
 (noun-part LD0030091)))

(defconcept WNN0206338
 :is-primitive WNN02066195
 :annotations
 ((word-list (hat chapeau lid))
  (scale s2)
  ($semantic-feature $clothing)
  (has-part (brim crown hatband))
  (function
    (wear(E,noun,Y) & human(Y)
    & typ-location(E,noun,
    procedure(locate-in-vicinity
    (noun,top-of(locate-part(head(Y)))))))))))
```

Fig. 3. Partial lexicon generation code for the word 'hat'.

contains information from the LDOCE and a pointer to the corresponding WordNet synset concept. 'WNN0206338' represents information form WordNet. Visual information required to detect a hat (such as shape) is associated with the concept 'V0438'; this is explained in the next section. Synonyms for hat include 'chapeau' and 'lid'; 'WNN02066195' is the superconcept of 'hat'. The 'scale' and 'function' slots have been manually instantiated and are used in generating further, picture-specific visual information. Procedural information stored in the function slot specifies that if the event 'wear' is associated with 'hat', and the subject of 'wear' is a human, a typical location for hat is on the head of the associated person. The constraint generator uses this information to generate a locative constraint (described later) which is subsequently used by the control and vision modules in identifying the person wearing the hat.

4.2. *Visual Knowledge*

The knowledge (both declarative and procedural) which is required by a vision system in order to model a particular object and subsequently recognise it is referred to as an object schema. In the computational model being proposed here, object schemas are not static; they can be dynamically specialised (by the constraint generator) from default schemas residing in the visual KB. This is a departure from conventional computer vision systems where object schemas are fixed and cannot be accessed outside the image processing module. Figure 4 depicts the specialization of a face schema with size, orientation and locative information.[2] *Scene schemas* are constructed dynamically as opposed to predefined schemas like 'outdoor suburban scene' which fix a priori the relational model corresponding to the scene. In PICTION, the scene schema is constructed based upon the collateral information obtained from the picture specific caption.

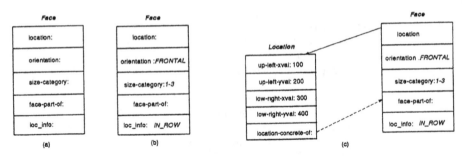

Fig. 4. Specialization of face schema with optional parameters and procedural information. (a) generic face schema in the visual knowledge base; (b) face schema specialised with collateral information (orientation, size and locative information); (c) face schema reflecting the output of the face locator.

The scene schema is implicit in the set of constraints generated by the NLP module based on an analysis of the caption.

4.3. *Visual Hierarchies*

We have seen that words can be organised in a network based on their meanings and semantic relationships. Similarly, visual descriptions of objects can also be organised based on hierarchies such as shape, texture, boundaries, etc.; such a scheme is discussed here. There are many objects for which it is difficult (or unnecessary) to construct detailed object schemas. In these cases it is sufficient to state some of their properties such as natural/man-made, boundary description, etc. Identification of these objects is based on a *blob* theory of object recognition: using constraints that specify size, expected location and a few object properties, the object can be roughly located, which is sufficient for our purposes.

We have defined visual hierarchies in terms of *visual superconcepts* which reflect these visual properties of an object. New links (*visual-is-a, visual-part-of*) have been added between existing WordNet synsets (representing concrete objects) and these superconcepts. Specialised attributes such as size, color, expected location, etc. are added at the synset level. This visual information allows recognition tools (such as segmentation tools, edge detectors, surface detectors) and specialised object detectors for certain common object classes (e.g., human face, tree, building, car) to be appropriately invoked.[3]

Our representation allows objects to be modeled at various resolutions. For example, at the most general level, a tree is a natural object. A more detailed visual model of tree defines the visual parts of a tree as well as the spatial relationships between these parts. These parts are classified according to the chosen set of visual superconcepts. At the most specific level, the description of a tree could include a specialised object schema for trees.

The has-part information in visual hierarchies may differ from the has-part information used in WordNet for the following reasons: (i) the has-part information in WordNet may be too fine-grained to be exploited by a vision system (e.g., shoes can have laces), and (ii) the names of the parts may differ (e.g., the

WordNet entry for 'tree' includes crown, trunk, branches and stump, however the visual description for tree will have a treetop and a trunk). This is illustrated in Figure 5. The node labelled 'foliage' in this figure refers to a specific object schema used to detect foliage.

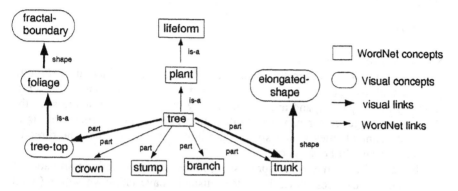

Fig. 5. Visual hierarchy superimposed on WordNet concept hierarchy.

A study in human cognition regarding the task of identifying objects reveals that there is justification for having different abstractions for words and pictures, (Linde 1982) postulates the existence of two separate semantic-memory representations. Joliceur *et al.* (1984) state that both words and pictures may use the same semantic-memory representation; they differ however in the *entry point*, namely the particular level of abstraction in the hierarchy at which the association is made.

The visual KB is being superimposed on the lexical KB by (i) introducing new links between existing concepts, and (ii) by introducing new concepts and superconcepts where necessary. We are in the process of doing this for several objects, both natural and man-made.

As pictures are processed, the world KB is continually updated with new facts about people, objects and events. In PICTION, learning is limited to filling in missing slots as information becomes available. However, it is conceivable to have the system exhibit true machine learning by constructing object schemas for new objects which have been detected based on their relative location to known objects.

5. NLP MODULE

The task of the NLP module is to understand the caption and produce the following: (i) a semantic representation of factual information contained in the text, (ii) defining the task of image interpretation by pointing out objects/regions of interest in the picture, and (iii) generating constraints on the picture which are useful in identifying the objects of interest.

In PICTION, the NLP module (illustrated in Figure 2) is divided into three different stages: syntactic parsing, partial semantic interpretation and constraint generation. For the sake of completeness, we describe each of these stages. However, it is the constraint generator which is the important concept; the choice of a parsing strategy is not important to the overall computational model being described.

5.1. *Parsing*

5.1.1. *Pre-Processing Input*
There are two objectives to this phase. The first is the elimination of *directive* phrases such as 'left-of', 'front row, left to right', etc. These are not essential to the syntactic parsing and are placed directly in the output structure such that the constraint generator can deal with them. This is implemented through a set of attachment rules which specify the noun phrase to which the directive information should be attached.

The second objective of pre-processing is the detection and classification of proper noun sequences. Since input texts usually have unknown words (words not in the lexicon), and the parser requires that all the input words be known, the detection of unknown words, most of which are proper nouns, is critical. In the following example taken from a recent edition of *The Buffalo News*, the proper noun sequences are bracketed:

```
[Vladimir Horwitz] at [Steinway and Sons], [New York], . . .
```

In addition, 'Vladimir Horowitz' is classified as a name, 'Steinway and Sons' is classified as an organization name and 'New York' is looked up and classified as a location.

A hidden Markov model is used to detect proper noun sequences, with a portion of the Penn Treebank corpus (excerpts from *The Wall Street Journal*[4]) used as the training set. We are currently able to detect proper noun sequences with about 90% accuracy. This figure can be (and is being) improved by increasing the size of the training set. Proper noun lists containing appropriate classification information such as gender, location, organization, etc. as well as heuristic rules (involving typical suffixes such as 'Inc.') are employed in the categorization of proper nouns. Proper classification of these proper noun sequences still poses a significant challenge (Mani *et al.* 1993).

5.1.2. *Grammar and Parser*
The lexical function grammar being employed covers basic features of English grammar. Morphological analysis, which is a part of syntactic analysis, is embedded in the lexicon searching functions. We employ a table-driven parser augmented by pseudo/full unification packages (Tomita 1987). The parser is made efficient through compilation of the grammar into an LR Parsing Table. The parser outputs a recursive structure of pairs of features and values. The parser utilises some basic semantic features (e.g., animate/inanimate) in order to verify semantic restrictions during parsing. Such information is purely ontological and can be obtained (through lexicon lookup) without complex semantic analysis. These

```
((SUBJ
  ((CONJLIST
    (*MULTIPLE*
     ((PRED "Coleman Young")
      (OM 1)
      (DIR "right")
      (APADJUNCTS ((PRED "Mayor") (PNN +)))
      (PPADJUNCTS ((PRED "Michael Illitch") (OM 2) (PREP "with"))))
     ((PRED "Marian") (OM 3) (APADJUNCTS ((PRED "wife") (DET "his")))))))))
 (PPADJUNCTS
  ((PRED "dinner")
   (PPADJUNCTS ((PRED "week") (APADJUNCTS ((PRED "last"))) (PREP NIL)))
   (DET "a")
   (PREP "at"))))
```

Fig. 6. Output of parser on the caption of Figure 1.

semantic features are incorporated into the final output structure. Figure 6 illustrates some sample output of the parser.

5.2. *Partial Semantic Interpretation*

The purpose of this phase is to disambiguate among the several syntactic structures output by the parser. Specifically, this phase includes (i) prepositional phrase disambiguation, (ii) word sense disambiguation and (iii) anaphora resolution. Currently, we are only handling cases that can be disambiguated by ontological information present in the lexical database. We are experimenting with statistical techniques for handling (i) and (ii). Anaphoric references are being resolved by the use of weights assigned to various referents depending on their role in the sentence.

5.3. *Constraint Generator*

The constraint generator makes use of the various knowledge bases in the process of extracting visual information from text. In particular, we show how the integrated language/vision knowledge base is used. Input to the constraint generator is the disambiguated parse from the parser.

5.3.1. *Visual Semantics*

In computer vision, 'visual information' refers to the general knowledge about objects which is required in order for a computer vision system to detect them in a scene. This includes the 3D description of an object in terms of its components and the spatial constrains between them. Included in this category is information which relates objects by a common context to model a typical scene in that context. An example of this is the modeling of a typical neighbourhood scene (comprised of streets, houses, trees, etc.) (Weymouth 1986) used in the interpretation of outdoor photographs.

Visual information in collateral text answers the questions who or what is present in the accompanying scene and provides valuable information on how to locate and identify these objects or people. When combined with *a priori* knowledge about the appearance of objects and the composition of typical scenes, visual information conveys the semantics of the associated scene. The resulting semantics provides the basis for top-down scene understanding. We refer to the theory of extracting visual information (and the associated semantics) from text as *visual semantics* (Srihari and Burhans 1994).

We have modeled visual semantics as a set of constraints on the accompanying scene. The set of constraints are divided into four types:

- **Spatial Identifying Constraints** are geometric or topological constraints, such as left-of, above, inside, etc. They can be binary or *n*-ary and describe inter-object relationships. They are used to identify/disambiguate among objects of the same class (e.g., people).
- **Locative constraints** express information about the location of objects in the picture with respect to a particular frame of reference. The information conveyed is procedural in nature; for example, if you are told there is a chair in the corner, it results in the following high-level procedure construct: *loc_in_vic(chair, region(corner(entire_image)))*.
- **Characteristic Constraints** are those which describe properties of objects, hence are unary in nature. Examples include gender and hair color.
- **Contextual Constraints** are those which describe the setting of the picture, and the objects which are expected to appear. For example, the people present (explicitly mentioned in the caption), whether it is an outdoor scene, and general scene context (apartment, airport, etc). Contextual constraints are principally derived from the caption but can also be derived from the photograph (e.g., use of textural properties to determine indoor/outdoor).

Some visual constraints are expressed explicitly as assertions, for example *left_of(Person_a, person-b)*. Locative and characteristic constraints are implicit in the object schema.

As an example, consider the photograph and caption of Figure 1 which was processed successfully by the face-identification system *PICTION*. Figure 7 illustrates the performance of the constraint generator.

```
CONTEXTUAL                                    CHARACTERISTIC
    in_picture(label:Coleman Young, class:human;     has_prop(name:Coleman Young;gender:male;
              label:Michael Illitch, class:human;              race:black)
              label:Marian, class:human)            has_prop(name:Michael Illitch;
              classification(indoor)                          gender:male)
                                                    has_prop(name:Marian (Illitch);
SPATIAL                                                       gender:female)
right_of(Coleman Young,Michael Illitch)
right_of(Coleman Young,Marian (Illitch))
adjacent(Michael Illitch,Marian (Illitch))
```

Fig. 7. Output of the constraint generator on caption of Figure 1. Note that a priori information pertaining to Coleman Young has been utilised.

5.3.2. *Automatic Generation of Visual Constraints*

In PICTION, the constraint generator has been written as a top-down rule-based system which uses LOOM concepts to drive the semantic 'parsing'. LOOM concepts have been written which represent various syntactic parse structures which can be encountered, at both the top and inner levels of the parse tree. LOOM methods which drive the constraint generator have corresponding actions which are invoked depending on whether the input matches a particular concept.

There are three main categories of rules:

- **Word-based**
  Spatial and characteristic constraints are frequently indicated by single words. Examples include left, right, above and below, as well as characteristics such as hair colour and titles like President.
- **Phrase-based**
  Locative and characteristic constraints are often indicated by directive phrases. Examples include 'between the two buildings' and 'wearing the striped shirt'. Such rules make extensive use of procedural information stored in the linguistic knowledge base which relate objects (such as 'shirt') to typical predicates such as 'wear'.
- **Sentence-based**
  Contextual constraints can generally be inferred at the sentence level, taking into account the various objects mentioned and their relations and properties. An example of this is the 'SVOPP' rule which states that if the sentence is of the form subject-verb-object-prepositional_phrase, and, if both the subject and object represent humans, and, if the PP represents a time and/or location, then, propose that both the subject and the object are in the picture.

The top-level rules are based on syntactic structure and attempt to predict which people (or objects) are in the picture. Verifying the antecedents of these rules (e.g., is the person deceased?) causes other rules to be fired. The final action is to generate identifying information for every person/object predicted to be in the picture.

6. CONTROL MODULE

Previous sections have described the automatic generation of collateral information from accompanying, descriptive text. From this point on, the focus is on the efficient exploitation of collateral information in the task of image interpretation. This task is jointly handled by the control and image understanding modules. Strat and Fischler (1991) discuss the use of context in visual processing but focuses solely on the exploitation of low-level collateral information (e.g., lighting conditions). Furthermore, it does not address the generation of these constraints.

The control module is a combination of data, namely, working memory and control. The interaction between this module and both the NLP and IU modules is described in separate sections. Working memory contains information related to the processing of the current input image and caption. In particular, it consists of (i) object schemas specific to those objects/people predicted to be in the picture, (possibly specialised by instantiating optional parameters or by procedural attachments) and (ii) spatial, characteristic, locative and contextual constraints generated by the constraint generator. Working memory also holds data representing intermediate states of the constraint satisfier. Finally, it is here that information from the caption (e.g., name of person) is consolidated with information from visual processing (e.g., coordinates of face location).

6.1. *Interaction with NLP Module*

The control module calls on the constraint generator which in turn calls the parser, assists in parsing, generates constraints and returns information to working memory. Control passes to the NLP module only once to process the caption. Currently there is no feedback to the NLP module from the control module in terms of disambiguating parses, etc. although this may be developed in the future. The output of the constraint generator may require further processing before it can be processed by the IU module. This is the case with locational constraints which are embedded as procedural information in visual object models (e.g., $loc\_in\_vic(a, b)$); the control module translates these into a set of directives for the IU module. Typically, this consists of instantiating optional parameters in object schemas.

6.1.1. *Spatial Primitives*

The NLP module employs a rich set of spatial primitives including qualitative prepositions such as 'near' and 'next to'. The control module gives a quantitative interpretation to these spatial primitives based on the relationship between the bounding boxes of the objects involved. Since spatial primitives are used in this task for interpreting scenes rather than for generating natural language descriptions of a scene, the spatial primitives are 'weaker' than those seen in other applications. We are investigating the use of fuzzy logic in this area (Abella and Kender 1993). At this point, the only object shape representation being used in PICTION is a rectangular bounding box which suffices for human faces. As new object classes are added, a more flexible shape representation is required (e.g., based on area, center, axes, elongation, etc.).

6.2. *Interaction with IU Module*

Our computational model for collateral-based vision is built 'on top of' existing IU architectures, employing top-down control in an efficient manner. It uses picture-specific information rather than general scene information. There are three key modifications (and/or enhancements) proposed to traditional IU architectures which enable the efficient exploitation of collateral information. These are in the areas of: (i) Visual Object modeling, (ii) Constraint Satisfaction as a paradigm for higher-level control, and (iii) Communication with IU Module. As stated earlier, object schemas can be accessed/modified by the NLP module; scene schemas are constructed dynamically.

6.2.1. *Constraint Satisfaction: A Paradigm for High-Level Control*

In computer vision, scene interpretation is the process of labeling salient objects in a given image. Traditional image understanding systems employ mixed top-down/bottom-up control strategies (e.g., blackboard systems) incorporating techniques such as inexact graph matching, rule-based systems and relaxation in the process of low-level feature detection (e.g., edges, surfaces, etc.) and high-level relational model verification (e.g., house model, typical neighbourhood scene model). Since the exact contents of the image are not known *a priori*, a significant amount of bottom-up computation is necessary before the appropriate high-level models can be invoked. Furthermore, the high-level models are used primarily to establish context, i.e., to drive the low and intermediate-level feature detection. As a result, complex control strategies combining top-down and bottom-up control are necessitated.

The computational model exploits the fact that the set of objects to be identified in the image is known with certainty (assuming that NLP analysis is correct). This enables the treatment of the scene labeling problem as a 2 step process where the first step consists of *locating/detecting* objects of specified classes (e.g., human faces), and the second step consists of *recognition/labeling*, i.e., labeling individuals of an object class. Furthermore, the control strategies used in these two stages are different. In the previous section we have described how PICTION uses collateral information such as the size and location of an object in performing the first step, namely, locating objects. In the second step, namely, object identification, the proposed model takes a new approach designed to exploit top-down information more efficiently by performing the labeling of objects at a higher level, rather than the IU level. More specifically, verification of high-level relational models (representing scene descriptions) is formulated as a constraint satisfaction problem (CSP) and handled by the control module. This provides a single framework for incorporating spatial, characteristic, locational and other general domain constraints without having to overspecify control information. In particular, it permits efficient backtracking where required. However the location of objects is still performed at the IU level thereby facilitating existing object detectors to be integrated into the overall model.

A *static* constraint satisfaction problem (V, D, C, R) involves a set of n **variables,** $V = \{v_1, v_2, \ldots, v_n\}$, each with an association **domain** D_i of possible **values**. The search space consists of the Cartesian product of the variables' domains, $D = D_1 \times D_2 \times \ldots \times D_n$. A set of **constraints** C is specified over some subsets of these variables, where each constraint C_p involves a subset $\{i_1, \ldots, i_q\}$ of V and is labeled by a relation R_p of R, subset of the Cartesian product $D_{i_1} \times \ldots \times D_{i_q}$ that specifies which values of the variables are compatible with each other. A **solution** to a CSP consists of an assignment of values to variables such that all constraints are satisfied. Current approaches to solving CSP's involve achieving local (i.e., node and arc (Mohr and Henderson 1986)) consistency first thereby reducing the amount of backtracking required in solving the global consistency problem.

In PICTION, each variable v_i corresponds to an object or person hypothesis, i.e., object or person predicted to be in the picture by the constraint generator and has associated with it an object class $Class_i$. The domain D_i for each variable is initialised to the set of all **candidates** $\{c_{i_1}, \ldots, c_{i_m}\}$ generated by the call $locate\_object(Class_i)$. There are 3 types of constraints used in the labeling process:

Unary Constraints: Typically correspond to characteristic constraints output by the constraint generator (e.g., gender, color of hair, etc.)

Binary Constraints: Typically, these are spatial constraints.

N-ary Constraints: Typically rules obtained from the domain *a priori* but applied in a discretionary manner by the constraint satisfier. An example of an n-ary constraint is one which examines height relationships between people in the same row. It favours those solutions where the vertical positions of faces do not differ significantly and where there is a minimal amount of horizontal overlap.

There are two key differences between the statement of PICTION's constraint satisfaction problem from traditional CSP's. The first deals with the cost and reliability of the routines to verify each relation. Unlike traditional CS problems, certain node consistency checks (e.g., colour of hair) are performed after arc consistency checks (e.g., verification of spatial constraints) due to cost effectiveness. Furthermore, the routines used to verify characteristic constraints (e.g., gender) generate a *confidence measure* based on (i) how well the criteria were satisfied, and (ii) the reliability of the routine itself. Although thresholds are employed within these routines to enforce minimum criteria for constraint satisfaction, it is necessary to record the degree to which it was satisfied. The latter value is used in evaluating multiple solutions and deriving partial solutions to the object identification problem.

Secondly, a static CSP is not a sufficient model for PICTION. It is necessary to formulate the problem as a *dynamic* CSP. In a dynamic CSP (Cullen *et al.* 1992), it is possible to add or retract constraints as well as variables. The latter is necessitated when trying to arrive at partial labelings in PICTION. If there is not enough support for a particular variable (i.e., object or person hypothesis), it will be retracted and the system will attempt to label any remaining objects or people predicted to be in the picture. Examples of a variable's domain changing includes the situation where a particular set of face candidates results in inconsistent or otherwise unacceptable solutions; in such a case, the face locator can be called again with relaxed parameters enabling a new set of face candidates to be tried.

In processing the example of Figure 1, constraints are applied in the following order:
(i)   Face Verification: unary constraint
      Candidates c4 and c8 are eliminated since they don't satisfy the face verification test which is based on symmetry and homogeneity of gray-levels.
(ii) Spatial: binary constraints
      Simultaneous satisfaction of spatial constraints to remaining candidates

(c2, c3, c5, c6, c7) results in several possible labelings for the 3 named people (e.g., Marian could be any of c2, c3, c5, c6).

(iii) Gender Discrimination: unary

This is a filter which takes as input, face candidates, and outputs confidences for the candidate being a male or female face. This is described in section 7.2.1. Based on this, Marian receives the unique label of c2.

(iv) Similar face size: n-ary

Reflects a simplistic method of performing foreground/background discrimination. Based on this constraint, candidates c3 and c6, along with c2, constitute a more favourable labeling than those labelings involving c5 and c7.

Note: c1 is eliminated initially; the face locator sometimes generates multiple, overlapping candidates for the same face, where one is almost entirely enclosed in another.

6.2.2. Evidence Combination

In order to evaluate complete and partial solutions (i.e., identification of only a subset of those people/objects predicted to be in the picture), it is necessary to record the following types of evidence:

- $cand\_conf(i, j)$ which records the confidence associated with the jth candidate having the object class of v_i; currently this is the confidence returned by the object locator;
- $binding\_conf(v_{i_1}, c_{j_1}, \ldots, v_{i_q}, c_{j_q})$ which represents the confidence associated with one possible binding of a subset of V (variables) to candidates. These subsets are all the *valid* subsets $\{i_1, \ldots, i_q\}$ of V which participate in any constraint C_p (eliminating duplicate subsets, i.e. the same subset involved in 2 or more constraints). This confidence is updated as a result of applying constraints in C involving these variables using a simple averaging scheme (currently). We are looking here into the use of Dempster-Shafer theory of evidence combination which is good for modeling the cumulative effect of evidence and allows negative evidence to be incorporated.

Given the above, the final confidence for a solution (either total which involves all variables, or partial, involving a subset of variables), $combined\_conf(v_{i_1}, c_{j_1}, \ldots, v_{i_q}, c_{j_q})$, can be computed as follows. Let $S_1, \ldots, S_t$ be the set of all valid binding subsets (numbering t) contained within the given binding. Let U be the set of (i, j) pairs representing all candidates appearing in the binding. Then, $combined\_conf(v_{i_1}, c_{j_1}, \ldots, v_{i_q}, c_{j_q})$ is computed as

$$\prod_{i=1}^{t} binding\_conf(S_i) \times \prod_{i,j \in U} cand\_conf(i, j)$$

If the combined confidence of 2 or more solutions differs by less than a preset threshold, they are considered equivalent. This creates multiple correspondences for some or all of the faces/objects.

6.2.3. *Communication with IU Module*

There are three levels of communication, each corresponding to the coarseness of the command.

- High-level:
  High level commands treat the IU module like a 'black box' and consist of calls to locate objects, verify object properties,
  e.g. TEST_MALE_FACE(face-candidate)

- Intermediate-level:
  At the intermediate level, we have parameterised object locators and constrained search,
  e.g. LOCATE_FACE(size:1-3;orientation:non-frontal)

- Low-level:
  Creating specialised object schemas constitutes a low level command. It should be noted that this is possible only if visual object modeling in the IU module uses the same knowledge representation formalism as in the other modules of the system. This enables the NLP module to access these modules and create specialised versions of them by instantiating optional parameters such as size, texture and colour, as well as including procedure information such as instructions on where to look for the object. There has been recent work in using semantic networks for image understanding; specifically, domain-independent control, or interpretation strategies can be formally stated based on the semantics of a standardised representation (Niemann *et al.* 1990).

7. IMAGE UNDERSTANDING (IU) MODULE

The vision module in this system performs two main functions. The first is the task of locating objects and the second is the verification of visual properties (e.g., gender in human faces, colour, etc.). Currently, the only object class that PICTION is capable of locating is a human face. We expect to add more object classes in the near future. The most frequently used characteristic in identification of people in photographs is gender. For this reason, gender discrimination has been the focus of intensive research. We are also looking into other characteristics which are relatively easy to develop verification tools for such as baldness, wearing of eyeglasses and hair colour. Characteristics such as age and expression, although used quite frequently, pose an enormous challenge in terms of development of verification tools and hence have not been used so far.

7.1. *Face Location*

From the caption, we are able to determine the number of faces and some weak bounds on the size of faces. These constitute parameters to the face-location module (Govindaraju *et al.* 1992). For each image area hypothesised to be a face, this module returns the coordinates of a bounding rectangle for that area. False candidates are sometimes generated due to incidental alignment of edges (see Figure 1b) and true candidates are occasionally missed due to poor edge data.

Although the face locator exhibits reasonably good performance in finding faces, it is not able to return a precise fit, i.e., the bounding boxes do not frame the face accurately. Accurate identification of face boundary is required for subsequent post-processing of the image (e.g., identifying the facial features). A program utilizing active contours in an attempt to trace the contours of the face is being implemented. Given as input the bounding box from the face locator, this program attempts to discover the contours corresponding to the face within this box. Since the bounding box does not always totally enclose the face area, the active contours program is being modified to allow it to search outside the bounding box as well. Furthermore, face-specific shape constraints, such as the fact that a face is a near oval, are also being exploited in the algorithm.

7.1.1. Face Verification
Once a face 'candidate' has been identified by the locator, it must be verified that it is indeed a face. Two methods have been implemented for verification, a moment based system and a relaxation-based system. The moment-based system captures holistic properties of the image such as symmetry and homogeneity.

The relaxation-based system employs both contour and edge data (from the face locator) as well as gray-level segmentation data in order to return a confidence for a candidate being a face. A key operation is the detection of the segments corresponding to the eyes. This approach is a generalization of an earlier technique to recognise faces.

Both these methods are used in a hierarchical manner. The two systems return 'confidence-values' of the face candidates to the control structure. The moment based system has been built with a fuzzy graph based output in order to get continuous values instead of a 'yes/no' response.

7.2. Facial Characteristics

In general, the vision module is required whenever it becomes necessary to examine in detail the portion of the original image (i.e., the photograph) corresponding to a box representing a face candidate. The vision module is expected to make some qualitative judgment about this area. The process used to make each of these judgments will be referred to as a 'filter'. Specifically, the vision module is called on to verify visual characteristics that may be useful in the identification process. It is these filters that enabled the successful processing of the examples presented in Figure 1.

7.2.1. Gender discrimination
We are investigating the application of *eigenfaces* (Pentland *et al.* 1993) in this problem. Eigenfaces are based on 'principal component analysis' (Karhunen-Loeve expansion) and in this case, are based on the vectors that best account for the distribution of face images with the $N \times N$ image space. Eigenfaces have been successfully used in both recognizing faces (from a database of faces) as well as characterizing faces (e.g., expression detection)(Pentland *et al.* 1993).

We are initially investigating the use of eigenfaces in gender discrimination.

The assumption is that male and female faces form clusters in the face space. This hypothesis is being tested on a database of several hundred male and female faces.

The disadvantage of the eigenface technique is its sensitivity to exact location as well as size normalization. The tolerance of the eigenface technique to inaccurate location is being investigated. The advantage stems from having a uniform technique for both classification problems (gender, beard/mustache, wearing glasses, etc.) as well as face recognition. In some cases it is necessary to identify certain key people in photographs through individual face recognition techniques, thus enabling recognition of other people through simpler constraints.

8. TESTING

The system was tested on a dataset of 50 pictures and captions obtained from *The Buffalo News* and *The New York Times*. We selected only those photographs where identification could be performed based on spatial constraints and characteristics for which we had developed verification tools. There are three success codes used to evaluate the system: (a) success, indicating that everyone identified in the caption is identified by the system correctly and uniquely; (b) partial success, indicating multiple possibilities for one or more people where the actual face is included and (c) error, indicating that one or more people was identified incorrectly (i.e., true face not included). An overall success rate of 65 percent, partial success rate of 20 percent and error rate of 15 percent was obtained. Although the sample size is too small to be considered statistically valid, the results illustrate the viability of this approach to face recognition. The most common reason for a result of partial success or error was the failure of the face locator to locate one or more of the identified faces. In only one case, the error was due to an incorrect parsing (i.e. predicting the wrong number of people to be in the picture). Other reasons for a result code of partial success or error included (i) the failure of spatial heuristics and (ii) inability to properly characterise faces (e.g., male/female). The system is currently being tested on a larger database (500–1000 pictures in digital form) obtained from a news wire service. Thus, the problems associated with scanning half-tones, such as aliasing effects and bleedthrough from the reverse side are eliminated.

9. SUMMARY

This paper has presented a computational model for understanding pictures based on collateral information in accompanying text. The research contributions are (i) a theory of locating and extracting relevant visual information in text, and (ii) the efficient exploitation of the above information in image understanding. An attempt to construct an integrated language/vision knowledge base has also been presented. The relevance of this work to document understanding, particularly intelligent information retrieval from an integrated text/photo database has been discussed. As a test of the model, a face identification system, *PICTION* has been described, which uses captions to label human faces in newspaper pictures.

We are investigating the application of this computational model in other domains as well. Diagram understanding is one such domain; in documents, diagrams are always accompanied by descriptive text. Diagram understanding involves low-level processes such as raster to vector conversion as well as higher-level processes such as grouping of graphical and textual primitives into symbolic structures (such as flowchart boxes). The other area of interest is medical image processing. Since medical images are frequently accompanied by textual annotations (made by physicians), we are interested in exploring the ways in such information can be linked for various applications, including image interpretation.

Any attempt at integrating language and vision requires the incorporation of a wide range of techniques, including natural language processing, computer vision, knowledge representation and innovative control mechanisms. It is our belief that this work helps to define a new sub-discipline within Artificial Intelligence, one which is based on assimilating concepts and techniques from associated sub-disciplines, as well as the development of new concepts specific to the problem of integrating language and vision.

NOTES

[1]   This work was supported in part by ARPA Contract 93-F148900-000. I would like to thank William Rapaport for serving as my advisor in my doctoral work; Venu Govindaraju for his work on the face locator; and more recently, Rajiv Chopra, Debra Burhans and Toshio Morita for their work in the new implementation of PICTION as well as valuable feedback.

[2]   The locative constraint IN_ROW indicates that people appear in rows; this information is used by the face locator to constrain the area of search for faces in a second pass. A second pass in which parameters are relaxed, is necessitated when the required number of faces are not found in the first pass.

[3]   According to (Biederman 1988), there are about 3000 common entry-level objects which the human perceptual system can detect.

[4]   The Penn Treebank version of the Wall Street Journal Corpus is part of the contents of a CD-ROM released by the Association for Computational Linguistics/Data Collection Initiative. The development of the tag set and the tagging was done at the University of Pennsylvania.

REFERENCES

Abella, A. & Kender, J. R. (1993). Qualitatively Describing Objects Using Spatial Prepositions. In *Proceedings of The Eleventh National Conference on Artificial Intelligence (AAAI-93)*, 536–540. Washington, DC.

Beckwith, R., Fellbaum, C., Gross, D. & Miller, G. A. (1991). WordNet: A Lexical Database Organized on Psycholinguistic Principles. In *Lexicons: Using On-line Resources to Build a Lexicon*. Lawrence Erlbaum: Hillsdale, NJ.

Biederman, I. (1988). Aspects and Extensions of a Theory of Human Image Understanding. In Pylyshyn, Z. (ed.) *Computational Processes in Human Vision: An interdisciplinary perspective*. Ablex: Norwood, NJ.

Cullen, P. B., Hull, J. J. & Srihari, S. N. (1992). A Constraint Satisfaction Approach to the Reslution of Uncertainty in Image Interpretation. In *Proceedings of The Eighth Conference on Artificial Intelligence for Applications*, 123–133. Monterey, CA.

Dahlgren, K., McDowell, J. & Stabler Jr., E. P. (1989). Knowledge Representation for Commonsense Reasoning with Text. *Computational Linguistics* 15(3): 149–170.

Govindaraju, V., Srihari, S. N. & Sher, D. B. (1992). A Computational Model for Face Location based on Cognitive Principles. In *Proceedings of The 10th National Conference on Artificial Intelligence (AAAI-92)*, 350–355. San Jose, CA.

ISX Corporation (1991). *LOOM Users Guide, Version 1.4*.

Jolicoeur, P., Gluck, M. A. & Kosslyn, S. M. (1984). Pictures and Names: Making the Connection. *Cognitive Psychology* 16: 243–275.

Knight, K. & Luk, S. (1994). Building a Large Scale Knowledge Base for Machine Translation. In *Proceedings of AAAI–94* (forthcoming). Seattle, WA.

Linde, D. J. (1982). Picture-Word Differences in Decision Latency. *Journal of Experimental Psychology: Learning, Memory and Cognition* 8: 584–598.

Mani, I., MacMillan, T. R., Luperfoy, S., Lusher, E. P. & Laskowski, S. J. (1993). Identifying Unknown Proper Names in Newswire Text. In *Proceedings of The Workshop on Acquisition of Lexical Knowledge from Text*, 44–54. Columbus, Ohio.

Mohr, R. & Henderson, T. C. (1986). Arc and path consistency revisited. *Artificial Intelligence* 28: 225–233.

Neimann, H., Sagerer, G. F. Schroder, S. & Kummert, F. (1990). Ernest: A Semantic Network System for Pattern Understanding. *Pattern Analysis and Machine Intelligence* 12(9): 883–905.

Pentland, A., Starner, T., Etcoff, N., Masoiu, A., Oliyide, O. & Turk, M. (1993). Experiments with Eigenfaces. In *IJCAI–93 Workshop on Looking at People: Recognition and Interpretation of Human Action*. Chambery, France.

SPIE. (1994). *Proceedings of the Conference on Storage and Retrieval for Image and Video Databases (Vol. 2185)*, (forthcoming). SPIE Press: Bellingham, WA.

Srihari, R. K. (1991a). Extracting Visual Information from Text: Using Captions to Label Human Faces in Newspaper Photographs (Ph.D. thesis). Dept. of Computer Science Technical Report 91-17, State University of New York at Buffalo.

Srihari, R. K. (1991b). PICTION: A System that Uses Captions to Label Human Faces in Newspaper Photographs. In *Proceedings of The 9th National Conference on Artificial Intelligence (AAAI-91)*, 80–85. Anaheim, CA.

Srihari, R. K. (1993). Intelligent Document Understanding: Understanding Photos with Captions. In *Proceedings of The International Conference on Document Analysis and Recognition (ICDAR-93)*, 664–667. Tsukuba City, Japan.

Srihari, R. K. & Burhans, D. T. (1994). Visual Semantics: Extracting Visual Information from Text Accompanying Pictures. In *Proceedings of the 12th National Conference on Artificial Intelligence (AAAI-94)*, 793–798. Seattle, WA.

Strat, T. M. & Fischler, M. A. (1991). Context-Based Vision: Recognizing Objects Using Information from Both 2-D and 3-D Imagery. *IEEE PAMI* 13(10): 1050–1065.

Tomita, M. (1987). An Efficient Augmented-Context-Free Parsing Algorithm. *Computational Linguistics* 13(1–2): 31–46.

Weymouth, T. (1986). *Using Object Descriptions in a Schema Network for Machine Vision*. Ph.D. Dissertation, University of Masschussetts at Amherst.

Artificial Intelligence Review **8**: 431–445, 1994–5.
© 1995 *Kluwer Academic Publishers. Printed in the Netherlands.*

The DenK-architecture:
A Fundamental Approach to User-Interfaces

R. M. C. AHN, R. J. BEUN, T. BORGHUIS, H. C. BUNT and
C. W. A. M. VAN OVERVELD*

Abstract. In this paper we present the basic principles underlying the DenK-system,
a generic cooperative interface combining linguistic and visual interaction. The system
integrates results from fundamental research in knowledge representation, communication, natural language semantics and pragmatics, and object-oriented animation.
Our design incorporates a cooperative and knowledgeable electronic assistant that
communicates with a user in natural language, and an application domain, which is
presented visually. The assistant, that we call the *cooperator*, has an information
state that is represented in a rich form of Type Theory, a formalism that enables us
to model the inherent cognitive dynamics of a dialogue participant. Pragmatic issues
in man-machine interaction, concerning the use of natural language and knowledge
in cooperative communication, are central to our approach.

Key words: multimodal interaction, knowledge representation, natural language
semantics, pragmatics, type theory, object oriented animation.

1. INTRODUCTION

In 1989, the universities of Tilburg and Eindhoven initiated a joint research
program that aims at the development of a *multimodal cooperative interface
for interactive knowledge acquisition and -analysis*. Multimodality refers here
to a combination of linguistic and visual interaction. This 8-year program is called
'Dialoogvoering en Kennisopbouw', abbreviated DenK,[1] which means 'Dialogue
Management and Knowledge Acquisition'.

The program combines fundamental research in knowledge representation,
communication, natural language semantics, pragmatics and object-oriented
animation to develop generic user interface techniques. These techniques are
applied in the prototypical *DenK-system*. The design of this system reflects a
cooperative situation where two participants can exchange information about a
shared application domain and where both participants can point at, observe
and manipulate objects within this domain (cf., Grosz 1978).

The point of departure is that, from a user's point of view, a computer application should present itself as a combination of an 'electronic assistant' and a
tangible model of the task domain. The electronic assistant should interact in
an intelligent and cooperative way with the user, using a combination of linguistic
and visual modalities, and acting on the user's intentions as understood in the
context of the interaction.

267

In this paper we discuss the basic motivation and principles that underlie the architecture and functionality of the DenK-system. We concentrate on the three pillars on which the system rests:

- an approach to cooperative dialogue based on an analysis of communicative acts as operations that *change* the cognitive state of the participants;
- the use of a particular ('constructive') form of the rich and solid mathematical formalism of *Type Theory* to represent the cognitive state of the electronic assistant, which is a prominent aspect of the dialogue context;
- a novel object-oriented animation system, called the *Generalized Display Processor*, to model and visualize the task domain.

2. THEORETICAL BACKGROUND

Underlying the combination of linguistic and visual modalities in the DenK-system is the recognition that humans interact naturally with their environment in two ways: *symbolically* and *physically*. On the one hand, if there is an intermediary agent (human or electronic assistant), humans can interact symbolically and use language to give commands, ask for or provide information, etc. On the other hand, physically, one picks up objects, moves or fastens them, or observes them by seeing, feeling, hearing, or smelling. The essential difference between the two types of interaction is that actions of the first type (for instance, speech acts) need an interpreter who can bridge the gap between the symbols and their actual meaning and purpose, while actions of the second type are related in a more direct manner to human perception and action (Hutchins 1989, de Souza 1993).

The two types of interaction are clearly distinguished in the DenK-design, where two components play a crucial role: a. the so-called *cooperator* who interprets symbolic messages from the user, is capable of reasoning about various aspects of the domain and the user (e.g., discourse information, mutual beliefs, presuppositions) and produces communicative behaviour adequate with respect to the user's beliefs and goals, and b. the *task* or *application domain*, modeled by the *Generalized Display Processor*, in which spatio-temporal components and graphical tools for representation and visualization of the domain are implemented. The user can interact indirectly with the application domain through linguistic communication with the cooperator, who has internal access to the domain, and can interact directly through input and output devices, such as mouse and screen. This is depicted in what we call the *triangle metaphor* (Figure 1).

It should be noted that the basic architecture of the DenK-system deviates from the architecture of other intelligent multimedia systems, such as AIMI (Burger and Marshall 1994), WIP (Wahlster *et al.* 1993), MMI^2 (Wilson *et al.* 1991) and CUBRICON (Neal and Shapiro 1989), where a direct link between the user and the application domain is missing. An important advantage of our approach is that particular complex aspects of the interaction, such as the visualization of autonomous motion behaviour of objects, do not have to be considered by the cooperator and can be left to the interactive components of the application domain.

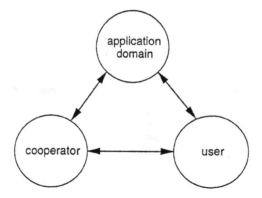

Fig. 1. The triangle metaphor: user, cooperator and application domain.

3. THE DESIGN OF THE COOPERATOR

The view underlying the design of the cooperator in the DenK-architecture is that dialogue participants use language to perform communicative acts, primarily aimed at changing the addressee's cognitive state in the direction of the speaker's goals (Bunt 1989, 1993). In line with Searle (1969), two aspects are distinguished in the communicative act: its *semantic content* and its illocutionary force, or, what we will call, its *pragmatic function*. The semantic content is related to the truth-conditional aspects of the action, such as the existence of particular objects, their properties and relations in the application domain. The pragmatic function determines, together with the semantic content, the effects of the communicative act on the cooperator's cognitive state.

The cooperator's (communicative) behaviour is controlled by the *pragmatic rule interpreter* (see Figure 2). To produce simple cooperative behaviour, the interpreter exploits three types of contextual information:
1. the cognitive state of the cooperator;
2. the most recent (communicative) action by the user;
3. the current state of the application domain.

First, the interpreter analyses the user's utterance within the current context and, if no communication failures are noticed, it updates the cognitive state of the cooperator with the new information. If the pragmatic function of the user's utterance was a command, a domain-related action is performed; if the function of the utterance was a question, the question is appropriately answered. Since we consider the cooperator as an expert about the domain, he accepts no new domain information from the user, and consequently all declaratives about the domain are interpreted as questions (see Beun 1990).

The cooperator's cognitive state – which is represented in Type Theory – consists of a sequence of mental objects that can be very diverse in both origin and kind. For instance, mental objects may refer to real objects in the application domain, may occur as discourse referents resulting from natural language

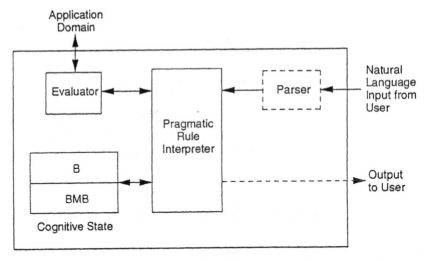

Fig. 2. The design of the cooperator.

interaction with the user (cf., Kamp 1981), and may even occur as so-called 'proof-objects', representing formal proofs of particular propositions.

In line with Kamp and Reyle (1993), we call a discourse referent that is connected with a particular real object in the application domain an *anchored referent*, i.e. the result of the evaluation of the discourse referent yields a concrete object in the application domain. It is important to note that not all discourse referents have to be anchored and thus may exist as abstract mental objects without real counterparts. Vice versa, real objects may exist without having a mental correlate.

Two types of belief are distinguished in the cooperator's cognitive state: a. the cooperator's *private beliefs* (B) and b. the cooperator's belief about *mutual beliefs* of the cooperator and user (BMB). The cooperator's belief about mutual belief is, by its very nature, a subset of the cooperator's private belief. The distinction between the different types of belief enables the cooperator to adapt and modify responses in accordance with the believed cognitive state of the user. For instance, the cooperator is not allowed, in accordance with the Gricean maxim of quantity (Grice 1975), explicitly to provide information that he believes to be mutually believed (Beun 1991).

We will return in the next section to the formal aspects of the dynamics of the cooperator's cognitive state and its communicative behaviour in response to the user's questions.

4. TYPE THEORY

To model the cognitive state of the cooperator and particular aspects of the communication process, we do not use predicate logic, but a formalism that is more versatile and more powerful: *Type Theory*. Type Theory refers to a whole class of formalisms, including Automath (de Bruijn 1980), Intuitionistic Type Theory (Martin-Löf 1984) and the Calculus of Constructions (Coquand 1985), which are all based on similar ideas (see also Barendregt 1991). These formalisms function as logical frameworks in which almost any form of mathematical reasoning can be expressed. They find their origin in foundational mathematical research, and have a strong constructivist flavour.

We will use Type Theory not only as a formalism to model the cooperator's (private or mutual) belief about the application domain, but also as a semantic representation of the utterances that are exchanged in the dialogue between the cooperator and the user. In Mäenpää and Ranta (1990) it was already pointed out that Type Theory is very useful as a semantic representation for natural language. Among the many advantages of Type Theory over other formalisms to represent the semantics of natural language utterances in a dialogue, there are two we will emphasize here: a. the inherent *dynamics* of the formalism and b. the build-in notion of *justifications* of propositional information (cf., van Benthem 1991).

Dynamics. A central notion in Type Theory is that of a *context*. A context is a sequential structure that contains the current information and can be extended in different ways to incorporate new information. The extension of contexts is laid down in a number of rules where two categories are clearly distinguishable: *introduction* rules and *inference* rules. Introduction rules describe how a context may be extended to accommodate new information. Inference rules describe how information may be combined in a sound way so that implicit information within a context can be made explicit. In a similar way, mental objects (e.g., discourse referents) are constantly introduced and added to the discourse structure in a dialogue. It has been shown in Ahn and Kolb (1990) that type theoretical contexts can even be regarded as natural generalizations of Discourse Representation Structures (Kamp 1981).

Justifications. Another important notion in Type Theory is the concept of *proofs*. Proofs are considered as mental objects, have concrete representations, and are completely integrated within the formalism itself. This means that within Type Theory we are not only able to represent *what* the cooperator believes, but also *how* he comes to believe it. Type Theory does not concern itself with truth, however. It records which information is present and what has been shown to follow from this information. This means that partiality is an inherent feature of the formalism.

4.1. Cognitive states as contexts in Type Theory

In this section we show, by means of an example, how the cognitive state of the cooperator can be represented by a context in Type Theory.

Throughout this paper we use a simple 'block-world' as our application domain, where pyramids, cubes and the like can move around and have properties like colour, size and so on. For our example, we assume the cooperator to have the following information about the 'block-world':

- there may exist pyramids and colours in the domain (the cooperator is familiar with the notions 'pyramid' and 'colour'),
- there is at least one particular pyramid,
- 'small' is a predicate on pyramids, and 'bright' is a predicate on colours,
- all pyramids have a colour, and every small pyramid has a bright colour (these are 'rules' that hold in the domain).

In Type Theory, a context is a sequence of (mental) objects, in which all objects have a *type*. Objects and types are denoted by expressions, and the infix operator ':' is used to relate objects and their types; 'O : T' should be pronounced as: 'O is an inhabitant of T'. Expressions of this form are called 'entries'. The entries in a context are separated by commas, and the beginning and end of the context are marked by '[' and ']' respectively.

To represent the cooperator's cognitive state, we start with an empty context and gradually introduce the information listed above. First, we have to introduce the necessary types, i.e. 'pyramid' and 'colour'. In Type Theory, new types may be introduced whenever they are needed. They must be introduced as the inhabitant of the *supertype*, denoted by the symbol '*', which functions as the 'type of the types'. Accordingly, we obtain a context with two entries:

[pyramid : *, colour : *]

After a type has been introduced, one may introduce inhabitants of that type. In this case we introduce an anchored specimen of a pyramid, by extending the context with the entry:

p318 : pyramid

The introduced pyramid is labelled by the expression 'p318' (all introduced objects must be uniquely identifiable).

In Type Theory, predicates are represented as functions to propositions. Viewed in this way, the predicate 'bright' is a function that given a particular colour, such as yellow, yields a proposition: 'Yellow is bright'. Within Type Theory propositions are introduced as types, i.e. they exist at the same level as the types 'pyramid' and 'colour' in the example; propositions have type '*'. An inhabitant of a proposition (type) represents a proof of that proposition. Proofs and other objects may be combined, in order to construct new proofs and new objects. The inference rules of the type system will restrict the way in which this can be done, and guarantee that all reasoning is sound.[2]

Given this interpretation of propositions, we can express the predicate 'small' as a function from pyramids to propositions, and the predicate 'bright' as a function from colour to propositions (objects of type '*'). These are added to the example context by extending it with the entries:

small(M) : * ⇐ [M : pyramid]
bright(C) : * ⇐ [C : colour]

These entries need some clarification, since they are not of the form 'O : T' specified earlier. In Type Theory these functions can be expressed in the required form, but in order to avoid a long and formal exposition we adopt a simplified Prolog-like notation. In this notation a limited fragment of Type Theory can be expressed in a rather intuitive way. The symbol '$\Leftarrow$' corresponds to the Prolog turnstile ':-'. Note how the two functions are expressed as Prolog-like clauses in this notation.

Using the clause notation and the predicates, we can express the last two pieces of information possessed by the cooperator. First, we extend the context with an entry representing a function, 'c', that associates a colour to every pyramid:

$$c(M) : colour \Leftarrow [M : pyramid]$$

Finally, we have to express that every small pyramid has a bright colour. To do this we introduce a function (represented by the object 'ax2') that, when given a pyramid (M) together with a proof that this pyramid is small (object 'P' of type 'small(M)'), returns a proof ('ax2(M, P)') that the colour of this particular pyramid is bright:

$$ax2(M, P) : bright(c(M)) \Leftarrow [M : pyramid, P : small(M)]$$

Combining all the above entries results in the following context, which represents the beliefs the cooperator has about the domain:

    [pyramid : *,
     colour : *,
     p318 : pyramid,
     small(M) : * $\Leftarrow$ [M : pyramid],
     bright(C) : * $\Leftarrow$ [C : colour],
     c(M) : colour $\Leftarrow$ [M : pyramid],
     ax2(M, P) : bright(c(M)) $\Leftarrow$ [M : pyramid, P : small(M)]
    ]

Once the information is represented in the form of a type theoretical context, the cooperator can make inferences by constructing new objects using the entries in the context. In fact one can extend the Prolog-like notation used in this article in such a way that it supports an effective proof construction method for Type Theory, combining resolution style proofs with natural deduction (Helmink and Ahn 1991). The cooperator contains a theorem prover based on this method, that solves queries that resemble the antecedents of a clause.

4.2. Communication in Type Theory

In communicating with the user, we want the cooperator to interpret the user's utterances and to generate responses, according to particular pragmatic principles.[3] To achieve this, the cooperator can make use of three main information sources, to wit:
- the application domain;
- the mutual beliefs as represented in Type Theory;[4]
- his private beliefs as represented in Type Theory.

In the current DenK-system, the cooperator distinguishes between the kinds of belief by maintaining *two* contexts: a *private* context representing his own beliefs, and a *common* context representing the mutual beliefs. Since the cooperator's mutual beliefs are also private beliefs, the entries in the common context are a subset of the entries in the private context. Recently, an extension of Type Theory has been developed which allows representation of and reasoning about different kinds of belief in one context (Borghuis 1993).

We present two cases in which the cooperator generates a pragmatically correct reply to an utterance of the user, using the information sources. In the first case the user makes a statement, in the second she asks a question. In both cases, we assume that the cognitive state of the cooperator is the one represented above, and that all beliefs of the cooperator are mutual beliefs except for the 'domain rule' that every small pyramid has a bright colour, which is a private belief of the cooperator. Remember that we assumed that the cooperator behaves as an expert about the domain and that all declaratives about the domain uttered by the user are interpreted by the cooperator as questions.

After having inspected the image on the screen, the user might utter the following sentence:

"The pyramid is small."

In order to interpret this utterance the cooperator first has to figure out which pyramid is meant. Due to the definiteness of the noun phrase, the cooperator may consult both the application domain and the mutual beliefs to find the particular pyramid. The cooperator's private beliefs are irrelevant here, because the user is unaware of those, and hence cannot refer to these beliefs in the utterance by means of a definite reference. Therefore the cooperator will assume that the user refers to the pyramid about which a mutual belief is stored in his common context ('p318 : pyramid'). He will interpret the user's utterance as saying that the user has evidence that 'small(p318)' holds. After checking the truth of this proposition in the application domain, the cooperator extends his *common* context with the following entry;

e435 : small(p318)

(where e435 represents the 'evidence' the cooperator has found for the proposition 'small(318)' in the domain). The cooperator will give the answer "yes", to indicate that he understands the utterance and agrees. The effect of the user's statement is that the proposition **the pyramid is small** has become a mutual belief of cooperator and user.

Suppose that the next utterance of the user is:

"Is the colour of the pyramid bright?"

The pragmatic function of the utterance is a **yes/no-question** and the user's goal is to signal to the cooperator that the user wants to know whether the proposition **the pyramid is bright** holds. The cooperator complies with this wish of the user by trying to construct an object for the proposition ('bright(c(p318)').

Using the theorem prover, the cooperator succeeds in constructing such an object from the entries in his private context:

ax2(p318, e435) : bright(c(p318))

Because the question was a **yes/no-question**, only the existence of a proof-object matters. The cooperator has found a proof-object, hence the question will be answered affirmatively.

If the user had asked:

"Why is the colour of the pyramid bright?"

the cooperator would be under the obligation to communicate how he came to believe 'bright(p318)'. This is recorded in the proof-object 'ax2(p318, e435)', but by the Gricean maxim of quantity the cooperator should only communicate those ingredients of the proof that are not already among the beliefs of the user. By checking the common context, the cooperator can find out that the user already believes that there exists a pyramid ('p318 : pyramid'), and that it is small ('e435 : small(p318)', this information became a mutual belief after the user's previous utterance). Hence, the cooperator generates an answer from the only ingredient in his proof (ax2(M, P): bright(c(M)) $\Leftarrow$ [M : pyramid, P : small(M)]) that is in the private and not in the common context:

"Because every small pyramid has a bright colour".

This answer is satisfactory since it provides the user only with the *new* information (the 'domain rule') needed to infer how the cooperator came to believe that the pyramid was bright.

In answering WH-questions, other complications also occur. It is particularly difficult to communicate the identity of an object, even if it occurs in the common context, because in the message to the user we can only refer to the *properties* of an object. This means that the cooperator has to find a unique description that can be interpreted by the user. Which description is actually most appropriate is a complicated matter, depending on aspects such as the difference in saliency of the properties of the objects, previous utterances or domain focus (Cremers 1994). We have not yet implemented the generation of such answers. In the current implementation the cooperator will simply 'point out' the desired object by highlighting it in the graphical representation of the domain on the screen.

5. THE APPLICATION DOMAIN: THE GENERALIZED DISPLAY PROCESSOR

The predominant requirement for the domain representation module is, of course, that it can represent the application domain. In general, the application domain will have essential visual (spatial) and dynamic (temporal) aspects, so an intuitive representation of this domain should consist of a convincing, real-time view on this changing domain. The domain-representation module is therefore implemented as an *animation system*.

For our purposes, an animation system that can serve as the domain representative of the cooperator has to meet with the following requirements:

to support a *generic* platform to simulate a large variety of application domains:

1. instructions have to exist to create objects[5] (both their geometric shape and their autonomous motion behaviour) and to pass messages to objects to alter their properties and behaviour; objects also have to be able to pass messages to each other;
2. to facilitate programming complex behaviour (e.g., the motions of mechanical devices, walking, grasping objects) a library of versatile built-in motion methods has to be available.

to support *multi-modal interaction*:

1. interrogation of the domain status has to be allowed at any time, i.e., asynchronously with respect to the time evolution of the animation;
2. the display image has to be refreshed continuously, so that the user has visual feedback of the animation irrespective of the state of the dialogue;
3. the user has to be able, at any time, to refer to aspects of the graphical model both via the cooperator (i.e., symbolic constructs that are translated from natural language into database interrogation instructions) and via direct manipulation, using a mouse and a 3-D simulated pointing device.

In order to meet with these requirements, we introduced the GDP-architecture (Generalized Display Processor (van Overveld 1991); see Figure 3). The GDP is a (virtual) processor consisting of a parser, an interpreter, rendering support, and a database.

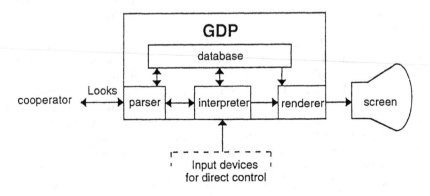

Fig. 3. The Generalized Display Processor.

The parser provides for the communication with the cooperator; it checks the incoming information and, if necessary, sends messages back from the interpreter to the cooperator. The interpreter calculates the values of the attributes of the objects (e.g., position, speed) in order to generate a new frame of animation, which is displayed on screen by means of the renderer.[6] The behaviour of the objects may be autonomous, or dictated by the cooperator or by input devices for direct control (e.g., the mouse).

At any discrete time, a complete description of all geometric attributes of a moving scene is stored in the database. The database consists of two tables: the class table and the object table. The class table contains the class definitions that state which attributes exist for a particular class as well as which methods it may execute.[7] The object table contains the (real) objects in the application domain, i.e. instantiations of an existing class.

5.1. *The Control Language LOOKS*

In order to program the GDP (i.e., in order to define what classes of objects will inhabit the application domain, to create these objects, to program the motion methods, to pass messages and to execute several other types of statements) the language LOOKS has been defined (Language for Object Oriented Kinematic Simulations (Peeters 1994)).

LOOKS supports a variety of object-oriented features, such as data hiding, abstract data types, strong typing, genericity and multiple repeated inheritance; it implements (quasi-)parallellism to facilitate the specification of concurrent motions.

At any time, fragments of LOOKS texts may be passed to the parser. Such a fragment can be either a class definition, an object definition or a message. If this fragment is successfully parsed, and if it was a

class definition, then an entry is created in the class table. Apart from the user-defined classes, LOOKS supports a variety of pre-defined classes, including integers, reals, vectors, movable geometric objects, cameras, (coloured) light-sources, windows, etc.

object definition, then an entry is created in the object table,

message to an object, then the corresponding method is handed to the interpreter to be executed.

Since the cooperator interacts via LOOKS with the GDP (see Figure 3), there is a close relation between LOOKS and the Type Theory formalism that was introduced previously in this paper. Virtually, type theoretical expressions are semantically grounded in LOOKS and the translation procedure comes down to a standard evaluation process[8] where complex type theoretical expressions are expanded into basic expressions that can be interpreted in LOOKS (Ahn 1994).

5.2. *Frame Generation*

In order to generate a frame of animation, the interpreter installs a method it receives from the parser into the list of active methods and executes the methods it encounters. Most active methods can be fully executed (e.g., assignments, expression evaluation, object transformations), after which they are removed from the list.

Methods may, however, also contain a 'synchronize' statement (typically within the body of an (infinite) loop). Execution of an active method proceeds until it is either fully executed, or until a 'synchronize' is encountered. In the latter case, execution stops, but the method is kept in the list; it will again receive the interpreter's attention when preparing the next frame. Since several methods may contain a 'synchronize', several of which may be kept in the active method list simultaneously, the synchronize mechanism may serve to achieve quasi-parallellism.

Also, the execution of a method, due to passing an asynchronous message, may invoke the execution of another method by calling this method. The latter method is also put into the list of active methods, and it will be executed as well during the preparation of the frame.

If no more active methods can proceed any further, the preparation of the frame is complete, and a snapshot of the objects is rendered into the active window(s) with respect to the active virtual camera(s), making use of the active light sources and simulated material properties (colour, shininess, etc.).

Part of the preparation of each frame is also the taking into account of user interaction. Via mouse events and appropriate LOOKS system methods, the user may interact with the ongoing animation (e.g., selecting an object and calling the mouse notifier method that has been assigned to this object).

The current GDP-implementation is designed to run on a high-end graphics workstation where it produces a flicker-free display of shaded images, illuminated by simulated light sources, consisting of several hundreds of polygons with a frame update rate between 15 and 20 frames/sec. It covers most of the requirements and functionality as described above (direct manipulation interaction tools and versatile built-in motion methods are presently under construction).

6. CONCLUSIONS

In the first four years of the program (1989–1993), most of the effort has been spent on formal pragmatic aspects of understanding and generating natural language dialogue, such as formal context modelling, representation of the beliefs of the dialogue participants, and rule-driven generation of dialogue acts. A first, provisional prototype of the DenK-system has been built and its architecture reflects the above view on the conceptual relations between user, cooperator and application.

A central issue in our approach was to develop an architecture for user-interfaces that enables us to formulate and to implement rules for cooperative behaviour, independent of a particular application domain. The design of the interface did not originate from the desire to model particular natural language phenomena, but from the need to establish *natural communication* between the application domain and its user, independently of the surface structure of the message. It is our opinion that phenomena well known in natural language semantics and pragmatics – such as context-dependency of the message, Gricean maximes, (in)definite reference, deixis – follow naturally from the fundamental properties of communication, even within the relatively simple model that has been presented in this paper.

In the next four years, apart from improving the natural language component, we will focus on the refinement of the cognitive state of the cooperator. We will especially study the extension of Type Theory with temporal aspects and modalities that are essential for describing adequate communicative behaviour, such as different types of belief and intentions. In close connection with this, we have planned to develop and evaluate different rules for cooperative behaviour, based on the notions that were introduced in this paper and supported by experimental work in dialogue research (in line with Grosz (1978)). Finally, the application domain will be extended by a so-called 'constraint-specification mechanism' that describes the properties of the domain that remain valid during the interaction. Of course, in the future the cooperator should be able to reason about these constraints.

ACKNOWLEDGEMENT

We would like to thank the anonymous reviewer for his or her valuable comments on earlier versions of this paper. The program is partly financed by the Tilburg-Eindhoven Organisation for Inter-University Cooperation.

NOTES

* Authors' addresses: R. M. C. Ahn and H. C. Bunt, Institute for Language Technology and Artificial Intelligence (ITK), Tilburg University, P.O. Box 90153, 5000 LE Tilburg, The Netherlands, e-mail: r.m.c.ahn@kub.nl, h.c.bunt@kub.nl; R. J. Beun, Institute for Perception Research (IPO), P.O. Box 513, 5600 MB Eindhoven, The Netherlands, e-mail: rjbeun@prl.philips.nl; T. Borghuis and C. W. A. M. van Overveld, Eindhoven University of Technology, Den Dolech 2, Eindhoven, The Netherlands, e-mail: tijn@win.tue.nl, wsinkvo@info.win.tue.nl.
[1] The word *denk* in Dutch means *think*.
[2] This ingenious idea is known as the Curry-Howard isomorphism (Curry and Feys 1958).
[3] It should be stressed here, however, that in the current implementation there is no natural language output (see Figure 2) and that all reponses are provided in Type Theoretical formulas.
[4] Note that besides the mutual beliefs, the cooperator also shares the first information source with the user has direct visual access to a graphical representation of the application domain.
[5] Here, we use terminology from object-oriented programming. An 'object' is a variable containing both data (its 'attributes') and optionally some program fragments (its 'methods'). Calling a method of an object is referred to as passing a 'message' to that object. An object is an instantiation of a 'class'; the class definition lists all available attributes and methods for all objects to be instantiated in this class. For a more complete introduction to object-oriented programming, we refer, e.g., to Meyer (1988).
[6] Provided the time granularity of the animation is sufficiently small and the renderer is sufficiently fast, the impression of a moving display results.
[7] A class may be defined from 'scratch' or it may inherit attributes and/or methods from other classes. The types of its attributes, as well as the types of the formal parameters in its method headings and the return types of its methods may either be earlier defined classes or generic types.
[8] See also the 'evaluator' in Figure 2.

REFERENCES

Ahn, R. M. C. (1994). *The Database*. Internal Report University of Tilburg (to appear).

Ahn, R. M. C. & Kolb, H. P. (1990). Discourse Representation Meets Constructive Mathematics. In Kálmán, L. & Pólos, L. (eds.) *Papers from the Second Symposium on Logic and Language*, 105–124. Akadémia Kiadó, Budapest.

Barendregt, H. (1991). Introduction to Generalized Type Systems. *Journal of Functional Programming* 1(2): 125–154.

Beun, R. J. (1990). The Recognition of Dutch Declarative Questions. *Journal of Pragmatics* 14: 39–56.

Beun, R. J. (1991). A Framework for Cooperative Dialogues. In Taylor, M. M., Néel, F. & Bouwhuis, D. G. (eds.) *Proceedings of the Second Venaco Workshop on the Structure of Multimodal Dialogue*. Maratea, Italy.

Van Benthem, J. (1991). Reflections on Epistemic Logic. *Logique et Analyse* 133–134: 5–14.

Borghuis, T. (1993). Interpreting Modal Natural Deduction in Type Theory. In de Rijke, M. (ed.) *Diamonds and Defaults*, 67–102. Kluwer Academic Publishers.

De Bruijn, N. G. (1980). A Survey of the Project Automath. In Seldin & Hindley (eds.) *To H. B. Curry: Essays on Combinatory Logic, Lambda Calculus and Formalisms*, 579–606. Academic Press.

Bunt, H. C. (1989). Information Dialogues as Communicative Action in Relation to Partner Modelling and Information Processing. In Taylor, M. M., Néel, F. & Bouwhuis, D. G. (eds.) *The Structure of Multimodel Dialogue*, 47–73. North-Holland, Amsterdam.

Bunt, H. C. (1993). Dynamic Interpretation and Dialogue Theory. In Black, W. J. (ed.) *Abduction, Belief and Context* (to appear).

Burger, J. D. & Marshall, R. J. (1993). The Application of Natural Language Models to Intelligent Multimedia. In Maybury, M. (ed.) *Intelligent Multimedia Interfaces*, 174–196. The MIT Press: Massachusetts.

Coquand, T. (1985). *Une théorie des Constructions*. Thèse de troisième cycle. Université de Paris VII: Paris.

Cremers, A. H. M. (1994). Referring in a Shared Workspace. In Brouwer, M. & Harrington, T. (eds.) *Basics of Man-Machine Communication for the Design of Educational Systems*, 71–78. Springer-Verlag: Berlin.

Curry, H. B. & Feys R. (1958). *Combinatory Logic, Vol. 1*, North Holland Publishing Company.

Grice, H. P. (1975). Logic and Conversation. In Cole, P. & Morgan, J. (eds.) *Speech Acts. Syntax and semantics, Vol. 11*, 41–58. Academic Press: New York.

Grosz, B. J. (1978). Discourse Analysis. In Walker, D. (ed.) *Understanding Spoken Language*, 229–345. Elsevier North-Holland: New York.

Helmink, L. & Ahn, R. M. C. (1991). Goal Oriented Proof Construction in Type Theory. In Huet, G. & Plotkin, G. (eds.) *Logical Frameworks*, 120–148. Cambridge University Press: Cambridge.

Hutchins, E. (1989). Metaphors for Interface Design. In Taylor, M. M., Néel, F. & Bouwhuis, D. G. (eds.) *The Structure of Multimodal Dialogue*, 11–28. North-Holland: Amsterdam.

Kamp, J. A. W. (1981). A Theory of Truth and Semantic Representation. In Groenendijk, J. & Stokhof, M. (eds.) *Formal Methods in the Study of Language*, 277–322. Mathematisch Centrum: Amsterdam.

Kamp, J. A. W. & Reyle, U. (1993). From Discourse to Logic: Introduction to Modeltheoretic Semantics of Natural Language, Formal Logic and Discourse Representation Theory. Dordrecht: Kluwer Academic Publishers.

Mäenpää, P. & Ranta, A. (1990). An Implementation of Intuitionistic Categorial Grammar. In Kálmán, L. & Pólos, L. (eds.) *Papers from the Second Symposium on Logic and Language*, 299–318. Akadémia Kiadó, Budapest.

Martin-Löf, P. (1984). *Intuitionistic Type Theory*. Bibliopolis: Naples.

Meyer, B. (1988) *Object-Oriented Software Construction*. Prentice Hall International.

Neal, J. G. & Shapiro, S. C. (1991). Intelligent Multimedia Interface Technology. In Sullivan, J. W. & Taylor, S. W. (eds.) *Intelligent User Interfaces*, 11–43. Addison-Wesley: Reading, MA.

Van Overveld, C. W. A. M. (1991). The Generalized Display Processor as an Approach to Real Time Interactive 3-D Computer Animation. *The Journal of Visualisation and Computer Animation* **2**(1): 16–21.

Peeters, E. A. J. (1994). LOOKS: *Syntax and Semantics*. Computing Science Note. Eindhoven University of Technology (to appear).

Searle, J. R. (1969). *Speech Acts*. Cambridge University Press: Cambridge.

De Souza, C. S. (1993). The Semiotic Engineering of User Interface Languages. *International Journal of Man-Machine Studies* **39**: 753–774.

Wahlster, W., André, E., Finkler, W., Profitlich, H.-J. & Rist, T. (1993). Plan-Based Integration of Natural Language and Graphics Generation. *Artificial Intelligence* **63**: 387–427.

Wilson, M. D., Sedlock, D., Binot, J-L. & Falzon, P. (1991). An Architecture for Multimodal Dialogue. In Taylor, M. M., Néel, F. & Bouwhuis, D. G. (eds.) *Proceedings of the Second Venaco Workshop on the Structure of Multimodal Dialogue*. Maratea, Italy.

Artificial Intelligence Review **8**: 447–468, 1994–5.
© 1995 *Kluwer Academic Publishers. Printed in the Netherlands.*

AI Meets Authoring:
User Models for Intelligent Multimedia

ANDREW CSINGER, KELLOGG S. BOOTH and DAVID POOLE

*Department of Computer Science, University of British Columbia, Vancouver,
Canada, V6T 1Z4; e-mail: {csinger, ksbooth, poole}@cs.ubc.cd*

Abstract. Authoring is a complex, knowledge-intensive activity which until recently
has been performed exclusively by humans. New computer-based techniques have
added horsepower rather than intelligence to traditional approaches, and have not
addressed their principal limitations, chief of which is the inability to tailor presentations to individual users at run-time.

We believe a model of the user is needed to support this kind of run-time determination of form *and* content. We describe our approach to the acquisition,
representation and exploitation of user models: the *most plausible* user model is the
result of an abductive *recognition* process and it incorporates assumptions about the
user which are then used to constrain the *design* by abduction of the best presentation. Both recognition and design processes are performed at run-time. We describe
a prototypical implementation designed to demonstrate these ideas in the domain of
video authoring.

Our approach to authoring is intended to apply across multiple media; we have
demonstrated these ideas with video because authoring in the video medium with
traditional approaches inherits and exacerbates the problems from traditional media,
and because the popularity of video as an authoring medium continues to grow.

Key words: authoring, artificial intelligence, multimedia, user-modelling, video

INTRODUCTION

Authoring is the honorable tradition of collecting, structuring and presenting
information in the form of a static "document" rendered in some medium or
media. Promising new technologies have recently come to light that could alleviate some of the limitations of this difficult, knowledge-intensive undertaking.

As an offshoot of his semiological analyses of the cinema, Metz (1974, p.
45) wrote that "the spectatorial demand cannot mould the particular content of
each film . . ." Such statements – though accurate in 1974 – are representative
of now out-dated, traditional approaches that take a technologically imposed
"supply-side" view of the authoring process, in which authors and publishers join
to decide both the form and the content of a document before readers ever make
their wishes known. The principal limitation of these traditional approaches is the
resulting "one-size-fits-all" static document, exemplified by the venerable book
format that we have been stuck with since well before Gutenberg. Most
approaches to authoring are even today just bigger and faster versions of the

printing press, and do nothing to overcome this early binding problem.[1] We now have fast graphics, powerful reasoning engines and other technology, but what are we going to do with them?

In order to tailor presentations to the needs and desires of individual readers, we believe we need consultable models of these readers. For the "demand-side" of the equation to have a direct effect on the form and content of the document, decisions about the final presentation must be delayed until "run-time," when the model of the reader can be brought to bear on the final stages of the design process. One difficulty is that user modelling is a new and complex problem.

We are developing techniques for user modelling that we apply to the authoring problem. Thinking of authoring in terms of the knowledge required to support the activity has resulted in a new approach that we call "intent-based authoring," which we believe can ultimately resolve the principal problems with the traditional approach.

We apply our approach to video authoring in particular, because authoring in the video medium is even harder than in conventional media, and we think that our approach can eventually work across media boundaries.

We begin in this article with an overview of authoring, distinguishing between traditional and the proposed intent-based paradigms, situating video authoring in these contexts. The problems with traditional authoring manifest themselves in the video domain in both of the distinct phases of transcription and presentation. We focus in this article on how the form and content of the presentation can be determined at run-time by reference to a model of the user/reader, and we discuss the acquisition, exploitation and representation of this model; a more detailed exploration of the issues involved in transcription is given by Csinger and Booth (1994) who discuss problems associated with the processing of information before its presentation.

The Encyclopaedia of Philosophy defines abduction as: "C. S. Peirce's name for the type of reasoning that yields from a given set of facts an explanatory hypothesis for them" (Edwards 1967, pp. 5–57). We use the term "abduction" throughout this article in the formal sense of Csinger and Poole (1993), which is consistent with Peirce's treatment; refer to Section 2.1.3 for details.

Finally, we describe *Valhalla*, a prototypical system implemented to demonstrate our ideas, and we provide our conclusions, drawn from our initial experiences using Valhalla.

1. AUTHORING

We first describe the traditional notion of authoring, independent of the target media for which the presentation is being designed, and then show how current approaches to video authoring lie within this traditional view, and thus suffer its drawbacks.

1.1. *Traditional Approaches*

Acquiring and presenting information are knowledge-intensive activities that in the past have been performed exclusively by humans. These activities in combination have come to be known as authoring. The task of an author is to collect a coherent body of information, structure it in a meaningful and interesting way, and present it in an appropriate fashion to a set of readers (or viewers) of the eventual work. This traditional notion of authoring commits the author to the form as well as to the contents of the work, well in advance of the actual time at which it is presented (see Figure 1). The familiar book format conveys this point; once printed, there is no way – short of second-editions and published errata – to change the presentation for the particular needs and desires of individual readers, or groups of readers. The author must both select and order the information to be presented. Presentations tailored to the needs of particular audiences are not possible in the traditional approach to authoring, with its "compile-time" commitment to form as well as to content.

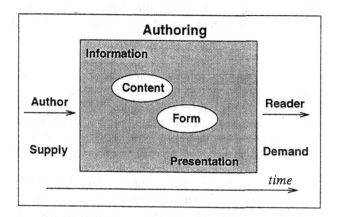

Fig. 1. **The Traditional Approach to Authoring.** There is no clear separation of information from presentation, and authors are committed to both the form and content of their message. Structured-document approaches separate form and content, but user-tailored presentation is still not possible; reader 'demand' only indirectly affects the authoring process.

Hypermedia

Although tables of contents and elaborate indexes are intended as remedies to this static format, the burden of the "one size fits all" approach falls heavily upon the reader. For instance, an encyclopedia is a hyperdocument that can be browsed using the indices and cross-references as navigational links. The browsing activity completes the selection and ordering functions normally performed by the author and brings with it an inherent overhead that must be assumed by every reader. The viewer completes the job of the author by selecting and ordering the information to be viewed through the process of navigating the links established by the author. This not only pushes the problem from one person (the author) to another person (the viewer), it also dramatically increases the demands on the author who must provide explicit navigation cues in addition to the traditional authoring tasks. Reducing the amount of human effort required from the author and viewer is still a significant problem with current approaches to (hyper-) authoring. These effects can be mitigated by the knowledge-based approach advocated in this paper.

Form Versus Content

An author chooses not only the information to be presented (the content) but also the order and style in which it will be presented (the form). Both contribute to the effectiveness of a presentation, yet few people are highly skilled in all aspects of these processes. This problem is at least partially addressed by the structured document paradigm, which attempts to separate the specification of the content of a document from the specification of its form. Markup languages like SGML (Standard Generalized Markup Language) and Hytime (Newcomb *et al.* 1991) are characteristic of this effort. They permit a delayed binding for what we might call the "surface structure" of a document (the format in which it is finally presented), but they still require the author to provide the "deep structure" (a hierarchical decomposition of the content as a structured document).

1.2. Intent-Based Authoring

A more complete de-coupling of specification and presentation processes is required, however, before truly personalized presentations are possible. We argue that in addition to the content of the document, the author must also supply an *intent*. This authorial intent is usually implicit in the work; a newspaper article is (sometimes) written to inform, an editorial to convince, a journal article such as this to argue for the acceptance of a new authoring paradigm, and so on.

Making explicit this intention at the time the document is specified opens the door to truly user-specific document presentation. Illustrated in Figure 2, we call this approach to authoring *intent-based authoring*, and describe here an application of the approach to the authoring of video documents. MacKinlay (1986), Karp and Feiner (1993) and others have argued similarly in the domains of graphical presentation and animation. Feiner explicitly uses the term "intent-based presentation". Previous work in automatic presentation has dealt with some aspects of the issues addressed herein, though it has been restricted for the most part to choosing "the right way" to display items based on their syntactic form (Mackinlay 1986, Roth and Mattis 1990). Semantic qualities of the data to be displayed are seldom considered.

The domain in which we are demonstrating our approach is the presentation of video data. Unlike Karp and Feiner (1993), who describe a system for intent-based animation, we do not start with a perfect model of the objects to be viewed and then decide on the sequence of video frames to be generated. Instead, we start with a typically large collection of pre-existing video frames (usually sequences of frames) and select and order these to communicate the intended information. Our task is one of (automatic) "assembly," rather than (automatic)

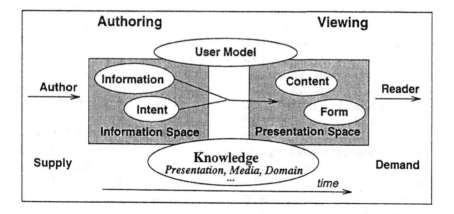

Fig. 2. **The Intent-based Approach to Authoring.** Information and presentation spaces are clearly separated, bridged by various knowledge sources. In particular, a model of the viewer permits user-tailored determination of content at run-time; supply meets demand.

"synthesis." A *presentation* for our purposes is an edit decision list which specifies the order in which a selection of video clips is to be played.[2]

Recently, other researchers have considered related problems. Hardman *et al.* (1993) undertake to free multimedia authors from having to specify all the timing relations for presentation events; some of these are derived by their system at run-time. Goodman *et al.* (1993) also build presentations on-the-fly from canned video clips and other information. Our work reported in this article focusses on user modelling, rather than the media and domain concerns that motivate most other work.

1.3. *Video Authoring*

The incentive to provide presentations which have been particularized to the viewer's needs and interests is even stronger with video than with traditional media because time is a precious human commodity, and time is what it takes to annotate, and to view video. Unfortunately, traditional authoring paradigms do not support such run-time determination of form and content.

Video is finding increasing use as a transcription medium in many fields because it arguably provides the richest record (the "thickest description" (Goldman-Segall 1989)) of the events of interest. Video recording offers high bandwidth, greatly exceeding human note-taking skills and speed; researchers can later review and annotate video at leisure. And, increasingly, video is cheap.

On the other hand, the limitations of the traditional approach to authoring are most obvious when these processes are applied in non-traditional media, such as in the video medium. The raw material must first be acquired, which involves filming or digitizing. From this raw source, video authors must assemble cuts into a cohesive presentation. The raw footage can be very voluminous, and very sparse. Ten hours of video taken during a field study for a new graphical user interface (GUI), for instance, may include many instances of coffee drinking and doughnut eating that may not be relevant to any conceivable presentation. Nevertheless, it takes someone at least ten hours to scrutinize the footage for something useful. The process of identifying these useful events and sequences has been called *annotation*, and a number of systems have been designed to expedite it. (See, for instance, Buxton and Moran (1990), Goldman-Segall (1991), Harrison and Baecker (1992), MacKay and Tatar (1989), MacKay and Davenport (1989) and Suchman and Trigg (1991)).

When the author has finally identified a useful set of cuts, the traditional notion of authoring requires assembling these into their final presentation order. Although quite adequate for creating rock music videos, this approach suffers from the aforementioned limitation, that such a presentation can not be tailored to the needs of individual viewers. In the case of video tape, it is a crippling limitation, due to the temporal linearity of the medium.

It is here that video data diverges significantly from text, graphics and even animation. Video data is inherently uninterpreted information in the sense that there currently are no general computational mechanisms for content-searching video data with the precision and semantic exactness of generalized textual search.[3]

Unlike video data, both graphics and animation can be searched for information using existing computer tools. Graphics usually rely on an underlying model or database that can be queried, while animations also have a model or database with temporal information added, which can be searched for information using existing computer tools. But frames and sequences of frames in video data cannot easily be queried for semantic content except in fairly specialized domains. At present, the only practical way of accessing a video database is for a human to first annotate it so that the annotation can be used to guide the author and the viewer. Creating this annotation, at least with the current tools, is an inherently linear operation (in terms of the time required to do it) and is a major bottleneck in the authoring of hypervideo documents.

We distinguish between the transcription processes of *logging* at the lexical level, which lends itself to some degree of automation, and *annotation*, a semantic/ pragmatic task which will require human intervention for the foreseeable future. A log of a meeting can be acquired automatically, for instance, by the Group Support System (GSS) software used by the participants. This log can be subsequently used to index a video record of the meeting to find instances of user actions at as low as the keystroke level and as high as the level of abstraction embedded into the GSS (e.g., 'brain-storming session," "open discussion," etc.) Annotation, on the other hand, is at a higher level of abstraction, defined by the eventual use to which the record of the meeting is to be put.

Two central problems related to annotation are the *semantic unpredictability* and the *syntactic ambiguity* problems, defined as follows and further described by Csinger and Booth (1994).

The Semantic Unpredictability Problem is that unanticipated uses of the database may not be supported by the procedures used to acquire the database.

The semantic unpredictability problem occurs when it is not known *a Priori* what will turn out eventually to be important (i.e., figuring out what events, and at what level of abstraction they should be recorded in the log). This problem is not solved by recording everything, nor by annotating every event in the record.

> The Syntactic Ambiguity Problem is that the names which refer to elements of the information record may not be used consistently within the record, and may not be consistent with systems external to the record.

The syntactic ambiguity problem applies to bodies of annotated video, and is not solved by adding a translation mechanism, or a lookup table; there is no necessary limit to the number of synonyms that would be required and the lookup table would need to be context sensitive.

This definition covers a variety of cases: incorrect or unintended *synonymy* is when there are multiple references to an individual (e.g., 'Smith,' 'smith,' 'jsmith,' 'John' . . .). *Homonymy* is when it may be impossible to resolve a reference (e.g., does 'smith' refer to John Smith or Mary Smith?). *Hypernymy* and *Hyponymy* are when references are at an inappropriate level in an abstraction hierarchy (e.g., 'sports-event,' 'baseball-game,' 'montreal-vs-boston' . . .). An example of where these kinds of problems can arise is when a computer-generated log is used to index a video record which has also been manually annotated; the log may employ Unix user-id's to refer to individuals (e.g., 'jsmith'), while the annotator may have used the more familiar 'John,' or 'Smith.' Some means of reconciling the references must be provided. Another example is where multiple annotators, or even a single annotator, use different labels to refer to the same event in the record.

Systems now available for video annotation do not address these problems. Each of the systems listed in the references to this article has its merits, but none of them deals directly with the syntactic ambiguity or the semantic uncertainty problem. Csinger and Booth (1994) describe how a knowledge based approach can at least mitigate some of the effects of these problems.

Even given a reasonable body of annotations, we believe navigation through a hypervideo document is more difficult than with other types of hypermedia. Pieces of information are difficult to extract from video because they often are meaningless when taken out of context (i.e., it usually does not make sense to view a non-consecutive subset of frames nor does it make sense to view only disconnected pieces of frames). Thus there is a major bottleneck in the presentation of hypervideo documents. The goal of our research is to alleviate the difficulties associated with both the annotation and presentation phases of video authoring, within the context of the intent-based authoring paradigm described above.

Davenport *et al.* (1993) describe their approach to interactive digital movie-making, a domain similar to ours in that they must log and annotate video footage for later retrieval by computer, in the absence of a human editor. Their domain differs in that it permits control over the acquisition of original raw footage. They are also not as interested in modelling the user *per se* as they are in giving the user meaningful interaction affordances to select variants of the movie. As moviemakers, Davenport *et al.* go to some effort to maintain the stylistic consistency of their presentation, an important element with which we have not yet concerned ourselves.

2. INTELLIGENT USER-TAILORED PRESENTATION

Presentation is the process of transforming information into stimuli that map into the perceptual space of human beings (Csinger 1992). There are innumerable problems associated with automating presentation processes (Karp and Feiner 1993, Mackinlay 1986). Basic issues include: (1) *What*: selecting the contents of the presentation, (2) *How*: determining the form and style of the presentation[4] and (3) *When*: deciding the temporal order of presentation events.

In the video medium, selecting the intervals of the record to be displayed, and the order in which they are to be displayed, are both serious problems.[5] Rendering the information in appropriate ways, relevant to the needs of individual users, will be achieved by recourse to models of these users, to knowledge about the media to be employed, and to other knowledge bases of various origin.

A rule-base of facts and assumables is supplied by *a knowledge engineer*. Some part of this database consists of intentional schema that intent-based *authors* can compose into high-level intentional representations. Other parts are world knowledge that the system uses in domain dependent and independent ways, and there can be knowledge as well that describes characteristics of the medium. The video record itself is provided by an *archiver*, and annotations that describe the contents of the video record are provided by an *annotator*. These databases, along with observations of the viewer's behavior, comprise the inputs to the intent-based authoring system.[6]

The outputs of the system are (1) an edit decision list of video clips which are played under user control on a video display device, and (2) a presentation to the user of the user model derived by the system. (Refer to Figure 3).

These processes, knowledge-bases and system outputs are described briefly in the following subsections.

2.1. *User Models*

Models of the viewers for whom the presentation is being prepared (Kobsa 1992, Wahlster and Kobsa 1990) are the most important knowledge-based ingredients in the recipe for intent-based presentation. Accordingly, our minimalist artificial intelligence approach (Poole 1990) to user modelling is to first build the most likely user model, and then from this user model to prepare the best presentation. This is a *recognition* task followed by a *design* task (Csinger and Poole 1993).

We use probabilities as the measure of likelihood of the user models, and use an instance of probabilistic Horn abduction to model the recognition task, finding the most likely explanation of the user's behavior in terms of a set of recognition assumptions which have associated probabilities.

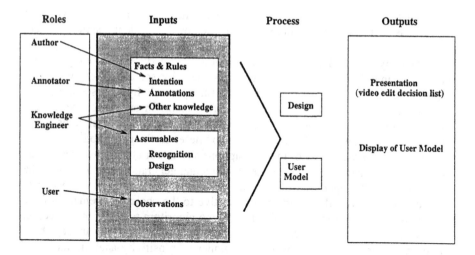

Fig. 3. **Roles, Inputs and Outputs.** Author(s) supply or select intentional descriptions of their communicative goals. Knowledge engineers provide general and specific knowledge, as well as the assumables for model recognition and presentation design. The system calculates the most likely user model from observations of the user's activity and uses that to design the best presentation. Both the presentation and components of the user model are displayed to the viewer.

We also need a way to perform the design task, and a way to evaluate designs (presentations): We use an abductive design approach (Finger and Genesereth 1985) with costs associated with design assumptions.

These recognition and design processes can be combined into a single abductive reasoning component, where some assumptions are recognition assumptions (with probabilities) and some are design assumptions (with costs). This scheme leads to a preference ordering over explanations which is described in Section 2.1.3.

Kass and Finin (1988) and others have suggested various dimensions along which user models might be categorized. We discuss in the rest of this section how our user models are acquired, exploited and represented by the system.

2.1.1. *Acquisition*

We regard the acquisition of a model of a user as a *recognition* task (Poole 1989, Csinger and Poole 1993), driven by the system's *observations* of the user's behavior at an interface, and by other information available in the user's run-time environment.

Acquisition techniques are often categorized by where they fall along a continuum from 'implicit' to 'explicit' in 'adaptive' and 'adaptable' systems, respectively (Fischer 1992). We employ a number of techniques that cover different parts of this spectrum.

At the explicit end of the continuum, we use a simple form-filling operation designed to elicit interest metrics. The system chooses at *run-time* both the fields and the layout of the form that is presented to the user, with the initial values determined by the system's current hypotheses about the user, which in turn are derived from the environment maintained by the resident operating system and other services (e.g., `finger`, `gopher`, `.plan` file, etc.), before the user has taken any action. The user implicitly validates the system's assumptions by his or her inaction, and explicitly corrects them by selecting new values or typing over the values displayed. Ideally, the system's hypotheses about the user are correct, and the user merely verifies them. In any case, the system makes 'observations' about the user consisting of what the user does when presented with a display of some of the hypotheses in the user model.[7]

The explicit presentation of the assumptions as a list of attribute values avoids complexities of natural language understanding and generation, and addresses the complaint that the operation of systems that employ user models is opaque to their users. However, this approach is sensitive to the choice of elements of the user model which are shown to the user. Some algorithm to make this selection is needed, as there may be very many hypotheses in the system's theory about the user. We are experimenting with a number of sensitivity-analytic measures that are compatible with the representation we are using.

At the implicit end of the continuum, we use recognition techniques to infer the user's goals and plans from observation of his or her actions at a virtual VCR interface panel (described later). This approach has the virtue of being completely unintrusive, but is difficult to implement because of well-known problems having to do with the large plan-library for realistic problems.

In summary, we build the most plausible model of the user based upon all the available evidence, which includes explicit, direct feedback from the user via the user-model window, implicit feedback from the user's manipulation of the virtual VCR controls, and other contextual information like the user's login and group id's. We perform this recognition task using abductive reasoning techniques (see Section 2.1.3), where probability is taken to be the measure of plausibility; assumptions used for recognition have associated probabilities, and our algorithms find the most likely model that explains the observations.

2.1.2. *Exploitation*

The exploitation of the user model in the intent-based authoring domain can be seen as a design task, where the model is used to design a presentation that meets the intention specified by the author. The user model is a 'theory' with which the design must be consistent (Poole 1989, Csinger and Poole 1993). Assumptions used for design have associated cost, and our algorithms minimize the cost of the design; the cost is a measure of the "badness" to the author of the design. We perform the design task by abduction.

The system tries to complete a constructive proof (from the user model, using design assumptions) that there exists an edit decision list that satisfies the intention of the author. When there are multiple proofs, the system selects the 'best' one, as described in Section 2.1.3.

For example, in the presentation of portions of a video record of a previously logged and annotated meeting, an important piece of information that might be found in the user model is the amount of time that a user is willing to devote to the presentation. This information will constrain the choice of cuts, and ensure that only the most important sequences are viewed.

The user model may not, of course, always be completely accurate, even after the user has been given the opportunity to modify selected fields in the acquisition phase. Dissatisfaction with the presentation may prompt the user to fast-forward, rewind, or simply stop the current presentation with the virtual VCR controls provided. The system can then reason about the user's goals and update the user model before designing a new presentation.

2.1.3. Representation

The contents of the knowledge-bases are expressed in a simple Horn-clause dialect (Poole 1993b), and the reasoning engine is a best-first probabilistic Horn-clause assumption based system (Poole 1993a).

Specifically, we use a variant of the Theorist framework for hypothetical reasoning (Poole 1987), defined in terms of two sets of formulae: the "facts" F, and the *assumables H*. An *explanation* of a closed formula g is a consistent set $F \cup E$ that implies g, where E is a set of ground instances of elements of H, called *assumptions*. Such a g, the formula that is explained, is called the *explanandum*. When the reasoning system calculates explanations for an *explanandum* it regards as given, the system is performing *abduction*. We sometimes refer to the set E itself as the explanation of g.

This work extends Theorist to include both probabilities and costs (see also Poole 1993a), and alters the notion of explanation to reflect a new combination of design and recognition.[8] H is partitioned into the set R of assumables available for user model recognition, and into the set D available for presentation design. Every assumable r in R is assigned a prior probability $0 \le P(r) \le 1$. R is partitioned into disjoint and covering sets (which correspond to independent random variables as in Poole (1993b)). Every assumable d in D is assigned a positive cost $U(d)$.

A *model* of the user is a set of recognition assumptions M: $M \subset R$, $F \cup M \not\models \emptyset$ such that $F \cup M \models Obs$, where Obs is a set of observations of the user; in other words, M is an explanation of Obs. The probability of a user model is the product of the probabilities of its elements assuming independence of recognition partitions: $P(M) = \prod_{r \in M} P(r)$. The best model is the one with the highest probability.

Given model M, a presentation *design* is a set of design assumptions W: $W \subset D$, $F \cup M \cup W \not\models \emptyset$ such that $F \cup M \cup W \models I(P)$, where $I(P)$ is a relation that is true when presentation P (a video edit decision list, for instance) satisfies the intention of the author. In other words, W, together with the model M, explains the existence of an edit decision list that satisfies the intention of the author; design W could be said to support presentation P in the context of model M. Note that here the user model M is treated as part of the facts for the design. The cost of a design is the sum of the costs of its constituent assumptions: $U(W) = \sum_{d \in W} U(d)$. The best presentation in the context of model M is the presentation supported by the least cost design.

Note that the partitioning of H partitions each explanation of $Obs \wedge \exists_p I(P)$

into a model and a design component which we denote as $\langle M, W \rangle$. We define a preference relation $\succ_p$ over explanations such that:

$$\langle M_1, W_1 \rangle \succ_p \langle M_2, W_2 \rangle,$$

iff

$$(P(M_1) > P(M_2) \text{ or } (P(M_1) = P(M_2) \quad \text{and} \quad U(W_1) < U(W_2)))$$

which results in a lexicographic ordering of explanations. So, the "best" explanation consists of the most plausible model of the user and the lowest cost design.

In other words, an explanation is composed of a user model and a presentation design. We prefer the explanation whose recognition assumptions constitute the most plausible user model (the one with the highest probability), and whose design assumptions constitute the best presentation (the one with the lowest cost). Our algorithms find the explanation that represents the best design for the most plausible model.

A single abductive reasoning engine is employed for both recognition of the user model, and for design of the presentation. Separating the assumables for model recognition from the assumables for presentation design not only helps knowledge engineers express what they really mean, but has interesting ramifications in the way presentations are chosen; in particular, we do not give up good models for which we can find only bad designs. For instance, consider the case where we have disjoint assumables *student* and *faculty*, where $P(student)$ $\gg P(Faculty)$, but the lowest cost design in the context of a model that assumes the user is a *student* is greater than the one in the context of a model that assumes the user is a *faculty* member (i.e., $U(W_{best} \mid \cdots student \cdots) \gg$ $U(W_{best} \mid \cdots faculty \cdots))$. We do not give up the assumption that the user is a student; the reasons for deciding in favor of *student* are not affected by the system's inability to find a good (low-cost) presentation.

Decision-theory has been applied by others to design tasks under uncertainty. Some of this literature (see Cheeseman (1990) for a discussion) argues that the best design is the one that results from averaging over all models (probabilistically weighted), i.e., that the expected cost function is to be minimized to find the best presentation design:

$$(1) \qquad E(W) = \mu(W|M_1)P(M_1) + \mu(W|M_2)P(M_2) + \cdots + \mu(W|M_n)P(M_n)$$

where $\mu(W|M)$ is the cost of design W in the context of model M.

Our current research suggests that this approach may not always be the best one; in particular, in our application, we want the user model to be explicit, so that it can be critiqued by the user and by computational agents. We also desire visibility of the model so that the system's design rationale is evident to the user, who can correct the model if necessary. Using the expected value definition of utility shown in Equation (1) does not support these goals.

2.2. Other System Knowledge

2.2.1. Domain-Independent Knowledge

We begin with a library of presentation plan schemata.[9] These schemata are variously elaborated, more or less domain-independent strategies or plans for delivering information in a variety of [stereo]typical scenarios. We could have, for instance, a "convince" plan, a plan intended to convince the viewer of a particular perspective, if this is deemed necessary. There are many ways in which viewers might become convinced of something; one strategy is to present examples as evidence in support of a conclusion. Stylistic or conventional factors might govern whether the evidence precedes the conclusion (prefix) or comes after it (postfix). We could also think of the "inform" plan, with its obvious speech-act connotations (Searle and Vanderveken 1985). A presentation plan is an arbitrarily complex argument structure designed to achieve a compound communicative goal.

A schema is chosen which is consistent with the model of the intention of the author. This schema must be refined, elaborated, and perhaps even modified non-trivially to arrive at the final presentation. Refinements take place by exploding the terminal leaves of the plan until they are instantiable components of the available (video) record. Structural changes to the tree can be made by extra-logical plan critics, or other generalized agents with an interest in the form or content of the presentation. Figure 4 illustrates two simple schemata, and Figure 5 shows some of the code used to implement the "describe" schema.

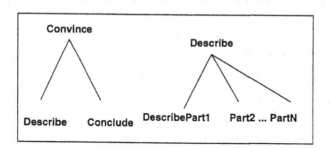

Fig. 4. **Example Presentation Schemata.** The leaves of the schemata can be video edit-lists, or can themselves be further elaborated.

2.2.2. Domain-Dependent Knowledge

Here we refer to axioms supplied by a domain specialist, which describe the manner in which domain-independent elements may be instantiated with domain-specific types of information. So, for instance, where the schema indicates that the viewer should be impressed or entertained at a specific point in the presentation, this body of knowledge would define the kinds of information in this particular domain that might qualify. For example, impressing a viewer at some point would depend upon what it takes to impress a user of a given type, as well as what the goals of the user are in consulting the presentation system. A

```
% Descr is a description of Thing
describe(Thing, Descr) <=
    editList([],Descr,descr(Thing),0,_L).
describe(BigThing, Descr) <=
    bagof(Thing, partof(Thing, BigThing), Things),
    desc(Things, [], Descr, 0, _Length).

desc([], Descr, Descr, Length, Length).
desc([H|T], InD, Descr, InL, Length) <=
    editList(InD,OutD,descr(H),InL,OutLength)
    desc(T, OutD, Descr, OutLength, Length).
```

Fig. 5. **Code sample: Part of the 'Describe' Schema.** A description of a *Thing* can be a video edit-list, or it can be the descriptions of its parts, each of which can be a video edit-list. This code is interpreted by the Horn-clause meta-interpreter that performs the probabilistic and cost-based abductive reasoning described in this article. The reasoner itself is written in Prolog.

set of axioms might permit the inference that a picture or a video of the latest results in computer-synthesized animation would impress a researcher in theoretical AI, although it might take more than that to impress the prospective graduate student in computer graphics.

Eventually, individual pieces of the video record must be chosen to fill the slots in the elaborated plan schema; the leaf nodes in the tree representing the plan schema for "convincing the user" are to be exploded (see Figure 6). We would be supplied with the knowledge required to retrieve instances of video that illustrate "graphics research results," and we would know at this point what

```
Convince(join-ubc-faculty)
  Describe(department)
      edit-list([(00:01:26, 00:02:27, head-klawe-intro)])

  Describe(laboratories)
    Describe(lci)
        edit-list([(00:43:41, 00:44:23, interview(alan-mackworth)),
                   (00:12:15, 00:15:54, tour-lci)])

    Describe(imager-lab)
        edit-list([(00:45:08, 00:46:16, interview(kelly-booth)),
                   (00:03:06, 00:03:13, rendered-dragon-speaks)])

  Conclude(general-appeal)

  Describe(vancouver)
      edit-list([(00:20:15, 00:20:20, cypress-mountain)])

  Describe(campus)
      edit-list([(00:25:07, 00:26:59, aerial-view-campus),
                 (00:27:43, 00:27:44, faculty-club)])
```

Fig. 6. **A Partially Elaborated Presentation.** The system instantiates the logical form *Describe(campus)* with actual video footage represented by the in- and out-points given in absolute time codes.

label in the annotation label field identifies visuals of computer-synthesized graphics, and so on.

2.2.3. Media-Specific Knowledge

Knowledge of particular media characteristics must be encoded as well. It may not do, for instance, to present intervals whose length is less than, say, a second in duration, and there is little point in flashing video stills for a thirtieth of a second. There is a limit to the speed with which video can be meaningfully displayed to human viewers, and transitions between cuts should be pleasing and consistent. The presentation component of the system should know at least this much about video. Similar considerations apply for other media. Certain cross-modal issues can be handled with this knowledge-base as well (Csinger 1994). Synchronization of different tracks, for instance, is a difficult task. How are the audio and video tracks to be synchronized, when a tape is presented faster than normal speed? Beyond what speed do special measures need to be taken? The eventual answers to these kinds of questions will be included in the media-specific knowledge base.

3. *VALHALLA*: A PROTOTYPE

Valhalla is a prototype implementation that addresses the problems associated with transcription (Csinger and Booth 1994), and decouples the specification from the presentation tasks of authoring, abandoning the traditional model in favor of the intent-based paradigm.

The author brings an intent, and information he thinks will be relevant to the eventual presentation. After annotation, a representation of this intent, and a set of indices into the raw video reside in a "document." This is all done at compile-time, in the absence of the viewer. Later, at run-time, the reasoner uses the document, along with the user model and other knowledge, to produce an edit-list. The viewer, even in the absence of the author, sees only relevant portions of the video.

Presentation is decoupled from specification by having the system prepare an edit-list of relevant events and intervals subject to the constraints in the available knowledge bases. The generation of this edit-list is performed at run-time, rather than compile-time, so that the author need not be physically present to ensure that the presentation is suitable. The intent of the author is currently encapsulated in a distinguished predicate that is attached to a show button on the interface, whose intended interpretation is that viewers should be given a basic overview of the material available, followed by a body which is relevant to their immediate information retrieval goals, and then by a conclusion; other author intentions could be similarly encapsulated and connected to the show button, or to other buttons on some custom interface. A number of constraints are applied to the design of the presentation, including for instance that its length not exceed a certain amount of time. We restrict the user's interaction with the system in this way to factor out variables that would make it difficult to test the impact of our modelling approach. Note, however, that there is an additional window, not shown in this article, that can be used to make arbitrary queries of the reasoning engine; the user can take the role of intent-based author by specifying his own intent in this window and instructing the system to find an appropriate presentation. See Figure 7 for an example.

```
? area(Student, graphics),              % Student studies graphics
  supervises(FacultyMember, Student),    %   and is supervised by FacultyMember
  relevant(FacultyMember, Topic),        %   to whom Topic is relevant
  editList([], Presentation, Topic, 0, L), % Get a video edit-list
  costLength(L, 300).                     %   close to 300 seconds
```

Fig. 7. **Authorial Intent as a Prolog query.** An author might form this query to ask for a presentation of footage (optimal length of five minutes), relevant in some way to a departmental supervisor of a graduate student associated with the Computer Graphics research laboratory . . . Obviously, the full power of intent-based authoring is not realizable in the prototype without some facility with Prolog, and with the underlying reasoning and representation methodology; this is why we expect the user testing of *Valhalla* to make use of the Show button, which abstracts away from these complexities.

The needs of individual users are met by referring to the user model, which is arrived at by the reasoning method outlined earlier in this article. As discussed earlier, the user is given the opportunity to critique a selected subset of the model via *Valhalla*'s user-model window, shown in Figure 8. The hypotheses actually displayed to the user are context-dependent, selected and ranked by a sensitivity analysis algorithm (to be described in a forthcoming article) that approximates the degree of importance to the design, of each assumption in the model. In addition, the techniques employed to display these assumptions reflect

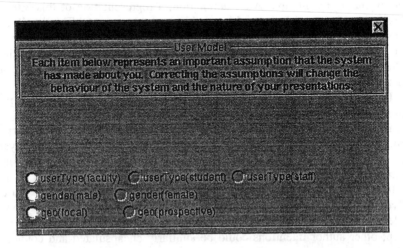

Fig. 8. **The *Valhalla* User Model Window.** This screen shows a number of sets of radio buttons, which is *Valhalla*'s display technique for variables whose values are drawn from an exclusive (disjoint) set. Here, *Valhalla* believes the user is a faculty member; a student can correct the system's misconception with a single click.

their relative importance; quantities to which the design is most sensitive are shown, for example, in bolder fonts, brighter colors, larger characters, and so on. Every effort is made to sanction the further assumption by the system that the user has actually seen and attended to the display in the user model window.

The *Valhalla* control window, shown in Figure 9, contains – in addition to the familiar virtual VCR control panel at the lower left – controls to advance to the next clip in the current edit-list, to return to the previous clip in the current edit-list, to replay the current clip, and to proceed with the presentation ("Go"). The "Show" button is a request that is passed on to the reasoning engine to calculate the next best presentation for the current model. "No!" is merely a direct way for the user to express dissatisfaction with the current presentation, freeing the reasoner to recalculate both model and design as required. Any activity at the control window is echoed to the reasoner, which can use plan recognition techniques to infer the motives of the user from these observations of user behavior.

The video delivery component of the system is designed to handle tape, video disk and digital video through a video server mechanism. Connections between the video server, user interface and reasoning engine are all client/server (TCP/IP) links, giving flexibility and platform independence; the user interface with form filling and virtual VCR control is implemented in Objective C and currently resides on a NeXT workstation, the Prolog reasoner as well as the video server on a Sparcstation. The knowledge bases are all written in a Prolog-like Horn clause language extended with assumptions (as described in Section 2.1.3), and the annotation database consists of only definite clause assertions.

We have begun testing the system with a body of video known as the UBC Computer Science Department Hyperbrochure, an hour-long video disk that includes an introduction to UBC's computer science department by its head, inter-

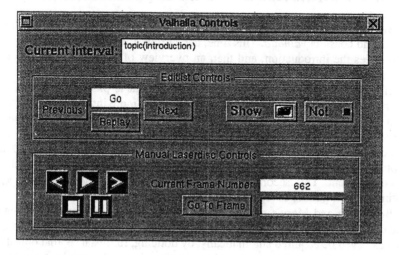

Fig. 9. **The *Valhalla* Control Window.** The label of the current interval as provided in the annotation database is displayed. Manual laser disk controls include absolute frame indexing.

views with most of the faculty and staff, as well as walk-throughs of the laboratories. Potential viewers of the material are prospective and current graduate and undergraduate students, faculty and staff, funding agencies and industrial collaborators. All these are potential users of *Valhalla*, and each brings idiosyncratic goals and interests that the system attempts to meet with tailored presentations.

3.1. *Scenario: Different Users, Different Models, Different Designs*

John, a prospective graduate student, starts up *Valhalla* after signing on as guest. The user model window pops up with the system's a priori hypotheses about John. Since usage of the guest account carries little information beyond the reasonable assumption that the user is not a current member of the department, some default hypotheses are based upon the knowledge that the terminal John is using is located in a faculty office, and that the departmental on-line calendar lists a faculty recruiting seminar that day. These coincidences conspire to produce the false assumption that John is a prospective faculty member.

If John notices by looking at the user model window that *Valhalla* thinks he is a prospective faculty member, he may correct this false assumption at this point by clicking on the button that represents that he is a prospective student. John can interact with user model window immediately, or he may wait until after pressing the show button and perhaps wondering why the presentation is not meeting his needs as a prospective student. In either case, after correcting the system's misconception, he is presented with a brief introduction to the department by its head, and then with a number of clips designed to motivate and increase his interest in the department. *Valhalla* makes numerous assumptions here about the interests of students and instantiates these goals with footage about sports facilities on campus, regular social events in the department, and a brief overview of research activities. John lets the presentation play to conclusion and logs out.

Mary, a prospective faculty member, signs on at the same terminal, also as guest, and consults *Valhalla*. This time, the a priori assumptions are more relevant. Mary sees the introduction, and then an overview of each of the laboratories in the department. She replays the clip of the Laboratory for Computational Intelligence (LCI) several times, information that is passed on by *Valhalla*'s interface to the reasoner, which infers that Mary is more interested in AI research than other activities in the department (although there *are* other explanations, like "sheer disbelief," etc.) Mary asks for another presentation (either before or after the current one runs to completion) and is then presented with more detailed footage about the LCI, as well as with interviews with key AI researchers in the department. This second presentation is shortened to accommodate Mary's optimal viewing time, as represented in the system's model of her.

Both John and Mary's presentations include clips about the Vancouver area, because it is considered by many to be very attractive. This kind of information can even be acquired automatically, by noticing, for instance, that out-of-town users tend to linger over scenic shots in the video presentations much more than do locals (who can just look out the window); the *a priori* probabilities of assumables can be upgraded according to well-known learning algorithms (Xiang *et al.* 1990). Had they been assumed by *Valhalla* to be current, rather than prospective members of the department, John and Mary would not have been presented with this extra information.

4. CONCLUSION

Video annotation and presentation are characterized in this paper as members of a class of authoring tasks. Most systems which are currently available to support this task inherit the limitations of the traditional model of authoring. The foremost such limitation is that since the composition/specification and presentation phases are inseparable in the traditional model, there is no way to provide user-tailored presentations at run-time. The problems are exacerbated in the video medium because it is temporally linear (and because humans have so little time), and because current techniques for automatic speech and visual recognition leave the contents uninterpreted. A knowledge-based solution was proposed to mitigate the serious effects of these problems, and a prototype called *Valhalla* was implemented and tested.

The central focus of our project continues to be the deployment of artificial intelligence techniques for user modelling. We work within the limits of what has been called "minimal AI" to explore the simplest useful applications of probability and decision theoretic reasoning strategies to the problems of modelling users of computer systems. Our approach is very simple, based as it is upon well-tested notions from decision theory and the AI literature. We will be evaluating the effectiveness of these and other techniques in future work. We are undertaking empirical testing of the *Valhalla* interface to see if the user modelling techniques it encapsulates help users accomplish certain well-defined information retrieval tasks, as we believe it will.

The intent-based authoring paradigm described in this article can be applied to different media, domains, and tasks. We believe it has potential to circumvent limitations of the traditional model of authoring.

ACKNOWLEDGMENTS

Thanks to Michael Horsch for a best-first Horn-clause reasoner that actually worked, and to Steve Gribble and Scott Flinn who are re-implementing the interface so that intent-based authors need not be Prolog programmers. We are grateful for the time and effort invested by the anonymous reviewers of this article.

NOTES

[1] We use 'binding' here in the sense of associating values with variables. The pun was unintended.

[2] Such a characterization deliberately excludes from discussion details of how clips are to be visually related (i.e., special editing effects like cut, fade or dissolve), attributes of the playback (e.g., screen contrast, color balance, etc.) and other aspects of video authoring that could easily fall within the purview of a framework of this sort.

[3] See, however, Cherfaoui and Bertin (1993), who use digital image processing techniques to extract some types of information from video. Refer to Joly and Cherfaoui (1993) for a recent survey of related approaches.

[4] There is also the important issue of 'allocating the media' (Arens *et al.* 1993), which involves hard-to-automate decisions about what medium in a multimedia environment best conveys the information value of a datum. Such decisions are very context-dependent, and are prone to unforeseen cross-modal effects (Csinger 1994, Wahlster *et al.* 1991).

[5] Although this discussion proceeds in terms of the video medium, the intent-based authoring framework is more general and widely applicable. Presentation plans can be elaborated not only with video sequences but with graphics, text and whatever other media and information resources are at the disposal of the presentation system.

[6] Note that a single agent may assume more than one of the roles mentioned (knowledge engineer, author, archiver, annotator, viewer); a user agent can author his own presentations by specifying or choosing an intention, and then viewing the ensuing presentation. An agent may be both author and knowledge engineer, annotator or archiver, and so on, at different times.

[7] The presentation of these hypotheses must be performed in perceptually salient ways. There is no point displaying this information with the aim of making things transparent for the user if the user is not going to understand it, or perhaps even worse, ignore it (Csinger 1994).

[8] The distinction here between design and recognition turns on whether the system is free to choose any hypothesis that it wants (design) or whether it must try to 'guess' some hypothesis that 'nature' or an adversary has already chosen (recognition). Both recognition and design can be performed abductively or deductively; we use abduction here for both. See (Csinger and Poole 1993) for details.

[9] This is similar in spirit to the presentation strategies employed in the WIP project at the German Research Center for Artificial Intelligence (DFKI) (Wahlster *et al.* 1991). Some of our approach has its intellectual roots in the work being done at DFKI, where the first author was a visiting scholar in 1992.

REFERENCES

Arens, Y., Hovy, E. & van Mulken, S. (1993). Structure and Rules in Automated Multimedia Presentation Planning. In *Proceedings of The 13th International Joint Conference on Artificial Intelligence*, 1253–1259, Chambéry, France.

Buxton, W. & Moran, T. (1990). EuroPARC's Integrated Interactive Intermedia Facility (IIIF): Early Experiences. In Gibbs, S. & Verrijn-Stuart, A. A. (eds.) Multi-user Interfaces and Applications, 11–34.

Cheeseman, P. (1990). On Finding the Most Probable Model. In Shranger, J. & Langley, P. (eds.) *Computational Models of Scientific Discovery and Theory Formation*, chapter 3, pp. 73–95. Morgan Kaufmann: San Mateo.

Cherfaoui, M. & Bertin, C. (1993). Video Documents: Towards Automatic Summaries. In *Workshop Proceedings of IEEE Visual Processing and Communications*, 295–298, Melbourne, Australia.

Csinger, A. (1992). The Psychology of Visualization. Technical Report 28, The University of British Columbia.

Csinger, A. (1994). *Cross-modal Reference and the Attention Problem* (in prep.).

Csinger, A. & Booth, K. S. (1994). Reasoning About Video: Knowledge-Based Transcription and Presentation. In Nunamaker, Jay F. & Sprague, Ralph H (eds.) *27th Annual Hawaii International Conference on System Sciences*, Volume III: Information Systems: Decision Support and Knowledge-based Systems, pp. 599–608, Maui, HI.

Csinger, A. & Poole, D. (1993). Hypothetically Speaking: Default Reasoning and Discourse Structure.

In *Proceedings of The 13th International Joint Conference on Artificial Intelligence*, 1179–1184, Chambéry,France.

Davenport, G., Evans, R. & Halliday, M. (1993). Orchestrating Digital Micromovies. *Leonardo* **26**(4): 283–288.

Edwards, P. (ed.). (1967). *The Encyclopaedia of Philosophy*. Macmillan and The Free Press.

Finger, J. J. & Genesereth, M. R. (1985). *Residue: A Deductive Approach to Design Synthesis*. Technical Report STAN-CS-85-1035, Department of Computer Science, Stanford University, Stanford, Cal.

Fischer, G. (1992). Shared Knowledge in Cooperative Problem-Solving Systems: Integrating Adaptive and Adaptable Systems. In *Proceedings of The Third International Workshop on User Modelling*. 148–161. Dagstuhl, Germany.

Goldman-Segall, R. (1989). Thick Descriptions: A Tool for Designing Ethnographic Interactive Videodiscs. *SigChi Bulletin*, **21**(2).

Goldman-Segall, R. (1991). A Multimedia Research Tool for Ethnographic Investigation. In Harel, I. & Papert, S. (eds.) *Constructionism*. Ablex Publishing Corporation: Norwood, NJ.

Goodman, B. A. (1993). Multimedia Explanations for Intelligent Training Systems. In Maybury, Mark T. (ed.) *Intelligent Multimedia Interfaces*, chapter 7, pp. 148–171. AAAI Press – MIT Press.

Hardman, L. van Rossum, G. & Bulterman, D. C. A. (1993). Structured Multimedia Authoring. In *Proceedings ACM Multimedia 93*, 283–289.

Harrison, B. L. & Baecker, R. M. (1992). Designing Video Annotation and Analysis Systems. In *Graphics Interface '92 Proceedings*, 157–166. Vancouver, BC.

Joly, P. & Cherfaoui, M. (1993). Survey of Automatical Tools for the Content Analysis of Video. IRIT 93-36-R, Bibliotheque de I'IRIT, UPS, 118 route de Narbonne, 31062 TOULOUSE CEDEX. Also available by anonymous FTP from ftp.irit.fr in PostScript, ascii and MS Word formats as private/svideo.[ps,as,wd], or by email direct from the authors (cherfaoui@ccett.fr or joly@irit.fr).

Karp, P. & Feiner, S. (1993). Automated Presentation Planning of Animation Using Task Decomposition with Heuristic Planning. In *Graphics Interface '93*, 118–127, Toronto, Canada.

Kass, R. & Finin, T. (1988). Modelling the User in Natural Language Systems. *Computational Linguistics* **14**(3): 5.

Kobsa, A. (1992). User Modelling: Recent Work, Prospects and Hazards. In *Proceedings of The Workshop on User Adapted Interaction*, Bari, Italy. Also available as a June 1992 Technical Report from Universität Konstanz Informationswissenschaft.

Mackay, W. E. & Davenport G. (1989). Virtual Video Editing in Interactive Multimedia Applications. *Communications of the Association for Computing Machinery* **32**(7): 802–810.

Mackay, W. E. & Tatar, D. G. (1989). Special Issue on Video as a Research and Design Tool. *ACM SIGCHI Bulletin* **21**(2).

Mackinlay, J. D. (1986). Automating the Design of Graphical Presentations of Relational Information. *Association for Computing Machinery Transactions on Graphics* **5**(2): 110–141.

Metz, C. (1974). *Film Language: A Semiotics of the Cinema*. Oxford University Press. Translated by Michael Taylor.

Newcomb, S. R., Kipp, N. A. & Newcomb, V. T. (1991). The "HyTime" Hypermedia/Time-based Document Structuring Language. *Communications of the Association for Computing Machinery* **34**(11): 67–83.

Poole, D. (1987). A Logical Framework for Default Reasoning. *Artificial Intelligence* **36**(1): 27–47.

Poole, D. (1989). Explanation and Prediction: An Architecture for Default and Abductive Reasoning. *Computational Intelligence* **5**(2): 97–110.

Poole, D. (1990). Hypo-Deductive Reasoning for Abduction, Default Reasoning and Design. In *Working Notes, AAAI Spring Symposium on Automated Abduction*, 106–110.

Poole, D. (1993a). Logic Programming, Abduction and Probability: A Top-Down Anytime Algorithm for Computing Prior and Posterior Probabilities. *New Generation Computing* **11**(3–4): 377–400.

Poole, D. (1993b). Probabilistic Horn Abduction and Bayesian Networks. *Artificial Intelligence* **64**(1): 81–129.

Foth, S. F. & Mattis, J. (1990). Data Characterization for Intelligent Graphics Presentation. In *CHI'90 Proceedings*, 193–200, Seattle, WA.

Searle, J. R. & Vanderveken, D. (1985). *Foundations of Illocutionary Logic.* Cambridge University Press.

Suchman, L. & Trigg, R. (1991). Understanding Practice: Video as a Medium for Reflection and Design. In Greenbaum & Kyng (eds.) *Design at Work: Cooperative Design of Computer Systems.*

Wahlster, W., André, E., Bandyopadhyay, S., Graf, W. & Rist. T. (1991). WIP: The Coordinated Generation of Multimodal Presentations from a Common Representation. Research Report RR-91-08, Deutsches Forschungszentrum für Künstliche Intelligenz, Stuhlsatzenhausweg 3, D-6600 Saarbrücken 11, Germany.

Wahlster, W. & Kobsa, A. (1990). *User Modelling in Dialog Systems.* Springer-Verlag.

Xiang, Y., Beddoes, M. P. & Poole, D. (1990). Sequential Updating Conditional Probability in Bayesian Networks by Posterior Probability. In *Proceedings of the Eighth Biennial Conference of the Canadian Society for Computational Studies of Intelligence,* 21–27.

Artificial Intelligence Review **8**: 469–470, 1994–5.

Book Reviews

Title: **Another 'Spaniard' in the works: About Ó Nualláin's treatise** *The search for mind: A new foundation for cognitive science*	*Editor/Author:* Seán Ó Nualláin *Publisher/Date:* Ablex, 1995

The book 'The search for mind: a new foundation for cognitive science' by Seán Ó Nualláin provides entertaining and/or provocative reading, depending on whether you wish to invest in reflexion or not. The reader has to be warned: this is rich, meaty, spicy, funny and according to the author, both description and prescription. It is at the very least good medicine against laziness of mind!

The book is divided in two parts: the constituent disciplines of Cognitive Science, encompassing philosophy, psychology, linguistics, neuroscience, AI and less expectedly enthnoscience and ethology. Part 2, A new foundation for Cognitive Science, deals in turn with Symbol systems, Consciousness and Selfhood, Cognitive Science and the search for mind.

Knowledge on the field is presented in a very synthetic way, with a very firm grasp on what the reader should remember. This well-balanced guidance implies freedom of judgement and courage, while offering an impressive number of alternative choices, through references and brief presentations of current lines of thought. There is much to chew, and a good lot of humour to ease the process (including drawings). Style is brilliant and very tonic. Difficult questions are put in plain language, but accuracy and correct methodology are never lost in the process.

Reviewing the different chapters in Part one will show that questions are raised while the settings are described. In the chapter on philosophical epistemology, the reader is invited to follow the author on a quick tour of the 'Great Gallery of famous philosophers of all times'; the exercise is pleasantly compared to the famous 'reduced Shakespeare' performance (including a thirty-second Hamlet), which we will find again in the chapter devoted to AI. At some crucial points, we are allowed to 'pause for breath', so we do not lose sight of the Big Questions of traditional epistemology. Such attempts are, from our point of view, always to be encouraged. However, they are difficult to appreciate for readers belonging to a different cultural area, especially when it comes to a judgment about 'Cartesianism' and related matters. It is generally admitted that, given a sufficient 'amount of indifference', the 'standard average European cognitive scientist' is a bona fide Cartesian. However, the French at least could object that given their fondness of debate, you can find at least five different kinds of anti-Cartesians for every single Cartesian in activity. The anti-Cartesians being themselves outnumbered by the Beotians, the usefulness of Ó Nualláin's 'Epistemology for beginners' is nevertheless not to be questioned.

Even if the Big Questions of Epistemology are usually asked by philosophers, those who try to answer them are mainly psychologists, hence Ó Nualláin's claim that psychology is experimental epistemology. He presents Psychology to us, perhaps even more convincingly that he did for Philosophy, since he is drawing a picture of his own field. To take but one

305

example, his account of the successes and shortcomings of the Piagetian approach is particularly bright and enjoyable, especially the comments on why 'natural logic' (Piaget's Holy Grail) is yet to be conquered. The whole of the chapter helps us understand why many authors (including Ó Nualláin) consider Psychology, rather than Linguistics or Philosophy, as central to Cognitive Science.

The chapter on Linguistics is probably the most frustrating, because the overall picture is almost painfully exact, while the discussion is less solidly integrated than we are already used to expect. It presents a computationalist view on the field, with examples of what is currently done. The conclusion is that linguistics should not be central to cognitive science. What is clearly pinpointed is that in the present state of the art, syntax largely fails, unless limited to a known context. More on the epistemological reasons why this is the case, or how context should be handled would be welcome. All the more so since language will be cited again in Chapter 5 and in Chapter 7 in relation with music. However this chapter gives an accurate view on the computational domain and a vivid account of the Chomskian revolution. It will no doubt lead to fruitful argumentation.

Neuroscience is very neatly presented, in a more distant fashion than the previous chapters. We directly plunge from there to connectionism (is that fair to neurobiologists? shouldn't they be a little bit more pricked at?) and a wealth of research paths to link the Big Questions in Epistemology to this approach.

AI researchers will find themselves well chastized in the hilarious reduced history of AI, and well loved, (though well known), in the more sober account of their achievements and shortcomings. Here the issues for CS are very clearly defined. The presentation of AI ends with a gallery of skeptics from Wittgenstein to Descartes, including Penrose, to teach us why and how computation and cognition can't be merely equated. If you missed the first chapter, you will be stuck here.

Ethology and ethnoscience come as a reminder that man is an animal living in relation with the natural environment and in a social community as any species and this is the necessary turn to the next part where the leitmotives of 'Mylesian theory' are developed.

In Part two, the discussion on symbols in Chapter 7 offers very deep insights on the question of mind and cognition, but the characteristics of symbol-systems lack clear distinction between a symbol-system in use as opposed to a system of notation and a system of interpretation (a problem which is lagging since Chapter 3). This might explain why some of the most far-fetching intuitions on cognition remain somewhat ethereal if seducing.

In his own 'Mylesian' theory of consciousness the author starts with 'the notion of cognition as an inevitable result of immersion in a life-world', an idea best formulated by Merleau-Ponty. He contends that 'we can either, as Cognitive scientists, focus on characterizing issues like the walls and pillars, or, like phenomenologists we can consider the discipline as the organization of space, rather than building materials'. Chapter 9 provides a general round-up of the question and leaves the reader with the appropriate impression that the field is just unfolding and that much work is to be done.

Thanks to this book, much has been done to delimitate the space where cognitive science should be developing. We will surely argue on many issues, but this presentation is humanist and passionate enough to precisely foster more effort to define what cognitive science should be about.

NADINE LUCAS and
JEAN-BAPTISTE BERTHELIN
LIMSI-CNRS, Orsay, France

Artificial Intelligence Review **8**: 471–472, 1994–5.

Title: **Computers and Creativity**
Editor/Author: Derek Partridge & John
  Rowe

Publisher/Date: Intellect Books (Oxford,
  England), 1994
Price: S/b £14.95

Computers and Creativity is centered around an elegant computational model of human creativity called GENESIS, devised by the book's second author, John Rowe. Influenced by Artificial Life approaches to AI, GENESIS is an *emergent memory* model, loosely based upon Minsky's notion (in *The Society of Mind*, 1985) of small, self-contained and cooperating 'agents', similar to Hofstadter's 'codelets' (1990) and Dennett's 'demons' (1991). The model works in a relatively knowledge-free domain (thereby ameliorating potential 'microworld' criticisms) of a revised version of the sequence-prediction card game *Eleusis*. This domain is rich enough to provide a convincing context for the model's performance, and simple enough to avoid unnecessary complexity.

The first two chapters are expository, the first a chatty introduction to the books subject matter, i.e. creativity, and the second a more detailed review of psychological theories of the creative process itself, notably the *four stage model* of Poincare and the *cortical arousal* theory.

Chapter 3 provides a short introduction to the benefits and drawbacks involved in the methodology of computational modelling, and then goes on to survey previous models of creativity. Instead of simply listing these other models however, the two authors seek to identify useful features by which to judge them, and other theories, including their own: the most important are judged to be the incorporation of analogical mechanisms in any putative model, the lack of a centralized control and the ability to support flexible representations. It is this last notion, what the authors call *representational fluidity* that is developed more fully in Chapter 4, along with the basic components of the GENESIS model. The model postulates two kinds of 'agents', *builders*

and *k-lines*. These agents do the work of constructing 'theory representations' of the 'perceptions' that they (i.e. the theory representations) are attempting to 'model'. A number of processes operate upon agents to constrain their behaviour, notably the processes of *censorship, suppression,* (notions, once more, adapted from Minsky) and (slightly differently) *credit assignment,* which is reward given to certain agents for achieving various model-specified subgoals. Finally, Chapter 4 considers two alternate ways in which agents are selected by the model to participate in theory building, the first based upon a measure of which agent is 'shouting the loudest', the second based upon Hofstadter's notion of a *terraced scan*, essentially a probablistic smearing of the previous measure allowing for greater initial flexibility in the model.

Chapter 5 elaborates upon the formal treatment in the earlier chapter, providing more details of the GENESIS implementation, and also considers the advantages of the chosen task domain, the sequence-prediction card game termed *micro-Eleusis* by Rowe. The task of GENESIS is to construct 'rules' or 'explanations' for sequences of cards (restricted to only four 'kinds' of card). That is, given the sequence **red-odd, red-even, black-odd, black-even, red-odd** . . . GENESIS must find a 'rule' that explains the sequence. Finite state automata are used to graphically illustrate the kinds of 'rule' that the model creatively finds. Chapter 5 concludes with a brief review of five other computational models used for comparison with the performance of GENESIS in the next chapter.

Following on, Chapter 6 is an extensive, detailed empirical study of the performance of GENESIS on a number of different sequence types, exhibiting various degrees of rule 'complexity'. The other computa-

Artificial Intelligence Review **8**: 472–473, 1994–5.

tional models introduced in Chapter 5, implemented by the second author for purpose of comparison with GENESIS, are considered here, both with GENESIS as 'player' and as 'dealer', and with two human players. Chapter 7 concludes the book, and discusses the various issues raised throughout the book, including a summary of the empirical study of the various models, the notion of creativity as 'controlled randomness', and a discursion into the advantages of Artificial Life and, to a lesser extent, connectionist (though the treatment here and earlier in Chapter 4, is cursory) approaches to computational modelling.

If I was to voice a complaint, it would not be with the work itself, but with the quality of the books appearance and pro-duction. An annoying number of omissions, additions and errors in the text display poor (if any) copyediting on the part of the publisher, notably the affiliations of the authors (cited differently on the back cover from that cited inside), as well as the persistent use of incorrect grammatical forms in the text, for example, 'i.e.' repeatedly reproduced as 'ie'.

In summary, however, this book is an interesting, accessible read, the computational work of the second author at its core both clever and intriguing, and I would recommend it.

STUART A. JACKSON
Department of Computer Science
University of Sheffield, U.K.

Title: **A Connectionist Language Generator**
Editor/Author: Nigel Ward

Publisher/Date: Ablex Publishing Corporation (Norwood, New Jersey), 1994
Price: H/b $55.00, P/b $27.50

When I began reading this book I was curious as to what a connectionist language generator might do. My curiosity has been satisfied as a result of reading the book, but I was disappointed to find that 'generation' in this case meant finding *appropriate* words and phrases to express a given idea in a single sentence. The book does make it clear that this task is difficult, and that FIG performs better than earlier generators which could only output one or two sentences. But although I felt more knowledgeable having read the book, my sense of disappointment didn't quite go away.

The book describes a connectionist natural language generator, FIG (Flexible Incremental Generator), which takes inputs from a simple parser of Japanese (or inputs assembled by hand), and outputs single sentences, in English or Japanese. The work is focused on issues of lexical choice and syntactic organisation, and does not address the complex questions of producing appropriate text for particular hearers, or producing texts longer than a sentence. FIG operates by means of an associative network, and as a localist connectionist model does not learn as the result of exposure to an environment, but is adjusted by hand. Mot of the chapters in the book describe aspects of FIG (in particular its lexical and syntactic knowledge). One of the most interesting chapters is a more general one on 'Design Issues', in which Ward outlines the desirable qualities of a language generator, regardless of whether or not FIG exemplifies them. Indeed Ward quite openly discusses some of the disadvantages of the FIG generator, conceding that its performance is not impressive compared with symbolic generators, and finally concluding that his main contribution is the drawing up of a set of design principles. The book also includes a chapter on Human Language Production (superficial coverage of human data), and one on Machine Translation (makes some interesting observations), and one on "Miscellany regarding Connectionism", in which Ward discusses his research methodology.

The style in which the book is written is quite lively and enthusiastic. It has extensive cross-references to other parts of the book, which can be useful, but which don't add to its readability. The tone is sometimes a bit glib, particularly where the author dismisses other approaches, or defends himself against potential criticisms. There is something attractive about following the development of a researcher's thoughts about what he is doing, but at the same time, a major weakness of the book is its research methodology. Ward refers to criticisms of his work that he has received, 'so it sounds like you build the network by hand, every link and every weight, and if it didn't work you fiddled various things to make it right'. He argues against this criticism, and in favour of a research methodology of computational implementation, or 'learning by implementing'. However, his argument is not very convincing – the implementer may well learn things, but will the rest of us? For instance, Ward tried several different approaches to incorporating syntax in the system before settling on one; but does his learning experience mean that the final one is the best one? Similarly, although he argues in favour of localist connectionism as opposed to a distributed system that learns, this reader at least was not persuaded.

In sum, this book is quite readable, and contains many observations about language, but it is nonetheless quite limited in scope. It describes a novel approach to language generation, and will therefore be of interest to researchers in the area, but is not aimed at a wider audience.

AMANDA J. C. SHARKEY
Department of Computer Science
University of Sheffield, U.K.